STRUCTURED COBOL

STRUCTURED COBOL
Second Edition

A. S. Philippakis
Arizona State University

Leonard J. Kazmier
Arizona State University

McGraw-Hill Book Company
New York   St. Louis   San Francisco   Auckland
Bogotá   Hamburg   Johannesburg   London
Madrid   Mexico   Montreal   New Delhi   Panama
Paris   São Paulo   Singapore   Sydney   Tokyo   Toronto

Library of Congress Cataloging in Publication Data

Philippakis, Andreas S
 Structured COBOL.

 Includes index.
 1. COBOL (Computer program language) I. Kazmier,
Leonard J., joint author. II. Title.
HF5548.5.C2P54 1981   001.64'24   80-12647
ISBN 0-07-049801-6

STRUCTURED COBOL

  4567890DODO89876543

This book was set in Optima by Cobb/Dunlop Publisher Services Incorporated.
The editor was Charles E. Stewart; the production supervisor was Donna Piligra.
R. R. Donnelley & Sons Company was printer and binder.

See Acknowledgment on page xv. Copyrights included on this page
by reference.

To Our Parents

CONTENTS

PREFACE

COBOL (COmmon Business Oriented Language) has been adopted as the standard programming medium for administrative applications of the computer in industry and government. The language has been continuously reviewed and modified under the sponsorship of the Conference on Data Systems Language (CODASYL), a working committee composed of representatives from major computer language users and computer manufacturers. The current version of COBOL was adopted as the standard by the American National Standards Institute (ANSI) in 1974 and is a revision and refinement based on 15 years of experience with the language.

This book has been designed to facilitate the learning of COBOL. It includes thorough coverage of concepts, as well as examples of applications at both elementary and intermediate levels of complexity. Review sections are included in the text as opportunities for the reader to enhance effective learning through self-testing. Students in business administration and computer science will find this book to be a suitable guide to the language.

Throughout this book, the concepts of structured programming are used. A structured program is one which follows certain principles of modular design and results in simplification of programming tasks and improved self-documentation. The COBOL language is particularly well-suited for the application of structured programming concepts, and use of these concepts has been incorporated in all of the computer programs that are described.

The book consists of 16 chapters. The first three chapters present a complete set of basic concepts, so that the student can begin to write complete programs in a relatively short time. Chapter 4 then presents concepts and methods of program design and lays a foundation for the structured programming approach employed throughout the text.

Beyond the introductory material of the first three chapters, the language concepts and options are developed at three levels. Chapters 4 and 5 present a basic subset of DATA and PROCEDURE statements. Chapter 6, 7, and 8 present more advanced features that enable the student to master the language at an intermediate level. Finally, Chapters 9 through 16 develop special language features as they relate to the general application areas of sequential file processing, sorting and merging, table handling, indexed sequential and relative file processing, subroutine programming, and the report writer feature.

As compared with the previous edition of this book, the application of structured programming has been expanded to include new concepts in program design, as well as program structure in general. Several chapters have been restructured so that students will be able to write intermediate-level programs sooner. New exercises have been added throughout the book, file processing has been extended to three separate chapters, and new coverage is included in the two new chapters on program structure and design and on the report writer feature.

The authors express their appreciation to Charles E. Stewart for his very capable supervision of this project. We also extend thanks to several anonymous reviewers for their comments and recommendations with respect to this revision.

A. S. Philippakis
Leonard J. Kazmier

ACKNOWLEDGMENT

The following acknowledgment is reprinted from *American National Standard Programming Language COBOL, X3.23-1974* published by the American National Standards Institute, Inc.

> Any organization interested in reproducing the COBOL standard and specifications in whole or in part, using ideas from this document as the basis for an instruction manual or for any other purpose, is free to do so. However, all such organizations are requested to reproduce the following acknowledgment paragraphs in their entirety as part of the preface to any such publication (any organization using a short passage from this document, such as in a book review, is requested to mention 'COBOL' in acknowledgment of the source, but need not quote the acknowledgment):

> COBOL is an industry language and is not the property of any company or group of companies, or of any organization or group of organizations.

> No warranty, expressed or implied, is made by any contributor or by the CODASYL Programming Language Committee as to the accuracy and functioning of the programming system and language. Moreover, no responsibility is assumed by any contributor, or by the committee, in connection therewith.

The authors and copyright holders of the copyrighted material used herein

> FLOW-MATIC (trademark of Sperry Rand Corporation), Programming for the UNIVAC I and II, Data Automation Systems copyrighted 1958, 1959, by Sperry Rand Corporation; IBM Commercial Translator Form No. F28-8013, copyrighted 1959 by IBM; FACT, DSI 27A5260-2760, copyrighted 1960 by Minneapolis-Honeywell.

have specifically authorized the use of this material in whole or in part, in the COBOL specifications. Such authorization extends to the reproduction and use of COBOL specifications in programming manuals or similar publications.

1

Programming for administrative data processing

WHAT IS A DATA PROCESSING SYSTEM?

A well-designed data processing system provides managers with information needed for decision making by providing for efficient data collection, data processing, and dissemination of the resulting information. Such a system can include manual procedures, the use of business forms, electronic data processing equipment, data files, and computer programs. Administrative data processing has a number of distinct features with respect to data input, the processing of data, and the output of such systems.

Data *input* typically is voluminous and consists of numeric and non-numeric data records of varying length. For example, a sales data record generally includes the name of the customer, the date, the amount of the purchase, the item description, and the like. In a retail business, these sales data records easily can total thousands per week.

The *processing* of business data input is characterized by the updating of files. Business activities require large files of data in order for the data processing system to be a fairly accurate reflection of these activities. Data files constitute a symbolic model of the activities taking place in an organization. Keeping this model current is the function of *file updating*. Input data are processed with respect to historical files in order to update the data in the files. For example, a bank maintains a file of its checking account customers that reflects the state of the bank's checking account function. When input data are accumulated in groups and processed periodically, we have a *batch processing* system, and the data files reflect the state of the activity at a point in time. When input data are processed as each transaction occurs, then the files reflect the current state of business activity, and we have a *real-time* system. File updating requires complex logic because files contain a variety of data and the processing logic must foresee all possibilities that can arise. For instance, a payroll system is a data processing task that often requires many months of effort, even though at first glance it seems a trivial matter involving simple arithmetic.

The *output* of administrative data processing is characterized by the production of reports that group and summarize data by meaningful categories which correspond to various functions.

In contrast to administrative data processing, scientific computing typically is characterized by a relatively low volume of input, small or nonexistent files, less complex processing logic but extensive arithmetic manipulations, and more limited report production needs.

Since administrative data processing has characteristics different from those of scientific computing, a special language has been developed to accommodate the particular needs associated with such processing of data. The language is COBOL (COmmon Business Oriented Language). The counterpart languages for scientific computation are FORTRAN (FORmula TRANslation) and ALGOL (ALGOrithmic Language). PL/I (Programming Language I) was designed for both administrative and scientific applications but has not been used widely. Although COBOL is the most widely used language for administrative data processing in conjunction with both small and large computers, two other languages also frequently used for data processing with small computers are BASIC (Beginner's All-purpose Symbolic Instruction Code) and RPG II (Report Program Generator II).

COMPUTER SYSTEMS FOR DATA PROCESSING

A system is a set of interrelated parts. Computers are referred to aptly as computer systems, since they consist of interrelated component parts. Figure

1-1 shows the basic component parts of a computer system: input, central storage, auxiliary storage, central processing, and output.

The input component performs the function of transmitting data from an external storage medium to the central storage of the computer. One well-known input device is the card reader, which transmits data from punched cards to central storage. The recording of data on punched cards is performed offline using a keypunch. Because punched cards continue to be used very widely, and because the chances are that the student of this text will use a keypunch for data and program preparation, the appendix at the end of Chapter 2 provides instruction on the use of the keypunch.

A variety of other input devices exists in addition to the card reader. These include magnetic tape, magnetic disk (often created by key-to-tape or key-to-disk devices), keyboard terminals, cathode-ray-tube (CRT) terminals, electronic "cash registers," paper tape, optical readers, and magnetic ink readers. Several types of input-output devices are presented in Figure 1-2.

Central storage is used to hold program instructions and data being processed by a given program. Central storage is measured in terms of *bytes* or *words*, depending on the hardware architecture of a computer system. Each byte or word is addressable by the central processor and can be made available for input or output.

Because central storage is relatively expensive and limited, business computer systems include auxiliary or secondary storage. The main use of auxiliary storage is to hold the data files of the data processing system. Magnetic tapes and disks are the commonly used devices, but magnetic

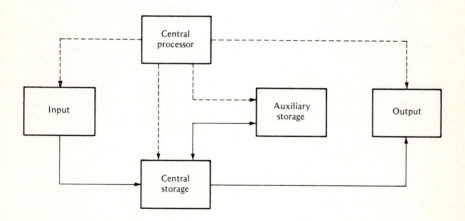

- - - - - Control relationship

———— Data flow

FIGURE 1-1 COMPONENTS OF A COMPUTER SYSTEM.

(a)

(b)

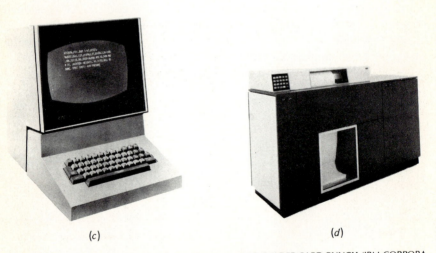

(c)

(d)

FIGURE 1-2   INPUT/OUTPUT DEVICES. (a) **IBM 2540 CARD READER/CARD PUNCH** (IBM CORPORA-
TION). (b) **UNIVAC MAGNETIC TAPE UNIT** (SPERRY RAND CORPORATION). (c) **IBM CATHODE-RAY
TUBE** (IBM CORPORATION). (d) **IBM 3211 PRINTER** (IBM CORPORATION).

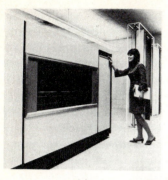

(a)

(b)

(c)

(d)

FIGURE 1-3   AUXILIARY STORAGE DEVICES. (a) UNIVAC FASTRAN III MAGNETIC DRUM (SPERRY RAND CORPORATION) (b) UNIVAC 8414 MAGNETIC DISK STORAGE (SPERRY RAND CORPORATION). (c) IBM 3321 DATA CELL UNIT (IBM CORPORATION). (d) IBM 3850 CARTRIDGE SYSTEM (IBM CORPORATION).

drums and extended cartridge storage systems also are used. A reel of magnetic tape when mounted on a tape drive becomes *online* and represents auxiliary storage. A reel of tape on a storage shelf is *offline* and does not constitute auxiliary storage as a component part of a computer system. Similar considerations apply to removable disks. Several types of auxiliary storage devices are presented in Figure 1–3.

A frequently used output device is the printer, which records data from central storage in printed form. In administrative applications, printed reports are common and voluminous. Recent developments have resulted in printer speeds approaching 20,000 lines of output per minute. Magnetic tapes and disks are also usable for output, as are punched cards, CRT display units, and microfilm.

The central processor controls and coordinates the functions of the other components of a computer system and includes the arithmetic and logical capabilities that characterize electronic computers.

It should be noted that most computers are *general purpose* digital computers, and a given computer system may be used equally well for administrative data processing or for scientific computing; however, the specific choice of components for a computer system is influenced by the nature of the expected application. A computer system used by a research laboratory consists of a mix of specific components different from that of a system used by an insurance company. The input, output, and file storage requirements are quite different.

REVIEW

1 The entry of data into a computer system is called data _____.

input

2 After data are input, the performance of such functions as file updating is included in the category of activities called data _____.

processing

3 When data are accumulated and processed periodically, _____ processing is involved. When input data are processed as each transaction occurs, a(n) _____ system is involved.

batch; real-time

4 Such activities as the production of printed reports and the display of information by means of a CRT are examples of computer _____.

output

5   The devices that can be used either for entering data into central storage or for obtaining information from storage are termed _____ _____ devices.

input-output

6   As contrasted to central storage, the magnetic drum, magnetic disk drive, and online magnetic tape are examples of _____ storage devices.

auxiliary

7   The arithmetic and logical capabilities that characterize electronic computers are contained in the _____ of the computer system.

central processor

LEVELS OF COMPUTER LANGUAGES

A computer program is a set of instructions that directs a computer in the performance of a data processing task. A computer language is a set of characters, words, and syntactic rules that can be used to write a computer program. One of the most revolutionary developments associated with computer systems is that instructions are conveyed to the machine by means of a language. A little thought will reveal that, except for computers, humans communicate with machines not by means of a language but by means of such physical operations as turning a value, striking a key, or depressing a pedal.

Every computer model has its own language, which is determined by its hardware structure. Such "native" computer languages are referred to as *machine* languages. These languages are, of course, machine dependent and are, at a first glance, highly obscure because they consist of long strings of numeric codes. Early computer programming was almost exclusively machine-language programming. Although machine language is natural to the hardware of a computer, it is quite unnatural to human programmers. A step in the direction of facilitating programming was taken with the development of *symbolic* languages. Symbolic languages use mnemonic codes to represent machine instructions. For instance, a machine instruction such as 21300400, meaning to add the value stored in location 400 to location 300, could be written as A SUM, TOTAL. Mnemonic codes, of course, are not understood by a computer; therefore, they have to be translated into machine-language form. An *assembler* is a machine-language program that translates symbolic language instructions into machine-language instructions. Symbolic languages are machine dependent in that a set of mnemonic codes is applicable only to a particular computer model; therefore, the programmer has to be familiar with the particular instruction repertoire of the machine being programmed. This is a serious disadvantage when programming efforts are extensive and hardware is changing.

The next stage in the development of programming language was the advent of *higher-level* languages that are procedure oriented rather than machine oriented. Such languages focus on the data processing procedure to be accomplished rather than on the coding requirements of particular machines. Further, higher-level languages are *not* machine dependent: such programs are not restircted to use with particular computer models. Even though such instructions are not designed to correspond to the way a particular computer model operates, they of course must be executed on a particular machine. Again, the process of translation is used to obtain the required machine-language program. A computer program written in a higher-level language is referred to as a *source* program. A *compiler* is a machine-language program that translates (or compiles) the source program into a machine-language program, which is referred to as an *object* program. The object program is then input into the machine to perform the

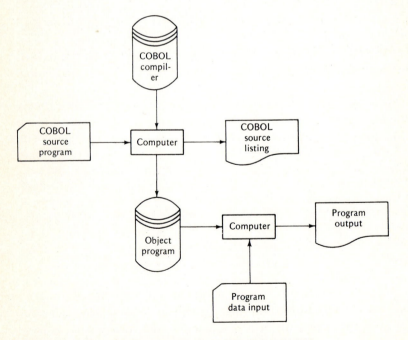

FIGURE 1-4   COBOL PROGRAM COMPILATION-EXECUTION PROCESS.

required task. Thus, a compiler is a program whose function it is to convert source programs to object programs. The main difference between a compiler and an assembler is that *compilation* is a more complex process than *assembly*. Assembly typically involves a one-for-one translation from a mnemonic to a machine code; compilation involves a many-for-one translation. One higher-level instruction may be the equivalent of several machine-level instructions.

Figure 1–4 illustrates the compilation and execution process. In the first phase, the source program and the compiler serve as input into the central processing unit (CPU) of the computer. The output includes the object program, which is stored on a magnetic disk or tape device, and a listing of the source program on the printer, along with diagnostic error messages. If no serious errors are detected, the object program is automatically entered into the CPU of the computer. Based on the program instructions, input data are then read and analyzed, culminating with the required output.

REVIEW

1   A computer program is essentially a set of instructions that directs the operation of a machine. When the set of instructions is written in a language that consists of a series of numeric codes that can be used with a particular computer model only, the language is referred to as a _____ language.

machine

2   The next stage in the development of computer languages made possible the use of mnemonic codes, such as SUM, in place of numeric codes. As is the case for machine languages, such languages are also machine dependent. Because of the type of code system used, such languages are called _____ languages.

symbolic

3   The third stage in the development of computer languages was the formulation of higher-level, or procedure oriented, languages that [are also / are not] machine dependent. An example of such a language is _____.

are not; COBOL (*or* FORTRAN,
BASIC, ALGOL, *etc.*)

4   Both symbolic languages and procedure oriented languages have to be translated into machine-language form before they can be used to direct computer operations. The program that translates a symbolic language

program into machine-language form is called a(n) _____
_____, whereas the manufacturer-supplied program that translates a
procedure oriented language program is called a(n) _____.

assembler; compiler

5   In the context of using a procedure oriented language, the program
written in such a language is often referred to as the _____
program, and the translated version of the program is referred to as the
_____ program.

source; object

THE PROGRAMMING PROCESS

Programming can be thought of best as a series of steps. As identified in
Table 1-1, these steps are *task analysis* and *description, program design,
program coding, program testing, documentation,* and *implementation.*

It is imperative that the programmer have a clear understanding of the
purpose of a program and all the detailed considerations that relate to the
program, such as source of input, computational logic, form of output, and
the like. The term *task analysis and description* refers to all the activities
associated with finding out what is to be done, how, for whom, and when.
Generally, systems analysis and design precedes programming. Although
systems analysts often are responsible for task analysis and description, the
programmer has to be equally clear about these matters before beginning
program design and coding.

The second step in the programming process is *program design.* The
logical structure of a program has to be designed before program coding is
done, just as an architect designs the functional components of a building
well in advance of a contractor's actual construction. Program design includes a delineation of the functions to be performed by the program and
their logical interrelationships. The end product of the design often is a
graphic representation, such as a program structure chart or flowchart.

**TABLE 1-1   STEPS IN THE
PROGRAMMING PROCESS**

- Task analysis and description
- Program design
- Program coding
- Program testing
- Documentation
- Implementation

Program coding is the act of writing the detailed instructions that consti-tute the program per se. These instructions are written in a particular lan-guage and in accordance with the program design.

Just as a building has to be inspected to ascertain that it was constructed in accordance with the design and the building codes, so a program has to be tested. *Program testing* is the process of checking the program to make sure that it was indeed designed and coded to comply with its intended function. The term *debugging* is used widely in the context of program testing. During testing, the programmer retraces the program logic and makes runs of the program, first with test data and eventually with "live" data.

After the program has been tested, it is documented. *Documentation* is the process of writing down explanations or classifications about the pro-gram by using ordinary language and such graphic aids as charts. Program documentation is necessary because a program in itself may be difficult to understand, especially by a person other than the author, or even by the author of the program after some time has elapsed.

The final step in programming is *implementation,* in which the program is put into production for actual use. This is mainly an administrative func-tion that does not involve the programmer directly, but the programmer should be aware of such implementation and be available if needed.

REVIEW

1 The first step in the computer programming process, concerned with a study of the required data processing, the type of input, and the required output, is called _____.

task analysis and description

2 A delineation of the functions to be performed by the program and their logical interrelationships is included in the second step in the program-ming process, called _____.

program design

3 The actual writing of the detailed instructions that constitute the com-puter program is called _____.

program coding

4 After the program has been written, it is executed with various data input in order to detect and correct any programming errors or omissions. This process is called _____.

program testing (or debugging)

5 The step in the programming process that is concerned with attaching

explanations to the program so that the program and its parts are understandable to another individual is called _____.

documentation

6   The final step in the programming process, in which the program is put to actual use, is called _____.

implementation

PROGRAM FLOWCHARTING

A flowchart is a graphic outline of a computer program. As the title suggests, the flowchart identifies the steps needed in a data processing task and presents them with connecting lines and arrows to indicate the direction of flow or the sequence. Figure 1–5 illustrates some of the most frequently used flowcharting symbols.

To illustrate the use of some flowchart symbols, Figure 1–6 presents an example of a flowchart for a simple program designed to read 50 cards. Each card has a value representing a quantity. If the quantity is 99 or less, the price is set at $10.00. If the quantity is 100 or greater, the price is set at $9.50. For each card record, we print the quantity, the price, and the total. The program terminates when 50 cards have been read.

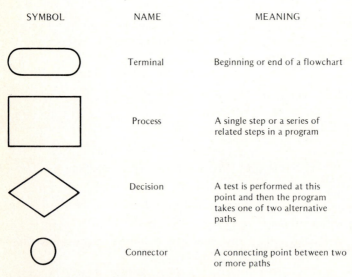

SYMBOL	NAME	MEANING
	Terminal	Beginning or end of a flowchart
	Process	A single step or a series of related steps in a program
	Decision	A test is performed at this point and then the program takes one of two alternative paths
	Connector	A connecting point between two or more paths

FIGURE 1-5   COMMON FLOWCHARTING SYMBOLS.

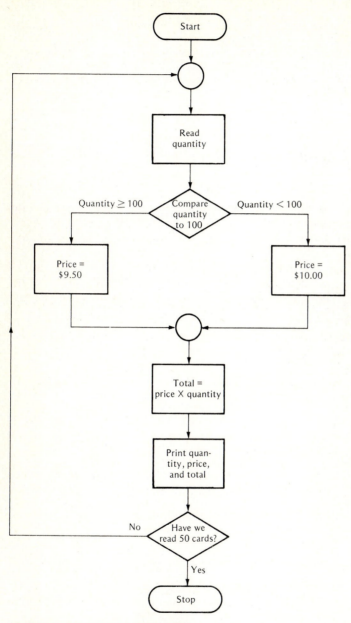

FIGURE 1-6   EXAMPLE OF A FLOWCHART.

REVIEW

1   The sample flowchart in Figure 1-6 involves the use of all of the flow-charting symbols. With reference to this figure only, one example of the use of the *decision* symbol is associated with the verbal description, "_____."

> *Compare quantity to 100 (or Have*
> *we read 50 cards?)*

2   An example of the use of the *terminal* symbol is associated with the verbal description "_____."

> *Start (or Stop)*

3   The first example of the use of the *process* symbol is associated with the verbal description "_____."

> *Read quantity*

4   In terms of the logic of the program, note that the program will "stop" if all 50 cards have been read. On the other hand, if all 50 cards have not been read at the point in the flowchart where this test is made, the next verbal instruction executed will be "_____."

> *Read quantity*

EXERCISES

1.1   What are the main differences between administrative data processing and scientific computing? How do these differences affect the choice of computer equipment?

1.2   Describe briefly the main characteristics of the following computer languages: COBOL, FORTRAN, PL/I, BASIC, RPG II, and ALGOL.

1.3   Briefly describe the principal components of any computer system.

1.4   In your own words, explain what is meant by a computer language.

1.5   Name and briefly discuss three levels of computer languages.

1.6   Explain these three related concepts: *source program, object program,* and *compiler*. How do these three interrelate in a typical COBOL program run?

1.7   Programming is not a single step but is thought of best as a process. Describe the steps included in the programming process.

1.8 Draw a flowchart to correspond to the following verbal description: start; set SUM and NUMBER-OF-VALUES to zero; input a record containing a value of INCOME, add this INCOME to the SUM, add 1 to NUMBER-OF-VALUES; if more records are available, input another record repeating the process, otherwise divide NUMBER-OF-VALUES into SUM giving an AVERAGE-INCOME; print the value of AVERAGE-INCOME and then stop.

2
Overview of COBOL

INTRODUCTION

COBOL (COmmon Business Oriented Language) is a programming language that has been designed expressly for administrative data processing. It is a higher-level language and, as such, generally is machine independent.

The idea of developing the language was conceived at a Pentagon meeting in May 1959. At that meeting, representatives from the government, from business users, and from computer manufacturers decided that it was feasible to proceed with the development of a higher-level language that would satisfy the specific needs of administrative data processing, as contrasted to scientific computing. A preliminary version of COBOL appeared in December 1959. This version was followed in 1961 by COBOL-61, which became the cornerstone for the development of later versions of the language. In 1968 a standard version of the language was approved by what now is called the American National Standards Institute (ANSI). COBOL is continuously evolving and being enhanced by the addition of new programming capabilities and the deletion of obsolete functions. Proposed changes in the language are documented annually in the *Journal of Development.* These changes are tentative, however, until ANSI adopts a new standard. The latest version of ANS COBOL was adopted in 1974. Appendices A and B in the back of this book provide a description of ANS COBOL; however, these appendices will be meaningful to you only after you have become acquainted with the elements of COBOL programming.

One advantage of COBOL computer programs is that they can be substantially *self-documenting.* Self-documentation is a characteristic of a language that allows a reader of a program to understand its function and follow its processing steps. Documentation is very important because, like other aspects of administration, data processing needs do not remain static. Making changes in programs, or *program maintenance,* is an ongoing activity in computer installations and may be performed by different people at different points in time. Thus, documentation is essential in order to avoid reprogramming. Although COBOL programs can be self-documenting, whether or not a particular COBOL program is self-documenting depends on the programmer. The language instructions are much like English, but the programmer has substantial choice as to whether to make a program self-documenting or obscure.

Although COBOL has been available for a long time, its use greatly increased during the 1970s. Widespread acceptance coincided with the appearance of the standard versions of the language and with the development of efficient COBOL compilers. Many of today's compilers translate quickly and generate an efficient object program. In earlier years it was not unusual to find that compilation of a small program required about half an hour and that the resulting object program ran slowly. Under such circumstances, computer installation managers tended to use lower-level symbolic languages that could be assembled (translated) more quickly and resulted in more efficient object programs. Today a COBOL program can be written in a shorter time than an assembly program for most data processing applications, and it can be run with about the same efficiency as a symbolic program written by a programmer of comparable competence. Thus, COBOL is now *the* language for administrative data processing, and one can reasonably predict that it will continue in this role for some time to come.

REVIEW

1 COBOL is unique as a programming language in that it was designed specifically to satisfy the needs associated with _____
_____.

administrative data processing

2 Development of the COBOL language is monitored by, and new versions of the language are approved periodically by, the _____
_____.

American National Standards
Institute (ANSI)

3 A principal reason for the substantial increase in the use of COBOL during the 1970s was [the availability of efficient compilers / the development of new data processing needs].

*the availability of efficient
compilers*

COBOL CHARACTERS AND WORDS

The most basic and indivisible unit of the COBOL language is the *character*. The set of characters used to form COBOL source programs consists of the 51 characters identified in Figure 2–1.

A sequence of characters can form a *word*. There are two types of COBOL words: *reserved words* and *user-defined words*. Reserved words are defined by the COBOL language. (Appendix A presents a complete list of ANS COBOL reserved words.) The programmer cannot use any of these words except in the form specified by the language. Much of this text is devoted to explaining the use of such reserved words.

User-defined words are supplied by the programmer (language user) in

CHARACTER	MEANING
0, 1, . . . , 9	Digit
A, B . . . , Z	Letter
	Space (blank)
( ) . "	Special symbols
+ – * /	
= $, ;	
< >	

FIGURE 2–1   THE SET OF CHARACTERS IN COBOL PROGRAMMING.

order to satisfy the format of a clause or statement in the language. A user-defined word may be 1 to 30 characters in length and may consist of letters, digits, and hyphens, except that a hyphen may not appear as the first or last character.

There are 17 types of user-defined words, examples of which are: condition-name, data-name, paragraph-name, record-name, and file-name. The reader will be exposed to different types of user-defined words as the text progresses. Special attention is given to data-names in the section that follows, because data-names are used so frequently.

REVIEW

1   The basic units of the COBOL language, such as the numbers 0 through 9 and the capital letters of the alphabet, are referred to as _____.

characters

2   COBOL words specifically defined by the COBOL language and used only for particular purposes are called _____ words.

reserved

3   COBOL words that are formulated by applications programmers are called _____ words.

user-defined

DATA-NAMES

Central storage or main storage in a computer can be thought of as a long string of character positions, with direct access available to any position. Both data and instructions are stored in internal storage, but, from the programmer's viewpoint, data storage is the most important concern. Data are stored in certain positions such that they can be referred to by a name or an address. In COBOL, the addresses are symbolic names and are called *data-names*. One way to view a computer program is to say that it consists of a set of instructions to manipulate central storage areas that are referenced by their corresponding data-names. The idea will become clear as we proceed.

Data-names are coined at the discretion of the programmer, except that there are certain rules that must be followed.

1   A data-name can be up to 30 characters in length and can include alphabetic characters, numeric characters, and hyphens.

2   At least one character must be alphabetic.
3   The only special symbol permitted is the hyphen. A hyphen always must be embedded; that is, it cannot be the first or last character of the data-name.
4   Blanks cannot be included in the data-names.
5   Within the above rules the programmer may use any data-name, with the exception of the approximately 300 COBOL reserved words listed in Appendix A. (Manufacturers often add some of their own words to the ANSI list.)

Some examples of legitimate data-names are:

HOURS

ENDING-INVENTORY

SALES-TAX-TOTAL

PREMIUM

A527157

31576X5

Of course, data-names do not have to be meaningful English words. A programmer can choose to use such data-names as X, Y, Z, X1, X2, and the like. However, even though such data-names are typically shorter than those that are inherently meaningful as names, they increase the likelihood of subsequent confusion. COBOL was designed specifically to allow self-documentation, which means that by reading the program one should be able to understand what the program does and what data it uses. The problem with using cryptic data-names is that their meanings are forgotten by the programmer and are never understood by others unless a list of definitions is supplied.

Part of the programming job is to subdivide central storage into data units, such as characters, elementary or group items, and records. This is accomplished by using data-names in ways that can reflect the structure of the data involved. As a matter of fact, COBOL derives much of its suitability for administrative applications from the opportunity it provides to take explicit account of the structure of data.

As an example of the use of data-names, consider the following information that is to be stored internally:

RONALD JOHNSON
1057 MONTEREY DRIVE
TEMPE, ARIZONA 85282

Recall that internally the information will be stored as a continuous sequence of characters rather than as three lines. Assuming that it will be

FIGURE 2-2 CONCEPTUAL STRUCTURE OF INFORMATION IN INTERNAL STORAGE.

stored starting with storage position 101, we have the conceptual structure presented in Figure 2–2. The bottom row in the figure identifies the data as well as the data positions in internal storage, and the other rows refer to the labels by which reference can be made to the storage locations that contain particular kinds of information. In other words, in this figure we have defined storage fields and labeled them by the use of different data-names. For example, the label FIRST-NAME refers to storage positions 101–110. Correct computer programming relies on the use of unique data-names to identify unique positions in storage. Thus, we can write instructions that direct the computer to take the data in columns 1–10 of a punched card and enter it in the storage location called FIRST-NAME. Obviously, the data-name FIRST-NAME must be unique to avoid ambiguity. Similarly, we could instruct the machine to print the contents of STREET on the high-speed printer, which would thereby make reference to the information held in storage positions 123–142.

Remember that a label or data-name, such as STREET, does not have any conceptual meaning for the computer, as it would have for a person. We could just as well have used the data-name XYZ in our example. We simply indicate to the machine that something is to be done to or with the content of a storage location that has been labeled for reference purposes. Even if the label implies something about the meaning of the content to the pro-grammer, it does not imply anything like that to the machine. Of course, it is a good habit to coin labels that convey meaning about the content to the programmer.

Referring again to Figure 2–2, notice that FIRST-NAME refers to storage positions 101–110, NAME refers to storage positions 101–122, and CUSTOMER-ADDRESS refers to storage positions 101–167, which include all the positions of this example. The way we have used the data-names allows us to reference data in accordance with their hierarchical structure. We can refer to the whole record, the group items in the record, or to the elementary items.

REVIEW

1   In COBOL, a label for a field of data appropriately is called a(n) _____
_____.

data-name

2   A data-name must not be more than _____ (number) characters in length and can include [alphabetic characters only / alphabetic and nu-meric characters].

30; alphabetic and numeric characters

3   Every data-name must include at least one [alphabetic / numeric] character, and the only special symbol permitted is the _____.

alphabetic; hyphen

4   Place a check mark before any of the following that is a legitimate data-name in COBOL.

a   _____ INVENTORY
b   _____ END OF YEAR BALANCE
c   _____ 2735B5
d   _____ 27-35B5
e   _____ BALANCE-DUE-
f   _____ 57
g   _____ END-OF-YEAR-BALANCE-DUE-ON-ACCOUNT
h   _____ CODE
i   _____ BALANCE

a   ✔
b   *spaces not allowed*
c   ✔
d   ✔
e   *hyphens must be embedded*
f   *at least one alphabetic character must be included*
g   *must be less than 30 characters in length*
h   *a reserved COBOL word (a bit of a trick question—see Appendix A)*
i   ✔

5   Each field of internal storage has a unique data-name, or label, associated with it. Each data-name [must / need not] be unique and [must / need not] imply something about the meaning of the content.

must; need not

6   Data-names can be so structured that data can be referenced according to a hierarchical organization. When this is done, the labeled data fields will [all be separate and distinct / involve some overlap].

involve some overlap (e.g., "STREET" vs. "NUMBER" in Figure 2–2

HIERARCHICAL ORGANIZATION OF DATA

The example in Figure 2-2 in the preceding section demonstrates how data-names such as NAME can refer to groups of contiguous data-names. COBOL derives a great deal of its suitability for business applications from the fact that it allows the programmer to construct hierarchies of data structures.

A useful distinction is made between *elementary* and *group* items in COBOL. An elementary item has no subordinate parts. With reference to Figure 2-2, FIRST-NAME and ZONE exemplify the first and last of the eight elementary items from left to right. The data-name NAME, on the other hand, is an example of a group item. A group item may consist of one or more other group items, as is the case with CUSTOMER-ADDRESS in the illustration.

Reference to Figure 2-2 makes the concept of group item rather obvious, but in a programming language we cannot construct figures, and so we need a means of communicating the same information in symbolic form. The language provides such a symbolic form by means of the *level-number* form. Here is an example of how level numbers can represent the same hierarchical (grouping) structure as in Figure 2-2.

```
01   CUSTOMER-ADDRESS
       02   NAME
              03   FIRST-NAME
              03   LAST-NAME
       02   STREET
              03   S-NUMBER
              03   STREET-NAME
       02   CITY-STATE
              03   CITY
              03   STATE
       02   ZIP-CODE
              03   PO
              03   ZONE
```

The first level number, 01, is associated with CUSTOMER-ADDRESS. An 01 level number indicates the highest level in a data hierarchy. Reference to the data-name at the 01 level is a reference to the entire data set, or *record,* as it is commonly called. There is only one data-name at the 01 level for each record, as it is the all-inclusive data-name. All data-names that follow this one and are part of this record have level numbers that are higher than 01 and, more specifically, are in the allowable range 02-49.

The 02 NAME introduces NAME as a data-name subordinate to the 01 level. Reading from top to bottom corresponds to left to right in Figure 2-2. We observe a total of four data-names at the 02 level: NAME, STREET, CITY-STATE, and ZIP-CODE. Since they are all at the same level, 02, none of them is subordinate to the others in the group (but each is subordinate to the 01 level).

As in Figure 2-2, we are interested in specifying that NAME is a group item and that it consists of two other data-names, FIRST-NAME and LAST-NAME. This relationship is expressed by assigning the 02 level number to NAME and the 03 level number to FIRST-NAME and LAST-NAME. Notice that, as we read from top to bottom, STREET is not confused as being subordinate to NAME because both are assigned to the 02 level.

The indentations are preferred but not required. In addition, the level number need not increase by consecutive numbers. The following example illustrates these two points:

```
01   CUSTOMER-ADDRESS
03   NAME
05   FIRST-NAME
03   STREET
04   S-NUMBER
04   STREET-NAME
```

Notice the absence of indentation in this example and observe that it is much harder to read and understand the expressed data hierarchy than in the preceding example. Also notice that level numbers do not increase by 1. The 03 NAME specifies that NAME is subordinate to CUSTOMER-ADDRESS, because 03 is greater than 01. Similarly, 05 FIRST-NAME is subordinate to NAME, because 05 is greater than 03. In the case of 04 S-NUMBER, it is understood that S-NUMBER is subordinate to the data-name just above it, which has a lower level number. Thus, the 04 level is perfectly proper in the example, and it preserves the hierarchy of Figure 2-2. It also should be emphasized that, once NAME is assigned to the 03 level, STREET *must* also be assigned to the same level, since NAME and STREET have the same immediate superior, CUSTOMER-ADDRESS.

REVIEW

1   In COBOL programming, a data-name that has no subordinate items is called a(n) _____ item, while one that does have subordinate items is called a(n) _____ item.

elementary; group

2 The hierarchical level of a data item is indicated by the level number assigned to it. The item at the highest hierarchical level always has the [highest / lowest] level number assigned to it.

lowest

3 Whenever a data item in a record is a group item, the items subordinate to that item are assigned level numbers which are [higher / lower] than the level number of that item.

higher

CONSTANTS

It may have occurred to you that a data-name in COBOL is analogous to the concept of a variable in algebra. It is a general symbol or name that can have many possible values. In addition to data-names, COBOL uses constants, and they are of three types: numeric literals, figurative constants, and nonnumeric literals. As an example of a *numeric literal,* suppose that the sales tax rate in a particular state is 0.04 of sales. Therefore, within the COBOL program we need a way in which we can multiply the amount of sales by 0.04. One way of accomplishing this *without* using a numeric literal is to define a storage field, assign to it a data-name, such as TAX-RATE, and input the value 0.04 in the field. Conceptually, the internal storage location has the following structure:

TAX-RATE			(Data-name)
0	0	4	(Content)

The decimal point is not shown but is understood to be located in the appropriate position. With this approach, the reference to TAX-RATE will always make available the 0.04 value stored in this field. Another option available in COBOL, however, is simply to write the numeric literal 0.04 in the program itself and use this value directly. Essentially, we are saying that, if a value is a numeric constant, its data-name in internal storage is the same as its value. Conceptually, the internal storage location has the following structure:

004			(Data-name)
0	0	4	(Content)

Numeric literals without a decimal are understood to be integers (whole numbers). If a decimal is used, it must not be the last character. Thus, 35. is not correct, whereas 35.0 is acceptable. The reason for this rule is that in COBOL programming the period is always used to signal the end of a sentence, just as in English, and it would be ambiguous whether a point following a number were a decimal point or a period.

The second type of constant used in COBOL is the *figurative constant*. The most common figurative constants are ZERO, ZEROS, ZEROES, SPACE, and SPACES, although a few others are available. These refer to zeros or blanks, respectively. Their general use can be illustrated by the following brief examples. Suppose we want to set AMOUNT equal to zero. We can write MOVE ZERO TO AMOUNT to accomplish this objective. Similarly, if we wish to ascertain that blanks are contained in the field called TITLE, we can write MOVE SPACES TO TITLE. Figure 2–3 lists and defines the standard figurative constants used in COBOL programs.

In addition to numeric literals and figurative constants, the third class of constants is the *nonnumeric literal*. As contrasted to numeric literals and figurative constants, the nonnumeric literal is any alphanumeric value enclosed in quotation marks. For example, suppose we want to print the title INCOME STATEMENT. The words INCOME and STATEMENT are not intended to refer to data-names; rather, we simply want these exact words

ZERO ZEROS ZEROES	All three forms are equivalent, and they reference the value of zero. In an instruction such as MOVE ZEROS TO AMOUNT, the storage field AMOUNT would be filled by as many zeroes as there are positions in that field. Thus the context determines the number of occurrences of the character 0.
SPACE SPACES	Both forms are equivalent, and they reference one or more blanks, similar to the ZERO constant.
QUOTE QUOTES	Both forms are equivalent, and they reference the quotation mark.
HIGH–VALUE HIGH–VALUES	Both forms are equivalent, and they reference the highest value in the collating sequence for the particular computer system.
LOW–VALUE LOW–VALUES	Both forms are equivalent, and they reference the lowest value in the collating sequence for the particular computer system.
ALL literal	References one or more occurrences of the single character nonnumeric literal, as in MOVE ALL "A" TO HEADER, which results in the storage field HEADER being filled with A's.

FIGURE 2–3   FIGURATIVE CONSTANTS AND THEIR MEANINGS.

printed. This can be done by enclosing them in single quotation marks and using them as explained in the next chapter, in which the PROCEDURE DIVISION of COBOL will be described.

As an example of how a nonnumeric literal might be used in a decision context, suppose we want to know if a customer's last name is BROWN. We could write something like this:

IF LAST-NAME EQUAL 'BROWN' (etc.)

Any letter, number, or special symbol can be enclosed in quotation marks with the exception of a quotation mark itself. if we want to use quotation marks as part of the literal, we can accomplish this by use of the QUOTE figurative constant as follows:

QUOTE 'TOTAL AMOUNT' QUOTE

In this example the word QUOTE indicates a quotation mark. The use of the figurative constant QUOTE before and after the nonnumeric literal will result in quotation marks being printed. The quotation marks are printed as single or double marks, depending on the specific printer used.

Unlike a data-name, a nonnumeric literal can include blanks. The nonnumeric literal also can be composed entirely of numeric characters. This may seem like a contradiction, but it is not, since the term "nonnumeric" refers to how the characters are handled within the computer and not to their alphanumeric form as such.

REVIEW

1   In all, three classes of constants were discussed in this section. They are the _____, _____, and _____
_____.

> *numeric literal; figurative
> constant; nonnumeric literal*

2   In the following listing, place an NL before those expressions that can serve as numeric literals in a COBOL program, an FC for figurative constants, and a NON-L for nonnumeric literals; leave a blank for expressions not exemplifying any of the classes of constants.

a   _____ 'DEPRECIATION SCHEDULE'
b   _____ '12%'
c   _____ 237
d   _____ INTEREST-DUE
e   _____ 125.

f _____ ZEROS
g _____ 25.32
h _____ SPACES
i _____ 100.0
j _____ 'SPACE'
k _____ '325'

a NON-L
b NON-L
c NL
d *no quotation marks*
e *cannot end with a decimal point*
f FC
g NL
h FC
i NL
j NON-L
k NON-L

OVERALL STRUCTURE OF COBOL PROGRAMS

COBOL programs are written according to a special structure that is organized into a hierarchy of parts. In terms of an overall outline, the structure of this hierarchy is described as follows. Much of this text is concerned with developing the detail associated with this structure.

A *character* is the lowest form in the program structure.

A *word* is made up of one or more characters.

A *clause* consists of characters and words and is used to specify an attribute of an entry.

A *statement* is a syntactically valid combination of words and characters written in the PROCEDURE DIVISION of a COBOL program and beginning with a verb.

A *sentence* is a sequence of one or more statements, the last of which is terminated by a period followed by a space.

A *paragraph* consists of one or more sentences.

A *section* consists of one or more paragraphs.

A *division* consists of one or more paragraphs or sections. Every COBOL program consists of four divisions in the following order: IDENTIFICATION DIVISION, ENVIRONMENT DIVISION, DATA DIVISION, and PROCEDURE DIVISION.

SAMPLE COBOL PROGRAM

Figure 2-4 illustrates a complete COBOL program. As is true for all COBOL programs, it consists of four divisions. The IDENTIFICATION DIVISION is written first, and it consists of one paragraph-name, in this case PROGRAM-ID, which identifies this program by the name LABELS.

The ENVIRONMENT DIVISION is written next. The basic function of this division is to specify the hardware required for this program.

The DATA DIVISION follows. It is used to identify the data-names that will be used in the program, as well as their data characteristics and hierarchical structure.

The last division is the PROCEDURE DIVISION, which constitutes the executable part of the program. In this division the programmer writes the specific instructions to be carried out by the computer. Note that the instructions have the appearance of everyday language, which illustrates the self-documentation feature of the COBOL language.

The function of this sample program is to read cards containing three data fields and to print these three fields on separate lines. Each card contains a name in columns 1-25, a street address in columns 26-50, and the city and state in columns 51-80. Output from two input data cards appears as follows:

ALLEN M. JOHNSON
1532 E. WASHINGTON ST.
CHICAGO, ILLINOIS 53186

PATRICIA K. WALTON
2252 PALM BOULEVARD
MIAMI, FLORIDA 31322

The program could be used with special gummed labels so that a mailing could be made to a group of individuals whose names and addresses are recorded on punched cards.

THE COBOL CODING FORM

A special coding form used in writing COBOL source programs is illustrated in Figure 2-5, on which the program described in the preceding section is entered. This form has been prepared to coincide with the standard 80-column format of the punched card and therefore is oriented particularly toward applications in which the COBOL program is to be punched onto cards before input into the computer. This method of input is still typical in COBOL programming, although visual display keyboard terminals are becoming the trend.

```
IDENTIFICATION DIVISION.
PROGRAM-ID. LABELS.
*
ENVIRONMENT DIVISION.
*
CONFIGURATION SECTION.
SOURCE-COMPUTER. ABC-480.
OBJECT-COMPUTER. ABC-480.
*
INPUT-OUTPUT SECTION.
FILE-CONTROL.
    SELECT ADDRESS-FILE ASSIGN TO CARD-READER.
    SELECT PRINT-FILE   ASSIGN TO PRINTER.
*
DATA DIVISION.
*
FILE SECTION.
*
FD  ADDRESS-FILE
    LABEL RECORDS ARE OMITTED
    DATA RECORD IS ADDRESS-RECORD.
01  ADDRESS-RECORD.
    02 NAME                         PIC X(25).
    02 STREET                       PIC X(25).
    02 CITY                         PIC X(30).
*
FD  PRINT-FILE
    LABEL RECORDS ARE OMITTED
    DATA RECORD IS PRINT-LINE.




01  PRINT-LINE                      PIC X(132).
*
WORKING-STORAGE SECTION.
*
01  END-OF-DATA-INDICATOR           PIC XXX VALUE 'NO'.
/
PROCEDURE DIVISION.
*
MAIN-LOGIC.
    OPEN INPUT ADDRESS-FILE
    OPEN OUTPUT PRINT-FILE
*
    PERFORM READ-AN-ADDRESS
*
    PERFORM PRINT-AND-READ-NEXT
            UNTIL END-OF-DATA-INDICATOR = 'YES'.
*
    CLOSE ADDRESS-FILE
          PRINT-FILE
*
    STOP RUN.
*
READ-AN-ADDRESS.
    READ ADDRESS-FILE RECORD
        AT END
            MOVE 'YES' TO END-OF-DATA-INDICATOR.
*
PRINT-AND-READ-NEXT.
    MOVE NAME TO PRINT-LINE
    WRITE PRINT-LINE
            BEFORE ADVANCING 1 LINE
*
    MOVE STREET TO PRINT-LINE
    WRITE PRINT-LINE
            BEFORE ADVANCING 1 LINE
*
    MOVE CITY TO PRINT-LINE
    WRITE PRINT-LINE
            BEFORE ADVANCING 4 LINES
*
    PERFORM READ-AN-ADDRESS.
```

FIGURE 2-4   SAMPLE COBOL PROGRAM.

FIGURE 2-5 COBOL CODING FORM WITH SAMPLE COBOL PROGRAM.

IBM

COBOL Coding Form

SYSTEM

PROGRAM LABELS

PROGRAMMER   DATE FEB. '81

PUNCHING INSTRUCTIONS

| GRAPHIC | | CARD | |
| PUNCH | | FORM # | |

PAGE 1 OF 3

IDENTIFICATION
73 _____ 80

COBOL STATEMENT

```
SEQUENCE   CONT  A  B
(PAGE)(SERIAL)

010010        IDENTIFICATION DIVISION.
010020        PROGRAM-ID. LABELS.
010030*
010040        ENVIRONMENT DIVISION.
010050*
010060        CONFIGURATION SECTION.
010070        SOURCE-COMPUTER. ABC-480.
010080        OBJECT-COMPUTER. ABC-480.
010090*
010100        INPUT-OUTPUT SECTION.
010110        FILE-CONTROL.
010120            SELECT ADDRESS-FILE ASSIGN TO CARD-READER.
010130            SELECT PRINT-FILE ASSIGN TO PRINTER.
010140*
010150        DATA DIVISION.
010160*
010170        FILE SECTION.
010180*
010190        FD  ADDRESS-FILE
010200            LABEL RECORDS ARE OMITTED
010210            DATA RECORD IS ADDRESS-RECORD.
010220        01  ADDRESS-RECORD.
010230            02  NAME    PIC X(25).
010240            02  STREET  PIC X(25).
```

(continued)

FIGURE 2-5 (*continued*).

IBM

COBOL Coding Form

SYSTEM	
PROGRAM LABELS	
PROGRAMMER	DATE FEB. '81

PUNCHING INSTRUCTIONS				PAGE 2 OF 3
GRAPHIC		CARD FORM #	*	IDENTIFICATION
PUNCH				73 [ ] 80

COBOL STATEMENT

SEQUENCE (PAGE) (SERIAL)	CONT	A	B	
020010			02 CITY	PIC X(30).
020020	*			
020030		FD	PRINT-FILE	
020040			LABEL RECORDS ARE OMITTED	
020050			DATA RECORD IS PRINT-LINE.	
020060		01	PRINT-LINE	PIC X(132).
020070	*			
020080			WORKING-STORAGE SECTION.	
020090	*			
020100		01	END-OF-DATA-INDICATOR	PIC XXX VALUE 'NO'.
020110	/		PROCEDURE DIVISION.	
020120	*			
020130	*			
020140			MAIN-LOGIC.	
020150			OPEN INPUT ADDRESS-FILE	
020160			OPEN OUTPUT PRINT-FILE	
020170	*			
020180			PERFORM READ-AN-ADDRESS.	
020190	*			
020200			PERFORM PRINT-AND-READ-NEXT	
020210			UNTIL END-OF-DATA-INDICATOR = 'YES'.	
020220	*			
020230			CLOSE ADDRESS-FILE,	
020240			PRINT-FILE.	

IBM

COBOL Coding Form

SYSTEM				PUNCHING INSTRUCTIONS			PAGE 3 OF 3
PROGRAM LABELS				GRAPHIC		CARD	IDENTIFICATION
PROGRAMMER		DATE FEB. '81		PUNCH		FORM #	73 [80]

SEQUENCE (PAGE) (SERIAL)	CONT	A	B	COBOL STATEMENT
0 3 0 0 1 0	*			
0 3 0 0 2 0			STOP RUN.	
0 3 0 0 3 0	*			
0 3 0 0 4 0		READ-AN-ADDRESS.		
0 3 0 0 5 0			READ ADDRESS-FILE RECORD	
0 3 0 0 6 0			AT END	
0 3 0 0 7 0			MOVE 'YES' TO END-OF-DATA-INDICATOR.	
0 3 0 0 8 0	*			
0 3 0 0 9 0		PRINT-AND-READ-NEXT.		
0 3 0 1 0 0			MOVE NAME TO PRINT-LINE	
0 3 0 1 1 0			WRITE PRINT-LINE	
0 3 0 1 2 0			BEFORE ADVANCING 1 LINE	
0 3 0 1 3 0	*			
0 3 0 1 4 0			MOVE STREET TO PRINT-LINE	
0 3 0 1 5 0			WRITE PRINT-LINE	
0 3 0 1 6 0			BEFORE ADVANCING 1 LINE	
0 3 0 1 7 0	*			
0 3 0 1 8 0			MOVE CITY TO PRINT-LINE	
0 3 0 1 9 0			WRITE PRINT-LINE	
0 3 0 2 0 0			BEFORE ADVANCING 4 LINES	
0 3 0 2 1 0	*			
0 3 0 2 2 0			PERFORM READ-AN-ADDRESS.	

The first six positions of the COBOL Coding Form are reserved for the optional sequence number. The programmer may assign a sequence number to each program line so that they are numbered in order. A common practice is to use the first three columns as a page number corresponding to the number of coding form pages used. Then the next three columns indicate line numbers, such as 010, 020, 030, and so on. Gaps are left in the sequence so that when program changes are made later new lines can be inserted without disrupting the previous sequence. For instance, a new line could be inserted between the second and third lines by assigning a line number of 025.

Column 7 is used mainly for continuation, and it is called the *indicator area*. When a word or literal cannot be completed on a line, it is continued on the next line, starting with column 12 or to the right of it, and a hyphen (-) is entered in column 7 of that line to indicate the continuation. When a nonnumeric literal is being continued, not only do we enter a hyphen in column 7, but we also start the continued line with a quotation mark in column 12 or to the right of it and conclude with a quotation mark. For instance, we could have:

7	12						72
					MOVE 'EXAMPLE CONTI		
-	'NUATION'						

In this example, the literal 'EXAMPLE CONTINUATION' does not fit on the line. Notice that in the continued line there is a hyphen in column 7, a quotation mark in column 12 (it could have been to the right of 12 as well), the remainder of the literal, and the closing quotation mark, for a total of three quotation marks. As a simplifying rule, the programmer should avoid continuations by not beginning a word or a literal that cannot be written fully on a given line.

Column 7 also is used to indicate that a line contains a comment entry, shown by writing an asterisk (*). Whatever is written on such a line is listed with the source program but is not compiled. Comments can be used to enter explanations about a portion of the program; however, a well-written program should have a limited need for comments. As exemplified in Figure 2-5, the readability of a program is enhanced by leaving blank lines. This can be accomplished by leaving blank cards in the source program or by including cards with an asterisk in column 7. Finally, readability will be enhanced by causing a portion of the program to be listed on a new page on the printer; this can be accomplished by entering a slash (/) in column 7.

REVIEW

1 The four divisions of a COBOL program are, in order, _____,
_____, _____, and _____.

IDENTIFICATION;
ENVIRONMENT;
DATA;
PROCEDURE

2 The first six positions on the COBOL Coding Form are reserved for a
sequence number, which typically includes a(n) _____ number
and a(n) _____ number.

page; line

3 When a word or literal cannot be completed on a given line, a(n) _____
_____ is entered in column 7 of [that line / the line on which the word is
continued].

hyphen; the line on which the
word is continued

4 When a line contains only a comment entry, a(n) _____ is
entered in column 7 of that line.

asterisk

5 When a line is to be printed on a new page in the printer listing of the
program, a(n) _____ is entered in column 7 of that line.

slash

THE OPERATING SYSTEM AND THE EXECUTION OF COBOL PROGRAMS

All modern computer systems are controlled by an *operating system*
that consists of a set of programs designed to facilitate the automatic operation of the computer system and to reduce the programming task for system
users. The heart of an operating system is the resident *supervisor* (*executive*
and *monitor* are synonymous terms), which is a program that acts as the
control module in the operating system. The computer operator loads the
supervisor as the first task "each morning," and from then on the supervisor
controls the operation, with human intervention being required only to implement some exceptional procedure. The supervisor loads and executes
other programs that either are part of the operating system or are submitted

by users. When a program has been executed completely, control is resumed by the supervisor, which executes control functions until it transfers control to another program. When the machine is idle, the supervisor is in a "wait" state, waiting for the next program to be executed.

The motivation for the development of operating systems is related to the basic difference in speed between computer systems and human operators. In the early days of computing, a human operator took each program to be run, loaded it into the machine, and removed the associated output prior to loading the next program. As computers became faster and the number of users multiplied, it became obvious that the operation of computer systems had to be automated. In a modern computer system, this automation is achieved by the operating system. Human operators continuously input the programs to be processed (often simultaneously in different locations), while the operating system maintains control over the program-to-program execution sequence, checks availability of resources (tapes, disk space, printers) and, when needed, transfers control from one program to another in an attempt to maximize *throughput*.

The development of operating systems represented a major conceptual breakthrough and has required extensive programming efforts. In fact, programming is differentiated into systems programming (systems software is a synonym) and applications programming. *Systems programs* relate to operating systems and include supervisors, language processors, data management such as disk-space allocation, and utilities. (*Utilities* are programs that perform such standard tasks as transferring data from cards to tape and dumping a tape on the printer.) *Applications programs,* on the other hand, are oriented toward the use of the computer for some data processing task. A COBOL programmer is an applications programmer. All applications programs require the use of systems programs in their processing, and therefore it is essential to have a basic understanding of the operating system of the computer with which the applications programmer is working.

Operating systems consist of hundreds of thousands, or even millions, of program instructions and require millions of dollars and many years of effort to develop. For these reasons, operating systems are considered an essential part of the equipment, are developed and maintained by each computer manufacturer, and are provided as part of the total cost of the equipment. Under such circumstances, you can see why each manufacturer has an operating system that differs from the others and often has different operating systems for different computer models. Because of these differences, we cannot explain specifics in this text. We will, however, discuss the general concepts that relate COBOL programming to operating systems, and we will assume that the reader has access to information about the specific operating system used by his or her computer installation.

In order for a COBOL program to be run, the programmer needs to communicate certain things to the operating system. Typical areas of information include the following:

Identify the user as a legitimate user of the machine.

Indicate the fact that a COBOL program is being used. (In a typical installation, programs are written in several languages and they need to be differentiated.)

Request compilation.

Indicate whether the compilation output (object program) is to be saved on disk, cards, tape, etc.

Request the use of tapes, disks, readers, printers, and other devices.

Request execution of the compiled program.

The communication process between the programmer and the operating system is effected by means of system commands known collectively as the Job Control Language (JCL). The JCL of course is not standardized. In general, the JCL is entered on cards or through an online keyboard terminal. A typical procedure is to submit a COBOL program through the card reader. In any event, the terminology of a "program deck" is common, whether or not punched cards actually are being used. Figure 2-6 portrays a typical

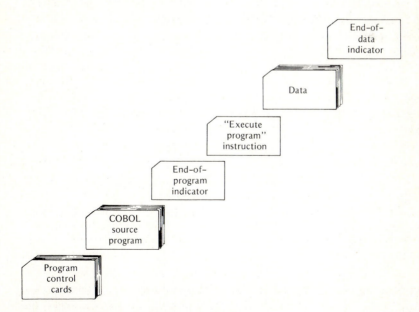

FIGURE 2-6   TYPICAL COBOL PROGRAM-DECK SETUP.

COBOL program-deck setup. The JCL statements are punched onto cards referred to as *program control cards*. In general, the first card identifies the user by account number or by name and may set parameters on maximum time, maximum number of pages, and the like. Then there are one or more JCL statements to invoke the compiler and to indicate the disposition of the object program. The source program follows, possibly with an end-of-program indicator. Then there are one or more JCL statements to ready the object program for execution. The "execute" type of instruction is followed by the data (if on cards) and often by an end-of-data indicator.

Overall, then, program control cards serve to transmit certain categories of information to the operating system. On the basis of this information, execution of the program is scheduled and monitored by the supervisor, which is the systems program concerned with controlling the operation of the computer.

REVIEW

1 The entire set of programs designed by the computer manufacturer to facilitate the automatic operation of the computer is called the _____ _____.

operating system

2 The particular program in the operating system that serves as a control module in the selection and scheduling of programs for execution is called the _____.

supervisor (or executive or monitor)

3 The types of computer programs concerned with such functions as disk-space allocation and copying data from cards to tape are called _____ programs.

systems (or utility)

4 The types of computer programs concerned with actual data processing tasks are called _____ programs.

applications

5 A programmer who uses COBOL as the programming language is a(n) [systems / applications] programmer.

applications

6 The communication process between the programmer and the operating system is carried out through the use of a set of commands called the _____.

Job Control Language (JCL)

7   Typically, the JCL is input by means of punched cards, with one statement entered on each card. The several cards that constitute a set of such cards are called _____ cards.

program control

8   In terms of the sequence of cards required for executing a COBOL program, the set of cards following the initial group of program control cards typically includes the _____. Then certain additional program control cards are included, followed by the cards which contain the _____.

source program; data

EXERCISES

2.1   What does the following statement mean? "COBOL programs should be substantially self-documenting."

2.2   What is the *operating system* of a computer? How do *program control cards* relate to such a system?

2.3   Explain the concept associated with the hierarchical grouping of data in COBOL programming and describe how the hierarchical structure is represented in a COBOL program.

2.4   What is the difference between data-names and constants in COBOL?

2.5   Explain what is meant by a *figurative constant* and name some such constants.

2.6   Give the name and the role of each of the divisions that make up a COBOL program.

2.7   Punch and run the sample program given in Figure 2–4, using several names and addresses of your own choice. Even though this exercise will not involve programming effort on your part, it will provide you with the opportunity to familiarize yourself with the program-submission procedures of your installation.

APPENDIX: KEYPUNCH OPERATING INSTRUCTIONS

Figure 2–7 presents an overall view of a keypunch, and Figure 2–8 portrays the keyboard of this unit. Refer to these figures as you read the following instructions.

1   Make sure that the power switch is on. Turn the PRINT toggle switch on;

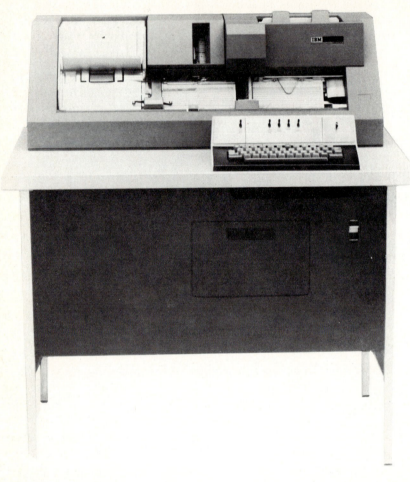

FIGURE 2-7   IBM 29 KEYPUNCH (IBM CORPORATION).

it is located just above the keyboard. Make sure that the feed hopper has an adequate number of cards.

2   Press the FEED key to feed a card from the feed hopper.

3   Press the REG (register) key to position the card under the punching station.

4   *Punch alphabetic* information by pressing appropriate keys. Keys are labeled. In order to determine the column ready to be punched next, observe the indicator inside the glass cover located to the left of the feed

FIGURE 2-8 KEYBOARD CHART FOR THE IBM 29 KEYPUNCH (IBM CORPORATION).

hopper. *Punch numeric* information by holding the NUM (numeric) key down. Keys are labeled. *Space* by means of the long space bar.

5 To remove a card from the punching station, press the REL (release) key. (In some keypunches, the label is EJECT instead of REL.) If you want to punch another card, go to reference point 2 above and repeat the cycle. If you have finished, press REL, then REG, then REL. The card will move to the output stacker in the upper left of the keypunch.

6 To duplicate a card that has just been punched, press the REL key to advance the card to the reading station. Press FEED, then REG, to position a blank card under the punching station. Depress the DUP (duplicate) key. Holding the DUP key down causes duplication at the rate of 10 columns per second. Tapping the DUP key advances the card one column at a time.

7 To duplicate portions of a card and to punch corrections or additions, place the original card in the reading station. Press FEED, then REG. To duplicate a number of columns, press the DUP key. To punch in some columns, punch as usual.

8   To backspace, depress the backspace key located directly below the reading station of the punch.

9   For more efficient punching, turn on the AUTO FEED toggle switch. Then depress FEED twice. After that, every time you depress REL, a new card is fed and registered automatically, thus eliminating the need to depress FEED and REG every time. When making duplications or corrections, however, turn off the AUTO FEED switch.

3

Writing complete programs

INTRODUCTION

The purpose of this chapter is to provide a complete but rudimentary set of COBOL instructions so that the student can begin to write complete programs. In subsequent chapters we will present additional statement types, as well as additional variations of statements presented in this chapter.

The chapter, by necessity, is lengthy. We recommend a quick initial reading of the entire chapter so as to grasp the entire set of ideas and to form a general framework within which to study, upon a more careful second reading, the specific programming concepts that are included.

TASK ANALYSIS AND DESCRIPTION

As described in Chapter 1, the first step in the programming process is to analyze the task so that we will have a clear understanding of the purpose and scope of the program. We also discussed the need for systems analysis and design to precede the programming process; however, our objective here is to illustrate the development of a small program, so we have chosen a very limited task.

We wish to print a salary report for the employees of a department so that we can review the salaries for male and female employees. A manager has asked us to give a report listing employee salaries according to sex and has suggested that we list each employee's name and then enter the annual salary in one of two columns, one for men and the other for women. We therefore will sketch the outline of the report as follows:

	SALARY	
NAME	MEN	WOMEN
.	.	.
.	.	.
.	.	.

As we think this project through a little more, we realize that such a report would be useful for individual reference, but it would not be very useful for analysis. So we decide jointly with the manager that it would be more useful to compute the average salary for each category of employee in the department and, while we are at it, to print the total salaries for each category.

As we further analyze the task, we develop the report design presented in Figure 3-1. Notice that we have included an example showing asterisks instead of a salary for one of the employees. We asked ourselves the question: What should be done if an employee is not identified as either a woman or man? This could happen by initial failure to complete the classification code on a personnel form or by a later transcription error. For instance, if we use M and F for male and female respectively, we might enounter a letter that is neither M nor F, perhaps due to a typist hitting the wrong key. So we have decided that if a person is not properly classified we will still list the name, but leave a column asterisk-filled to alert the reader. Of course, we also would omit the corresponding salary from the computation of the averages.

Another factor included in task analysis is the identification of the source of the input data. In this example, we make the simplified assumption that the data are recorded on cards, each card representing an employee.

	ANNUAL SALARY	
EMPLOYEE NAME	MEN	WOMEN
JONES, A.	18200.00	
ANDERSON, P.	12000.00	
ROBERTS, M.		15000.00
PROUST, K. *****		
NICHOLSON, J.	19600.00	
PHILLIPS, P.		18500.00
WORK, A.		20000.00
TOTAL	49800.00	53500.00
AVERAGE	16600.00	17833.33

FIGURE 3-1   SAMPLE SALARY REPORT.

So we obtain a *record layout* of the data on each record, as shown in Figure 3-2.

Since we now feel confident that we understand the task well enough, we proceed to design the report format in more precise form. As presented in Figure 3-3, a *print-layout* chart is prepared to give exact specification to the report format. We decided to leave a margin of 15 columns to the left, and we allow for 15 columns for the employee name. Since the input record layout in Figure 3-2 indicates that the name field includes 15 characters, we do not need a field any larger than this for the output. The output fields for salary for each individual and for the total are the same size, which may seem risky since the total could grow larger. Notice, however, that in this case the salary field in the input record contains five positions to the left of the decimal, and we have allowed seven such positions in the output. Thus, we in fact have not made the two total fields too small. Instead, we have

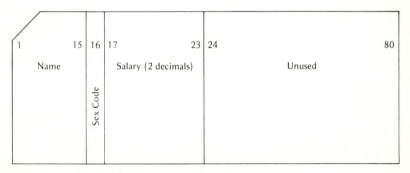

FIGURE 3-2   LAYOUT OF INPUT FOR SAMPLE COBOL PROGRAM.

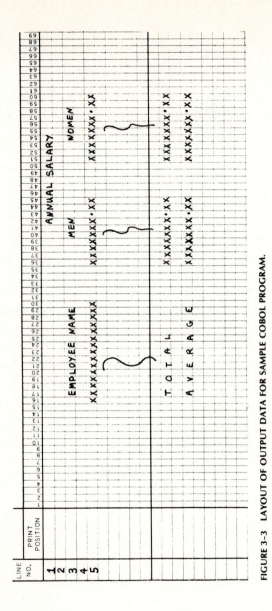

FIGURE 3–3   LAYOUT OF OUTPUT DATA FOR SAMPLE COBOL PROGRAM.

allowed the individual salary fields to be too large, which does no harm. Normally we would make these two types of fields different in size, but we are trying to keep the task simple in this program.

REVIEW

1 The purpose of the sample program described in this section is to perform an analysis using as input data the name, sex code, and _____ of each employee.

salary

2 Of the two types of record-layout forms that may be used in conjunction with writing a program, the one that describes the data to be processed is the input _____ layout.

record

3 Of the two types of record-layout forms, the one that describes the desired printer output is the _____-layout chart.

print

4 The output of the program is to list annual salaries for men and women in separate columns, and to calculate the _____ of the salaries and the _____ of the salaries for each group.

total; average

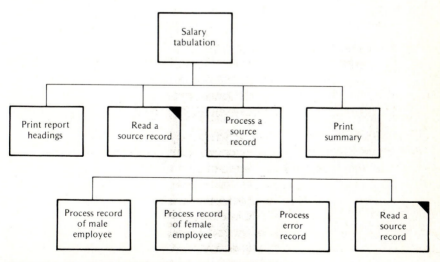

FIGURE 3-4   STRUCTURE CHART FOR THE SAMPLE PROGRAM.

```
IDENTIFICATION DIVISION.
PROGRAM-ID. SALARY.
*
ENVIRONMENT DIVISION.
*
CONFIGURATION SECTION.
SOURCE-COMPUTER. ABC-480.
OBJECT-COMPUTER. ABC-480.

INPUT-OUTPUT SECTION.
FILE-CONTROL.
     SELECT EMPL-FILE   ASSIGN TO CARD-READER.
     SELECT PRINT-FILE  ASSIGN TO PRINTER.
*
DATA DIVISION.

FILE SECTION.
FD   EMPL-FILE
     LABEL RECORDS ARE OMITTED
     DATA RECORD IS EMPL-RECORD.
01   EMPL-RECORD.
     02 NAME-IN                 PIC X(15).
     02 SEX-CODE                PIC 9.
        88 MALE                 VALUE 1.
        88 FEMALE               VALUE 2.
        88 ERROR-SEX-CODE       VALUE ZERO, 3 THRU 9.
     02 SALARY-IN               PIC 99999V99.
     02 FILLER                  PIC X(57).
*
FD   PRINT-FILE
     LABEL RECORDS OMITTED
     DATA RECORD IS PRINT-LINE.
01   PRINT-LINE                 PIC X(132).
*
WORKING-STORAGE SECTION.
*
01   SEX-COUNTERS.
     02  NO-OF-MEN              PIC 99 VALUE ZERO.
     02  NO-OF-WOMEN            PIC 99 VALUE ZERO.
01   SAL-TOTALS.
     02  MEN-TOTAL-SAL          PIC 9(7)V99 VALUE ZERO.
     02  WOMEN-TOTAL-SAL        PIC 9(7)V99 VALUE ZERO.
*
01   END-OF-FILE-TEST          PIC XXX VALUE 'NO'.
     88 NO-MORE-RECORDS VALUE 'YES'.
*
01   HEADER1.
     02 FILLER                  PIC X(41) VALUE SPACES.
     02 FILLER                  PIC X(13) VALUE 'ANNUAL SALARY'.
*
/
01   HEADER2.
     02 FILLER                  PIC X(16) VALUE SPACES.
     02 FILLER                  PIC X(13) VALUE 'EMPLOYEE NAME'.
     02 FILLER                  PIC X(10) VALUE SPACES.
     02 FILLER                  PIC X(3)  VALUE 'MEN'.
     02 FILLER                  PIC X(11) VALUE SPACES.
     02 FILLER                  PIC X(5)  VALUE 'WOMEN'.
01   REPORT-LINE.
     02 FILLER                  PIC X(15) VALUE SPACES.
     02 NAME-OUT                PIC X(15).
     02 ERROR-SIGNAL            PIC X(5)  VALUE SPACES.
     02 MEN-SAL-OUT             PIC ZZZ9999.99 BLANK WHEN ZERO.
     02 FILLER                  PIC X(5)  VALUE SPACES.
     02 WOMEN-SAL-OUT           PIC ZZZ9999.99 BLANK WHEN ZERO.
/
PROCEDURE DIVISION.
*
PROGRAM-SUMMARY.
*
     OPEN INPUT  EMPL-FILE
          OUTPUT PRINT-FILE
*
     PERFORM PRINT-HEADINGS
```

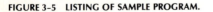

FIGURE 3-5   LISTING OF SAMPLE PROGRAM.

```
*
        PERFORM READ-EMPL-RECORD
*
        PERFORM PROCESS-A-RECORD
                UNTIL NO-MORE-RECORDS
*
        PERFORM PRINT-SUMMARY
*
        CLOSE EMPL-FILE
        CLOSE PRINT-FILE
*
        STOP RUN.
*
*
    PRINT-HEADINGS.
        WRITE PRINT-LINE FROM HEADER1
                AFTER ADVANCING PAGE.
        WRITE PRINT-LINE FROM HEADER2
                AFTER ADVANCING 2 LINES.
        MOVE SPACES TO PRINT-LINE
        WRITE PRINT-LINE
                AFTER ADVANCING 2 LINES.
*
    READ-EMPL-RECORD.
        READ EMPL-FILE
                AT END MOVE 'YES' TO END-OF-FILE-TEST.
*
    PROCESS-A-RECORD.
        IF MALE
            PERFORM PROCESS-MEN.
        IF FEMALE
            PERFORM PROCESS-WOMEN.
        IF ERROR-SEX-CODE
            PERFORM PROCESS-ERROR-CODE.
*
        MOVE NAME-IN TO NAME-OUT
        WRITE PRINT-LINE FROM REPORT-LINE
                BEFORE ADVANCING 1 LINE.
        MOVE SPACES TO REPORT-LINE.
*
        PERFORM READ-EMPL-RECORD.
*
    PROCESS-MEN.
        MOVE SALARY-IN TO MEN-SAL-OUT
        MOVE ZEROS TO WOMEN-SAL-OUT
        ADD 1 TO NO-OF-MEN
        ADD SALARY-IN TO MEN-TOTAL-SAL.
*
    PROCESS-WOMEN.
        MOVE SALARY-IN TO WOMEN-SAL-OUT
        MOVE ZEROS TO MEN-SAL-OUT
        ADD 1 TO NO-OF-WOMEN
        ADD SALARY-IN TO WOMEN-TOTAL-SAL.
*
    PROCESS-ERROR-CODE.
        MOVE ALL '*' TO ERROR-SIGNAL.
*
*
    PRINT-SUMMARY.
        MOVE ' TOTAL' TO NAME-OUT
        MOVE MEN-TOTAL-SAL TO MEN-SAL-OUT
        MOVE WOMEN-TOTAL-SAL TO WOMEN-SAL-OUT
        WRITE PRINT-LINE FROM REPORT-LINE
                AFTER ADVANCING 3 LINES.
*
        DIVIDE NO-OF-MEN INTO MEN-TOTAL-SAL
                GIVING MEN-SAL-OUT
        DIVIDE NO-OF-WOMEN INTO WOMEN-TOTAL-SAL
                GIVING WOMEN-SAL-OUT
*
        MOVE 'A V E R A G E' TO NAME-OUT
        WRITE PRINT-LINE FROM REPORT-LINE
                AFTER ADVANCING 2 LINES.
```

FIGURE 3-5 (*continued*).

SAMPLE PROGRAM

Figure 3-4 presents the *structure chart,* which identifies the main functions performed by the program. Such charts are discussed more extensively in the next chapter, but for now we can recognize that each box identifies one basic function in the program. The first main function is to print the headings of the report and the last function is to print the summary consisting of totals and averages. The repeated function is the one labeled Process a Source Record, which involves the appropriate processing for each record and the reading of the next record. In the structure chart, the fact that the Read a Source Record function is included in more than one place in the chart is indicated by shading the upper-right-hand corner of the respective blocks.

Figure 3-5 presents a listing of the sample program. This program will be referenced throughout the remainder of this chapter to allow the reader to relate the various types of language statements to a concrete case.

THE IDENTIFICATION DIVISION

The function of the IDENTIFICATION DIVISION is to supply information about the program to others who may read or use the program. On the COBOL Coding Form, we start in column 8 with the words INDENTIFICA-TION DIVISION. The first and only required paragraph is the PROGRAM-ID, which is followed by the program-name chosen by the programmer. As in the example, we may have:

IDENTIFICATION DIVISION.
PROGRAM-ID. SALARY.

In this case, the word SALARY is the name the programmer has chosen to identify the program. This name must start with an alphabetic character and may consist of up to 30 alphabetic or numeric characters unless the specific compiler limits the number to fewer. The two lines shown in the example are sufficient content for the IDENTIFICATION DIVISION. All other paragraphs are optional but, if they are used, must be written in the order shown. The following example includes optional paragraphs. The underlined words are COBOL reserved words, which are required; the other words are a matter of the programmer's choice.

IDENTIFICATION DIVISION.
PROGRAM-ID. SALARY.
AUTHOR. LEE WALTERS.
INSTALLATION. XYZ CORPORATION.
DATE-WRITTEN. JANUARY 14, 1981.

<u>DATE-COMPILED</u>.
<u>SECURITY</u>. THIS PROGRAM RESTRICTED TO PERSONNEL WHO HAVE BEEN
CLEARED BY THE CONTROLLER'S OFFICE.

All paragraph-names start in column 8 and, as indicated above, are all optional with the exception of PROGRAM-ID. The compiler does not process what follows the COBOL words but only prints this content. Thus, after DATE-WRITTEN we could have written DURING THE SPRING OF 81. The compiler derives no more meaning from JANUARY than from the nonsense syllables AMZXAB; therefore, the programmer should be concerned simply with choosing verbal descriptions that will be meaningful to the potential readers of the program.

Note that the DATE-COMPILED paragraph is left blank. The compiler will insert the actual date, and the source listing will include that date.

An entry in the IDENTIFICATION DIVISION may extend to more than one line, as illustrated in the case of the SECURITY paragraph. In such a case, the lines subsequent to the first one must all start in column 12 or to the right of column 12. The PROGRAM-ID paragraph, however, is restricted to one word, which must not exceed 30 characters in length.

REVIEW

1 The order in which the four divisions of a COBOL program appear is:
_____, _____, _____, and
_____.

> IDENTIFICATION;
> ENVIRONMENT;
> DATA;
> PROCEDURE

2 Other than the division name itself, the only paragraph required in the IDENTIFICATION DIVISION is the one named _____.

> PROGRAM-ID

3 Although other entries in the IDENTIFICATION DIVISION may extend to more than one line, the PROGRAM-ID paragraph is normally restricted to one word which must not exceed _____ (number) characters in length.

> 30

4 Overall, the purpose of the IDENTIFICATION DIVISION of a COBOL program is to _____.

> *describe the program to potential*
> *users (etc.)*

THE ENVIRONMENT DIVISION

A COBOL program written for one computer normally can be processed on another computer, with the exception of the ENVIRONMENT DIVISION portion of the program. The reason for this exception is that the specified equipment to be used in running the program is described in this division. Since the equipment at different computer centers differs in terms of manufacturer and model, the ENVIRONMENT DIVISION of a COBOL program has to be tailored to each computer installation. This may seem inconvenient, but consider also the advantages of this modular design of COBOL. Since equipment differences affect the ENVIRONMENT DIVISION only, this division of the program can be changed without rewriting any of the other three divisions.

The following illustration of an ENVIRONMENT DIVISION is reproduced from the sample program in Figure 3–5:

```
ENVIRONMENT DIVISION.
CONFIGURATION SECTION.
SOURCE-COMPUTER. ABC-480.
OBJECT-COMPUTER. ABC-480.
INPUT-OUTPUT SECTION.
FILE-CONTROL.
     SELECT EMPL-FILE ASSIGN TO CARD-READER.
     SELECT PRINT-FILE ASSIGN TO PRINTER.
```

There are two sections in this example division, the CONFIGURATION and the INPUT-OUTPUT. The SOURCE-COMPUTER and OBJECT-COMPUTER paragraphs serve documentation purposes. ABC-480 is fictitious in the example and would be replaced by a manufacturer's name and model number.

In this example, there is one paragraph in the INPUT-OUTPUT SECTION: the FILE-CONTROL paragraph. The SELECT statement identifies the name of a file, in this case CARD-FILE. This file-name is the programmer's choice and is formed in compliance with COBOL name formation rules (although some compilers place further restrictions, such as that the first 12 characters must be unique). The ASSIGN statement declares that this file will be associated with the hardware device whose name follows, in this case CARD-READER. Similarly, PRINT-FILE identifies another file-name, and the hardware device with which this file will be associated is PRINTER (thus, this file will include the output information). Device names are neither COBOL words nor programmer supplied; they are *implementor-names,* which means they are specific to the compiler used. Instead of the natural words shown in the example, the user of IBM compilers is likely to have entries of the following type:

SELECT CARD-FILE ASSIGN TO SYS005-UR-2540R-S.
SELECT PRINT-FILE ASSIGN TO SYS006-UT-1403-S.

In this case the terms SYS005-UR-2540R-S and SYS006-UT-1403-S stand for card reader and printer, respectively. The appendix at the end of this chapter illustrates some device designations for a few selected computer systems.

Apart from the specific computer name and the card reader and printer designations, the entries shown in the example are sufficient to guide the student in writing an ENVIRONMENT DIVISION for a program that involves input from the card reader and output on the printer. Later in the text, additional considerations and options will be described.

REVIEW

1 Of the four divisions of a COBOL program, the one written with an orientation to a particular computer center and its equipment is the _____ DIVISION.

ENVIRONMENT

2 The two sections of the ENVIRONMENT DIVISION are the CONFIG-URATION SECTION and the INPUT-OUTPUT SECTION. Of these, the one that serves to identify the equipment to be used and is the only section specifically required is the _____ SECTION.

CONFIGURATION

3 The section of the ENVIRONMENT DIVISION concerned with the as-signment of specified files to particular devices is the _____ SECTION.

INPUT-OUTPUT

4 Overall, the division of a COBOL program concerned with supplying general information about the program is the _____ DIVISION, whereas the division that specifies the equipment to be used is the _____ DIVISION.

IDENTIFICATION;
ENVIRONMENT

THE DATA DIVISION

The DATA DIVISION identifies storage fields and their names. Com-monly, it consists of two sections: the FILE and the WORKING-STORAGE sections. In its simplest form, the function of the FILE SECTION of the DATA DIVISION is to describe each file used in the program by specifying:

1 The name of the file
2 The name assigned to the record in the file
3 The hierarchical structure of the data fields in the record
4 The field size and type of data in each storage field of the record.

The FILE SECTION of Figure 3–5 is reproduced here:

```
FILE SECTION.
FD  EMPL-FILE
        LABEL RECORDS ARE OMITTED
        DATA RECORD IS EMPL-RECORD.
01  EMPL-RECORD.
        02  NAME-IN                 PIC X(15).
        02  SEX-CODE                 PIC 9.
            88  MALE                 VALUE 1.
            88  FEMALE               VALUE 2.
            88  ERROR-SEX-CODE       VALUE ZERO, 3 THRU 9.
        02  SALARY-IN                PIC 99999V99.
        02  FILLER                   PIC X(57).
*
FD  PRINT-FILE
        LABEL RECORDS OMITTED
        DATA RECORD IS PRINT-LINE.
01  PRINT-LINE                       PIC X(132).
```

The designation FD is needed at the beginning of each file description; it stands for File Description. FD is always followed by a file-name, in this case EMPL-FILE for the first FD entry. The statement LABEL RECORDS ARE OMITTED indicates that this file has no labels. In a magnetic tape or disk file, label records are not omitted; in a card file or print file labels have no meaning. The use of labels is described in Chapter 9: "Sequential File Processing." For the time being, we will assume that labels are omitted. The next clause in the FD entry, DATA RECORD IS EMPL-RECORD, identifies the name of the record in the file as EMPL-RECORD. The word EMPL-RECORD is the programmer's choice.

Following the FD entry, a record description is written. The 01 level number introduces the record-name: EMPL-RECORD. The following four entries describe the fields that are subordinate, or parts of the record. Each is introduced with the 02 level number, indicating that it is a subordinate field. PIC is an abbreviated form of PICTURE, an alternative form and a COBOL reserved word. The PIC clause is used to describe the size and data characteristics of the field; the use of this clause is described in some detail later in this section.

NAME-IN, SEX-CODE, and SALARY-IN are data-names referencing fields on the record. MALE, FEMALE, and ERROR-SEX-CODE are *condition-names* used to reference conditions identified by the contents of the field that they follow. For instance, MALE VALUE 1 identifies the condition-name MALE as the condition of SEX-CODE having a value (content) of 1. This concept is further explained later in this section.

FILLER is a COBOL reserved word. It is an optional name for a field to which no specific mention will be made in the program. The use of FILLER eliminates the need to coin more data-names than needed. Since it is not used directly, FILLER can be used to name several fields without causing any problems of unique identification. An imperative rule of the language is that all references in a program must be made to unique field names. This rule is not violated by use of the nonunique name FILLER, because this field is not referenced in the program.

The second FD entry describes the PRINT-FILE associated with the printer. The record-name is PRINT-LINE, and it has no subordinate data field.

Storage fields associated with the file records receive data from, or are used to send data to, external input-output devices, such as card readers and printers. In addition to such storage fields, there also is a need for storage fields to store partial results, to save data for later computations, to store header data, and the like.

The following excerpts from Figure 3–5 illustrate the WORKING-STORAGE SECTION:

```
WORKING-STORAGE SECTION.
    *
 01   SEX-COUNTERS.
      02   NO-OF-MEN            PIC 99 VALUE ZERO.
      02   NO-OF-WOMEN          PIC 99 VALUE ZERO.
 01   SAL-TOTALS.
      02   MEN-TOTAL-SAL        PIC 9(7)V99 VALUE ZERO.
      02   WOMEN-TOTAL-SAL      PIC 9(7)V99 VALUE ZERO.
    *
 01   END-OF-FILE-TEST          PIC XXX VALUE 'NO'.
      88   NO-MORE-RECORDS VALUE 'YES'.
 01   HEADER1.
      02   FILLER               PIC X(41) VALUE SPACES.
      02   FILLER               PIC X(13) VALUE 'ANNUAL SALARY'.
```

The two fields NO-OF-MEN and NO-OF-WOMEN are used in the program as accumulators to count the number of men and women tabulated. They have been grouped under the 01 SEX-COUNTERS group data-name to give visibility to their common function, as also was done in the case of the two salary totals under the entry 01 SAL-TOTALS.

WORKING-STORAGE fields may be initialized to desired values, as is illustrated in the two excerpted examples of END-OF-FILE-TEST and HEADER1. In the case of the END-OF-FILE-TEST, we have specified VALUE 'NO', which means that we want this field to contain the characters 'NO' at the start of program execution. In the case of HEADER1, we specified a field of 41 [PIC X(41)] blanks (VALUES SPACES) and another field that is to contain the characters 'ANNUAL SALARY'. Such initial values are specified for WORKING-STORAGE SECTION entries, not for FILE SECTION entries. In the case of input files, fields in file records receive their data from the external storage device; thus, it makes no sense to specify initial values. In the case of output record fields, initial values cannot be specified because of "double-buffering" practices of operating systems, as is explained in Chapter 9.

We also should add a note that there is a special level-number, 77, that can be used instead of 01 for elementary data items (ones not having 02 or higher levels underneath them). The practice was universal in "older" programs and still is allowed in all compilers; however, it has been dropped because the 77 level serves no necessary purpose. Still, it is likely that anyone involved with COBOL programs will encounter programs having 77 level numbers in the WORKING-STORAGE SECTION of programs written previously.

REVIEW

1   Of the four divisions of a COBOL program, the one concerned with the identification and description of storage fields is the _____ division.

                                                                                    DATA

2   After the DATA DIVISION and FILE SECTION have been identified in the program, the designation FD is used and always is followed by a file-name. FD is a reserved COBOL word and stands for _____ _____.

                                                                        File Description

3   A label as such typically is *not* attached to a file when the data are entered on [punched cards / magnetic tape].

                                                                        punched cards

4   After the name of the file, the next item of information given in the FD entry is the name of the _____ contained in the file.

                                                                                    record

5 The level number assigned to the whole record is always _____ (number).

> 01

6 All fields in the record that are directly subordinate to the overall record commonly are assigned the level number _____ (number).

> 02 *or higher*

7 When a WORKING-STORAGE field is at the elementary level and therefore contains no subordinate fields, the level number assigned to the field is _____ (number).

> 01 (*or 77*)

8 An initial value can be established in a WORKING-STORAGE field by use of the _____ clause.

> VALUE

9 The VALUE clause can be used in the WORKING-STORAGE SECTION to establish field values that are [numeric only / numeric or nonnumeric].

> *numeric or nonnumeric (for*
> *example, a nonnumeric literal*
> *such as 'ANNUAL SALARY' can*
> *be assigned)*

THE PICTURE CLAUSE

Level numbers define the hierarchical structure of data items in a record, whereas data-names identify each field in the record by name. Beyond this, the PICTURE clause associated with each item is used to describe the field size and indicates such information as whether the field is numeric, alphabetic, or alphanumeric; whether it is computational or display; whether it contains editing characters; whether it contains a decimal point; and whether a numeric field can contain a negative value. All this is accomplished by use of the PICTURE clause.

The abbreviated form, PIC, is equally valid and is the form used in the example for no other reason than personal preference.

Referring to the sample program, we have an entry:

```
02   NAME-IN      PIC X(15).
```

The X is a PICTURE character that stands for an alphanumeric field. The (15) stands for the number of positions in the field, in this case 15. Thus X(15) indicates an alphanumeric field of 15 positions. Incidentally, data are referred to as alphanumeric, numeric, or alphabetic. In COBOL, an alphanumeric field can contain any legitimate COBOL character. A numeric field may contain only the digits 0–9 and an algebraic sign. An alphabetic field may contain the blank and any of the letters A–Z.

Another example of the PICTURE clause is:

02   SEX-CODE   PIC 9.

In this case the 9 indicates a numeric field of one position. The fact that there is only one 9 is the reason for the field size being 1. Contrast this to:

02   NO-OF-MEN   PIC 99 VALUE ZERO.

The statement above identifies a two-position numeric field. Thus, the number of 9s indicates the size of the field.

A decimal point is indicated with a V. The V PICTURE character shows the location of an *implied* decimal point. Consider the example:

02   SALARY-IN   PIC 99999V99.

The position of the V indicates that the first five character positions contain integer values and that the last two positions in the field contain decimal values. It may be recalled that SALARY-IN refers to the data input from card columns 16–22 of the card input record. If on a given card these columns have 1254325 punched in them, the data will be read and stored as if it were 12,543.25 in ordinary language. Notice that the decimal point is not punched. Rather, the PICTURE provides the information to read in the last two digits as if they were entered to the right of a decimal point.

A PICTURE character may be repeated to indicate field size, or we may use parentheses enclosing a constant. We thus can have the following equivalent pairs of designations:

PIC 9999   is equivalent to 9(4)
PC 99999V99   is equivalent to 9(5)V9(2)
PIC X(5)   is equivalent to XXXXX.

However, PIC X(42) cannot be written in the form of 42 X's because a rule of the language states that no more than 30 PICTURE characters can be used in a given clause—and it is a sensible rule, at least for the example.

So far we have discussed examples and rules concerned with forming alphanumeric and numeric fields, the latter with or without a decimal point. We now will consider *numeric edited* fields. In COBOL there is a definite distinction between numeric data used for computation and numeric data used for printing; the latter are referred to as edited data. Chapter 6 contains an expanded discussion of editing. At present we will consider two options exemplified in:

02   MEN-SAL-OUT   PIC ZZZ9999.99 BLANK WHEN ZERO.

The Z's are zero-suppress PICTURE characters. They imply that in this field of seven integers and two decimal positions any leading zeros in the first three positions should be replaced with blanks. Recall that numeric data do not include blanks. Thus, if we had a field that contained 0001234.56 and we wanted to print this data without the leading zeros, we first would move the data to an edited numeric field and then print the edited field. The other point to notice in this example is that a decimal point is included in the PICTURE character string. This is an editing decimal point and will be printed as such. In contrast, if we print a field that contains a V, no decimal point will be printed.

The BLANK WHEN ZERO clause specifies that if the value of MEN-SAL-OUT is zero then the whole field should be filled with blanks. There will be 10 blank characters, since the editing decimal point is one of the positions in the field.

In a limited context, we have discussed the PICTURE clause for the following uses:

1   To define alphanumeric fields using the X PICTURE character
2   To define numeric fields using the 9 character
3   To define an implied decimal point using the V character
4   To suppress leading zeros by moving data to an edited numeric field using the Z character
5   To print a decimal point by moving data to an edited numeric field using the decimal (.) character.

These rudimentary rules will suffice for the present. They will enable the student to write complete programs without being in full command of the PICTURE options, which will be discussed further in Chapter 5: "Basic DATA DIVISION Features."

REVIEW

1   The character in the PICTURE clause used to indicate that the field can contain alphabetic, numeric, or special symbols is the _____ character.

X

2   The character in the PICTURE clause which indicates that a field has numeric content only is the _____ character.

9

3   The character in the PICTURE clause which indicates the position of an assumed decimal point is the _____ character.

V

4   Either the V PICTURE character or the decimal (.) PICTURE character can be used to indicate the position of the decimal point. Of these, the one that requires use of a numeric edited field is the _____ character.

decimal (.)

5   The PICTURE character that serves the editing function of replacing leading zeros in a value with blanks is the _____ character.

Z

CONDITION-NAMES

In the sample program, we have used condition-names as in this example:

```
02  SEX-CODE              PIC 9.
    88  MALE              VALUE 1.
    88  FEMALE            VALUE 2.
    88  ERROR-SEX-CODE    VALUE ZERO, 3 THRU 9.
```

The special level number, 88, signifies a condition-name, not a storage field. In this example, MALE is not a field but a name given to the condition of SEX-CODE being equal to 1. Such condition-names make the program more readable. It is easier to say IF MALE . . . than to say the equivalent IF SEX-CODE = 1, which would require that we stop to consider the meaning of the numeric code.

REVIEW

1   The level number 88 always defines a [storage field / condition-name].

condition-name

2   The main advantage of using condition-names instead of numeric codes is _____.

program readability

THE PROCEDURE DIVISION

The IDENTIFICATION, ENVIRONMENT, and DATA divisions in a COBOL program perform "housekeeping tasks" in that they provide background information so that the program can be executed after compilation. On the other hand, the instructions that directly result in execution of the program are given in the PROCEDURE DIVISION. Most of the instructions in the PROCEDURE DIVISION are instructions to operate on storage locations, or fields, that have been defined in the DATA DIVISION. Some verbal counterparts of PROCEDURE DIVISION instructions go like this: "Take the data punched onto a card and enter it into storage, according to the fields described by a record in the DATA DIVISION. Add the value of one data-name to that of another and place the result in a third data-name, all three data-names and their corresponding storage descriptions having been given in the DATA DIVISION. Output the contents of a storage location on the printer." The key words, PROCEDURE DIVISION, identify the beginning of this division and begin at the A Margin of the COBOL Coding Form, followed by a period. The division consists of paragraphs, each paragraph containing at least one sentence. Each paragraph starts with a paragraph-name beginning in column 8 (A Margin). Paragraph-names are coined by the programmer following the rules of data-name formation, with one additional option: paragraph-names may be all-numeric. Sentences and statements are written in columns 12-72.

A PROCEDURE DIVISION also may consist of several sections, each one starting in column 8 with a section-name followed by the key word SECTION, as in TAX SECTION, where TAX is a programmer-chosen section-name. A section may contain several paragraphs: the need for sections occurs, however, in large or sophisticated programs that are not likely to fall within the scope of a beginner's programming exercises.

In this chapter, we present some basic instructions used in the PROCEDURE DIVISION. Additional PROCEDURE DIVISION statements are described in Chapters 6 through 8.

The two most commonly used types of PROCEDURE DIVISION statements are *imperative* and *conditional* statements. An *imperative* statement consists of a verb that indicates action, plus appropriate operands involved in the action. In this chapter, the following imperative verbs are discussed:

Input-output verbs: OPEN, READ, WRITE, CLOSE

Data transfer verb: MOVE

Arithmetic verbs: ADD, SUBTRACT, MULTIPLY, DIVIDE

Control verbs: PERFORM, STOP, GO TO.

In addition to the four types of verbs, two basic *conditional* expressions are covered in this chapter: The IF and the AT END conditional expressions.

INPUT-OUTPUT VERBS

In this section we consider four input-output verbs: OPEN, READ, WRITE, and CLOSE.

Before an input or an output file can be used by the program, it must be *opened*. It is not our purpose to go into any detail at this point, except to say that opening a file involves checking the availability of the device associated with the file. The following statement can be seen in the first paragraph in Figure 3-5:

OPEN INPUT   EMPL-FILE
    OUTPUT PRINT-FILE.

The file named EMPL-FILE is opened as input, and the file named PRINT-FILE is opened as output. Thus, the OPEN verb declares the input or output function of the file. It will be recalled that the file names appear in two other divisions of the program. In the ENVIRONMENT DIVISION the two files were assigned to the card reader and printer, respectively, and in the DATA DIVISION the FD entries referenced each file. Thus, when references to files are made in the PROCEDURE DIVISION, it is understood that information about the files already has been given in the ENVIRONMENT and DATA divisions.

The basic format of the READ instruction is: READ file-name RECORD AT END imperative statement. In Figure 3-5, in the READ-EMPL-RECORD paragraph, the input instruction is:

READ EMPL-FILE RECORD
    AT END MOVE 'YES' TO END-OF-FILE-TEST.

In the example program in Figure 3-5, we wish to read data punched onto cards. Each card is a record of the EMPL-FILE whose record was named EMPL-RECORD in the DATA DIVISION. It will be recalled that each card has the following fields:

CARD COLUMNS	CONTENT	DATA-NAME
1–15	Employee's name	NAME-IN
16	Sex code	SEX-CODE
17–23	Salary	SALARY-IN
24–80	Unused	FILLER

The representation of the data in internal storage and the assignment of data-names to storage positions can be represented by the following conceptual structure:

	EMPL-RECORD			
Data-name	NAME-IN	SEX-CODE	SALARY-IN	FILLER
Columns	1 15	16	17 23	24 80

Thus, when the command READ EMPL-FILE RECORD is executed, the data contained in the next card in the card reader will thereafter be available by use of the data-name EMPL-RECORD. Further, the data formerly contained in card columns 1–15 will be internally available by use of the data-name NAME-IN; the content of column 16 will be available under the name SEX-CODE; and the contents of columns 17–23 will be available under the name SALARY-IN.

Each execution of the READ statement causes the contents of a new card to go into EMPL-RECORD and to erase the previous data contained in EMPL-RECORD. This means that we normally process one record at a time, and, when we read the next record, we have no use for the preceding one. If we do have further use for this record, then the data should be copied into another field to be saved for subsequent use.

As part of the READ instruction, we also need to indicate what the computer should do after all the input records have been read. The AT END clause serves this purpose. When a card is read, it is examined to see if it is an end-of-file card. The specific form of an end-of-file card differs according to the computer used, but in general it contains data codes that designate it as such. Only when such a card is read is the imperative statement following AT END executed. Thus AT END is a conditional clause; it indicates that the following statement should be executed if the card just read is an end-of-file card. In our sample program, the imperative statement following AT END enters a YES in the END-OF-FILE-TEST field so that the program will be able to determine when all the data have been read in.

The output verb WRITE is similar to the input verb READ, except that reference is made to a record-name rather than a file-name. There are two basic forms illustrated in the sample program. The first one is

WRITE PRINT-LINE FROM HEADER1
    AFTER ADVANCING PAGE.

This in essence says to transfer the data in the field HEADER1 (FROM HEADER1) to PRINT-LINE, which is the record-name of the file associated with the printer, and to write the data in PRINT-LINE after skipping to the top of a new page (AFTER ADVANCING PAGE). PAGE is a COBOL reserved word which means the top of a new page on the printer.

Notice that in COBOL we do not write data directly. First we transfer it to the record of the output file, and then we write it. Now we can see why the DATA DIVISION definition of PRINT-LINE consisted of an X(132) field. It is simply a field to which we transfer whatever we want printed. For example, HEADER1 is a field that contains the first line of header data.

In the case of some IBM COBOL compilers, if programmers wish to use all of the printer character positions, then they must provide for one more position than the print line. Thus, if the printer we are using can print lines of 132 characters, we would write the following data record description:

01   PRINT-LINE   PIC X(133).

The first of these 133 positions is not printed. It is used for vertical spacing. The programmer should see to it that data fields to be printed have an extra first position containing a blank. For an IBM user, the recommended data description for HEADER1 are as indicated in the DATA DIVISION in Figure 3-5:

01   HEADER1.
     02   FILLER   PIC X VALUE SPACE.
     02   FILLER   PIC X(41) VALUE SPACES.
     02   FILLER   PIC X(13) VALUE 'ANNUAL SALARY'.

Of the 42 blank spaces, the first one will not be printed, but will be used by the system for carriage control instead. Thus, it is recommended that the programmer using IBM equipment write FILLER PIC X VALUE SPACE as the first field in all print records.

A second example from Figure 3-5 illustrates another option of the ADVANCING clause:

WRITE PRINT-LINE FROM HEADER2
     AFTER ADVANCING 2 LINES.

In this case we print the contents of HEADER2 after the printer advances two lines, which leaves one blank line between the current and the preceding output. Thus, to triple-space between lines we simply use AFTER AD-VANCING 3 LINES, and in general the integer preceding the word LINES (or LINE) specifies the vertical spacing.

We conclude this discussion of input-output verbs with the CLOSE verb, which is used after a file no longer is needed and which must be used before the end of the program. At the end of the PROGRAM-SUMMARY paragraph of Figure 3-5, we see:

CLOSE EMPL-FILE
     PRINT-FILE.

The CLOSE verb is more meaningful in the context of magnetic tapes and disk files, but it is required for card and printer files as well. File-names are written on separate lines simply to enhance readability. CLOSE EMPL-FILE PRINT-FILE would be equally acceptable in this case.

REVIEW

1   Input of data into the central storage of the computer is accomplished by executing a READ statement. Before a READ statement can be executed, a checking procedure must be carried out to determine file availability by executing a(n) _____ statement.

OPEN

2   As each record of a file is read into storage, the previous content of that storage location, which typically represents data from the preceding record that was read, is automatically [moved / erased].

erased

3   The part of the READ statement that indicates what should be done after all the records of the input file have been read is the _____ clause.

AT END

4   Output of data from a designated output file is accomplished by executing a(n) _____ instruction.

WRITE

5   Before a WRITE statement can be executed, availability of the output file must be ascertained by executing an appropriate _____ statement.

OPEN

6   Data contained in a storage location can be transferred to an output file for subsequent output by use of the _____ option, which is available with the WRITE statement.

FROM

7   A further option available with the WRITE statement allows control of the vertical spacing in the printed output. The clause used to designate spacing instruction is the _____ clause.

ADVANCING

8   When a data processing operation is completed, the availability of both the input and output files that have been used should be terminated. This is accomplished by an appropriate _____ instruction.

CLOSE

THE MOVE INSTRUCTION

The MOVE verb is used to copy data from a *sending field* to a *receiving field*. Despite what the word MOVE implies, data in fact are *not* moved but, rather, simply are copied. Thus, the instruction MOVE A to B designates that B should contain a copy of the content of A. Examples of the MOVE instruction in Figure 3-5 are:

MOVE SPACES TO PRINT-LINE
MOVE 'YES' TO END-OF-FILE-TEST
MOVE ZEROS TO WOMEN-SAL-OUT
MOVE MEN-TOTAL-SAL TO MEN-SAL-OUT

When using the MOVE verb, caution must be exercised to ascertain that the sending and receiving fields have appropriate corresponding sizes and data characteristics. This matter is explained in Chapter 6: "Basic PROCEDURE DIVISION Statements."

REVIEW

1 Execution of a MOVE instruction results in the content of a sending field being [moved / copied] in the receiving field.

copied

2 The sending field should not be [smaller / larger] than the receiving field, and the two fields should have the same data characteristics.

larger

ARITHMETIC VERBS

In this subsection we consider the use of four arithmetic verbs: ADD, SUBTRACT, MULTIPLY, DIVIDE.

The verb ADD is used to accomplish addition. As an example, suppose we have defined two storage fields in the DATA DIVISION, to which we have given the data-names SUBTOTAL and TOTAL. If we write ADD SUBTOTAL TO TOTAL, the effect will be to increase the value of TOTAL by the value of SUBTOTAL, leaving the value of SUBTOTAL unchanged.

To illustrate another option in using the ADD instruction, suppose we want to add TOTAL and SUBTOTAL and to store the result in a field we call GRAND-TOTAL. To do this we can execute the instruction:

ADD TOTAL SUBTOTAL GIVING GRAND-TOTAL.

When this statement is executed, the original contents of TOTAL and SUBTOTAL are unaffected; therefore, the order of these two is immaterial.

In the Figure 3-5 sample program, we find these examples:

ADD 1 TO NO-OF-MEN
ADD SALARY-IN TO MEN-TOTAL-SAL

The first example illustrates the use of a numeric constant as an operand of the ADD verb. Both examples illustrate the use of *accumulators*. If we check back in the WORKING-STORAGE SECTION of the DATA DIVISION, it will be observed that NO-OF-MEN and MEN-TOTAL-SAL were both initialized with a VALUE ZERO. This is necessary, since in the PROCEDURE DIVISION we say ADD . . . TO. . . . The initial contents of memory are, in general, not zero. Thus, if we have neglected to initialize the NO-OF-MEN field, for instance, we add 1 to nonzero and likely nonnumeric data, with erroneous or unpredictable results. It should be emphasized that, when a field is defined as numeric (use of the 9 PICTURE character), it does not mean that it will necessarily contain numeric data. A good example is the common student error of not filling a numeric punched card field with leading zeros. Suppose that a field SALARY-IN PIC 99999V99 receives data from card columns 17–23 which have been punched as | |8|0|0|0|0|0|. The first position was left blank. The blank is a distinct character in the memory of a computer, and it is not the same as zero. Execution of ADD SALARY-IN TO MEN-TOTAL-SAL would result in erroneous arithmetic, since the addend would not be 8000.00 but "blank 8000.00" which is entirely incorrect.

In light of the above discussion, it also should be obvious now that arithmetic must be performed using fields defined as numeric fields in the DATA DIVISION. What may not be so obvious is that arithmetic *must not* be performed using numeric edited fields. Thus, fields whose PICTURE clauses contain Z's or editing decimal points (as well as other editing characters to be learned later) must not be operands in arithmetic statements. The 9 and the V, on the other hand, do define numeric items.

The verb SUBTRACT is used to accomplish arithmetic subtraction. It parallels the ADD verb in the two forms we discuss in this section:

SUBTRACT AMOUNT FROM SUM
SUBTRACT AMOUNT FROM SUM GIVING BALANCE

The first example will cause the value of AMOUNT to be subtracted from the value of SUM, causing the content of SUM to change (unless AMOUNT is equal to zero). The second example causes the subtraction to take place, but the result now is stored in BALANCE, leaving AMOUNT *and* SUM unchanged.

At this point we take the opportunity to introduce the subject of negative numbers in COBOL. It is the responsibility of the programmer to define a field so that it can contain a negative value. Suppose we have:

```
02   AMOUNT      PIC 999
02   SUM         PIC 999
```

If AMOUNT contains the value 500 and SUM contains the value 100, the instruction SUBTRACT AMOUNT FROM SUM will cause SUM to contain 400, not −400. To avoid such problems we should have defined SUM in the DATA DIVISION as:

02   SUM PIC   S999

The S PICTURE character designates a *signed* field and allows representation of negative values. As a general rule, all numeric fields should be signed. In the example, Figure 3–5, we did not do this because of the nature of the problem.

When punching negative data, the negative sign is *overpunched* in the rightmost column of the field. To overpunch the negative sign, do as follows: when punching the rightmost digit, depress the MULTIPUNCH key on the upper left corner of the keyboard and hold it down while punching the digit *and* the negative sign. In this fashion both characters are entered in one column.

The verb MULTIPLY is used to accomplish multiplication. Consider these two forms:

MULTIPLY QUANTITY BY PRICE
MULTIPLY QUANTITY BY PRICE GIVING AMOUNT

The first instruction will cause the product of QUANTITY and PRICE to be stored in PRICE. The second instruction will leave QUANTITY and PRICE unaffected, storing their product in AMOUNT.

The DIVIDE verb can be used as in:

DIVIDE PRICE INTO AMOUNT
DIVIDE NO-OF-MEN INTO MEN-TOTAL-SAL GIVING MEN-SAL-OUT

The first instruction will store the quotient of AMOUNT divided by PRICE in AMOUNT. The second example, taken from Figure 3–5, will store the quotient of MEN-TOTAL-SAL divided by NO-OF-MEN in MEN-SAL-OUT.

REVIEW

1   Assume that the storage locations with data-names X, Y, and Z contain, both initially and before each statement, the values indicated on the first line of the following table. For each of the COBOL statements in the table, indicate the value contained in each storage location after state-

ment execution. Place a check after any statement that is not an executable ADD instruction.

	STATEMENT	VALUE IN		
		X	Y	Z
	Initial values:	10	12	100
a	ADD X TO Y			
b	ADD X Y GIVING Z			
c	ADD XY			
d	ADD Z TO Y			

   a   10; 22; 100
   b   10; 12; 22
   c   ✔(TO or GIVING *is missing*)
   d   10; 112; 100

2   Assume that storage locations with data-names X, Y, and Z initially contain the values indicated on the first line of the following table. For each of the table's COBOL statements, indicate the value contained in each storage location after statement execution. Place a check after any statement that is not an executable SUBTRACT instruction.

	STATEMENT	X	Y	Z
	Initial values:	90	30	20
a	SUBTRACT Y FROM Z			
b	SUBTRACT Z FROM Y			
c	SUBTRACT Z FROM X GIVING Y			
d	SUBTRACT X FROM Y GIVING Z			

   a   90; 30; −10
   b   90; 10; 20
   c   90; 70; 20
   d   90; 30; −60

3   Assume that the storage locations with data-names X, Y, and Z initially contain the values indicated on the first line of the following table. For each of the table's COBOL statements, indicate the value contained in each storage location after statement execution. Place a check after any statement that is not an executable MULTIPLY or DIVIDE instruction.

		RESULTING VALUE IN		
STATEMENT		X	Y	Z
Initial values:		90	30	10
a	MULTIPLY Y BY Z			
b	MULTIPLY Y BY Z GIVING X			
c	MULTIPLY Z BY Y			
d	DIVIDE X BY Z			
e	DIVIDE Z INTO X			
f	DIVIDE Z INTO X GIVING Y			

a   90; 30; 300
b   300; 30; 10
c   90; 300; 10
d   ✔ (incorrect form)
e   9; 30; 10
f   90; 9; 10

4   If a field conceivably could contain a negative value, then in the DATA DIVISION the PICTURE clause for such a field should include the _____ PICTURE character as the leftmost character in the field.

S

CONDITIONAL EXPRESSIONS

Conditional expressions allow the program to test for a condition and, depending on the result, to do one thing or another. In the example program of Figure 3-5, we wanted to test whether an employee record referred to a man, a woman, or neither (the latter being an error), so we wrote statements such as:

IF MALE
    PERFORM PROCESS-MEN.
IF FEMALE
    PERFORM PROCESS-WOMEN.

The first conditional statement tests for the condition signified by the condition-name MALE which, it will be recalled, is the condition that SEX-CODE equals 1. If the condition is true, we will do the statement that follows (PERFORM PROCESS-MEN) until we encounter the period. If the condition is false, we will do nothing and will continue with the next sentence in the program, recognizing that the next sentence begins after the period.

Other examples of the IF conditional expression are:

IF BALANCE IS GREATER THAN 82.50
IF NAME IS EQUAL TO "THOMPSON"
IF M-DATA IS NOT EQUAL TO "DECEMBER"
IF 35 IS LESS THAN COUNTER
IF "ABC 123" IS NOT EQUAL TO PARTCODE
IF AMOUNT IS EQUAL TO ZERO

A second form of the conditional IF utilizes ELSE to specify the actions to be taken when the condition is not met. Suppose that the supplier gives a 0.01 discount to all customers, but a 0.03 discount to purchasers of 1,000 or more units. We would write:

IF QUANTITY IS LESS THAN 1000
    MULTIPLY 0.99 BY PRICE
ELSE
    MULTIPLY 0.97 BY PRICE.
MULTIPLY PRICE BY QUANTITY GIVING TOTAL.

The statement following the condition and preceding ELSE is executed if the condition is true. The statement following ELSE and preceding the next period is executed if the condition is false. In any case, the period following the ELSE statement is crucial since it marks the end of the conditional sentence. Note that in this quantity discount example the MULTIPLY PRICE BY QUANTITY GIVING TOTAL statement is executed regardless of the truth or falsity of the condition. To understand the point even better, consider what would happen if the period after the words MULTIPLY 0.97 BY PRICE were removed. The answer is that the total would be computed only if the condition QUANTITY IS LESS THAN 1000 were false.

The following operators may be used to form conditional expressions:

GREATER THAN	or	$>$
NOT GREATER THAN	or	NOT $>$
LESS THAN	or	$<$
NOT LESS THAN	or	NOT $<$
EQUAL TO	or	$=$
NOT EQUAL TO	or	NOT $=$

The words and symbols are equally valid, and the choice depends strictly on programmer preference.

A special conditional expression is the AT END clause, which always is associated with the READ statement. In terms of function, AT END simply means "IF you read the end-of-file code."

REVIEW

1 Whereas the AT END clause is an example of a specialized conditional expression, more general conditional expressions make use of the _____ statement.

IF

2 If the condition specified in the IF clause is *not* met, then program execution continues with [the statement that directly follows the IF / the next sentence / the next paragraph].

the next sentence

3 The option used in conjunction with the IF clause that makes it possible to execute one of two alternative statements (or sets of statements) without having to use two separate IF conditionals is the _____ option.

ELSE

4 Suppose that, if AMOUNT is greater than 10, PRICE should be discounted by 0.20; and if AMOUNT is not greater than 10, PRICE should be discounted by 0.10. Write the COBOL program statement to achieve this result by using the ELSE option.

_____

_____

_____

_____

IF AMOUNT IS GREATER THAN 10
MULTIPLY 0.80 BY PRICE
ELSE
MULTIPLY 0.90 BY PRICE.
(*Note that* "MULTIPLY
PRICE BY 0.80" *is not
correct, because a literal
cannot follow* BY *when*
GIVING *is not used.*)

5 Using the previous question, accomplish the same computational objective by using two separate IF statements.

_____

_____

_____

_____

IF AMOUNT IS GREATER THAN 10
MULTIPLY 0.80 BY PRICE.
IF AMOUNT IS NOT GREATER THAN 10
MULTIPLY 0.90 BY PRICE.

CONTROL VERBS

Program instructions in the PROCEDURE DIVISION are executed in the order in which they are written, from top to bottom, except when control verbs interrupt this normal flow. In this section we will describe some basic forms of program control.

The PERFORM verb provides a powerful mechanism for program control. Referring to the PROGRAM-SUMMARY paragraph in Figure 3-5, one can observe the instruction:

PERFORM PRINT-HEADINGS.

PRINT-HEADINGS is a paragraph-name. The effect of the instruction is to branch to the indicated paragraph, execute the instructions in that paragraph, and then return to the statement that immediately follows the PERFORM instruction (which in this case happens to be another PERFORM statement).

It can be seen that use of four PERFORM statements in the PROGRAM-SUMMARY paragraph of Figure 3-5 has indeed enabled us to make it a summary. The details of processing are specified in the PERFORMed paragraphs, which in turn also may PERFORM other paragraphs. For instance, PROGRAM-SUMMARY PERFORMs PROCESS-A-RECORD, which in turn PERFORMs PROCESS-MEN, and so forth.

The PERFORM verb also can be used to execute an iterative procedure, or loop, as in the case of the following example from Figure 3-5:

PERFORM PROCESS-A-RECORD
    UNTIL NO-MORE-RECORDS.

It will be recalled that NO-MORE-RECORDS is true when the end-of-file condition has been reached in the EMPL-FILE assigned to the card reader. The PERFORM just given operates as follows: the condition NO-MORE-RECORDS is tested; if it is true nothing happens, and the program then leaves this PERFORM and continues with the next statement, which happens to be the PERFORM PRINT-SUMMARY; if the condition is not ture, then PROCESS-A-RECORD is executed, and the whole process is repeated until the NO-MORE-RECORDS condition becomes true.

In flowchart form we have:

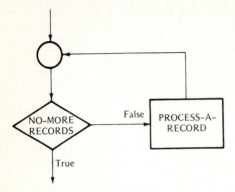

Another control verb in COBOL is GO TO. Until recently it was one of the most used verbs in all programming languages; however, it has been found that its unrestricted use is likely to create difficulty in reading a program and may contribute to the development of error-prone programs. A controversy exists between those who feel that GO TO must never be used and those who feel that it should continue to be used under certain circumstances. In this book we refrain from the use of GO TO as much as possible; still, programs written in the first quarter-century of programming history are full of GO TO statements, and the momentum of tradition is likely to result in some continued use of this control verb.

GO TO is an unconditional branch to a paragraph (or section) name. The object of a GO TO statement is a paragraph-name, and we can execute an individual sentence with a paragraph only by entering the paragraph from its beginning. Consider Figure 3-6, and note that there are two GO TO statements in the READING-DATA paragraph and that they both make reference to paragraph-names. In one case, reference is made to the paragraph-name in which the GO TO statement itself is included, because it is desired to repeat the instructions of that paragraph. Execution of a COBOL program always flows from the first to subsequent paragraphs, unless a transfer-of-control statement interrupts the flow. Therefore, at the end of the STARTER paragraph in Figure 3-6, we need not say GO TO READING-DATA, since program execution automatically will continue with the next paragraph.

Finally, a control statement used in every COBOL program is STOP RUN, which terminates program execution. A program may contain more than one STOP RUN statement, depending on the logic of the program. As an example, we may wish to terminate execution upon reading an error record, or we may wish to use STOP RUN after the program has completed its normal course. In Figure 3-6, the STOP RUN statement is the last one in the program. This does not have to be the case. STOP RUN signifies the logical end of the program. It should not be confused with the physical end

```
PROCEDURE DIVISION.
STARTER.
    OPEN INPUT ACCOUNTS-RECEIVABLE OUTPUT SUM-REPORT.
READING-DATA.
    READ ACCOUNTS-RECEIVABLE RECORD AT END GO TO WRAP-UP.
    IF AMOUNT IS GREATER THAN 500.00 MOVE RECEIVABLE TO REP-LINE.
    WRITE REP-LINE.
    ADD AMOUNT TO TOTAL.
    ADD 1 TO COUNTER.
    GO TO READING-DATA.
WRAP-UP.
    MOVE TOTAL TO EDTOTAL.
    DIVIDE COUNTER INTO TOTAL.
    MOVE TOTAL TO AVERAGE.
    MOVE SUMMARY TO REP-LINE WRITE REP-LINE.
    CLOSE ACCOUNTS-RECEIVABLE SUM-REPORT.
    STOP RUN.
```

FIGURE 3-6   AN EXAMPLE OF A PROCEDURE DIVISION USING GO TO.

of the program, which is indicated by a program control card that varies with the operating system used.

All files should be closed with the CLOSE verb prior to execution of the STOP RUN instruction.

REVIEW

1   The COBOL verbs that interrupt the normal sequential execution of program statements are called _____ verbs.

control

2   The control verb that makes it possible to branch to a specified paragraph, execute it, and then return to the statement immediately following the statement containing the control verb is _____.

PERFORM

3   The COBOL verb that provides the programmer with the capability of achieving branching in a program without returning to the point of original branching is _____.

GO TO

4   In order to continue program execution with the instructions in the next sequential paragraph of the PROCEDURE DIVISION, a GO TO statement [is / is not] required at the end of the preceding paragraph.

is not

5 The control statement used to terminate program execution is _____
_____.

STOP RUN

6 A STOP RUN statement [must appear only once / can appear in several places] in a program.

can appear in several places

7 STOP RUN [is / need not be] the last statement in a program.

need not be

DEBUGGING AND TESTING A PROGRAM

The programmer goes through a number of steps in completing a programming project. These steps are summarized in Table 3–1 and serve as the basis for the description of program debugging and testing that is presented in this final section of the chapter. Look now, therefore, at the steps included in Table 3–1, before reading the fuller explanation below.

The first step, that of designing the overall program structure, includes a number of elements that can serve to simplify the overall programming task. Because of the importance of this step, it is described in some detail in the next chapter: "Program Structure and Design."

After the program has been written on the COBOL coding form, the programmer should review the program to correct errors and to ascertain that the program is complete. Often there will be data-names that were left out of the DATA DIVISION and there may be entire paragraphs left out of the PROCEDURE DIVISION. For instance, we may encounter a PERFORM statement that refers to a paragraph-name that we have forgotten to write.

After all apparent errors and omissions in the handwritten program have been corrected, a keypunch or an online terminal is used to key-in the program into machine-readable form. The keyed-in version then is listed

TABLE 3–1 STEPS INCLUDED IN A PROGRAMMING PROJECT

- Design the overall program structure.
- Write the program on a COBOL coding form.
- Review and correct the handwritten program.
- Key-in the program in machine-readable form.
- Obtain a listing of the program for review.
- Compile the program and review any diagnostic error messages.
- Recompile the program until no error diagnostics are issued.
- Execute the program with some limited test data.
- Review the output for the test data and determine the causes of any erroneous output.

on paper, allowing for another review in search for any further errors or omissions.

The next step in the general procedure is to compile the program and to obtain a source listing of the program from the COBOL compiler. Such a listing includes *diagnostic error messages* as part of the output. The most common types of diagnostics result from spelling errors or improper syntax, such as missing periods, parentheses, or data-names. The diagnostic messages vary from compiler to compiler, and often require some experience for interpretation of their meaning. Some examples of spelling-related and syntactical errors are included in the following statements:

1. ... LABEL RECORDS OMMITTED
          DATA RECORD IS CARD-RECORD.
2. 01 CARD-RECORD
3.   02   EMPL-NAME   PICX(30).
4.   02   EMP-SALARY   PIC 9(4V99.
5. ADD TOTAL-MALES TO 1
6. MOVE EMP-NAME TO EMPL-NAM-OUT

The errors in the previous list of statements are:

1   OMMITTED is misspelled; it should be OMITTED.
2   The period was left out after CARD-RECORD.
3   The space is missing between PIC and X(30).
4   There is no corresponding right parenthesis in 9(4V99; it should be 9(4)V99.
5   The ADD statement is syntactically incorrect. A data-name must follow TO. The statement should be corrected to ADD 1 TO TOTAL-MALES.
6   EMP-NAME is misspelled. The data name definition in line 3 is EMPL-NAME.

The preceding error diagnostics are *not* of the form that would be obtained from a compiler. The messages received are more general, never tell the programmer how to correct the error, and do not interrelate parts of the program. For instance, in the case of the error given in statement 6, the compiler simply would indicate that EMP-NAME is an unidentified data-name.

Based on the diagnostics and review of the program, corrections and changes are made, the program is recompiled, and the process is repeated until no error diagnostics are issued by the compiler. The program then is executed and tested with some limited test data. The data should be representative of the data with which the program eventually will be run but should be limited in the number of data items so that the programmer can determine manually the correct output to be obtained. For instance, for the sample salary tabulation program in this chapter, we would construct some test data that includes women, men, and some errors in the sex-code. Further, we would calculate the totals and averages as a basis for comparison with the program output.

If the test run gives any erroneous output, the programmer must find the source of the problem. This step often is the most difficult part of programming. The approach most programmers use is to "desk-check" or "walkthrough" the program. In other words, we utilize a listing of the program and the test data and we read the program instructions and apply them to the test data. As we go through the program mentally, we compare our results to the results of program execution, step by step. Often the problem will be somewhere "in the middle" of the program. In such a case, we trace and compare the program execution in the suspected area of the program, rather than from the very beginning, to save time and avoid unnecessary effort. There may be an early error, however, that only surfaces at a later point in the program. For instance, it may be that a total is incorrect at the end of program execution because we forgot to initialize an accumulator to zero. Thus, if we had forgotten to set the value of NO-OF-WOMEN to zero in the sample program, the average salary for women would be incorrect.

In the sample program in Figure 3-5, the task requires that a line of output be printed as each record is read. In this way we happen to have a natural trace of the input stream. In other programs we may not be printing output as each input record is read; in such a case it often is very useful to modify the program so that we have a trace of the input records. The trace permits us to know whether the program "went bad" as we were processing the first, the 10th, or the last record. Accordingly, we could modify the reading paragraph to list each record on the printer as it is read; for example:

```
READ-EMPL-RECORD.
    READ EMPL-FILE
        AT END MOVE 'YES' TO END-OF-FILE-TEST.
    MOVE EMPL-RECORD TO PRINT-LINE
    WRITE PRINT-LINE AFTER ADVANCING 2 LINES.
```

The program now will list every record. Even though the report will be in poor format due to the interspersed printing of report lines and the trace records, we have an easy method of tracing the input.

Of course, we can do a similar trace of any data or computational results. For instance, if we wanted to trace the values of MEN-TOTAL-SAL, we would similarly MOVE MEN-TOTAL-SAL TO PRINT LINE WRITE PRINT-LINE each time that we processed a record. There actually are alternate ways of accomplishing this all-important trace. Most computer sites have special debugging processors that allow the programmer to specify with ease desired tracings of many or all data- and record-names. Further, COBOL itself contains specialized instructions in its so-called Debugging Module that allow tracing. While both the COBOL and other debugging features are efficient for professional programmers or advanced students, the suggestions just given are an easier way to obtain desired tracing for beginning COBOL programmers.

Experience and situational insight are very useful attributes in debugging and testing; however, the best way to avoid debugging and testing problems is to be very careful in the initial design and writing of the program. It is a tested fact that the student who writes a program with little design and review effort is the one who gets caught in endless attempts to correct a poorly written program. A programmer who spends 10 hours designing, writing, and reviewing a program may spend two hours correcting compiler diagnostics and testing. On the other hand, a programmer with similar abilities who spends just five hours designing, writing, and reviewing for the same program, will likely spend 15 hours in debugging the program.

REVIEW

1   After designing the overall program structure, the program is written on a
COBOL _____.

coding form

2   The program on the coding form is reviewed to check for errors and omissions. The program is then keyed-in into machine-readable form by means of a _____ or online _____.

keypunch; terminal

3   After the keyed-in version of the program is listed and reviewed, the program is compiled in order to obtain a source listing and diagnostic
_____.

error messages

4   Corrections and changes to the program are made by reviewing all of the diagnostics. When no diagnostic error messages are obtained upon recompiling the program, the program then is executed using limited
_____.

test data

5   If the output resulting from the test data is erroneous, the programmer typically desk-checks the program by comparing mental calculations to
_____ on a step-by-step basis.

program output

6   When a programmer arranges to list every record or the result of every calculation that is associated with an output error, the procedure is called program _____.

tracing

EXERCISES

3.1   Write COBOL statements for the following computational tasks.

 a   Set TOTAL equal to the sum of SUBTOTAL-1 and SUBTOTAL-2.
 b   Add the value of BONUS to PAY.
 c   Calculate COMMISSION as the product of RATE and SALES.
 d   Make the value of SHARES equal to the number of shares that can be bought by DOLLARS at PRICE per share.

3.2   Write COBOL statements for the following data transfer tasks.

 a   Set the value of a data-name A equal to 150.
 b   Set the value of ACCUMULATOR equal to zero.
 c   Set HEADER equal to a string of the letter X.

3.3   Write COBOL statements to exchange the contents of two fields, A and B.

3.4   Write COBOL statements to terminate a program if BALANCE is equal to zero.

3.5   Correct the following COBOL program segment:

PROCEDURE DIVISION.
FIRST-PARAGRAPH. READ CARD-FILE RECORD AT END (etc.)

3.6   Write a statement to make an output file called TRANSACTIONS-FILE available for subsequent use.

3.7   Write statements to determine if an output file called PAYABLES has been read in completely and, if it has, to terminate the program at that point.

3.8   Write statements to print the (last) record of a file called FINAL-REPORT, making sure that the file is closed properly before the program terminates. The record of FINAL-REPORT is called MONTHLY-REPORT.

3.9   Write statements to print two records from a file whose record is called MONTHLY-REPORT, leaving two blank lines between the records. The first record will print the contents of HEADER-1 and the second will print the contents of HEADER-2.

3.10 Give a program instruction to execute next a paragraph called INTEREST-COMPUTATION.

3.11 If a paragraph consists of four sentences, can we write an instruction outside that paragraph to execute the third sentence next?

3.12 Write instructions to test if the MARITAL-STATUS-CODE is equal to 1 and, if it is, to execute a paragraph called SINGLES.

3.13 A storage field called SEX-CODE indicates whether a person is male or female (1 = male, 2 = female). Another field, OCCUPATION, contains the occupation of the person. Assuming the output record below, write COBOL statements to move the occupation to the appropriate place, making sure that, if a person is male, FEMALE-OCCUPATION is blank, and vice versa.

OTHER-DATA	MALE-OCCUPATION	FEMALE-OCCUPATION

3.14 A student is enrolled in HISTORY, ENGLISH, and ACCOUNTING. These three fields contain his corresponding numeric grades in those courses, using this scale: 4 = A; 3 = B; 2 = C; 1 = D; 0 = E. The history course is a two-credit course and the other two are three-credit courses. Write COBOL statements to calculate the grade-point average and store it in GRADE-POINT. Use other storage fields of your choice.

3.15 The GROSS-PAY of an employee is calculated by multiplying REGULAR-HOURS by RATE and OVERTIME-HOURS by 1.50 of RATE. Write COBOL instructions to compute GROSS-PAY, using only one work-area field for intermediate results: WORK-AREA.

3.16 A deck of cards is being read from a file called CARDS. Each card contains, among other things, a field called AMOUNT. Write COBOL PROCEDURE DIVISION statements to find the smallest value of AMOUNT read in and to store it in SMALLEST. Disregard ties. When all the cards have been read in, the program goes to the PROCESS-SMALLEST paragraph.

3.17   Is the following PROCEDURE DIVISION statement correct? ADD 3 TO FILLER.

3.18   Assume the following DATA DIVISION entries:

01   AMOUNT   PICTURE 9(4).
01   DAYS-ELAPSED   PICTURE X(9).

Are the following PROCEDURE DIVISION statements correct?

a   MOVE "ZERO" TO AMOUNT.
b   MOVE SPACES TO AMOUNT.
c   ADD 50 TO DAYS-ELAPSED.
d   MOVE ZERO TO DAYS-ELAPSED.
e   MOVE "ZERO" TO DAYS-ELAPSED.

3.19   Complete the DATA DIVISION description for the following WORKING-STORAGE record so that it corresponds to the following record layout. Use your own choice of data-names.

01   TOTALS-LINE.
    02   PIC   VALUE
    02   PIC   VALUE
    02   PIC   VALUE
    02   PIC
    02   PIC   VALUE
    02   PIC

1–16	17–25	26–35	36–45	46–50	51–60
Blank	T O T A L	Blank	Men's total salary, showing decimal point and 2 decimal places	Blank	Women's total salary, showing decimal point and 2 decimal places

3.20   Referring to the following schematic representation, write a DATA DIVISION record description using the following information:

DEPT	2 letters
NAME	5 digits
RATE	4 digits, 2 decimal places, used for arithmetic
SKILL	1 letter
REGULAR	7 digits, 2 decimal places, used for arithmetic
OVERTIME	6 digits, 2 decimal places, used for arithmetic
SS-TAX	5 digits, 2 decimal places, used for arithmetic

PAY-RECORD						
EMPLOYEE		RATE	SKILL	YEAR-TO-DATE		
DEPT	NAME			GROSS		SS-TAX
				REGULAR	OVERTIME	

3.21 A program contains the statement:

PERFORM REPORT-PRINTING UNTIL END-OF-DATA.

Explain how END-OF-DATA is defined in the program, and illustrate how it is used as a control mechanism. Assume that END-OF-DATA refers to an input file called CUSTOMER-FILE.

3.22 Using the PERFORM verb, write PROCEDURE DIVISION instructions to read 10 cards from a file called CARD-FILE, accumulating the sum of the values in a field called AMOUNT. (*Hint:* Set up a counter to count the cards read in and test for the value of the counter to determine termination.)

3.23 Punch and run the sample program given in Figure 3-5. Use as input the sample data shown in Figure 3-1. Even though this exercise will not involve programming effort on your part, it will provide you with the opportunity to familiarize yourself with the ENVIRONMENT DIVISION entries pertinent to your computer, and the program-submission procedures of your installation.

3.24 Write a COBOL program that will take any deck of punched cards and list its contents on the printer. Another way of describing the program function is to say: write an "80-80 card-to-printer lister."

APPENDIX: SAMPLE ENVIRONMENT DIVISION ENTRIES FOR SELECTED COMPUTER SYSTEMS

ENVIRONMENT DIVISION FOR IBM 370

ENVIRONMENT DIVISION.
CONFIGURATION SECTION.
SOURCE-COMPUTER. IBM-370.
OBJECT-COMPUTER. IBM-370.

INPUT-OUTPUT SECTION.
FILE-CONTROL.
    SELECT   CARD-FILE   ASSIGN TO SYS012-UR-2540R-S.
    SELECT   PRINT-FILE   ASSIGN TO SYS014-UR-1403-S.
    SELECT   TAPE-FILE   ASSIGN TO SYS008-UT-2400-S.
    SELECT   DISK-FILE   ASSIGN TO SYS161-DA-3370-I.

ENVIRONMENT DIVISION FOR UNIVAC 1100

ENVIRONMENT DIVISION.
CONFIGURATION SECTION.
SOURCE-COMPUTER. UNIVAC-1110.
OBJECT-COMPUTER. UNIVAC-1110.
INPUT-OUTPUT SECTION.
FILE-CONTROL.
    SELECT   CARD-FILE   ASSIGN TO CARD-READER.
    SELECT   PRINT-FILE   ASSIGN TO PRINTER.
    SELECT   TAPE-FILE   ASSIGN TO UNISERVO . . .
    SELECT   DISK-FILE   ASSIGN TO MASS-STORAGE . . .

ENVIRONMENT DIVISION FOR DEC PDP-11

ENVIRONMENT DIVISION.
CONFIGURATION SECTION.
SOURCE-COMPUTER. PDP-11.
OBJECT-COMPUTER. PDP-11.
INPUT-OUTPUT SECTION.
FILE-CONTROL.
    SELECT   CARD-FILE   ASSIGN TO 'SY:'.
    SELECT   PRINT-FILE   ASSIGN TO 'SY:'.
    SELECT   DISK-FILE   ASSIGN TO 'SY:'.

ENVIRONMENT DIVISION FOR BURROUGHS 1700

ENVIRONMENT DIVISION.
CONFIGURATION SECTION.
SOURCE-COMPUTER. BURROUGHS B-1700.
OBJECT-COMPUTER. BURROUGHS B-1700.
INPUT-OUTPUT SECTION.

```
FILE-CONTROL.
     SELECT    CARD-FILE      ASSIGN TO READER.
     SELECT    PRINT-FILE     ASSIGN TO PRINTER.
     SELECT    DISK-FILE      ASSIGN TO DISK.
```

ENVIRONMENT DIVISION FOR CDC 6600

```
ENVIRONMENT DIVISION.
CONFIGURATION SECTION.
SOURCE-COMPUTER. 6600.
OBJECT-COMPUTER. 6600.
INPUT-OUTPUT SECTION.
FILE-CONTROL.
     SELECT    CARD-FILE      ASSIGN TO INPUT.
     SELECT    PRINT-FILE     ASSIGN TO OUTPUT.
     SELECT    TAPE-FILE      ASSIGN TO TAPE01A.
     SELECT    DISK-FILE      ASSIGN TO DISK01.
```

4

Program structure and design

CHARACTERISTICS OF GOOD PROGRAMS

The traditional approach to the programming process was to view a computer program as a personal creation by an individual. Often, the characteristic of a good programmer was the ability to write clever programs—"clever" often being synonymous with complex and obscure. The trouble with such programs is that it is difficult for persons other than the author to understand them, and even the author may have difficulty when months or years intervene. In recent years, therefore, particular emphasis has been given to the principles and concepts by which good programs can be written. The following is a list of several characteristics associated with a good computer program:

1   It is correct.
2   It is understandable.
3   It is easy to change.
4   It has been written efficiently.
5   It should execute efficiently.

Of course, the identification of these characteristics does not in itself tell us how to write such programs. However, after identifying these programming objectives, we describe the concepts and techniques by which these objectives can be achieved in the subsequent sections of this chapter.

The first, and usually most important, characteristic of a good program is that it is *correct*. The program should carry out the task for which it was designed and do so without error. In order to achieve this objective, a complete and clear specification of the purpose and functions of the program must be obtained, as discussed in the section "Task Analysis and Description" in Chapter 1. Thus, program "errors" can be due to outright mistakes on the part of a programmer or be due to a lack of a clear description regarding the required output of the program.

The second characteristic of a good program is that it is *understandable*. Although a computer program is a set of instructions for a computer, it also should be comprehensible to other people. A person other than the author should be able to read and understand the purpose and functions of the program. Higher-level programming languages such as COBOL are intended for human use and interpretation in their direct form, and are intended for machine use only indirectly, through compilation.

Next, a computer program should be *easy to change*. Changes in products, changes in company procedures, new government regulations, and the like all lead to the necessity of modifying existing computer programs. As a consequence, most established computer installations devote considerable time and effort to changing existing programs. A good program not only fulfills its original purpose but also is adopted easily in response to a changing environment.

The fourth characteristic of a good program is that it has been *written efficiently*. This refers to the amount of time spent in writing the program. Of course, this objective is secondary to the program being correct, understandable, and easy to change. In practice, the easiest way to write a program quickly is to write it partly correct, leave it difficult to understand, or allow its obscurity to make it difficult to change. Still, the principal cost of a programming project is the programmer's time; thus, the best programming techniques economize this time while still satisfying the objectives that the program be correct, understandable, and easy to change.

The final characteristic of a good program that we should consider is that it should *execute efficiently*. The program should be written so that it does not use more computer storage nor more computer processing time than is necessary. Again, this objective also is secondary to the primary objectives that a program be correct, understandable, and easy to change. Furthermore, as hardware costs have decreased relative to programmers' salaries, overall cost considerations often justify minimizing the concern about a high level of efficiency in program execution. A programmer should be alert, nevertheless, to the techniques by which efficient program execution can be achieved.

REVIEW

1   The most important characteristic of a good computer program is that it is _____.

correct

2   Probable reference to the program by individuals other than the original programmer dictates that it should be _____, while unavoidable changes in data processing requirements in most organizations make it desirable that the program be _____.

understandable; easy to change

3   In order to economize the programmer's time, a program should be _____ efficiently; in order to economize the use of computer hardware, the program should _____ efficiently.

written; execute

PARTITIONING THE PROGRAMMING TASK

A fundamental approach to programming by which good programs can be developed is that of *partitioning* the overall task. This refers to breaking up a large programming task into several smaller and more specific tasks or functions. A program should not be viewed as a monolithic entity; rather, it should be subdivided into several *modules,* or procedures. By this approach, the programmer can concentrate her or his efforts on one specific part of the overall programming task at any one time.

A key question, of course, is: What is a program module? First, each module must be *cohesive,* which means that it must relate to the performance of *one* programming function. We therefore should partition the overall programming task into functions and create as many modules as there are functions. The next question is: What is a function? Generally speaking, a *function* is a specific task that can be described in a line or two of plain language. A good example is, "Compute this week's FICA tax for this employee"; but what about the function, "process the payroll for this week"? We would say that this is a composite function that should be partitioned into more specific tasks or functions. On the other hand, the printing of a line of information or the adding of two numbers would be too specific a function for the purpose of developing a program module. As you may have surmised, there is no hard and fast definition as to what constitutes a programming function. In practice, knowledge of the overall task, combined with some programming experience, is a sufficient basis for subdividing task into functions. As a general rule, when a single function is coded into PROCEDURE DIVISION statements, it should not exceed one page of computer printout (about 50 lines of code) in length; however, the function may be represented by just one line of code in some cases.

In a COBOL program, a module, which represents a single function, typically is coded as a paragraph or as a section consisting of several paragraphs. The beginning programmer will find that most of the functions performed in a typical small program are represented by just a few lines of code. Reviewing the sample program in Chapter 3 (Figure 3–5), it is easy to identify the modules as consisting of several lines in each case. For example, the shortest module in this program is PROCESS-ERROR-CODE, which consists of just one line; while the longest module, PRINT-SUMMARY, consists of 12 lines.

REVIEW

1   The process by which the overall programming task is subdivided into several more specific tasks is called _____.

partitioning

2   Both in program writing as well as in program review, a COBOL program can be said to be comprised of several program _____.

modules

3   In writing a COBOL program, a module is developed for each programming _____ that has been identified.

function (or *task*)

4   As a general rule, when a single function is coded into PROCEDURE DIVISION statements, it should not exceed about _____ lines of code.

50

THE HIERARCHY OF PROGRAM MODULES

In the preceding section we described the concept of partitioning a program into several modules, each performing a single, identifiable function. A related concept that is used in order to achieve a good program structure is the concept of *hierarchy*. Application of this concept requires that the functions or modules in a program be related to one another in a hierarchical structure. A hierarchical structure classifies some modules as being *subordinate* to other modules, while the latter modules are *superior,* or *superordinate,* to the subordinate modules. A given module may be subordinate to one module but be superior with respect to another module. The concept of a hierarchical program structure is illustrated in Figure 4–1. Such a chart is called a *structure chart, hierarchy chart,* or *visual table of contents* (VTOC, pronounced "vee-tok").

Figure 4–1 shows that one module, Process Payroll, is superior to all of the other modules. It is always true that there is one—and only one—module that represents the entire program function, in this case the processing of a payroll system. The module at the top of the hierarchy is designated as being at level 0. Level 1 in the hierarchy is the level immediately below level 0. In Figure 4–1 there are four modules at level 1 that are subordinate to the module Process Payroll. One of the modules at level 1, Edit Input Data, has two subordinate modules that constitute level 2 in the hierarchy.

Just as we emphasized that partitioning of the overall programming task should be purposeful, so also must the hierachical arrangement be based on logic and purpose in order to achieve a good program structure. How do we develop such a hierarchy? Development of a logical and purposeful hierarchy of modules is achieved by applying the *top-down design* approach.

In accordance with the top-down design, we begin by identifying the

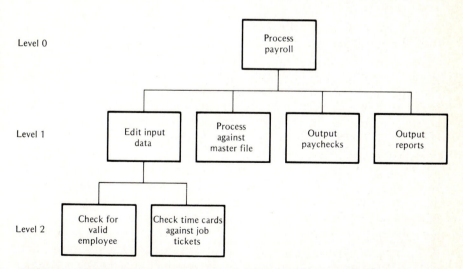

FIGURE 4-1   PARTIAL STRUCTURE CHART DEPICTING THE HIERARCHICAL PROGRAM STRUCTURE FOR PAYROLL PROCESSING.

top module, which describes the overall function of the program. Then we partition this overall function into its main components. For example, we ask ourselves: What has to be done to process the payroll? In response to this question we identify four main functions in Figure 4-1: Edit Input Data, Process against Master File, Output Paychecks, and Output Reports. We then review these functions and consider whether any modules can be added or deleted. For instance, we might question whether or not the two separate output modules are really different functions, with the thought that they possibly should be replaced by one module, which could be called Produce Output.

When we are satisfied that the determination of modules at level 1 is complete, we consider each of these modules in turn and repeat the process of analysis as if we were at level 0. That is, for each function at level 1 we attempt to identify specific subfunctions that comprise that function. With respect to the example in Figure 4-1, we first ask: What are the main subfunctions included in Edit Input Data? Two subfunctions were identified: Check for Valid Employee, and Check Time Cards against Job Tickets. Although we need not continue with the analysis in Figure 4-1, the next step would be to determine subfunctions for the remaining level-1 functions.

The general process of identifying subfunctions continues by taking each lower level in turn. We stop when no function at any level can be partitioned any further. Recall that in the preceding section we said that a single function is a cohesive task that ultimately can be expressed in no more than about 50 lines of PROCEDURE DIVISION code, but most often requires a lot fewer.

The top-down design, by which functions and modules are determined, is an effective approach because it permits the programmer to concentrate on a single module at a time and consider the relationship of that module to its one superior. By this approach, a large programming project that is very complex is reduced to a set of projects, each of which is relatively easy. The partitioning of the overall task and the programming effort also makes it possible to have different programmers devote their efforts separately to different modules, thereby making possible timely completion of large and complex programming projects.

During the top-down analysis, the *span* of each superior module should be checked. Span refers to the number of immediate subordinate modules associated with one superior module. A good hierarchical structure is one that generally includes spans that are neither too narrow nor too wide, although specific exceptions often are justified. If most of the spans include less than three subordinates, then the spans are too narrow and the functions that are being identified are probably too broad. If most of the spans include more than five subordinates, then the spans are too wide and the functions being identified are probably too specific. Figure 4–2 portrays structure charts that represent the two extremes: spans that are too narrow and too wide. If the spans are too narrow, we should examine the possibility of further partitioning of tasks. If the spans are too wide, we should review the possibility of combining existing modules at a given level into fewer modules. Of course, the purpose of observing and changing spans is not to achieve a "correct" span for its own sake. The objective is to have a correct partition, and the spans that are developed should serve as an indicator of correct partitioning.

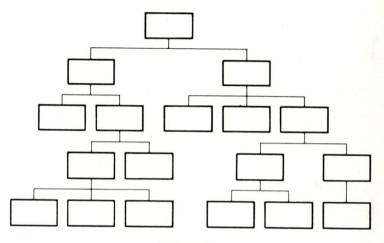

(a) Narrow Span

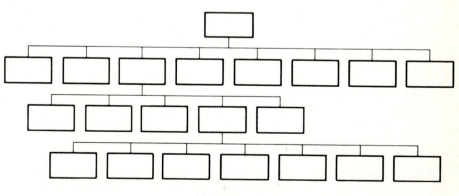

(b) Wide Span

FIGURE 4–2   STRUCTURE CHARTS DEPICTING DIFFERENT SPANS IN A HIERARCHY.

Another useful concept in developing a hierarchical structure of tasks and modules is that of *independence*. Each module at a given level should be independent of its "peers" at that level. The concept of independence requires that each module represent a function that clearly is distinct from all other modules that have a common immediate superior. Further, a module that is subordinate should be *dependent* on its immediate superior, which means that the module would be executed only under the control of that superior. Thus, a module at level 3 in a hierarchy should never call for the execution of another module at level 3, nor should it call for the execution of a module at a superior level to it. A module may be subordinate to more than one superior module, however, and perhaps at different levels in each case. For instance, a common function such as reading a record from a file may be invoked by several superior modules. Such a subordinate module would be repeated at the appropriate places in the structure chart, with a recognition that the same task is represented in each case.

Application of the concepts associated with partitioning and developing a hierarchy of program modules will be presented in the last section of this chapter, "An Illustration of Program Design," after we first consider the use of flowcharts to depict the flow of program logic.

REVIEW

1   In terms of the hierarchical relationship between modules, a program module can be described as being either _____ to another module or _____ to another module.

> subordinate; superior (or superordinate)

2   The chart that portrays hierarchical program structure is called a _____.

> structure chart (or hierarchy chart, or visual table of contents, VTOC)

3   The module that represents the overall program function and is superior to all other program modules is designated as being at level _____.

> 0

4   The approach to developing a hierarchical program structure by which analysis begins at level 0 and systematically is extended to the lower levels is called the _____ design.

> top-down

5   If the functions identified generally are too broad, then the spans in the structure chart will be very _____; functions that generally are too specific result in spans that are very _____.

narrow; wide

6   As a rule of thumb, spans are too narrow if most superior modules have fewer than _____ subordinates, and they are too wide if most superior modules have more than _____ subordinates.

three; five

7   That each module should represent a function that is clearly distinct from all other modules that have a common superior is the concept of _____.

independence

8   The concept of dependence dictates that execution of a given module should be under the control of _____ only.

its immediate superior

FLOWCHARTING THE PROGRAM LOGIC

As introduced in Chapter 1, a flowchart is a graphic representation of the flow of program logic. Whereas the structure chart or hierarchy chart depicts program *structure,* the flowchart depicts logical *flow.* Thus, the flowchart is concerned with the *sequence of execution* of the individual statements or groups of statements in the program. Depending on the required detail and programmer choice, a flowchart may orient only toward the logic flow across or between modules or may include consideration of program flow with respect to the minute details included within the modules.

There are three basic forms of program flow that can be used to describe the logical processes included in any program. These are called the SEQUENCE, DECISION, and DOWHILE, and they are presented in Figure 4–3.

The SEQUENCE form of flow indicates a *sequential* flow of program logic. Each block may stand for a statement, a whole module, or even a collection of modules. In COBOL we illustrate with statements in series, such as:

```
ADD TOTAL SUBTOTAL GIVING GRAND-TOTAL
MOVE GRAND-TOTAL TO EDIT-FIELD
WRITE PRINT-RECORD.
```

A fundamental concept in flowcharting is that a function block (a rectangle in the flowchart) may represent a very specific task or a function that

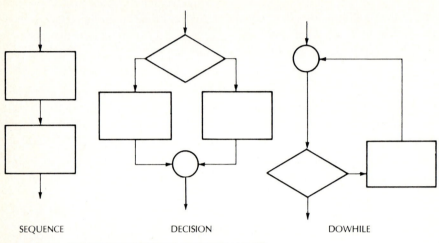

SEQUENCE   DECISION   DOWHILE

FIGURE 4-3   THE THREE BASIC FORMS OF PROGRAM FLOW.

includes relatively complex processes. In all cases, the function block is treated as a *black box*. We enter it, it does something, and we leave it. The detail of what it does is of no concern from the standpoint of the use of the function block. However, what is done within the function block (say, within a program module) could be the focus of attention in a separate, detailed, flowchart. The function block can be used as a black box in place of any process, as long as there is *one* entry point and *one* exit point associated with the process.

As the name implies, the DECISION form of flow indicates *conditional* program flow. The program takes one path or another, depending on whether a condition, often referred to as the *predicate,* is true or false. In COBOL we implement the structure as follows:

IF AMOUNT IS GREATER THAN 100
    MULTIPLY 0.20 BY PRICE
ELSE
    MULTIPLY 0.10 BY PRICE.

We may have a case whereby if a condition holds we do something and if not we continue in the program sequence. In such a case the modified DECISION flow can be represented as in Figure 4-4. In COBOL we implement this form of flow by omission of the ELSE clause, as in the following:

IF AMOUNT IS GREATER THAN 100
    MULTIPLY 0.20 BY PRICE.

Finally, the DOWHILE form of flow provides for a looping operation; that is, it provides for repetitive execution of a program segment. Of course,

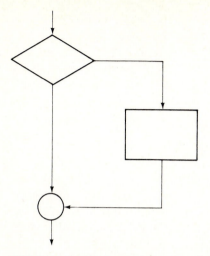

FIGURE 4-4   MODIFIED DECISION FORM OF PROGRAM FLOW.

the loop should never be infinite. Referring to the diagram for the DOWHILE flow in Figure 4-3, note that the decision block tests for a condition. If the condition holds, we exit from the loop; if not, we execute the instruction in the functional block. The following example of the DOWHILE flow is diagrammed in Figure 4-5:

PERFORM PROCESS-AND-PRINT
    UNTIL END-OF-DATA-INDICATOR = ZERO.

    The SEQUENCE, DECISION, and DOWHILE forms of program flow serve to represent most program functions and thus are considered to be the

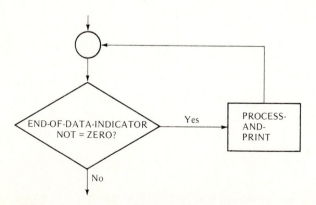

FIGURE 4-5   EXAMPLE OF DOWHILE PROGRAM FLOW.

basic forms of flow. It often is convenient, however, to recognize two additional types of program flow: DOUNTIL and CASE.

The DOUNTIL form of program flow is represented in Figure 4-6. Notice that it resembles the DOWHILE form of flow, except that the block of statements to be executed precedes the test. Thus, the block will be executed at least once. An example is:

```
PERFORM PROCESS-AND-PRINT.
PERFORM PROCESS-AND-PRINT
UNTIL END-OF-DATA-INDICATOR = ZERO.
```

Notice that coding the DOUNTIL form of flow in COBOL is a bit awkward, since an instruction has to be repeated. A function is executed unconditionally and then is executed conditionally. Essentially, the DOUNTIL flow includes a combination of the SEQUENCE and DOWHILE forms of program flow.

The second additional form of program flow is the CASE. Use of this type of flow is convenient when there is a large number of alternatives to be tested. For example, suppose that the marital status of an employee is coded as 1, 2, 3, or 4, representing single, married, divorced, or widowed, respectively. We wish to count the number of employees belonging to each class. The flowchart for this task is presented in Figure 4-7 and illustrates the program execution in the CASE form of program flow.

In COBOL there are three common ways of coding the CASE form of flow. The first way involves use of the verb EXIT, which refers to a place in the program but really does nothing. Along these lines, don't be misled by the usual meaning of the word "exit." The EXIT verb does not mean "go

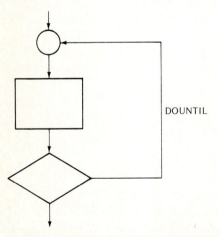

DOUNTIL

FIGURE 4-6   THE DOUNTIL FORM OF PROGRAM FLOW.

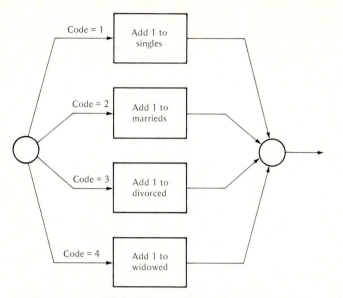

FIGURE 4-7   AN EXAMPLE OF THE CASE FORM OF PROGRAM FLOW.

out;" it really means "do nothing." The following program segment illustrates the use of the EXIT verb:

```
CHECK-MARITAL-STATUS-START.
    IF MARITAL-CODE = 1
        ADD 1 TO SINGLES
        GO TO CHECK-MARITAL-STATUS-END.
    IF MARITAL-CODE = 2
        ADD 1 TO MARRIEDS
        GO TO CHECK-MARITAL-STATUS-END.
    IF MARITAL-CODE = 3
        ADD 1 TO DIVORCED
        GO TO CHECK-MARITAL-STATUS-END.
    IF MARITAL-CODE = 4
        ADD 1 TO WIDOWED
        GO TO CHECK-MARITAL-STATUS-END.
CHECK-MARITAL-STATUS-END.
    EXIT.
```

Notice that the last GO TO in the program segment is not necessary, because natural sequential execution will lead to CHECK-MARITAL-STATUS-END in any event. It is good practice, however, to include this GO TO statement. For instance, if we now wanted to check for incorrect marital status code, we could add statements at the end of the first paragraph (CHECK-MARITAL-STATUS-START) without altering the last IF sentence.

The second way to express the CASE form of flow in COBOL is to use the special form of the GO TO . . . DEPENDING ON verb. The following program segment illustrates the use of this verb:

```
          GO TO     ADD-TO-SINGLE
                    ADD-TO-MARRIED
                    ADD-TO-DIVORCED
                    ADD-TO-WIDOWED
          DEPENDING ON MARITAL-CODE.
NEXT-PROCEDURE.
     (etc)
       ⋮
ADD-TO-SINGLE.
     ADD 1 TO SINGLES
     GO TO NEXT-PROCEDURE.
ADD-TO-MARRIED.
     ADD 1 TO MARRIEDS
     GO TO NEXT-PROCEDURE.
ADD-TO-DIVORCED.
     ADD 1 TO DIVORCED
     GO TO NEXT-PROCEDURE.
ADD-TO-WIDOWED.
     ADD 1 TO WIDOWED
     GO TO NEXT-PROCEDURE.
```

The GO TO . . . DEPENDING ON simply states that program execution should go to the first paragraph (ADD-TO-SINGLE) if MARITAL-CODE = 1, to the second paragraph if MARITAL-CODE = 2, and so on. Since we named four paragraphs, if the value of MARITAL-CODE is not in the range 1–4, the GO TO . . . DEPENDING ON in effect will be bypassed.

In both previous examples we utilized the GO TO to return to the same place regardless of which paragraph was executed. Such use of the GO TO is consistent with the fundamental rule of "one entry—one exit." Uses of GO TO that branch to different places are error-prone and are not included in well-structured programs.

The third way of implementing the CASE form of program flow is to use a "nested if" structure, as illustrated in Figure 4–8. Such nested ifs are described in Chapter 7: "Conditions and Conditional Statements." As can be seen in Figure 4–8, each nested decision has one entry and one exit. In terms of program code, we could write:

```
IF MARITAL-CODE = 1
    ADD 1 TO SINGLE
ELSE
    IF MARITAL-CODE = 2
        ADD 1 TO MARRIED
    ELSE
        IF MARITAL-CODE = 3
            ADD 1 TO DIVORCED
        ELSE
            ADD 1 TO WIDOWED.
```

Traditionally, flowcharts have been used for two main purposes: to help the programmer develop the program logic, and to serve as documentation

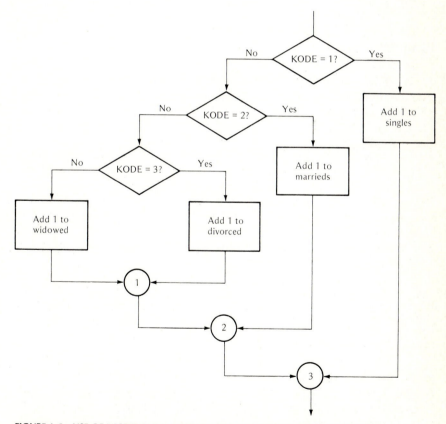

FIGURE 4-8 USE OF NESTED-IF TO ACHIEVE THE CASE FORM OF PROGRAM FLOW.

for a completed program. In recent years, however, the development of structured programming has minimized the need for and the usefulness of flowcharts. A case can be made that, if a programmer utilizes principles of good program design and structure, the program is self-documenting and a flowchart therefore is superfluous. Further, in an environment in which program modifications are frequent, redrawing flowcharts becomes cumbersome. On the other hand, there are programs available that read source code and generate flowcharts automatically, so it also can be said that drawing flowcharts for revised programs can be easy. We believe that flowcharts are effective means of communicating program logic in some cases, but in general they are superfluous. In this text we have used a very small number of flowcharts, relying instead on program design and structure as a means of communicating the function of sample programs.

REVIEW

1   Whereas program structure is represented in a structure chart, or hierarchy chart, the sequence of execution of program statements is represented in a _____.

flowchart

2   The three basic forms of program flow are the SEQUENCE, DECISION, and DOWHILE. Of these, the one in which program execution follows one path or another, depending on whether or not a condition is met, is the _____ form of flow.

DECISION

3   The form of program flow that results in repetitive execution of a program segment is the _____.

DOWHILE

4   The form of program flow that simply involves a series of instructions, or sets of instructions, which are executed in the order in which they are presented in the program, is the _____.

SEQUENCE

5   In addition to the three basic forms of program flow, two other forms are the DOUNTIL and the CASE. The form of program flow that incorporates the DOWHILE, except that the program segment that can be executed repeatedly always will be executed at least once, is the _____.

DOUNTIL

6 The form of program flow in which program execution follows one of several paths, typically depending on the value of a coded data item, is the _____.

CASE

7 Three common ways of coding the CASE form of flow in COBOL are by the use of the EXIT verb, the GO TO . . . DEPENDING ON verb, or a nested-if structure. Of these, the two ways in which each of the alternative paragraphs to be executed concludes with the same GO TO statement are by the use of the _____ and _____ _____.

EXIT verb; GO
TO . . . DEPENDING ON verb

8 When using the nested-if structure to achieve the CASE program flow, each nested decision should have _____ (number) entry point(s) _____ (number) exit point(s).

one; one

AN ILLUSTRATION OF PROGRAM DESIGN

We conclude our presentation on program structure and design by presenting an illustration of the program design that served as the basis for the sample program in Chapter 3. It will be recalled that we wanted to write a program to produce a salary report, as illustrated in Figure 3–1 in Chapter 3. We will assume here that we have already completed the task analysis as described at the beginning of Chapter 3 and are now ready to design the program.

Perhaps the best and most natural way to begin the program design is to compile a list of the main functions to be performed. For our salary report program, the main functions would be listed as:

1 Print the report heading
2 Process each employee record
3 Print the report summary

We then would make a second pass (iteration), adding more detail to the list:

1 Print report heading
2 Process each employee record
  a Read a record
  b Check whether man or woman
  c Accumulate separate totals for men and women
  d Print a line in the report

3   Print the report summary
   a   Print the accumulated totals
   b   Compute the averages
   c   Print the averages

Next we prepare a structure chart to portray the hierarchical structure of the program, as presented in Figure 4-9. Each block represents a function. The connecting lines show the hierarchical relationships between subordinate functions and their superiors. Notice, however, that the Read a Record function is subordinate to two functions. We alert the reader of the chart to this duplication of the function by shading the upper-right-hand corner of the respective blocks. We have included the Read a Record function in the Process a Record function because, in order to process a record for each employee, we need to read the record. It would seem that the Read a Record function could be removed from being a direct subordinate of the top function, Produce Salary Report; however, you would find that if you removed this function you would complicate your programming later, even though it seems natural to do so at this point.

Because almost every program reads data from a file and does so repeatedly, it is good to learn the proper approach to structure at this point: design your logic so that you read the first record as a special record and follow this with a loop that processes the record that has just been read and

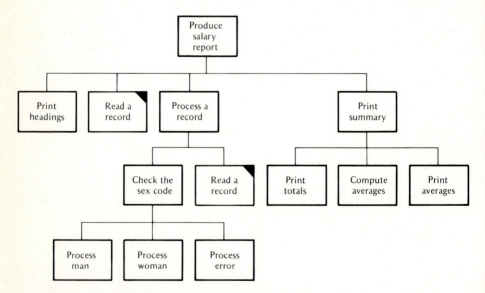

FIGURE 4-9   STRUCTURE CHART FOR THE SAMPLE PROGRAM.

reads the next record as the last thing in the loop. The loop will be repeated until we have reached the end of the file.

We can portray the flow of program execution as shown in Figure 4-10. By this design, the Process Record function will be executed only when there is, in fact, a record to process, and processing stops when the end of the file is reached.

Having made the structure chart for our program, we proceed to develop the program as a series of interrelated procedures. We not only list the functions, but we also specify the order in which they are to be executed. Table 4-1 presents a program outline. We have written the program using "pseudocode," meaning that it is written in more-or-less ordinary language; but we also have incorporated some terms and functions that anticipate the form of the program that will be written.

Just as in a structure chart, there is only *one* top function in Table 4-1, which we choose to call Program-Summary. It starts the program, controls its execution, and finally stops it. The first instruction, Open Files, specifies a task that is simple enough that it is fully expressed by this one instruction. The second instruction, however, refers to another (subordinate) paragraph. It says, Perform Print-Headings, which is the name of another procedure. At any point in the program, we have the choice of listing all of the instructions needed to do a subtask right there or of putting them in another place in the program and referring to them by a Perform Paragraph command. The general rule is to partition the program so that each function is a separate paragraph; thus, it is better to write short paragraphs that refer to other, subordinate, paragraphs. In this example, the Print-Headings function is

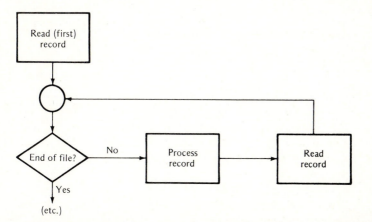

FIGURE 4-10 RECOMMENDED FLOW STRUCTURE FOR READING AND PROCESSING RECORDS FROM A FILE.

TABLE 4–1   PSEUDOCODE FOR THE SALARY REPORT PROGRAM

```
PROGRAM-SUMMARY
    Open Files
    Perform Print-Headings
    Perform Read-Record
    Perform Process-Record until no more records
    Perform Print Summary
    Close Files
    Stop
PRINT-HEADINGS
    Write two lines on top of new page and double space after the second line
READ-RECORD
    Read a Record
    If it is the end of the file set an indicator on
PROCESS-RECORD
    If the record represents a man
        Perform Process-Man
    If the record represents a woman
        Perform Process-Woman
    If the record represents neither man nor woman
        Perform Process-Error
    Print a report line
    Perform Read-Record
PROCESS-MAN
    Add 1 to number of men
    Add the salary to the total salary for men
    Move the salary data to the men's column
PROCESS-WOMAN
    Add 1 to the number of women
    Add the salary to the total salary for women
    Move the salary data to the women's column
PROCESS-ERROR
    Move asterisks to the salary fields
PRINT-SUMMARY
    Print the accumulated total salaries
    Compute the averages (e.g., divide number of men into total salary of men)
    Print the averages
```

rather trivial and could be included in its entirety in the Program-Summary paragraph; still, it would be distractive to our reading because it deals with printing details that interfere with our ability to understand the overall function of the program.

Another important reason for modularizing the structure of a program is to facilitate program modifications. If we should want to make a change in the printing of report headings, we would find it much easier to work with a paragraph whose sole function is limited to that function. Otherwise, we would have to be concerned about whether one change would impact something else in that paragraph. There is an exception to every rule, of course. Notice that the Print-Summary paragraph does not have the subordinates identified in the structure chart. Even though three distinct functions are carried out, we have decided to leave them all in one paragraph because each function is so simple.

Having developed the structure chart and the program outline, we essentially have completed the program design. We now have a good grasp of

PRODUCE-SALARY-REPORT
.
.
PRINT-HEADING
.
.
READ-A-RECORD
.
.
PROCESS-A-RECORD
.
.
CHECK-THE-SEX-CODE
.
.
PROCESS-MAN
.
.
PROCESS-WOMAN
.
.
PROCESS-ERROR
.
.
PRINT-SUMMARY
. .
.
PRINT-TOTALS
.
.
COMPUTE-AVERAGES
.
.
PRINT-AVERAGES

FIGURE 4-11   REVISED MODULE (PARAGRAPH) STRUCTURE FOR SAMPLE PROGRAM (FIGURE 3-5), BASED ON THE STRUCTURE CHART IN FIGURE 4-9.

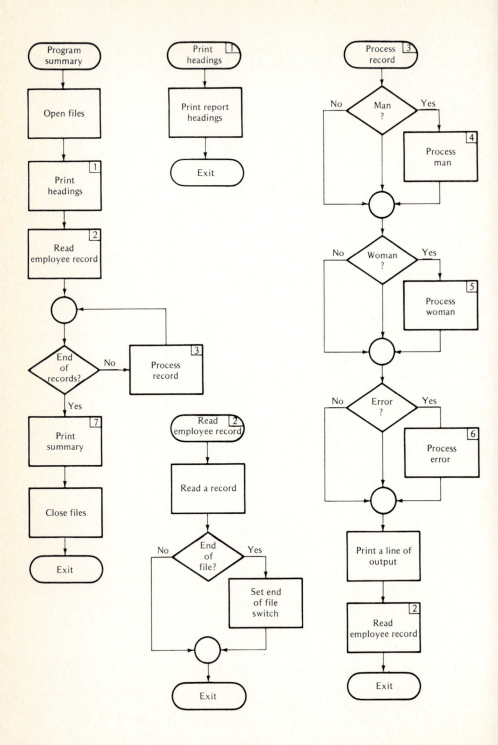

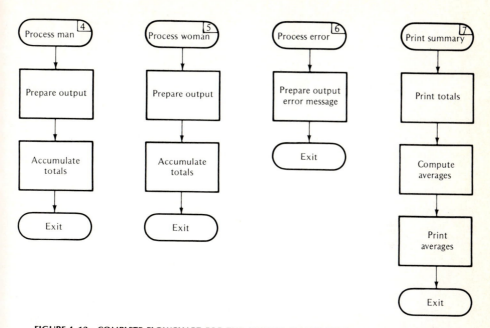

FIGURE 4-12   COMPLETE FLOWCHART FOR THE ANNUAL SALARY PROGRAM. (THE NUMBERS IN THE UPPER RIGHT-HAND CORNER OF SOME ENTRIES SERVE AS CROSS-REFERENCES BETWEEN MODULES AND THEIR RESPECTIVE BLOCKS.)

the functions to be performed and their procedural relations; therefore, we are ready to write the specific COBOL code that will do the desired task.

The sample program in Chapter 3, Figure 3-5, should be reviewed now and related to the structure chart in Figure 4-9. It will be observed that we do not have a direct one-for-one correspondence between the structure chart and the program. The reason is that the size and the simplicity of the program led us to combine some functions. For instance, Figure 4-9 contains a module labeled Check the Sex Code. The program incorporates that function in the form of the first six lines (three IF statements) in the PROCESS-A-RECORD paragraph. This revised structure is justified because of the simplicity of the task in this case, but we do want to point out that the structure in Figure 4-9 is preferable as a general approach. As we read the program in Figure 3-5, the cohesive function of the first six lines in PROCESS-A-RECORD is not immediately obvious. Figure 4-11 illustrates the module structure of the program in strict correspondence to the structure chart in Figure 4-9. (Exercise 4.3 asks the student to rewrite the program using the modules identified in Figure 4-11.)

We conclude our example by presenting a complete flowchart in Figure 4-12 that corresponds to the program logic. The chart illustrates the application of the basic forms of program flow, such as the SEQUENCE, DECISION, and DOUNTIL. Although the flowchart seems to add little in this case, it does bring out clearly the program-flow logic, and it helps us to better understand and review the correctness of the program.

REVIEW

1   We began the design of the program to produce a salary report by listing the main _____ to be performed by the program.

functions

2   After the program functions were identified, the hierarchical structure of the program was determined by preparing a _____

structure chart

3   Based on the structure chart, a program outline was prepared using more-or-less ordinary language, or _____.

pseudocode

4   The general rule that is followed in writing a program outline is to partition the program so that each function is a separate _____.

paragraph

5   After the program outline was completed, the last step in program design was done, which was _____.

to write the COBOL *program*

EXERCISES

4.1   In your own words, list and explain briefly the characteristics of a good program.

4.2   Discuss the concepts of *partitioning, hierarchy,* and *top-down design* as they relate to program structure.

4.3   Rewrite the sample program in Chapter 3 so that it is in strict correspondence with the structure chart of Figure 4-9, using the outline in Figure 4-11.

4.4   A sales file consists of records having the following format:

Salesperson Name	Date	Amount of Sale	Other Data

The records are sorted so that the records of each salesperson are together, in sequence. A program is to be written to produce a report having the following format:

SALESPERSON NAME	DATE	AMOUNT OF SALE	
JOHNSON, A. J.	03/15/81	132.29	
	03/20/81	150.15	
	04/01/81	300.00	
	.	.	
	.	.	
	.	.	
TOTAL			4,125.89

This report will be repeated for as many salespeople as there are in the file, with total sales for each salesperson reported on a new page.

a Design a structure chart for such a program, using the top-down approach.

b Write a pseudocode outline for such a program.

4.5 A program is to be developed to represent the basic logic and function of a vending machine that accepts nickels, dimes, and quarters; dispenses a 30-cent candybar; and provides the correct change, if any. Coins other than nickels, dimes, and quarters are either rejected or do not fit. We assume that we want to develop a program that reads data cards, with each data card representing one coin. The program reads the data, processes it, and either "delivers" a product and the change or reads another card representing another coin. The last card in the input deck contains a special code that indicates the end of data. After processing such a card, the program stops. Develop a flowchart of the program logic, using the basic program structures discussed in this chapter.

5
Basic DATA DIVISION features

INTRODUCTION

As described in the introductory section on the DATA DIVISION in Chapter 3, the purpose of this division of a COBOL program is to identify storage fields and their names. The DATA DIVISION commonly includes two sections: the FILE SECTION and the WORKING-STORAGE SECTION. In this chapter we describe in greater detail the features associated with these two sections of the DATA DIVISION, including the use of various types of PICTURE clauses to define the type of data in storage and the use of several other specialized clauses.

In addition to the FILE SECTION and the WORKING-STORAGE SECTION, the DATA DIVISION also can include a LINKAGE SECTION, RE-

PORT SECTION, and COMMUNICATION SECTION. The LINKAGE SEC-
TION is described in Chapter 15: "Structured Programs and Subprograms."
The REPORT SECTION is used with a special feature, the *report writer*,
which is described in Chapter 16. The COMMUNICATION SECTION can
be used to access, process, and create messages for communicating with
local and remote communication devices; coverage of this feature is beyond
the intended scope of this book.

THE FILE SECTION

Reviewing briefly the introduction in Chapter 3, the function of the FILE
SECTION is to describe each file used in the program by specifying:

1   The name of the file
2   The name assigned to the record in the file
3   The hierarchical structure of the data fields in the record
4   The field size and type of data in each storage field of the record.

In this chapter we will continue with the basic format used in Chapter 3:

```
FD  file-name
    LABEL RECORDS ARE OMITTED
    DATA RECORD is record-name.
```

Until we consider magnetic tape and disk files later in the text, it will be
assumed that the file device associated with file-name is the card reader or
printer. There is an FD entry for each file involved in a program, which is
followed by its record description. The record description begins with the
record name, which is always at the 01 level, and includes the data specifications for the data fields in the record. For instance, in the sample program
in Chapter 3 we had:

```
FD  EMPL-FILE
        LABEL RECORDS ARE OMITTED
        DATA RECORD IS EMPL-RECORD.
01  EMPL-RECORD.
    02   NAME-IN       PIC X(15).
    02   SEX-CODE      PIC 9.
    02   SALARY-IN     PIC 9(5)V99.
    02   FILLER        PIC X(57).
```

Level numbers are used to describe the hierarchical structure of data in
a record. A field without any subordinate fields is an *elementary item*, while

a field with subordinate fields is a *group item*. In the program segment above, there is one group item, EMPL-RECORD, and there are four elementary items that in this case are at the 02 level. If the NAME-IN field were structured to contain the last name in columns 1–13, the first initial in column 14, and the middle initial in column 15, we could describe the NAME-IN field as follows:

```
02  NAME-IN.
      03   LAST-NAME        PIC X(13).
      03   FIRST-INITIAL    PIC X.
      03   MIDDLE-INITIAL   PIC X.
```

Notice that in the revised program segment above, the group item NAME-IN does not have a PICTURE description. The PICTURE description is used only with elementary items.

REVIEW

1 The division of a COBOL program that includes a description of the storage fields and their names is the _____ DIVISION.

DATA

2 The two sections commonly included in the DATA DIVISION are the _____ SECTION and the _____ SECTION.

FILE; WORKING-STORAGE

3 In the FILE SECTION, we always begin a file description by identifying the name of the file in the entry, which is designated by the COBOL reserved word _____.

FD *(for File Description)*

4 After the name of the file is given, the next item of information given in the FD entry is the name of the _____ included in the file.

record

5 The level number assigned to the whole record is always _____.

01

6 In the record, a field that has subordinate fields is called a _____ item, whereas a field with no subordinates is an _____ item.

group; elementary

THE WORKING-STORAGE SECTION

The WORKING-STORAGE SECTION immediately follows the FILE SECTION in the program. Although it is possible for a program to have neither a FILE SECTION nor a WORKING-STORAGE SECTION, such a program would be very unusual. Whereas the FILE SECTION describes the files used in the program, the WORKING-STORAGE SECTION provides for the storage of data items that are not part of any file, such as intermediate calculations, report headings for printing, and numeric constants for use in calculations.

The WORKING-STORAGE SECTION consists of group items and elementary items, as is also the case in the FILE SECTION. In older versions of COBOL it was common to use a special level number, 77, to describe all elementary independent items; that is, elementary items that are not part of a group. These elementary independent items preceded all the group (or record) items which were introduced at the 01 level. However, whether the elementary independent items are designated by the level 77 or 01 makes no difference in program processing, and this is the main reason why the use of level 77 was abandoned in the late 1970s.

There is little to say about the organization of the WORKING-STORAGE SECTION except that it is a recommended practice to group related items together under a common superior in order to enhance reader awareness of their relationships. For example, in the sample program in Chapter 3 we had:

```
01   SAL-TOTALS.
     02   MEN-SAL-TOTAL      PIC 9(7)V99 VALUE ZERO.
     02   WOMEN-SAL-TOTAL    PIC 9(7)V99 VALUE ZERO.
```

The 01 group item in this program segment is used only for readability, or documentation, since we do not ever make use of the data-name SAL-TOTALS in the program. An alternative to this structure would be to write the two elementary independent items as follows:

```
01   MEN-SAL-TOTAL      PIC 9(7)V99 VALUE ZERO.
01   WOMEN-SAL-TOTAL    PIC 9(7)V99 VALUE ZERO.
```

In this alternative program segment, the similarity in the data-names and their physical consecutive order implies a relationship between them, but the relationship is much clearer when a hierarchical set of statements is written in the WORKING-STORAGE SECTION.

REVIEW

1   The section of the DATA DIVISION that provides for the storage of such data items as intermediate calculations and report headings is the _____ SECTION.

WORKING-STORAGE

2   In lieu of the older practice of using the special level number, 77, for elementary independent data items, current practice favors use of the level number _____ for such items.

01

3   When two or more elementary items are related, rather than place them in the program as elementary independent items, documentation is improved by _____.

grouping them under a common
superior

THE PICTURE CLAUSE FOR DATA DESCRIPTION

The general form of the PICTURE clause was introduced in Chapter 3 in the example of a complete program. The purpose of this DATA DIVISION feature is to describe the data included in the data items. We use the word PICTURE, or its abbreviated form PIC, and the optional word IS, followed by a string of characters that describe the data. In the following subsections, we consider in turn each of the PICTURE characters that can be used to describe data fields that are defined in the DATA DIVISION.

THE 9 PICTURE CHARACTER

The numeric 9 indicates that a storage position will only contain any of the numeric digits from 0 to 9. In this context, a blank is *not* considered equivalent to the numeric 0 and thus is not a numeric character. The field size of the item is indicated by the number of successively written 9s in the PICTURE clause; thus, PICTURE IS 999 means a field of three numeric positions. As indicated in Chapter 3, an alternative is to write a 9 followed by parentheses enclosing the number of positions in the field. For example, the statement 03 SUM PICTURE IS 9(5) indicates that SUM is a five-position numeric field. Some examples of using the 9 PICTURE character are as follows:

DESCRIPTION	NUMERIC VALUE	REPRESENTED IN STORAGE AS
02 SCHOOL-ENROLLMENT PICTURE IS 9(6)	12,327	012327
02 STOCK-ON-HAND PICTURE 9999	8,956	8956
04 POPULATION-OF-CITY PICTURE 9(10)	1,563,813	0001563813
03 UNION-MEMBERSHIP PICTURE IS 9999	285	0285

Again, note that a numeric field can contain only the digits 0–9. Blanks are *not* numeric characters. When punching data onto cards, you should be careful to zero-fill a field with leading zeros; otherwise you may be in for some surprising results. Thus, in a field of six positions, the numeric value 532 should be punched as follows:

0	0	0	5	3	2

THE V PICTURE CHARACTER

The V character indicates the position of an assumed decimal point. "Assumed" means that the decimal point is not written as part of the field and therefore is not included as part of the field size. Instead, the information about decimal-point location is stored elsewhere in the computer, so that any arithmetic computations can be done correctly. For example, if two items are multiplied and each is assumed to have two positions to the right of the decimal, the product will be understood to have four positions to the right of the decimal point. If the V character is omitted, it is understood that the decimal point is at the extreme right of the numeric field. It is not necessary, therefore, to place a V as the last character in a PICTURE clause. Of course, no more than one V is permitted in a field. Refer to the following table and note that, if we printed HOURS-WORKED without any editing, the value represented in storage, 385, would be printed *without a decimal*. Again, the V character establishes the *position* of the decimal for purposes of arithmetic manipulation but does not make the decimal point as such available for printout. Some examples of using the V character are given in this table. The caret (͜) indicates the position of the assumed decimal point.

DESCRIPTION	NUMERIC VALUE	REPRESENTED IN STORAGE AS
03 HOURS-WORKED PICTURE 99V9	38.50	38͜5
03 NET-PAY PICTURE 9(4)V99	452.39	0452͜39
02 TON-CAPACITY PICTURE 999	550	550͜
02 BALANCE PICTURE 99999V99	23561.00	23561͜00

THE P PICTURE CHARACTER

The P PICTURE character is used in conjunction with the V character to indicate the position of a decimal point in cases in which the decimal point is not within the number. This character is used, for example, when it is understood that a value held in storage represents thousands of units and we wish to indicate the decimal position for this value. The following examples indicate the use of this character. As before, the caret indicates the position of an assumed decimal point.

DESCRIPTION	NUMERIC VALUE	ARITHMETIC EQUIVALENT
02 AMOUNT PICTURE 99PPPV	12	12000.
02 AMOUNT PICTURE VP(3)9(4)	1023	.0001023

The P character is not used very much in COBOL applications to administrative problems. It is suited best to scientific computational needs, which are not likely to be satisfied by COBOL anyway.

THE S PICTURE CHARACTER

The S character is used to designate a numeric field that is signed; i.e., one that can be negative in value. In COBOL, all fields are considered positive unless the S has been used. For instance, for a field containing the checking account balance of a bank customer, when the account is overdrawn, the only way the balance will become negative is to designate the balance field as a signed one by use of the S character. Otherwise, if the balance is $23.50 and a check is written for $50.00, the balance will become $26.50!

Only one S character may be used in a field, and it must be the leftmost character. The S is not counted in the size of the field, and therefore S99 is a field of two positions. In the following examples, the negative sign in machine representation is shown as a "−" on top of the rightmost digit, in order to preserve the concept that it does not take up an extra position. Incidentally, you might as well become familiar with this now: *for punched-card data to be processed by use of a COBOL program, any negative number is so identified by punching the negative sign over the rightmost digit by multipunching.* This means that, when you punch the rightmost digit, you depress the MULTI-PUNCH key and punch both the desired digit and the "−" sign in the same card column.

DESCRIPTION	NUMERIC VALUE	REPRESENTED IN STORAGE AS
02 BALANCE PICTURE S9999V99	156.29	015629
02 BALANCE PICTURE S9999V99	−1251.16	125116
02 BALANCE PICTURE S9(4)V99	−0.10	000010
02 BALANCE PICTURE 9(4)V99	−325.18	032518

THE X PICTURE CHARACTER

The X PICTURE character denotes that alphanumeric positions are contained in a field. NAME X(20), for example, signifies a field of 20 alphanumeric positions, which can include alphabetic characters, numeric characters, and special symbols. In the following examples, a "b" represents a blank space in the storage location. Notice that when the characters do not fill an X field completely they are left-justified, with blanks filling the remaining positions on the right.

DESCRIPTION	EXAMPLE	REPRESENTED IN STORAGE AS
02 PART-NAME PICTURE XXXXX	DIODE	DIODE
02 PART-NAME PICTURE X(5)	TUBE	TUBEb
02 NAME PICTURE X(20)	JOHN F. ANDREWS	JOHNbF.bANDREWSbbbbb
02 MESSAGE-CODE PICTURE X(8)	AB13C,$M	AB13C,$M

THE A PICTURE CHARACTER

The A PICTURE character is similar to the X character, except that it indicates that only alphabetic characters and blanks are contained in a field. Excluded therefore are numeric characters and special symbols. Since the first two statements in the preceding examples concerned storage locations containing only alphabetic information, the A PICTURE character could have been used instead of the X, as indicated in the following table:

DESCRIPTION	EXAMPLE	REPRESENTED IN STORAGE AS
02 PART-NAME PICTURE AAAAA	DIODE	DIODE
02 PART-NAME PICTURE A(5)	TUBE	TUBEb

The reader is cautioned against using the A character in what seems a natural use: a field containing people's names. Names such as O'Neal do not consist of alphabetic characters alone. The X character is better suited for use in such fields.

REVIEW

1 We have discussed thus far six PICTURE characters that can be used in a PICTURE clause to describe the contents of a field. These are the 9, V, P, S, X, and A PICTURE characters. The character used to indicate that a field can contain either alphabetic, numeric, or special symbols is the _____ character; whereas the character that indicates alphabetic content only is the _____ character.

X; A

2 The character that indicates numeric content only is the _____ character. If the stored values can be negative as well as positive, the PICTURE clause should include the _____ character as the leftmost character.

9; S

3 In punching data, a negative value is indicated by multipunching a negative sign in the card column containing the [leftmost / rightmost] digit of the field.

rightmost

4 The character used to indicate the position of an assumed decimal point is the _____ character. This character is used only with PICTURE clauses that also contain the _____ PICTURE character.

V; 9

5 When we wish to identify the correct decimal position for a field whose numeric value is understood to be in thousands of units, we use the _____ PICTURE character.

P

6 When a value does not fill a numeric 9 field completely, the value is justified to the [right / left], and the extra positions are filled with [blanks / zeros].

right; zeros

7 When an item does not fill an A field or an X field completely, the item is justified to the [right / left], and the extra positions are filled with [blanks / zeros].

left; blanks

THE PICTURE CLAUSE FOR DATA EDITING

As contrasted to the field definition characters we have described so far, the PICTURE characters that follow are editing symbols. The editing function involves a change in the form of data. For example, we may suppress leading zeros, we may use commas to make long numeric values more legible, we may insert a dollar sign in front of a value, and so forth. The purpose of editing is to make data more suitable for human reading. Thus, in its most common use, editing is associated with printing data on the printer. A great many of the applications of COBOL involve the production of reports that are to be read by people, and data editing greatly enhances the visibility of data in such reports.

THE $ PICTURE INSERTION CHARACTER

By use of the $ PICTURE character, the dollar sign is written in the position in which it is to appear in the output. Since the $ sign is counted in the size of the field, the field should be assigned at least one more position than the maximum number of significant digits expected. The $ sign also may be floated, by which we mean that it will not necessarily be entered in the leftmost position of a field but, rather, will be entered to the left of the first significant digit in the field and be preceded by blanks. For example, if we have the statement 02 SUM PICTURE $$$99V99, when a data value is to be entered in SUM, a test is performed. The leftmost digit is examined first. If it is zero, the next digit is examined. If this next digit is not zero, then the dollar sign is inserted directly to the left of it. For the PICTURE clause above, the $ sign can appear in any one of the first three positions, according to the value stored in the field. The following examples further illustrate the use of the $ PICTURE insertion character. The last example shows that, when the $ sign appears in all positions and the value is zero, the effect is to blank the field.

DESCRIPTION	NUMERIC VALUE	REPRESENTED IN STORAGE AS
02 SUM PICTURE $999V99	125.13	$125ˌ13
02 SUM PICTURE $9(5)V99	100.0	$0010000
02 SUM PICTURE $$99V99	12.49	b$12ˌ49
02 SUM PICTURE $$$9V99	150.10	$150ˌ10
02 SUM PICTURE $$$$V99	0.15	bbb$ˌ15
02 SUM PICTURE $$$$V$$	0.0	bbbbbb

For the last example just given, let us consider what the result in storage would be if the value to be written in SUM were 0.05. In this case, the presence of the V would stop the float, and the value would be represented in storage as bbb$ˆ05. If the decimal point did not terminate the float, the result in storage would be bbbbbˆ$5, which is clearly not the desired repre-

sentation. Therefore, the presence of the decimal point stops the float, except when the entire field is zero. Further examples involving use of the $
PICTURE character are included in the discussion immediately following.

THE DECIMAL AND THE COMMA PICTURE INSERTION CHARACTERS

Each of these insertion characters is used to indicate the position of the
indicated character in the storage location. Because the ․ (decimal) PIC-
TURE character indicates the position of the decimal point and serves to
align the actual decimal values in the field, only one such character may
appear in a field. Further, a field cannot contain both a V and a ․ PICTURE
character. On the other hand, a field may include more than one ‚ (comma)
PICTURE character if the size of the field warrants it. The following examples
illustrate the use of the ․ and the ‚ PICTURE insertion characters in conjunction with the $ insertion characters. Notice some of these points. The $ float
stops when either the first nonzero digit or the ․ or V is encountered. Again,
the only exception is when the $ is written in all positions and the value is
zero, in which case the entire field (including any ․ and ‚) is blanked. If a
comma happens to precede the first nonzero item, the comma is replaced by
the dollar sign, which is the format generally desired for purposes of output.

	DESCRIPTION	NUMERIC VALUE	REPRESENTED IN STORAGE AS
02	SUM PICTURE $9,999.99	2,350.22	$2,350.22
02	SUM PICTURE $9,999.99	150.31	$0,150.31
02	SUM PICTURE $$,999.99	150.31	bb$150.31
02	SUM PICTURE $$,$$$.99	25.40	bbb$25.40
02	SUM PICTURE $$,$$$.999	0.019	bbbbb$.019
02	SUM PICTURE $$,$$$.$$$	0.009	bbbbb$.009
02	SUM PICTURE $$,$$$.$$$	0.0	bbbbbbbbbb
02	SUM PICTURE $$,$$9.999	2,210.2	$2,210.200
02	SUM PICTURE $$,999.9	2,210.2	$2,210.2
02	SUM PICTURE $$,999.9	2,210.256	$2,210.2
02	SUM PICTURE $9,999.9999	23	$0,023.0000
02	SUM PICTURE $$,$$$.$$9	0.002	bbbbb$.002

THE Z PICTURE CHARACTER

The Z PICTURE character is used to replace leading zeros by blanks and
thus performs a function identical to that of the floating $ character, except
for insertion of the $ itself. As for the floating $, zero-suppression terminates
when the first nonzero digit or the ․ character is encountered, whichever
occurs first. As with the $ PICTURE character, the only exception occurs
when Z's have been designated for all positions in a field and the value to be

inserted in that field is zero, in which case the entire field is blanked. The following examples illustrate the use of the Z PICTURE character:

DESCRIPTION		NUMERIC VALUE	REPRESENTED IN STORAGE AS
02 SUM PICTURE	Z99	25	b25
02 SUM PICTURE	ZZZ.99	25	b25.00
02 SUM PICTURE	ZZZ.99	0.10	bbb.10
02 SUM PICTURE	ZZZ.ZZZ	0.052	bbb.052
02 SUM PICTURE	ZZZ.ZZZ	0.0	bbbbbbb
02 SUM PICTURE	$ZZZ.9	13.2	$b13.2
02 SUM PICTURE	$ZZZZ.Z	13.2	$bb13.2
02 SUM PICTURE	$Z,ZZZ,ZZZ.ZZ	156,320.18	$bb156,320.18
02 SUM PICTURE	$Z,ZZZ,ZZZ.ZZ	3,156,320.18	$3,156,320.18
02 SUM PICTURE	$$,$$Z.ZZZ	0.001	bbbb$b.001

THE + AND − PICTURE INSERTION CHARACTERS

Each of these editing characters can be inserted in the leftmost or rightmost position in a PICTURE. When the + character is used, any value that does not have an arithmetic sign associated with it is assigned a + sign. On the other hand, when the − PICTURE character is used, any value that does not have an arithmetic sign associated with it is represented in storage without a sign. In either case, a negative sign associated with a value always is represented in storage. The − PICTURE insertion character differs from the S character in that the use of the S character identifies a field as a signed one for computational purposes, but the sign does not occupy a position as such. Use of the − PICTURE character leads to a field in which the sign occupies a character position. The + character and the − character also can be floated; in this respect they are similar to the $ PICTURE character. However, the +, −, and $ are mutually exclusive as floating characters. If we want to have both $ float and + or − sign representation, we write the + or − to the right of the field, as illustrated in the last two of the following examples:

DESCRIPTION		NUMERIC VALUE	REPRESENTED IN STORAGE AS
02 BALANCE PICTURE	+999.9	35.2	+035.2
02 BALANCE PICTURE	999.9+	35.2	035.2+
02 BALANCE PICTURE	999.9+	−35.2	035.2−
02 BALANCE PICTURE	++9.9	−001.3	b−1.3
02 BALANCE PICTURE	+++9.99	.05	bb+0.05
02 BALANCE PICTURE	+++9.99	−.05	bb−0.05
02 BALANCE PICTURE	++++.++	.01	bbb+.01

(continued)

DESCRIPTION		NUMERIC VALUE	REPRESENTED IN STORAGE AS
02 BALANCE PICTURE	− − − − − −	0.0	bbbbbbb
02 BALANCE PICTURE	− −99.99	−10.25	b−10.25
02 BALANCE PICTURE	−999.99	100.25	b100.25
02 BALANCE PICTURE	999.9−	−10.2	010.2−
02 BALANCE PICTURE	$$$$.99−	20.35	b$20.35b
02 BALANCE PICTURE	$$$$.99+	20.35	b$20.35+

REVIEW

1 Several $ signs included in a PICTURE clause signify that [several dollar signs should appear in the output / the output should contain the dollar sign in one of several possible positions].

the output should contain the dollar sign in one of several possible positions

2 Both the V PICTURE character and the . PICTURE character indicate _____ positions.

decimal point

3 The difference in the use of the V and the . PICTURE characters is that the V signifies an _____ decimal point, whereas the . signifies an _____ decimal point.

assumed; actual

4 In general, the $ float stops when the first nonzero digit is encountered or when the _____ PICTURE character is encountered. The only exception occurs when the value in the field is zero and the $ is written in all positions, in which case the field is filled with _____.

V or . (decimal); blanks

5 The PICTURE insertion character that is similar to the . PICTURE character but can appear more than once in a field is the _____ PICTURE character.

, (comma)

6 The character in a PICTURE clause which is used to replace with blanks the leading zeros in a value is the _____ PICTURE character.

Z

7   Representation of the algebraic sign of a numeric value is accomplished by the use of the _____ or _____ PICTURE character.

$+; -$

8   If the $-$ PICTURE insertion character is used, a value held in storage will have associated with it either a $-$ sign or [$+$ / no] sign. If the $+$ PICTURE character is used, a value held in storage will have associated with it either a $+$ sign or [$-$ / no] sign.

no; $-$

THE DB AND CR PICTURE CHARACTERS

In accounting applications there is often need to identify values that represent debits or credits. The COBOL language facilitates such differentiation by means of the DB (debit) and CR (credit) editing characters. As indicated in the following examples, the DB or CR symbol is written only to the right of a field in the PICTURE clause, and in both cases it is represented in storage for the purpose of subsequent output only when the value is negative.

DESCRIPTION	NUMERIC VALUE	REPRESENTED IN STORAGE AS
02 RECEIPT PICTURE $999.99DB	135.26	$135.26bb
02 RECEIPT PICTURE $999.99DB	−135.26	$135.26DB
02 RECEIPT PICTURE $,$$9.99CR	−10.50	bb$10.50CR

Notice that the edited field does not provide for negative values as such. A value such as 10.50 would have been stored previously in a signed numeric field and then sent to the edited field. For example, if the original field is described by 03 PAY PICTURE S9(4)V99, then executing the instruction MOVE PAY TO RECEIPT will generate the stored content represented on the last line of the preceding table.

The following table summarizes the effects of the storage location associated with the use of the $+$, $-$, CR, and DB PICTURE editing symbols. Note that for positive values the $+$ is included in the edited field only when the $+$ PICTURE character appears in the PICTURE clause. Note also that for negative values the $-$ sign is included in the edited field if either the $+$ or $-$ PICTURE character has been used, and that the CR or DB appears only if the numeric value is negative.

PICTURE CHARACTER USED	STORAGE REPRESENTATION WHEN VALUE IS POSITIVE	STORAGE REPRESENTATION WHEN VALUE IS NEGATIVE
+	+	−
−	Blank	−
DB	Blank	DB
CR	Blank	CR

THE B PICTURE CHARACTER

This is an insertion editing character resulting in blanks being centered in the designated positions. For example, suppose the first two characters in the storage location NAME always represent the initials of a person's first name and middle name, as follows: RBSMITH. If we wish to print the name with spaces included between the two initials and between the initials and the last name, we can set up the editing field 02 EDNAME PICTURE ABABA(10). If we then execute the instruction MOVE NAME TO EDNAME and subsequently print the contents of EDNAME, the output will be R B SMITH.

THE 0 PICTURE CHARACTER

The zero insertion character causes zeros to be inserted in the positions in which it appears. For example, we can use this option if the value represented in the storage is understood to be in thousands and we want to edit it to show the full value. Thus if we had 1365 as the value of sum and we set up EDSUM PICTURE 9(4)000, we could execute MOVE SUM TO EDSUM, giving the following result in EDSUM: 1365000.

THE * PICTURE CHARACTER

The * character is referred to as a check-protect character and normally is used to protect dollar amounts written on checks or other negotiable documents. As indicated by the following examples, it works very much like the floating $ or the Z PICTURE character. In this case, however, instead of the $ sign being floated or positions being filled with blanks, the * character is entered in each zero-suppressed position as designated in the PICTURE clause.

DESCRIPTION	NUMERIC VALUE	REPRESENTED IN STORAGE AS
02 CHECK-VALUE PICTURE $***.99	256.18	$256.18
02 CHECK-VALUE PICTURE $***.99	10.13	$*10.13
02 CHECK-VALUE PICTURE $***.99	0.15	$***.15

THE / PICTURE CHARACTER

Each / (stroke) in the PICTURE character string represents a character position into which the stroke character will be inserted. For example, suppose we have:

02   NUMERIC-DATE   PIC 9(6) VALUE 040782.
02   EDITED-DATE   PIC 99/99/99.

The instruction MOVE NUMERIC-DATE TO EDITED-DATE will cause EDITED-DATE to contain 04/07/82.

REVIEW

1   The editing characters that can be used in a PICTURE clause to identify debits and credits, respectively, are the _____ and the _____ characters.

DB; CR

2   In order for a DB or CR to be included in an editing field, the value entered in that field must be [positive / negative / positive for DB but negative for CR].

negative

3   The insertion editing character that results in blanks being entered in the designated positions is the _____ PICTURE character, whereas the insertion editing character that results in zeros being entered in designated positions is the _____ PICTURE character.

B; 0

4   The insertion editing character that is referred to as the check-protect character is the _____ PICTURE character.

*

5   Use of the / (stroke) insertion character results in the stroke character being inserted in designated character positions [only when those positions are blank / to achieve visual separation of numeric values].

*to achieve visual separation of
numeric values*

SUMMARY OF PICTURE CLAUSE OPTIONS

Table 5-1 lists all the PICTURE characters. As indicated, the characters that identify the type of content in a storage field are the 9, A, and X characters. Special purpose characters associated with numeric fields only

TABLE 5–1   TYPES OF CHARACTERS AVAILABLE FOR USE IN PICTURE CLAUSES

TYPE OF CHARACTER	SYMBOL	USE
Field definition characters	9	Numeric field
	A	Alphabetic field
	X	Alphanumeric field
Numeric field special character	V	Assumed decimal point
	P	Decimal scaling
	S	Operational (arithmetic) sign included
Editing characters	$	Dollar sign
	Z	Zero suppression
	*	Check protection
	.	Decimal point
	,	Comma
	+	Plus sign
	−	Minus sign
	DB	Debit
	CR	Credit
	B	Blank insertion
	0	Zero insertion
	/	Stroke insertion

are the V, P, and S characters. All the other characters listed in Table 5–1 are used for editing purposes.

Instead of listing the characters that can be used in PICTURE clauses, another way of summarizing the material presented in this section is to consider the categories of data that can be contained in a storage location and the PICTURE characters that can be used with each category. Accordingly, Table 5–2 identifies five categories of data: numeric, alphabetic, alphanumeric, numeric edited, and alphanumeric edited. Notice that the PICTURE clause for alphanumeric items cannot contain all 9s or all A's; all 9s would be indicative of a numeric field, and all A's would indicate an alpha-

TABLE 5–2   THE FIVE CATEGORIES OF DATA

Numeric items	The PICTURE may contain suitable combinations of the following characters: 9 V P and S.
Alphabetic items	The PICTURE clause contains only the A character.
Alphanumeric items	The PICTURE clause consists of A 9 and X characters. It cannot contain all A or all 9 characters, but it may contain a mixture of A and 9 characters.
Numeric edited items	The PICTURE clause can contain suitable combinations of the following characters: B P V Z 0 9 , . + − CR DB $ and /.
Alphanumeric edited items	The PICTURE clause can contain combinations of the following characters: A X 9 B 0 and /.

betic field. Note also that numeric edited items can include appropriate combinations of all 12 editing characters included in Table 5-1. On the other hand, alphanumeric edited items can include the B and 0 (zero insertion) and / (stroke) editing characters only.

REVIEW

1 Three of the PICTURE characters discussed are used for the purpose of defining the type of content in a storage field, namely, the _____, _____, and _____ characters. On the other hand, the three special characters used in conjunction with computational numeric fields are the _____, _____, and _____ PICTURE characters. (Refer to Table 5-1 if you wish.)

9, A, X; V, P, S

2 The only editing PICTURE character used in conjunction with an alphabetic field is the _____ character, whereas the three editing characters that can be used in conjunction with an alphanumeric field are the _____, _____, and _____ PICTURE characters.

B; B, 0, /

THE BLANK WHEN ZERO CLAUSE

Use of this clause achieves the same result as Z PICTURE, but it is more general. Consider the statement 02 AMOUNT PIC ZZ9.99 BLANK WHEN ZERO. If AMOUNT contains a zero value, the field will be blanked (six blanks); otherwise the PICTURE string will provide the editing.

REVIEW

1 In the event that an entire data field contains a zero value, the field can be output as all blanks by use of the _____ clause.

BLANK WHEN ZERO

CONDITION-NAMES

Recall that figurative constants are words that signify constant values. For example, the figurative constants ZERO and SPACES mean a value of zero and blanks, respectively. In effect, the use of condition-names enables the programmer to define additional figurative constants for use in the COBOL program. The use of this option always is indicated by the special level 88 entry, whose format is:

As an example of the use of condition-names, suppose that the personnel record used in a company contains, among other things, the number of years of education. The information is contained in a variable called EDUCATION and is so coded that the number indicates the last school grade completed. Thus, a code number less than 12 indicates that the person did not complete high school, 12 indicates a high school graduate, 13–15 indicate some college education, 16 indicates a college graduate, and a number greater than 16 indicates some graduate or postgraduate work. If we wish to process for educational level using these categories, we could write such PROCEDURE DIVISION statements as: IF EDUCATION IS LESS THAN 12 . . . IF EDUCATION IS EQUAL TO 12 . . . etc. However, an alternative is to define figurative constants in the DATA DIVISION, which will then stand for the indicated values. Thus, we can write:

```
01  PERSONNEL-DATA.
    02  ID-NUMBER . . .
    02  NAME . . .
    02  ADDRESS . . .
    02  EDUCATION PICTURE IS 99.
        88  LESS-THAN-H-S-GRAD    VALUES ARE 0 THRU 11.
        88  H-S-GRAD              VALUE IS 12.
        88  SOME-COLLEGE          VALUES ARE 13 THRU 15.
        88  COLLEGE-GRAD          VALUE IS 16.
        88  POST-GRAD             VALUES ARE 17 THRU 20.
        88  ERROR-CODE            VALUES ARE 21 THRU 99.
```

When the preceding condition-names are defined in the DATA DIVISION, they then can be used in PROCEDURE DIVISION statements. For example, the statement IF H-S-GRAD ADD 1 TO TOTAL is identical in result to the statement IF EDUCATION IS EQUAL TO 12 ADD 1 TO TOTAL1. Furthermore, the statement IF SOME-COLLEGE ADD 1 TO TOTAL2 is equivalent to a series of *nested* conditional statements (see Chapter 7). An example is:

```
IF EDUCATION IS < 16
    IF EDUCATION > 12
        ADD 1 TO TOTAL2
        .
        .
        .
```

Thus, one advantage of using condition-names is that they allow the programmer to write complex tests in simple form in the PROCEDURE DIVISION. At the beginning of this section, we indicated that the condition-name is like a figurative constant. After reviewing the previous example, it should be clear that this comparison holds true, except that the condition-name refers to a specific data-name only (EDUCATION in this case).

The use of condition-names improves the readability of a computer program and also makes it easier to change programs. Statements such as IF EDUCATION < 12 and IF SEX-CODE = 1 require that we remember the arbitrary meaning of the numeric codes. Their equivalent condition-names, however, are self-documenting when reference is made to LESS-THAN-H-S-GRAD or MALE. In terms of program changes, suppose that we decide to change the code for "male" from 1 to 2. In the absence of having used a condition-name, we would have to search the entire PROCEDURE DIVISION to make sure that every instance of the use of this code is changed. If the condition-name has been used, all we have to do is to change the definition of the condition-name from VALUE IS 1 to VALUE IS 2 in the DATA DIVISION.

REVIEW

1   The programmer can define figurative constants to be used in conjunction with a particular data-name by the use of _____ _____.

condition-names

2   An entry in which a condition-name is defined always is assigned the level number _____ (number).

88

3   Suppose that for the data-name MARITAL-STATUS the possible values are 1 = married, 2 = divorced, 3 = widowed, 4 = single, and all other values are errors. Write suitable 88 level entries to define condition-names for

a condition of being or having been married
b condition of being single
c condition of error code.

03 MARITAL-STATUS PICTURE 9.
88 _____
88 _____
88 _____

> **a** IS-OR-WAS-MARRIED VALUES ARE 1 THRU 3.
> **b** SINGLE VALUE IS 4.
> **c** ERROR-CODE VALUES ARE ZERO 5 THRU 9.

THE VALUE CLAUSE

In addition to defining storage fields with respect to form by using the PICTURE clause, it often is desirable to assign initial values to WORKING-STORAGE fields. Such a value may remain unchanged throughout the program, as in the case of a tax rate, or it may change in the course of program execution. Such initial values are not assigned to FILE SECTION items, since such fields receive their data either from the external medium or from some other storage location as the result of program execution.

As you may recall from previous examples, an initial value is assigned by the use of the VALUE clause. The general form of this clause is:

$$\text{VALUE IS} \begin{Bmatrix} \text{numeric literal} \\ \text{figurative constant} \\ \text{nonnumeric literal} \end{Bmatrix}$$

The use of the VALUE clause is illustrated in the following examples. Notice that the order of the PICTURE and VALUE clauses is irrelevant, and that the use of the word IS is optional for each type of clause.

02 PAGE-TITLE VALUE IS 'SAMPLE PROGRAM'   PICTURE IS A(14).
02 TENTH-BAL   PICTURE IS 99 VALUE 10.
02 TAX-RATE VALUE IS 0.03   PICTURE V99.
02 FILLER VALUE IS SPACES   PICTURE X(20).
02 ACCUMULATOR   PICTURE IS 9(8)V9(4) VALUE IS ZEROES.

At this point it should be emphasized that the VALUE clause associated with 88 level condition-names, as described in the preceding section, is different from the VALUE clause used to assign initial values to storage positions.

REVIEW

1   Initial values can be assigned to WORKING-STORAGE fields by use of the _____ clause.

VALUE

2   The VALUE clause [always precedes / always follows / can either precede or follow] the PICTURE clause in a WORKING-STORAGE entry.

can either precede or follow

EXERCISES

5.1   True or false: The PICTURE clause can be used only with elementary items. Indicate the reason for your answer.

5.2   Indicate the size of each of the following fields:

PICTURE	SIZE
99V99	
9(3).9	
S999V9	
ZZ,ZZZ	
+(3).99	
$***,**9.99	
VPP99	
ZZZ000	

5.3   Suppose it has become necessary to change an existing COBOL program. The original version of the relevant DATA DIVISION entries is as follows:

```
02  FIELD-A
      03  FIELD-B
      03  FIELD-C
      03  FIELD-D
02  FIELD-E
```

In the revised version it is required that the fields be restructured so that (a) reference can be made to all the fields as one unit; (b) reference can be made to fields B and C as a unit; and (c) reference can be made to fields D and E as a unit. Show how this can be done.

5.4   Write DATA DIVISION entries for the WORKING-STORAGE record named SALES-DATA whose description is given in the following table. Data are moved from the items whose PICTURE description is shown.

SOURCE ITEM PICTURE	RECEIVING ITEM-NAME	PRINT POSITIONS	EDITING REQUIRED
99999	SALE-NUMBER	1–5	Suppress all leading zeros.
		6–7	Blank
(X)25	NAME	8–32	None
		33–34	Blank
S9999V99	DOLLARS	35–?	Insert comma, decimal point. Dollar sign immediately to the left of leftmost nonzero digit. Show negative sign if negative.
		2 positions	Blank
S9(3)V9(4)	PROFIT		Show decimal point. Suppress leading zeros. Show negative sign to left of leftmost nonzero digit.

5.5 The following are DATA DIVISION entries for fields that contain the data to be printed as the CHECK-REGISTER record. The output resulting from printing of the CHECK-REGISTER record should have approximately the following format (header titles are shown for clarity only):

VENDOR NAME	VENDOR NUMBER	CHECK NUMBER	DATE	DEBIT	DISCOUNT	CASH
ACME CORP.	1234	12345	01/03/82	$1,030.57	$20.13	$1,010.44

```
01  CHECK-NUMBER        PICTURE 9(5).
01  DEBIT               PICTURE 9(6)V99.
01  DISCOUNT            PICTURE 9(4)V99.
01  CASH                PICTURE 9(6)V99.
01  VENDOR-DATA.
    02  V-NAME          PICTURE X(15).
    02  V-NUMBER        PICTURE X(4).
01  DATE.
    02  MONTH           PICTURE 99.
    02  DAY             PICTURE 99.
    02  YEAR            PICTURE 99.
```

Write DATA DIVISION entries to form the CHECK-REGISTER record so that the output is printed approximately in the desired format. (Make sure the data is in the form MM/DD/YY.)

5.6 It is required that two lines having the following general format be printed:

SUMMARY STATISTICS

AVERAGE BAL. $XXX,XXX.XX   MAX$XXX,XXX.XX   MIN$XXX,XXX.XX

Assume the following DATA DIVISION entries:

```
FD  PRINT-FILE LABEL RECORDS OMITTED DATA
        RECORD IS PRINT-LINE
01  PRINT-LINE      PICTURE X(132).
WORKING-STORAGE SECTION.
01  MAX-BAL         PICTURE 9(6)V99.
01  MIN-BAL         PICTURE 9(6)V99.
01  AVER-BAL        PICTURE 9(6)V99.
```

Write WORKING-STORAGE SECTION entries to set up the required fields to print these two lines.

5.7 A wholesale distributor employs a number of salespeople in the five designated territories of a state. A coding method is used to denote a territory and a salesperson. The first digit indicates the territory and the second digit the individual salesperson, as shown in the following:

TERRITORY	CODE
Southwest	11–16
Northwest	21–25
Central	31–38
Northeast	41–49
Southeast	51–54

a Write condition-name entries so that, given a value of SALES-CODE, we can determine the territory and can identify an error code. For example, codes 08 and 19 would be error codes.

b For certain purposes, we are interested in testing whether a SALES-CODE value refers to the central territory or to the other territories. Set up condition-names that will enable us to test for central and noncentral territories.

6

Basic PROCEDURE DIVISION statements

COBOL LANGUAGE FORMATS

Before turning our attention to PROCEDURE DIVISION statements, we need to describe the method by which programming options are presented in this book. COBOL is characterized by great flexibility in the form of options available to the programmer. In order to communicate these options we use a *metalanguage,* a language about a language. The form of presentation used here is not unique to this book but generally is followed in all books concerned with COBOL program statements. The method is used in order to describe how each type of statement should be structured, and to identify the options available to the programmer for each type of statement. In other words, the style of presentation is necessary because we wish to talk about types of statements in general, rather than about specific and particular program instructions. For this purpose, then, the following set of conventions is followed:

1   Words presented entirely in uppercase letters are always reserved COBOL words.
2   Uppercase words that are underlined are words that are required in the type of program statement being described. Uppercase words that are not underlined are optional and are used only to improve the readability of the program.
3   Lowercase words are used to indicate the points at which data-names or constants are to be supplied by the programmer. In addition to the words "data-name" and "literal," the term "identifier" is used to indicate a data-name, but it has a slightly broader meaning. It refers to either of the following cases: data-names that are unique in themselves, or data-names that are not unique in themselves but are made unique through *qualification*. Qualification is discussed in Chapter 8: "Additional DATA and PROCEDURE DIVISION statements." For now, you may safely assume the words "data-name" and "identifier" to be equivalent. Other lowercase words used to indicate items to be inserted by the programmer are:

file-name
record-name
integer
formula
condition
statement
any imperative statement
any sentence

4   Items enclosed in braces { } indicate that *one* of the enclosed items *must* be used.
5   Items enclosed in brackets [ ] indicate that the items are optional, and one of them *may* be used at the option of the programmer.
6   An ellipsis (...) indicates that further information may be included in the program instruction, usually in the form of repeating the immediately preceding element any desired number of times.

As an example of the use of these conventions, consider the ADD statement. With the COBOL language format, a basic form of ADD is:

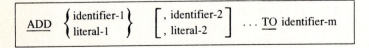

If we apply the rules just presented, the word ADD is a reserved COBOL word because it is in uppercase, and it is required because it is underscored. The word TO is governed by the same rules. The braces following ADD indicate that one of the two alternatives enclosed *must* be used. Thus, the required word ADD must be followed by either an identifier or a literal. Incidentally, it also is understood that, for this specific instruction, the identifier must be an elementary numeric (nonedited) field and the literal must be a numeric literal. The square brackets indicate that identifier-2 and literal-2 are both optional. In other words, the identifier or literal that immediately follows ADD may or may not be followed by a second identifier or literal. The commas also are optional; they may be included to improve readability, or they may be omitted. The ellipsis indicates that the preceding element (in square brackets) may be repeated as many times as desired. Finally, the identifier-m indicates that there *must* be an identifier following the word TO. Note that it is not enclosed in braces, because it is the only option; braces are used when we may choose among alternatives.

Utilizing this general format, we see that the following examples are legitimate ADD statements:

ADD AMOUNT TO TOTAL
ADD 100 TO TOTAL
ADD REGULAR OVERTIME TO GROSS
ADD 10 BONUS 100.25 TO GROSS

REVIEW

1 In presenting COBOL statement instructions, words that are entirely in uppercase letters designate _____ words.

reserved COBOL

2 When a reserved COBOL word is underlined in the format presentation, this indicates that the word [may / must] be used as part of a program instruction.

must

3 Items to be inserted in the program instruction, such as data-names, identifiers, constants, and expressions, are indicated by [lowercase / uppercase] words.

lowercase

4 When two or more items are enclosed within brackets [ ], this indicates that one of them [may / must] be included in the program instruction.

When two or more items are enclosed within braces {   }, this indicates that one of them [may / must] be included.

may; must

5   To indicate that further information, such as additional data-names, can be included in an instruction, a(n) _____ is used.

ellipsis

ARITHMETIC VERBS

Figure 6-1 presents the standard formats for the four principal arithmetic verbs: ADD, SUBTRACT, MULTIPLY, and DIVIDE. As can be seen in this figure, a variety of statement formats can be written. Before we present examples of how to use these verbs, we will discuss two specialized clauses that can be used with arithmetic statements: the ROUNDED and ON SIZE ERROR clauses.

THE ROUNDED CLAUSE

A need frequently exists for rounding numeric values. For example, even though prices or rates of interest may be quoted to three or four decimal places, any billing must be rounded to two decimal places, since the smallest monetary unit is the cent. COBOL provides automatic rounding by use of the ROUNDED clause, which can be used with all arithmetic verbs.

Execution of the statement ADD A TO B ROUNDED will result in a rounded number in B. If B were specified as containing two decimal places in the DATA DIVISION description, rounding would be accomplished by adding 0.005 to the result of the addition and truncating the third place. Therefore, when the remainder that is to be dropped begins with a 5 or higher value, the number is rounded up; otherwise it is rounded down. If B were specified to contain one place to the right of the decimal, 0.05 is added to the result of the addition, and the second place is truncated.

THE ON SIZE ERROR CLAUSE

The case may arise in which an arithmetic result is larger than anticipated, in terms of the number of digit positions available. For example, a construction worker earning $10.00 per hour should have a weekly gross pay well under $999.99. But suppose that by some mistake in the program, or more likely in the input, the computed weekly pay figure is over $1,000.00. Rather than allow truncation of this figure to occur, such "overflows" can be

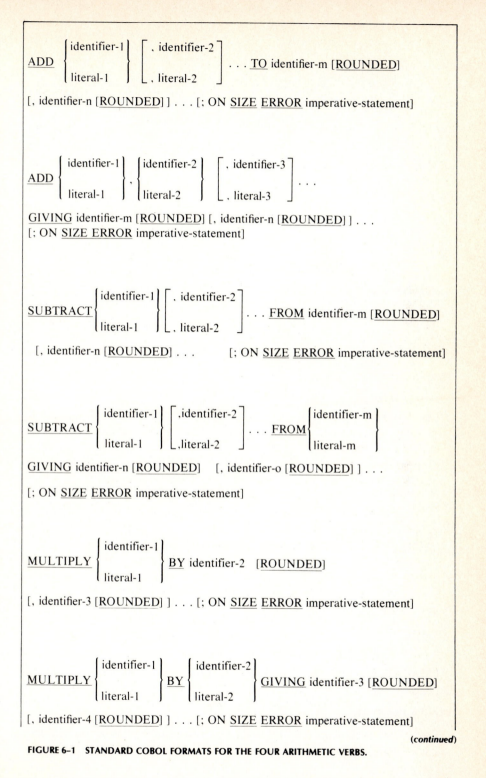

$$\text{ADD} \begin{Bmatrix} \text{identifier-1} \\ \text{literal-1} \end{Bmatrix} \begin{bmatrix} \text{, identifier-2} \\ \text{, literal-2} \end{bmatrix} \dots \underline{\text{TO}} \text{ identifier-m } [\underline{\text{ROUNDED}}]$$

[, identifier-n [<u>ROUNDED</u>]] . . . [; ON <u>SIZE</u> <u>ERROR</u> imperative-statement]

$$\text{ADD} \begin{Bmatrix} \text{identifier-1} \\ \text{literal-1} \end{Bmatrix} , \begin{Bmatrix} \text{identifier-2} \\ \text{literal-2} \end{Bmatrix} \begin{bmatrix} \text{, identifier-3} \\ \text{, literal-3} \end{bmatrix} \dots$$

<u>GIVING</u> identifier-m [<u>ROUNDED</u>] [, identifier-n [<u>ROUNDED</u>]] . . .
[; ON <u>SIZE</u> <u>ERROR</u> imperative-statement]

$$\underline{\text{SUBTRACT}} \begin{Bmatrix} \text{identifier-1} \\ \text{literal-1} \end{Bmatrix} \begin{bmatrix} \text{, identifier-2} \\ \text{, literal-2} \end{bmatrix} \dots \underline{\text{FROM}} \text{ identifier-m } [\underline{\text{ROUNDED}}]$$

[, identifier-n [<u>ROUNDED</u>] . . .   [; ON <u>SIZE</u> <u>ERROR</u> imperative-statement]

$$\underline{\text{SUBTRACT}} \begin{Bmatrix} \text{identifier-1} \\ \text{literal-1} \end{Bmatrix} \begin{bmatrix} \text{,identifier-2} \\ \text{,literal-2} \end{bmatrix} \dots \underline{\text{FROM}} \begin{Bmatrix} \text{identifier-m} \\ \text{literal-m} \end{Bmatrix}$$

<u>GIVING</u> identifier-n [<u>ROUNDED</u>]   [, identifier-o [<u>ROUNDED</u>]] . . .

[; ON <u>SIZE</u> <u>ERROR</u> imperative-statement]

$$\underline{\text{MULTIPLY}} \begin{Bmatrix} \text{identifier-1} \\ \text{literal-1} \end{Bmatrix} \underline{\text{BY}} \text{ identifier-2 } [\underline{\text{ROUNDED}}]$$

[, identifier-3 [<u>ROUNDED</u>]] . . . [; ON <u>SIZE</u> <u>ERROR</u> imperative-statement]

$$\underline{\text{MULTIPLY}} \begin{Bmatrix} \text{identifier-1} \\ \text{literal-1} \end{Bmatrix} \underline{\text{BY}} \begin{Bmatrix} \text{identifier-2} \\ \text{literal-2} \end{Bmatrix} \underline{\text{GIVING}} \text{ identifier-3 } [\underline{\text{ROUNDED}}]$$

[, identifier-4 [<u>ROUNDED</u>]] . . . [; ON <u>SIZE</u> <u>ERROR</u> imperative-statement]

(continued)

FIGURE 6–1 STANDARD COBOL FORMATS FOR THE FOUR ARITHMETIC VERBS.

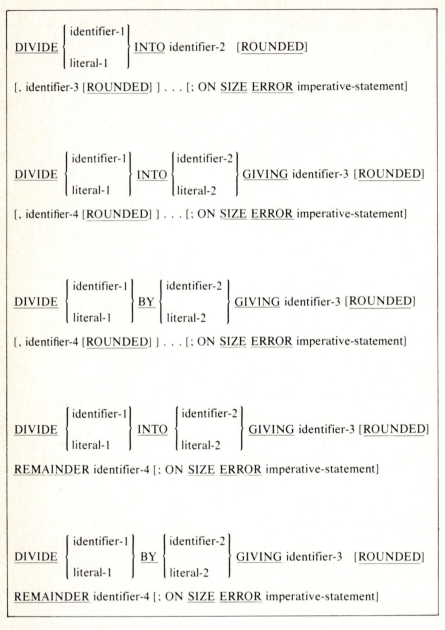

FIGURE 6-1 (*continued*)

detected by use of the ON SIZE ERROR clause. For example, assume GROSS has PICTURE 999V99. We can write:

MULTIPLY RATE BY HOURS GIVING GROSS
    ON SIZE ERROR
    MOVE "GROSS PAY EXCEEDS $999.99" TO MESSAGE.

The ON SIZE ERROR clause is simply a conditional statement that says, if the size of a value does not fit in the field, do whatever is indicated in the statement that follows in that sentence. The statement that follows must be imperative; that is, it cannot be conditional. When ON SIZE ERROR is used and the condition is fulfilled, the arithmetic operand intended to receive the result is not altered from its previous value. In other words, it is as if the arithmetic operations had not happened.

In addition to "large" results, the ON SIZE ERROR condition also is fulfilled by a zero division. As you may recall from algebra, division by zero is an undefined operation yielding an "infinitely" large quotient.

USE OF ARITHMETIC VERBS

Figure 6-2 presents a set of examples involving the use of arithmetic verbs. Review these examples and note the effects of the various forms of instructions on the data fields. In addition, the following paragraphs direct your attention to some particular results.

Example 4 illustrates the effect of the ROUNDED clause. The result of 132.456 has been rounded to 132.46 because Y has two decimal positions.

Example 5 shows the effect of the ON SIZE ERROR clause. Since Y has three positions to the left of the decimal point, the result 1030.25 is too large. Incidentally, if the ON SIZE had not been used, the result in Y would have been stored as 030.25, due to truncation of the first significant digit.

Example 7 illustrates that a negative result is stored as an absolute value (without sign) if the numeric field does not include the S PICTURE character.

Example 8 illustrates the application of the rule of arithmetic that subtracting from a negative value is equivalent to adding the number to be subtracted to that negative value.

Example 12 illustrates that truncation will occur if the number is larger than the defined field.

Example 18 shows the effects of the absence of ROUNDED in the result in X and the presence of ROUNDED in the result in Y. Incidentally, it is permissible to write DIVIDE 12.2 INTO X ROUNDED Y ROUNDED.

Example 19 illustrates the storage of the integer result in Z (since the PICTURE of Z is integer) and storage of the remainder in X. The remainder is

	W	X	Y	Z
PICTURE:	S999V99	999V99	999V99	999
INITIAL VALUE:	010.0̄0	090.00	030.00	040

		W	X	Y	Z
1	ADD X TO Y			120.00	
2	ADD X, Y TO Z				160
3	ADD 5 Y GIVING W	035.00			
4	ADD X, 12.456 to Y ROUNDED			132.46	

5	ADD 1000.25 to Y ROUNDED
	   ON SIZE ERROR
	     MOVE ZERO TO Z
					000

6	SUBTRACT Y FROM X		060.00		
7	SUBTRACT X FROM Y			060.00	
8	SUBTRACT X Y FROM W	130.0̄0			
9	SUBTRACT W FROM X GIVING Y			100.00	

10	SUBTRACT 1260.256 FROM Y
	   ROUNDED
	   ON SIZE ERROR
	     MOVE ZERO TO Z
					000

11	MOVE 10 TO X MULTIPLY X BY Y		010.00	300.00	
12	MULTIPLY X BY Y			700.00	

13	MULTIPLY X BY Y
	   ON SIZE ERROR
	     MOVE ZERO TO Z
					000

14	MULTIPLY Y BY 0.2453 GIVING X ROUNDED		007.36		
15	DIVIDE Y INTO X		003.00		
16	DIVIDE X INTO Y			000.33	
17	DIVIDE Z INTO 100 GIVING Y			002.50	
18	DIVIDE 12.2 INTO X Y ROUNDED		007.37	002.46	
19	DIVIDE 12.2 INTO Y GIVING Z REMAINDER X		005.60		002
20	DIVIDE Z BY 12.2 GIVING Y ROUNDED REMAINDER X		000.10	003.28	

FIGURE 6-2 EXAMPLES OF THE USE OF ARITHMETIC VERBS.

determined as follows. Because the *integer* quotient is $30.00 \div 12.2 = 2$, the remainder is $30.00 - (2 \times 12.2) = 5.6$.

Example 20 shows that the value is stored in the REMAINDER field *before* the rounding takes place. Thus, the unrounded quotient is 3.278, which if stored in Y would have been stored unrounded as 3.27. The remainder is, then, $40 - (3.27 \times 12.2) = 0.106$, which is stored (right-truncated) in X as 0.10.

REVIEW

1   If the result of an arithmetic operation is 45.4545, rounding to three decimal places will result in the value _____ being placed in a storage location, whereas rounding to two places will result in the value _____ being placed in the storage location.

45.455; 45.45

2   If the ROUNDED option is not used, 45.4545 reported to three places would result in the value _____, whereas the value reported to two places would be _____.

45.454; 45.45

3   When the number of digits of an arithmetic result is greater than the number defined in the DATA DIVISION specifications, the likely reason is an error in the data input. Such an overflow can be signaled by use of the _____ clause.

ON SIZE ERROR

4   Complete the following table by entering the numeric result of each arithmetic operation:

		W	X	Y	Z
	PICTURE:	99V9	99	99V9	S999.9
	INITIAL VALUE:	15.0	10	12.8	100.0
1	ADD W, Y TO X				
2	ADD W, Y GIVING X ROUNDED				
3	SUBTRACT W FROM Y				
4	SUBTRACT W FROM Y GIVING Z				

(*continued*)

	W	X	Y	Z
PICTURE:	99V9	99	99V9	S999.9
INITIAL VALUE:	15.0	10	12.8	100.0

5 MULTIPLY W BY Y

6 MULTIPLY X BY Y GIVING Z
   ROUNDED

7 DIVIDE X INTO Y ON SIZE
   ERROR MOVE ZERO TO X

8 DIVIDE X INTO Y ROUNDED
   REMAINDER Z

1 $X = 37$
2 $X = 28$
3 $Y = 02.2$
4 $Z = 002.2$
5 $Y = 92.0$
6 $Z = 128.8$
7 $Y = 1.2$
8 $Y = 1.3; Z = 008.8$
    $[= 12.8 - (1.2 \times 10)]$

FILE INPUT AND OUTPUT

The general functions performed by an input statement and an output statement are, respectively, to transfer data from an external storage medium to central storage, and to transfer data from central storage to an external storage medium. In the present context, we transfer data from the punched card to central storage, and from central storage to printed paper. The file storage medium involved in each case is specified in the ENVIRONMENT DIVISION by the corresponding SELECT file-name and ASSIGN TO . . . statements.

Before a file can be used, we must OPEN that file and designate whether it is an input file or an output file. The format is:

The meaning and purpose of the OPEN verb is explained in Chapter 9: "Sequential File Processing"; for now, we simply will say that it must be used prior to writing into or reading from a file.

We can use an OPEN statement for each file, or we can use one OPEN statement for several files as a group:

```
OPEN INPUT EMPL-FILE
OPEN OUTPUT REPORT-FILE
OPEN INPUT FILE-A FILE-B
     OUTPUT FILE-C FILE-D FILE-E.
```

Before a program terminates execution with a STOP RUN statement, we must use a CLOSE statement for each file that was opened. Again, the meaning and purpose of this statement will be explained further in Chapter 9.

The following is the format for the CLOSE verb; just as for the OPEN verb, we can use one CLOSE statement for each file or we can reference several files from one CLOSE.

```
CLOSE file-name-1    [file-name-2] . . .
```

Data are transferred into central storage by use of the READ verb:

```
READ file-name RECORD [INTO identifier] AT END imperative statement
```

Each execution of the READ transfers the data contained in the next physical record of the external file (card deck in this case) to the record described in the FD entry for that file.

The AT END is a conditional statement that applies when an end-of-file record is used. In the case of the card reader, an end-of-file record is one that has a special code word punched on it. Every READ statement must have the AT END specified.

The INTO option is a short form for moving the data that has been read. For example, suppose we want to print each record as it is read. One way we could accomplish this result is through the following:

```
READ INPUT-FILE RECORD INTO OUTPUT-RECORD
     AT END MOVE 'YES' TO END-OF-FILE.
IF END-OF-FILE = 'NO'
     WRITE OUTPUT-RECORD . . .
```

The INTO OUTPUT-RECORD function could be replaced by the equivalent use of MOVE:

READ INPUT-FILE RECORD
    AT END MOVE 'YES' TO END-OF-FILE.
IF END-OF-FILE = 'NO'
    MOVE INPUT-RECORD TO OUTPUT-RECORD
    WRITE OUTPUT-RECORD . . .

The WRITE statement, as used with the printer, has the following format:

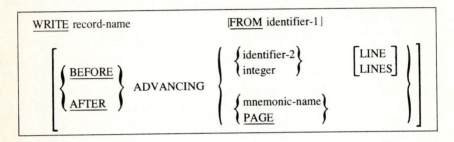

The FROM option is the counterpart of the INTO option for the READ verb. For example, we could write:

MOVE HEADER TO OUTPUT-RECORD
WRITE OUTPUT-RECORD . . .

or we could use the FROM:

WRITE OUTPUT-RECORD FROM HEADER . . .

The ADVANCING clause is used to control the vertical spacing on the printer. We already have seen examples of fixed spacing, such as when we write WRITE . . . AFTER ADVANCING 2 LINES. We also can have variable spacing, as the sample in the following paragraph illustrates.

Suppose that a sales invoice form has space for 10 items on each invoice, and we always wish to print the total billing on the last line of the invoice. We can use a storage field as a counter to keep track of the number of items on each invoice. Let us call this field KOUNT. If an invoice contains four items, the value stored in KOUNT will be 4; if an invoice contains six items, the value will be 6, and so on. In order to print the total billing on the last line of the invoice, the number of lines to be skipped always will be 10 spaces minus KOUNT. For this example, we of course are assuming that there will never be more than 10 items; therefore, the following statements provide the basis for skipping the appropriate number of lines:

SUBTRACT KOUNT FROM 10 GIVING LINE-COUNT
WRITE REP-LINE AFTER ADVANCING LINE-COUNT LINES.

When a mnemonic-name is used, it is specified in the SPECIAL-NAMES paragraph of the ENVIRONMENT DIVISION. Such mnemonic names are specified by the manufacturer. As an example, consider an IBM system where C01 is defined to mean channel 1 on the printer carriage control tape, where channel 1 defines the top of a printer page. We could have:

```
ENVIRONMENT DIVISION.
CONFIGURATION SECTION.
SOURCE-COMPUTER. IBM-370.
OBJECT-COMPUTER. IBM-370.
SPECIAL-NAMES.
    C01 IS TOP-OF-PAGE.
INPUT-OUTPUT SECTION.
(etc.)
```

In the PROCEDURE DIVISION, the statement WRITE PRINT-RECORD AFTER ADVANCING TOP-OF-PAGE is understood to mean to skip to the top of a new page. Actually, the need to be able to skip to the top of a new page is universal enough for COBOL to include the reserved word PAGE as an option in WRITE, the use of which results in skipping to a new page.

REVIEW

1 Prior to inputting data from a file, a(n) _____ statement must be executed.

OPEN INPUT

2 Prior to writing data from a file, a(n) _____ statement must be executed.

OPEN OUTPUT

3 Before a program terminates execution with STOP RUN, a _____ statement must be executed for every file that was opened.

CLOSE

4 Data are entered into central storage by use of the _____ verb.

READ

5 The option that results in the same data being available in two different places after a READ statement has been executed (often in one input record and one output record) is the _____ option.

INTO

6   The verb that is used to output data from central storage is the _____ verb.

WRITE

7   In conjunction with a WRITE statement, data are moved from an identifier to an output record by use of the _____ option.

FROM

8   Variable vertical spacing of output on the printer can be accomplished by using the _____ clause in conjunction with a WRITE statement.

ADVANCING

DATA TRANSFER

Data transfer in COBOL is accomplished by use of the MOVE verb. Actually, both the term "data transfer" and the word MOVE are misnomers, because the function performed is *duplicating,* not moving. When we write MOVE A to B, the contents of A are duplicated in B, with the contents of A remaining unchanged. Common usage of the concept of data transfer therefore recognizes that duplication of the contents of a storage location is involved.

The format for the MOVE instruction is:

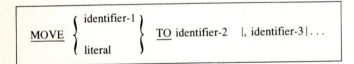

In any use of the MOVE instruction, caution should be exercised so that the receiving field is not smaller than the sending field. If the receiving field is too small, truncation will result in the loss of part of the value or information being transferred. The rules for moving data are many and relate to the form of data moved. One important point to remember is the following: numeric data are aligned according to the decimal point. If the receiving field is larger than the sending, the extra positions are filled with zeros. If the receiving field is smaller, then truncation takes place as needed, to the right, left, or both right and left of the decimal point. In the following illustration the caret (∧) implies a decimal point:

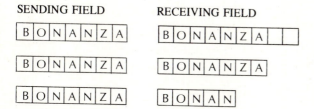

SENDING FIELD	RESULT IN RECEIVING FIELD
0 1 3 5 2	0 0 1 3 5 2 0
2 5 2 3 5	2 5 2 3 5
2 5 2 3 5	5 2 3 5
2 5 2 3 5	5 2 3

A second important point is that alphabetic or alphanumeric data are left-justified in the receiving field (unless the programmer uses the JUSTIFIED RIGHT clause in the DATA DIVISION). If the receiving field is larger than the sending field, the additional positions are filled with blanks. If the receiving field is smaller, then truncation takes place from the right. The following examples illustrate some typical cases:

SENDING FIELD	RECEIVING FIELD
B O N A N Z A	B O N A N Z A
B O N A N Z A	B O N A N Z A
B O N A N Z A	B O N A N

Table 6–1 indicates the types of data transfer that are and are not permitted in COBOL. The reader may want to review Table 5–2 in the preceding chapter, which defines the various categories of data to which

TABLE 6–1   LEGAL AND ILLEGAL MOVE COMMANDS

CATEGORY OF SENDING DATA DATA ITEM	CATEGORY OF RECEIVING DATA ITEM		
	ALPHABETIC	ALPHANUMERIC; ALPHANUMERIC EDITED	NUMERIC INTEGER; NUMERIC NONINTEGER; NUMERIC EDITED
Alphabetic	Yes	Yes	No
Alphanumeric	Yes	Yes	No
Alphanumeric edited	Yes	Yes	No
Numeric integer	No	Yes	Yes
Numeric noninteger	No	No	Yes
Numeric edited	No	Yes	No

reference is made in Table 6–1. Most compilers have incorporated the rules presented in this table, so that the programmer will be warned of illegal MOVE statements; still, it is not difficult to internalize most of these rules. Particularly, you should remember that numeric edited data cannot be moved correctly to a numeric field.

REVIEW

1   When data are transferred by use of the MOVE instruction, one might say more correctly that the data have been _____, rather than "moved."

duplicated

2   When numeric data are moved from a sending field to a receiving field, alignment takes place with respect to the _____.

decimal point

3   When nonnumeric data are moved from a sending field to a receiving field, alignment takes place at the [left / right] margin.

left

4   In terms of the legality of data transfer, the one type of numeric data that cannot be moved to a numeric field is _____ data.

numeric edited

THE PERFORM VERB

In general, the PERFORM verb is used to specify the sequence of execution of a modular program, represented by paragraphs or sections, or to specify the repeated execution of such modules to achieve program looping. We already have seen the use of the PERFORM verb in the program examples in Chapters 2 and 3. In this section, we review and expand our description of the uses of this verb by presenting the basic formats associated with the PERFORM verb. This is a highly flexible verb, and additional formats for its use will be presented in later chapters.

The simplest format of the PERFORM is:

```
PERFORM    procedure-name
```

The procedure-name referenced in this format is either a paragraph- or section-name. Simply stated, the PERFORM directs program execution to the named procedure, at which point the procedure is executed and program execution returns to the next statement following the PERFORM. In this respect, it follows that the named procedure must allow the program to return; that is, the procedure must not contain a GO TO or a STOP RUN statement. However, the paragraph that is performed may itself contain another PERFORM instruction.

Another format of PERFORM is:

PERFORM procedure-name-1 THRU procedure-name-2

In this format, the PERFORM verb indicates that a series of two or more procedures (paragraphs or sections) is to be executed consecutively. Consider the example on the CASE form of program flow in Chapter 4, in the section on "Flowcharting the Program Logic." We could check the marital code by using the PERFORM verb as follows:

```
PERFORM CHECK-MARITAL-CODE-START THRU
     CHECK-MARITAL-CODE-END.
     .
     .
     .


CHECK-MARITAL-CODE-START.
    IF MARITAL-CODE = 1
        ADD 1 TO SINGLE
        GO TO CHECK-MARITAL-CODE-END.
    IF MARITAL-CODE = 2
        ADD 1 TO MARRIED
        GO TO CHECK-MARITAL-CODE-END.
    IF MARITAL CODE = 3
        .
        .
        .


CHECK-MARITAL-CODE-END.
    EXIT.
```

A third version of the PERFORM verb allows us to specify repetitive execution. The format is:

PERFORM procedure-name-1   [THRU procedure-name-2] $\left\{ \begin{array}{l} \text{identifier} \\ \text{integer} \end{array} \right\}$ TIMES

Examples of the use of this format are:

PERFORM PROCESS-RECORD 10 TIMES.
PERFORM PROCESS-RECORD N TIMES.
PERFORM PROCESS-START THRU PROCESS-END 12 TIMES.

As an example, consider the case in accounting where we need to form the "sum of the digits," for depreciating an asset over N years, where N has an integer value. We need to form the sum of $1 + 2 + 3 + \ldots + (N-1) + N$. Thus, if N is 5, we have $1 + 2 + 3 + 4 + 5$. Here is a routine for doing this task:

> MOVE ZERO TO SUM-OF-DIGITS
> MOVE 1 TO YEAR-COUNTER
> PERFORM FORM-SUM N TIMES.
> .
> .
> .

FORM-SUM
> ADD YEAR-COUNTER TO SUM-OF-DIGITS
> ADD 1 TO YEAR-COUNTER.

A fourth version of the PERFORM verb allows for conditional execution of a procedure or a series of procedures. The format is:

PERFORM procedure-name-1 [THRU procedure-name 2] UNTIL condition

The UNTIL condition is checked first, before the procedure(s) is executed. If the condition is true, then the procedure(s) is *not* executed. In flowchart form, it looks like this:

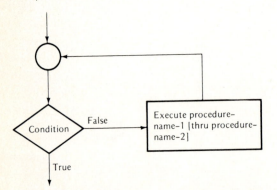

This format allows repetitive execution as long as the condition is not met. It follows that, if the condition is false, it must become true at some point as a result of procedure-name-1, or else we would have an infinite loop.

REVIEW

1   The COBOL verb used to execute a paragraph and return to the instruction immediately following is the _____ verb.

PERFORM

2   Whereas the basic format of the PERFORM verb concerns the execution of a single paragraph (or section), a second format allows execution of [two / two or more] paragraphs.

two or more

3   Suppose four consecutive paragraphs were to be executed as a group. The PERFORM statement would include [two / four] procedure-names.

*two (only the first and last
paragraphs in the series are
named)*

4   After execution of the paragraph(s) identified in the PERFORM instruction, execution of the program continues with the statement immediately following [the identified paragraph(s) / the PERFORM instruction].

the PERFORM instruction

5   When the UNTIL option is used with the PERFORM verb, the condition is tested [before / after] the object of PERFORM is executed.

before

SAMPLE PROGRAM

We conclude this chapter by presenting a sample program to help the reader review many of the statements discussed, as they apply to a particular application.

The objective of this program is to read records in a file and produce a report such as that shown in Figure 6-3. The input records are sorted so that all records pertaining to a given product are grouped together. The input records have the format presented in Figure 6-4. The report is relatively simple, but it is representative of the kind of report required for administra-

```
PRODUCT NO.    SALES AMOUNT    TOTAL SALES
    123            125.27
                   100.00
                                  $225.27
    345             50.50
                   110.25
                    10.09
                                  $170.84
```

FIGURE 6-3   OUTPUT OF THE REPORT PROGRAM.

Record Format

PRODUCT-NO	SALES-AMOUNT	FILLER
PIC 999	PIC 9(4)V99	PIC X(71)

Sample Input

```
123012527
123010000
345005050
345011025
345001009
```

FIGURE 6-4   INPUT RECORD FORMAT AND SAMPLE RECORDS.

tive use. In a more typical case, we would have several classes of data objects, such as department and salesperson, in addition to the product classes; therefore we would want to present grouped data and totals for each class. For instance, we could have the sales for each product, for each salesperson, and for each department. We will illustrate such an expanded version of the current program in Chapter 9: "Sequential File Processing."

Now that we are at the stage of analyzing and designing such a program, we can observe several key points that are typical of such report-generating programs. First, the initial record that is input is treated separately. We have to check all subsequent records to ascertain whether or not the current record is for the same product as the previous record; this is not the case for the first record, for which there is no previous record. When the end of the file is reached, we should print the total sales for the product immediately preceding, before the program terminates. A final observation is that we will want to print a page heading at the top of each page. For this reason, it will be useful to develop a module whose function it will be to print each line and a page heading, as appropriate. We will assume that each page will consist of 25 lines and will define a constant PAGE-SIZE for this value. Should we want to generate the report in a different PAGE-SIZE, all we would have to do is change the VALUE clause of PAGE-SIZE.

The structure chart for the program is presented in Figure 6-5. It can be seen that Print Line is a module that is subordinate to five different modules. The reason for the repeated use of this module is that the page-heading logic is included in this module; therefore, it involves more than just printing a line. In a report-oriented program it always is best to do the printing in one module, rather than dispersing this function throughout the program. Report formats often need to be changed, and it is much easier to change one cohesive module than to attempt to change scattered statements throughout the program.

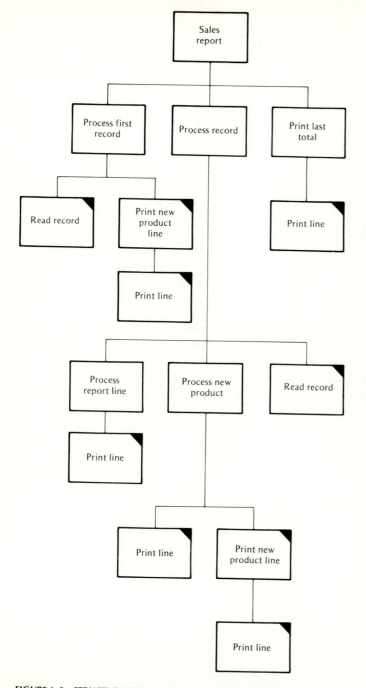

FIGURE 6-5   STRUCTURE CHART FOR THE REPORT PROGRAM.

```
IDENTIFICATION DIVISION.
PROGRAM-ID.  SALESREPORT.
*
ENVIRONMENT DIVISION.
*
CONFIGURATION SECTION.
SOURCE-COMPUTER.  ABC-480.
OBJECT-COMPUTER.  ABC-480.
*
INPUT-OUTPUT SECTION.
*
FILE-CONTROL.
    SELECT SALES-FILE ASSIGN TO CARD-READER.
    SELECT REPORT-FILE ASSIGN TO PRINTER.
/
DATA DIVISION.
*
FILE SECTION.
*
FD  SALES-FILE
    LABEL RECORDS ARE OMITTED
    DATA RECORD IS SALES-RECORD.
01  SALES-RECORD.
    02 PRODUCT-NO                PIC 999.
    02 SALES-AMOUNT              PIC 9(4)V99.
    02 FILLER                    PIC X(71).
*
FD  REPORT-FILE
    LABEL RECORDS ARE OMITTED
    DATA RECORD IS REPORT-RECORD.
01  REPORT-RECORD               PIC X(132).
*
WORKING-STORAGE SECTION.
*
01  END-OF-FILE-INDICATOR       PIC XXX VALUE 'NO'.
    88 END-OF-FILE VALUE 'YES'.
    88 NOT-END-OF-FILE VALUE 'NO'.
*
01  PREVIOUS-PRODUCT-NO         PIC 999.
*
01  PRODUCT-TOTAL               PIC 9(5)V99.
*
01  PAGE-SIZE                   PIC 99 VALUE 25.
*
01  LINE-COUNTER                PIC 99 VALUE 25.
*
* BY INITIALIZING LINE-COUNTER TO 25-PAGE-SIZE, WE
* WILL GET THE PAGE HEADING PRINTED PRIOR TO THE FIRST
* LINE OF OUTPUT.
*
*
01  REPORT-HEADING.
    02 FILLER PIC X(10) VALUE SPACES.
    02 FILLER                   PIC X(11) VALUE 'PRODUCT NO.'.
    02 FILLER                   PIC X(3) VALUE SPACES.
    02 FILLER                   PIC X(12) VALUE 'SALES AMOUNT'.
    02 FILLER                   PIC X(4) VALUE SPACES.
    02 FILLER                   PIC X(11) VALUE 'TOTAL SALES'.
*
01  REPORT-LINE.
    02 FILLER                   PIC X(14) VALUE SPACES.
    02 PRODUCT-NO-OUT           PIC 999.
    02 FILLER                   PIC X(9) VALUE SPACES.
    02 SALES-AMOUNT-OUT         PIC Z,ZZ9.99.
    02 FILLER                   PIC X(7) VALUE SPACES.
    02 TOTAL-SALES-OUT          PIC $$,$$9.99.
/
PROCEDURE DIVISION.
*
PROGRAM-SUMMARY.
*
    OPEN INPUT SALES-FILE
         OUTPUT REPORT-FILE.
*
    PERFORM PROCESS-FIRST-RECORD
*
    PERFORM PROCESS-RECORD
            UNTIL END-OF-FILE
*
    PERFORM PRINT-LAST-TOTAL
*
    CLOSE SALES-FILE
          REPORT-FILE
*
    STOP RUN.
```

FIGURE 6-6 LISTING OF THE REPORT PROGRAM.

```
/
  PROCESS-FIRST-RECORD.
       PERFORM READ-RECORD.
       IF NOT-END-OF-FILE
          MOVE PRODUCT-NO TO PREVIOUS-PRODUCT-NO
          MOVE SALES-AMOUNT TO PRODUCT-TOTAL
          PERFORM PRINT-NEW-PRODUCT-LINE
          PERFORM READ-RECORD.
*
  READ-RECORD.
       READ SALES-FILE
            AT END MOVE 'YES' TO END-OF-FILE-INDICATOR.
*
  PRINT-NEW-PRODUCT-LINE.
       MOVE SPACES TO REPORT-LINE
       MOVE PRODUCT-NO TO PRODUCT-NO-OUT
       MOVE SALES-AMOUNT TO SALES-AMOUNT-OUT
       PERFORM PRINT-LINE.
*
  PRINT-LINE.
       IF LINE-COUNTER = PAGE-SIZE
          WRITE REPORT-RECORD FROM REPORT-HEADING
               AFTER ADVANCING PAGE
          MOVE SPACES TO REPORT-RECORD
          WRITE REPORT-RECORD AFTER ADVANCING 1 LINE
          MOVE 2 TO LINE-COUNTER.
       WRITE REPORT-RECORD FROM REPORT-LINE
            AFTER ADVANCING 1 LINE
       ADD 1 TO LINE-COUNTER.
/
  PROCESS-RECORD.
       IF PRODUCT-NO = PREVIOUS-PRODUCT-NO
          PERFORM PROCESS-REPORT-LINE
       ELSE
            PERFORM PROCESS-NEW-PRODUCT.
*
       ADD SALES-AMOUNT TO PRODUCT-TOTAL.
*
       PERFORM READ-RECORD.
*
  PROCESS-REPORT-LINE.
       MOVE SPACES TO REPORT-LINE
       MOVE SALES-AMOUNT TO SALES-AMOUNT-OUT
       PERFORM PRINT-LINE.
*
  PROCESS-NEW-PRODUCT.
       MOVE SPACES TO REPORT-LINE
       MOVE PRODUCT-TOTAL TO TOTAL-SALES-OUT
       PERFORM PRINT-LINE
*
       MOVE ZERO TO PRODUCT-TOTAL
*
       PERFORM PRINT-NEW-PRODUCT-LINE
*
       MOVE PRODUCT-NO TO PREVIOUS-PRODUCT-NO.
*
  PRINT-LAST-TOTAL.
       MOVE SPACES TO REPORT-LINE
       MOVE PRODUCT-TOTAL TO TOTAL-SALES-OUT
       PERFORM PRINT-LINE.
```

FIGURE 6–6 (*continued*)

The program listing is presented in Figure 6–6. You should study the program and its use of DATA and PROCEDURE statements now. Exercises 6.3 and 6.4, following, ask you to modify this program in certain ways.

EXERCISES

6.1   Write a COBOL program that will read punched cards, edit the data, and print a report as indicated on the following page.

Input:

CARD COLUMNS	CONTENT
1–11	Social security number
12–23	Last name
24–32	First name
33–40	Blank
41–47	Year-to-date earnings

Output: not more than a page. Header at the top of the page, as follows:

SOCIAL SECURITY	LAST	FIRST	EARNINGS
XXX-XX-XXXX			$XX,XXX.XX
XXX-XX-XXXX			$XX,XXX.XX
	(etc.)		

Data: create four records using social security numbers and names of your choice. However, use these earnings:

$10,352.81

$ 5,863.98

$ 3,800.00

$ 691.12

6.2 Write the PROCEDURE DIVISION statements to produce the output described in Exercise 5.6.

6.3 Modify the sample program in the last section of this chapter so that a grand total of all sales amounts is printed on a separate page at the end of the report, with the following format:

GRAND-TOTAL FOR SALES REPORT = $XXX,XXX.XX

6.4 Modify the sample program in the last section of this chapter so that at the end of the report a summary is given of amounts of sales, with the following format:

PERCENT OF SALES LESS THAN $100	PERCENT OF SALES $100–$500	PERCENT OF SALES OVER $500
XXX.X	XXX.X	XXX.X

AVERAGE VALUE OF SALES ORDER = $X,XXX.XX

In other words, the program should tabulate the SALES-AMOUNT field so that the required percentage amounts can be computed. The program should determine what percent of the records had a SALES-AMOUNT less than $100, what percent had an amount in the range of $100–$500, and what percent exceeded $500. The final average is the sum of SALES-AMOUNT values divided by the number of records.

6.5 Write a COBOL program to read a file of records containing data about accounts-receivable and to print a summary of the overdue and forthcoming receivables. An extended description follows, including variable names and a partial DATA DIVISION. Thus, this exercise is of moderate programming difficulty.

INPUT
   This consists of a set of records having the following design:

COLUMNS	COBOL NAME
1–6	ACCOUNT-NO
7–8	FILLER (blank)
9–11	DAY-DUE†
12–13	YEAR-DUE
14–21	AMOUNT-DUE
22–80	FILLER (blank)

†The day on which the account is due is expressed as a 3-digit number (Julian calendar). Thus January 10 is 010, February 28 is 059, and December 25 is 360.

The first record is a special one containing today's date and year in columns 9–11 and 12–13, respectively. All other records pertain to accounts-receivable.

   The records are sorted in ascending sequence on ACCOUNT-NO, and there should be only one record per account. The program checks for correct sequencing. Records out of sequence are to be printed as shown on the sample output. Note that the data on such records are excluded from the total.

DATA DIVISION
   All DATA DIVISION entries are provided, except that you are asked to write WORKING-STORAGE entries to provide the header with the words STATUS, NUMBER OF ACCOUNTS, and DOLLAR VALUE.

```
DATA DIVISION.
FILE SECTION.
FD  REC-FILE LABEL RECORDS OMITTED
    DATA RECORD  RECEIV-RECORD.
01  RECEIV-RECORD.
    02  ACCOUNT-NO          PICTURE 9(6).
    02  FILLER              PICTURE XX.
    02  DAY-DUE             PICTURE 999.
    02  YEAR-DUE            PICTURE 99.
    02  AMOUNT-DUE          PICTURE 9(6)V99.
    02  FILLER              PICTURE X(59).
FD  REPORT-FILE LABEL RECORD OMITTED
    DATA RECORD REPORT-RECORD.
01  REPORT-RECORD           PICTURE X(132).
WORKING-STORAGE SECTION.
01  TODAY                   PICTURE 999.
01  THIS-YEAR               PICTURE 99.
01  PREVIOUS-ACCT-NO        PICTURE 9(6).
01  OVERDUE                 PICTURE S9(6).
01  OVERDUE-AMOUNT          PICTURE S9(6)V99.
01  RECEIVABLE-AMOUNT       PICTURE S9(6)V99.
01  END-OF-DATA             PICTURE 9 VALUE ZERO.
01  ERROR-MESSAGE.
    02  FILLER              PICTURE X(23) VALUE
                           'ACCOUNT OUT OF SEQUENCE.'
    02  FILLER              PICTURE XX VALUE SPACE.
    02  ERROR-NUMBER        PICTURE X(6).
01  RESULT.
    02  STATUS-TYPE         PICTURE X(13).
    02  FILLER              PICTURE X(9) VALUE SPACES.
    02  HOW-MANY            PICTURE ZZZ99.
    02  FILLER              PICTURE X(13), VALUE SPACES.
    02  DOLLAR-VALUE        PICTURE $$$$,$$$.99.
```

A few data-names merit explanation:

TODAY   Stores today's data as read in from the very first record of the
    input file

THIS-YEAR   Stores the current year as read in from the very first record
    of the input file

PREVIOUS-ACCT-NO   Stores the previously read account number so
    that each record can be compared with the preceding one to see

that they are in ascending sequence. Initially, PREVIOUS-ACCT-NO is set equal to zero

OVERDUE   Stores the number of overdue accounts

OVERDUE-AMOUNT   Stores the total dollar value of overdue accounts

RECEIVABLE   Stores the number of accounts that are not overdue

RECEIVABLE-AMOUNT   Stores the total value of accounts that are not overdue

SAMPLE INPUT

```
                        10181
012345                  0908100010000
023567                  1508000020020
001234                  1408000030030
123456                  0308200040040
```

SAMPLE OUTPUT

ACCOUNT OUT OF SEQUENCE 001234

STATUS	NUMBER OF ACCOUNTS	DOLLAR VALUE
OVERDUE	02	$300.20
RECEIVABLE	01	$400.40
TOTALS	03	$700.60

6.6 A record file contains data on the number of vehicles passing a certain point on the highway. Each record contains a whole number in columns 1–4 that corresponds to one day's traffic. We are interested in reading the record file and producing a report such as that shown below. For each week, we list the daily data and a statistical summary for the week. It is assumed that, at the most, there will be 10 weeks of data; however, the last week of data may be a partial week—that is, less than seven days. The output format is as follows:

DAILY TRAFFIC REPORT

    WEEK XX

    X, XXX

    X, XXX

     .

     .

     .

     .

    X, XXX

MINIMUM =X, XXX MAXIMUM =X, XXX WEEKLY TOTAL =XX, XXX

7

Conditions and conditional statements

INTRODUCTION

Computer processors derive their logic capability from their ability to test for the truth or falsity of conditions. We can appreciate the fundamental nature of this ability by considering what computer programs would be like without conditional logic. It would be impossible, in fact, to write most computer programs without the use of conditional instructions. The COBOL language recognizes the importance of this capability and provides a rich repertoire of conditions and conditional statements. We present the subject as a separate chapter because of the number of conditions that can be tested and because we wish to highlight the logical unity of various types of conditional statements.

We already have studied a number of conditional statements. First, we studied the IF conditional statement in Chapter 3: "Writing Complete Programs." In the same chapter, we also discussed the AT END conditional clause, which is used in conjunction with input files. Finally, we studied the ON SIZE ERROR conditional clause, which is concerned with overflows resulting from arithmetic operations. In this section, we expand on the subject of conditions and conditional statements by discussing six types of conditions: (1) relation conditions, (2) nested conditions, (3) class conditions, (4) sign conditions, (5) condition-name conditions, and (6) complex conditions. In general, a condition is an expression that is either true or false in a particular circumstance; that is, the condition either holds or it does not hold.

RELATION CONDITIONS

Such conditions are concerned with comparisons between two items. The type of comparison is indicated by the relational operator, which may be in the form of words or symbols. The relational operators available in COBOL are:

LESS THAN   <

EQUAL TO   =

GREATER THAN   >

The general format for relation conditions is:

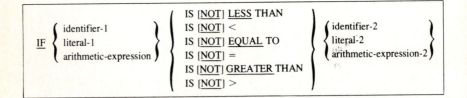

Examples of the use of these additional features are:

IF AMOUNT > 100 . . .

IF A + B = PRICE . . .

IF A − B + 20 IS LESS THAN Q * A . . .

In the general format just presented, the first and second operands often are referred to as the subject and object of the condition, respectively. One additional point in this regard is that these two operands cannot both be literals. Thus, the statement IF 3 IS GREATER THAN 2 is invalid. Of course, there is no reason why such a statement ever need be written, since the equality or inequality is predetermined by the statement itself and does not constitute an actual relational comparison.

The meaning of relational tests involving numeric values is obvious. If RATE-1 and RATE-2 are numeric fields, the conditional expression IF RATE-1 > RATE-2 GO TO PAR-A leads to PAR-A whenever the numeric (algebraic) value of RATE-1 is greater than the numeric value of RATE-2, *regardless of the field size.*

With respect to nonnumeric comparisons, however, certain things are not so obvious. A comparison involving two alphabetic items proceeds from left to right in pairs of characters until the first unequal pair occurs. Thus, in comparing $\boxed{T|H|O|R|P}$ to $\boxed{T|H|A|L|E|S}$, the first field is determined to be greater than the second when the O-A pair is compared. The size of the fields in this case is irrelevant, but suppose we are comparing the following two fields:

$\boxed{S|A|N|D|E|R|S}$ $\boxed{S|A|N|D|E|R|S|O|N}$

In this case, the first field is considered smaller, since the first blank (from left to right) is considered smaller than the letter O.

As a third case of alphabetic comparison, consider this:

$\boxed{S|M|I|T|H}$ $\boxed{S|M|I|T|H| }$

The two items are considered equal, even though their field size is unequal. In this case, the blanks are ignored, which is consistent with the general logic of the comparison.

Consider the following two alphanumeric fields:

$\boxed{X|A|-|1|1|4}$ $\boxed{X|.|B|-|3}$

Convention for determining the "larger" of the two does not exist; still, these are legitimate fields in computer processing, and we must handle them. In this respect, we rely on the *collating sequence* of a computer system, which varies with the computer used. The collating sequence is simply a defined sequence that states the relative "size" of each possible character in a computer's storage. For example, in the widely used IBM System/370 computers, the collating sequence for the following characters is as indicated by the order of listing:

blank

. (period or decimal point)

(

+ (plus sign)

)

- (hyphen or minus)

/ (stroke)

, (comma)

' (single quote)

" (double quote)

letters A –Z

numbers 0 –9

Thus, when comparing 3-A/ and Z/9K, the 3-A/ is the greater.

There are several collating sequences in use, and one should be aware of the possible differences in program results arising from differences in collating sequences.

REVIEW

1   Relation conditions are concerned with comparisons between two items. The words or symbols that serve to indicate the type of comparison to be made are called relational _____.

operators

2   As indicated above, relational operators can be in the form of either words or symbols. In the following spaces, enter the symbols that are equivalent to the listed relational operators:

LESS THAN _____

EQUAL TO _____

GREATER THAN _____

<

=

>

3   Of the following three relation conditions, the one that is invalid as a COBOL expression is the one identified by the letter [**a** / **b** / **c**].

a   IF GROSS-PAY IS GREATER THAN 99 . . .

b   IF 100 < ORDER-AMT . . .

c   IF 500 > 400 . . .

c

4   An ordering that defines the relative rank of all the valid characters in a computer system is referred to as the _____ for the system.

collating sequence

NESTED CONDITIONS

Before discussing nested conditions, let us consider the general format for the IF statement.

The possible unique structures are many, and, since the IF statement is a very common and very useful program instruction, we will do well to spend some time studying it. Here are some of the forms we can have:

IF condition statement-1.
IF condition statement-1 ELSE NEXT SENTENCE.
IF condition statement-1 ELSE statement-2.
IF condition NEXT SENTENCE ELSE statement-2.

Note that the first case shows that we can omit the ELSE portion. For example, we can write IF SUM-TAX < 50.00 MOVE ZERO TO DEDUCTIONS. The period following DEDUCTIONS signifies that the current sentence has ended. Thus, the statement that follows will be the NEXT SENTENCE, and so it would be redundant to write ELSE NEXT SENTENCE, although it would not be wrong.

To enhance your understanding of conditional statements, study the following example:

IF AMOUNT IS GREATER THAN CREDIT LIMIT
    WRITE PRINT-LINE FROM CREDIT-OVERDRAW
ELSE
    MOVE AMOUNT TO BILLING-FIELD
    WRITE PRINT-LINE FROM BILL-AREA.
ADD AMOUNT TO TOTAL-VALUE.

The flowchart for this program segment appears in Figure 7–1. The program statements that correspond to the flowchart descriptions are as follows:

FLOWCHART DESCRIPTION	CORRESPONDING PROGRAM STATEMENT
Condition	IF AMOUNT IS GREATER THAN CREDIT-LIMIT
Statement-1	WRITE PRINT LINE FROM CREDIT-OVERDRAW
Statement-2	MOVE AMOUNT TO BILLING-FIELD WRITE PRINT-LINE FROM BILL-AREA
Next sentence	ADD AMOUNT TO TOTAL-VALUE

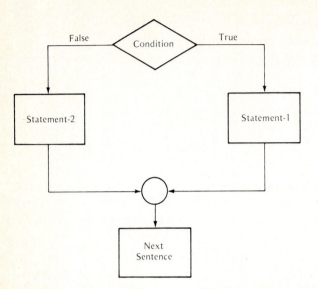

FIGURE 7-1   FLOWCHART FOR THE EXAMPLE OF A CONDITIONAL STATEMENT.

Notice that statement-1 and statement-2 need not be single statements. Statement-2 illustrates the case in which two statements are included.

The NEXT SENTENCE option is one way of expressing the null leg of a condition, as in this example:

```
IF DEBITS = CREDITS
    NEXT SENTENCE
ELSE
    PERFORM OUT-OF-BALANCE.
```

The NEXT SENTENCE provides a clear way of expressing the fact that no action is taken if the condition is true. Contrast the example just given to the equivalent:

```
IF DEBITS NOT = CREDITS
    PERFORM OUT-OF-BALANCE.
```

For most people, the first version is clearer.

In the general format for the IF statement, statement-1 and statement-2 are not restricted to being imperative statements; rather, they themselves may be conditional expressions, giving rise to the possibility of using nested IF statements. A relatively simple example of a nested IF statement, or a nested conditional, is the following:

```
IF AMOUNT IS LESS THAN 100
      IF AMOUNT IS GREATER THAN 50
            MOVE 0.3 TO RATE
      ELSE
            MOVE 0.4 TO RATE
ELSE
      MOVE 0.2 TO RATE
```

This COBOL statement corresponds to the following rule:

AMOUNT	RATE
Less than or equal to 50	0.4
Greater than 50 but less than 100	0.3
Equal to or greater than 100	0.2

You will find it useful in interpreting nested conditionals to look for the first ELSE; it always pertains to the immediately preceding IF. The second ELSE pertains to the IF just preceding the inner IF, and so on. Schematically, the relationships can be portrayed as follows:

```
IF ... IF ... .IF ... ELSE ... ELSE ... ELSE ...
  |      |_____|          |          |
  |_____|
```

The flowchart for this example is shown in Figure 7-2.

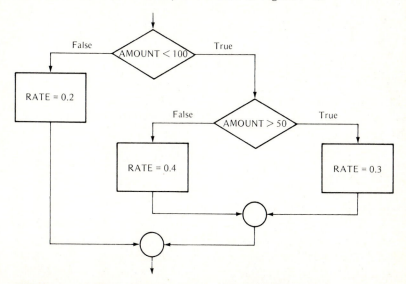

FIGURE 7-2   NESTED CONDITIONAL STRUCTURE TO DETERMINE RATE.

Nested conditions can be very useful in writing program statements, but they also can be misused. This is done by nesting conditions so deeply that program logic is not easy to follow. Because nested conditions are important, we present some additional examples.

First, consider a code that can have legitimate values in the range 1–5. Figure 7-3 depicts a nested conditional structure that tests for the value of

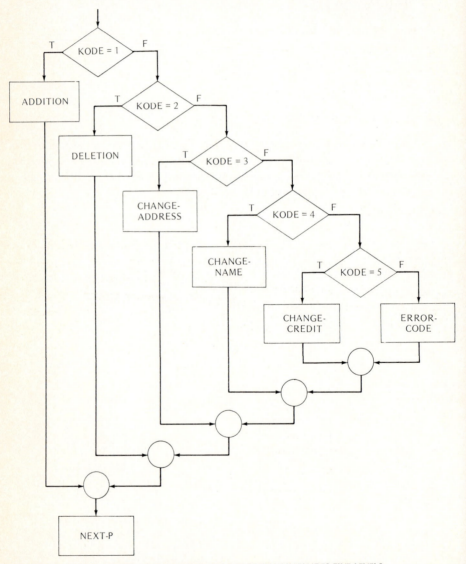

FIGURE 7-3 SAMPLE NESTED CONDITIONAL STRUCTURE THAT INCLUDES FIVE LEVELS.

the code and executes a suitable procedure. In language form, we could write:

```
IF KODE = 1
    PERFORM ADDITION
ELSE
    IF KODE = 2
        PERFORM DELETION
    ELSE
        IF KODE = 3
            PERFORM CHANGE-ADDRESS
        ELSE
            IF KODE = 4
                PERFORM CHANGE-NAME
            ELSE
                IF KODE = 5
                    PERFORM CHANGE-CREDIT
                ELSE
                    PERFORM ERROR-CODE.
PERFORM NEXT-P.
```

We have nested to five levels, which tests the limits of our ability to understand the program logic inherent in the nesting. In general, many programming managers advise against nesting more than three levels. In this particular example, the structure is rather easy, however, because of the null alternatives involved. In this sense, we can say that, even though we have nested to five levels, it is a "clean" program structure.

Alternatively, we could use the GO TO . . . DEPENDING ON verb:

```
GO TO ADDITION
        DELETION
        CHANGE-ADDRESS
        CHANGE-NAME
        CHANGE-CREDIT
    DEPENDING ON T-CODE.
PERFORM ERROR-CODE.
GO TO GO-TO-COLLECTION.
ADDITION.
    .
    .
    .
    GO TO GO-TO-COLLECTION.
```

DELETION.
.
.
.

CHANGE-CREDIT.
.
.
.

GO-TO-COLLECTION.
    PERFORM NEXT-P.

This example would be much more readable, of course, if we used condition-names instead:

```
01  ACTION-CODE     PIC 9.
       88  ADD-RECORD          VALUE 1.
       88  DELETE-RECORD       VALUE 2.
       88  ADDRESS-CHANGE      VALUE 3.
       88  NAME-CHANGE         VALUE 4.
       88  CREDIT-CHANGE       VALUE 5.
       88  CODE-ERROR          VALUES ARE ZERO, 6 THRU 9.
```

Use of condition-names not only would make the code more understandable but also would make it easier to change. To change the codes, we would need only to change them at the one place in the program where the condition-names were defined.

As yet another alternative, we could use simple conditions:

```
IF ADD-RECORD       PERFORM  ADDITION.
IF DELETE-RECORD    PERFORM  DELETION.
IF ADDRESS-CHANGE   PERFORM  CHANGE-ADDRESS.
IF NAME-CHANGE      PERFORM  CHANGE-NAME.
IF CREDIT-CHANGE    PERFORM  CHANGE-CREDIT.
IF CODE-ERROR       PERFORM  ERROR-CODE.
PERFORM NEXT-P.
```

In this case, the programming is simpler, but there are two minor disadvantages. First, it is not obvious immediately that only one of these seven conditions can be true, and therefore program clarity suffers. Second, all seven conditions will be tested before the PERFORM NEXT-P is executed; whereas in the nested and GO TO structures, as soon as one condition holds, control moves immediately to PERFORM NEXT-P.

Consider next the example presented in Figure 7–4. It can be seen that the flowchart implies nested conditionals such as these:

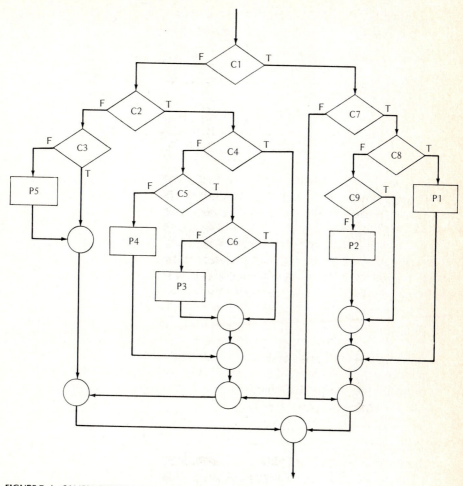

FIGURE 7-4   SAMPLE DEEPLY NESTED CONDITIONAL STRUCTURE.

```
IF   C1
    IF   C7
        IF   C8
            PERFORM P1
        ELSE
            IF NOT C9
                PERFORM P2
            ELSE
                NEXT SENTENCE
```

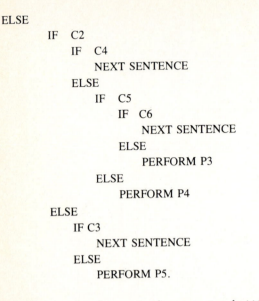

```
ELSE
        IF   C2
            IF   C4
                NEXT SENTENCE
            ELSE
                IF   C5
                    IF   C6
                        NEXT SENTENCE
                    ELSE
                        PERFORM P3
                ELSE
                    PERFORM P4
        ELSE
            IF C3
                NEXT SENTENCE
            ELSE
                PERFORM P5.
```

It is obvious that the nesting has gone too far! What can we do to simplify the program structure? Figure 7–5 suggests decomposition into several modules that are executed by use of PERFORM instructions. Notice that these modules are understandable, each by itself, and yet we preserve their dependencies. Thus, rather than deep nesting, we suggest breaking down the program into several paragraphs containing simple or lightly nested conditional statements.

REVIEW

1 Identify, for the following program instruction, the program statement that corresponds to each IF statement element. Refer to the general format for the IF statement if you wish.

```
IF   QUANTITY < 100
        NEXT SENTENCE
ELSE
        MULTIPLY DISCOUNT BY PRICE.
MULTIPLY PRICE BY QUANTITY GIVING NET.
```

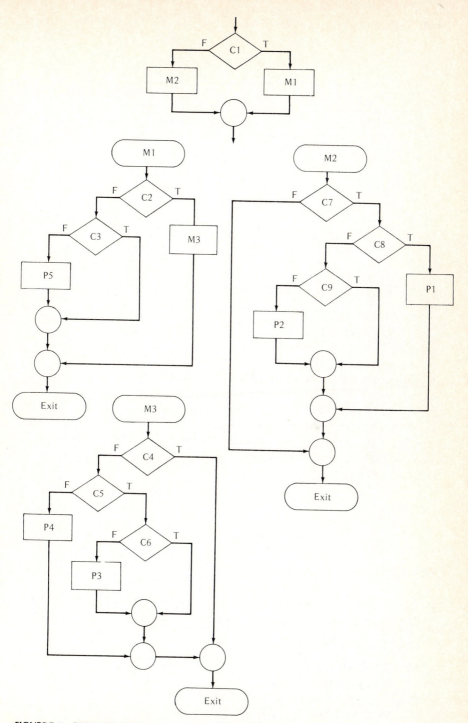

FIGURE 7-5 DECOMPOSITION OF A DEEPLY NESTED CONDITIONAL STRUCTURE.

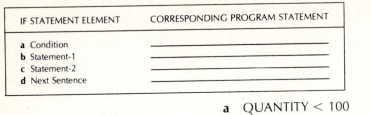

IF STATEMENT ELEMENT	CORRESPONDING PROGRAM STATEMENT
a Condition	_____
b Statement-1	_____
c Statement-2	_____
d Next Sentence	_____

a QUANTITY < 100
b *Not used*
c MULTIPLY DISCOUNT BY PRICE
d MULTIPLY PRICE BY QUANTITY GIVING NET

2   Construct a flowchart for this program segment:

IF   QUANTITY < 100
  NEXT SENTENCE
ELSE
  MULTIPLY DISCOUNT BY PRICE.
MULTIPLY PRICE BY QUANTITY GIVING NET.

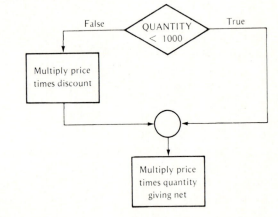

3   Using the following COBOL statement, complete the table below, summarizing the decision rule being used:

IF   GRSPAY < 1000.00
  IF   GRSPAY > 500.00
    MOVE 0.05 TO RETRMNT-DEDUC
  ELSE
    MOVE 0.03 TO RETRMNT-DEDUC
ELSE
  MOVE 0.07 TO RETRMNT-DEDUC.

AMOUNT OF GROSS PAY	RETIREMENT DEDUCTION RATE
Equal to or greater than 1,000	_____
Greater than 500 but less than 1,000	_____
Less than or equal to 500	_____

0.07; 0.05; 0.03

4 The type of conditional statement illustrated in the preceding question usually is referred to as a(n) _____ conditional.

nested

5 The logic associated with a deeply nested program structure can be clarified by decomposition of the program into several separate, but dependent, _____.

modules (or paragraphs)

CLASS CONDITIONS

The use of a class condition test makes it possible to determine whether the contents of a data field are numeric or alphabetic. Further, by the use of a combination of such conditionals, we also can determine if the field contains alphanumeric data. The general format for the class condition test is:

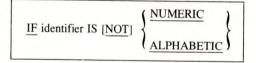

A data field is numeric if it contains only the digits 0–9, with or without an operational sign. Alphabetic items, on the other hand, consist of the letters A–Z and/or blanks. It is not valid to perform a NUMERIC class test on an alphabetic field or an ALPHABETIC class test on a numeric field. Thus, suppose we have the following DATA DIVISION specifications:

AMOUNT   PICTURE 9(4)V99.
NAME   PICTURE A(15).

It would be improper to write:

IF AMOUNT IS ALPHABETIC . . . or IF NAME IS NUMERIC . . .

Instead, the AMOUNT field just given can be tested to determine if the content is in fact NUMERIC or if it is NOT NUMERIC. Similarly, the NAME field can be tested only to determine if the content is ALPHABETIC or NOT ALPHABETIC. A common case of a numeric field not containing numeric data involves reading a field from a card that contains one or more blanks.

TABLE 7-1   VALID USES OF THE CLASS CONDITION TEST FOR DIFFERENT KINDS OF FIELDS

FIELD CLASS	VALID TEST
Numeric	NUMERIC, NOT NUMERIC
Alphabetic	ALPHABETIC, NOT ALPHABETIC
Alphanumeric	NUMERIC, NOT NUMERIC, ALPHABETIC, NOT ALPHABETIC

Specifying the PICTURE with 9s does not guarantee that the field will contain numeric digits. Table 7-1 summarizes the valid uses of the class condition test for different kinds of fields. Note that any of the condition tests may be used with an alphanumeric field.

In general, the class condition test is useful as a check to determine if particular data classes contain the type of data as defined in the DATA DIVISION: numeric, alphabetic, or alphanumeric. The tests for NUMERIC and ALPHABETIC are straightforward, such as:

IF AMOUNT IS NUMERIC . . .
IF NAME IS NOT ALPHABETIC . . .

In effect, the first statement directly tests the appropriateness of the content in the numeric field called AMOUNT, whereas the second statement tests for inappropriateness of the content in the alphabetic field called NAME. Since an alphanumeric field can have both alphabetic and numeric content, the alphanumeric content can be ascertained indirectly by determining that the content is not entirely numeric and that it is not entirely alphabetic, as follows:

IF   FIELD-A IS NOT NUMERIC
    IF   FIELD-A IS NOT ALPHABETIC
        PERFORM ALPHA-NUM-PAR . . .

The class condition test cannot be used with numeric items whose USAGE has been declared COMPUTATIONAL. Thus the usage must be explicitly or implicitly DISPLAY. The COMPUTATIONAL and DISPLAY clauses are discussed in Chapter 8: "Additional DATA and PROCEDURE DIVISION Statements."

REVIEW

1   The purpose of a class condition test is to determine if the actual content of a storage field is _____, _____, or _____.

numeric, alphabetic,
alphanumeric

2   Suppose that a field named VENDOR has been defined as an alphabetic field in the DATA DIVISION. If we wish to check for the possibility that numeric data have been entered into this field, we could do so by the statement: IF VENDOR IS _____.

NOT ALPHABETIC

3   Suppose that a field named ADDRESS has been defined as an alphanumeric field in the DATA DIVISION. If we wish to ascertain that the content of the field is in fact alphanumeric, we can do so by the statement _____.

IF ADDRESS IS NOT NUMERIC
IF ADDRESS IS NOT
ALPHABETIC

USING CONDITIONALS TO CHECK INPUT DATA

The well known GIGO (Garbage In Garbage Out) acronym summarizes effectively the importance of accurate input data. Before data can be processed, they must be checked for correctness and completeness. Errors creep into source data for a variety of reasons, but are due mainly to human error. A good data processing system accepts reasonable error rates in input data as a fact of life and screens the data through so-called "edit" programs. Such programs use conditional expressions that check input data to determine that they are complete and that they are valid or at least reasonable. Errors that are detected are listed for manual correction and resubmission.

Figure 7-6 presents a simplified program that checks employee records that contain payroll data. Sample input and output are shown in Figure 7-7. As the program illustrates, it is a good procedure to list the record that contains the error and to check for all possibilities. If there is one error, the chances are that there may be several errors, and we should identify all of them the first time through. An error message is printed for each error that is detected. It is worth noting that the PAY-RATE field is checked for reasonableness by comparing it to maximum and minimum limits, but such a test is meaningful only if the PAY-CODE is correct (either salaried or hourly).

REVIEW

1   A good data processing system is based on the assumption that there will be [no / some] errors in input data.

some

```
IDENTIFICATION DIVISION.
PROGRAM-ID.  DATAEDIT.
*
ENVIRONMENT DIVISION.
*
CONFIGURATION SECTION.
SOURCE-COMPUTER.  ABC-480.
OBJECT-COMPUTER.  ABC-480.
*
INPUT-OUTPUT SECTION.
*
FILE-CONTROL.
    SELECT EMPLOYEE-FILE ASSIGN TO CARD-READER.
    SELECT PRINT-FILE ASSIGN TO PRINTER.
/
DATA DIVISION.
*
FILE SECTION.
*
FD  EMPLOYEE-FILE
    LABEL RECORDS ARE OMITTED
    DATA RECORD IS EMPLOYEE-RECORD.
01  EMPLOYEE-RECORD.
    02 EMPL-NAME                PIC X(15).
    02 EMPL-NO                  PIC 9(4).
    02 PAY-CODE                 PIC X.
       88 SALARIED              VALUE 'S'.
       88 HOURLY                VALUE 'H'.
    02 PAY-RATE                 PIC 9(4)V99.
    02 FILLER                   PIC X(54).
*
FD  PRINT-FILE
    LABEL RECORDS ARE OMITTED
    DATA RECORD IS PRINT-RECORD.
01  PRINT-RECORD               PIC X(132).
*
WORKING-STORAGE SECTION.
*
01  END-OF-FILE-INDICATOR      PIC XXX VALUE 'NO'.
    88 END-OF-FILE             VALUE 'YES'.
*
01  RECORD-PRINT-SWITCH        PIC 9 VALUE ZERO.
    88 RECORD-HAS-BEEN-PRINTED VALUE 1.
*
01  PAY-LIMITS.
    02 MINIMUM-SALARY          PIC 9(4)V99 VALUE 600.00.
    02 MAXIMUM-SALARY          PIC 9(4)V99 VALUE 6800.00.
    02 MINIMUM-WAGE            PIC 9(4)V99 VALUE 3.50.
    02 MAXIMUM-WAGE            PIC 9(4)V99 VALUE 18.99.
*
01  ERROR-MESSAGE-RECORD.
    02 FILLER                  PIC X(20) VALUE SPACES.
    02 ERROR-MESSAGE           PIC X(60).
*
01  INPUT-RECORD-OUT.
    02 FILLER                  PIC X(5) VALUE SPACES.
    02 INPUT-RECORD            PIC X(80).
*
01  HEADING-1.
    02 FILLER                  PIC X(30) VALUE SPACES.
    02 FILLER                  PIC X(24) VALUE
       'INPUT DATA ERROR LISTING'.
*
01  HEADING-2.
    02 FILLER                  PIC X(27) VALUE SPACES.
    02 FILLER                  PIC X(36) VALUE
       '(RECORD PRECEDES ITS ERROR MESSAGES)'.
```

FIGURE 7-6   LISTING OF THE PROGRAM TO CHECK INPUT DATA.

```
PROCEDURE DIVISION.
*
 PROGRAM-SUMMARY.
*
     OPEN INPUT EMPLOYEE-FILE
          OUTPUT PRINT-FILE.
*
     PERFORM READ-RECORD.
*
     WRITE PRINT-RECORD FROM HEADING-1 AFTER PAGE
     WRITE PRINT-RECORD FROM HEADING-2 AFTER 1.
*
     PERFORM ERROR-CHECKING
          UNTIL END-OF-FILE.
*
     CLOSE EMPLOYEE-FILE
           PRINT-FILE.
*
     STOP RUN.
*
 READ-RECORD.
     READ EMPLOYEE-FILE RECORD
          AT END MOVE 'YES' TO END-OF-FILE-INDICATOR.
*
 ERROR-CHECKING.

     IF EMPL-NAME = SPACES
        MOVE 'EMPLOYEE NAME IS MISSING' TO ERROR-MESSAGE
        PERFORM ERROR-PRINT.
*
     IF EMPL-NO NOT NUMERIC
        MOVE 'EMPLOYEE NUMBER CONTAIN NON-NUMERIC CHARACTERS'
             TO ERROR-MESSAGE
        PERFORM ERROR-PRINT.
*
     IF (NOT SALARIED) AND (NOT HOURLY)
        MOVE 'PAY CODE IS NEITHER S NOR H' TO ERROR-MESSAGE
        PERFORM ERROR-PRINT.
*
     IF PAY-RATE NOT NUMERIC
        MOVE 'PAY RATE CONTAINS NON-NUMERIC CHARACTERS'
             TO ERROR-MESSAGE
        PERFORM ERROR-PRINT.
*
     IF (NOT SALARIED) AND (NOT HOURLY)
        NEXT SENTENCE
     ELSE
        IF SALARIED
           AND (PAY-RATE < MINIMUM-SALARY)
           OR (PAY-RATE > MAXIMUM-SALARY)
           MOVE 'UNREASONABLE PAY RATE FOR SALARIED EMPLOYEE'
                TO ERROR-MESSAGE
           PERFORM ERROR-PRINT
     ELSE
           IF HOURLY
           AND (PAY-RATE < MINIMUM-WAGE)
              OR (PAY-RATE > MAXIMUM-WAGE)
              MOVE 'UNREASONABLE WAGE RATE FOR HOURLY EMPLOYEE'
                   TO ERROR-MESSAGE
              PERFORM ERROR-PRINT
           ELSE NEXT SENTENCE.
*
     MOVE ZERO TO RECORD-PRINT-SWITCH.
*
     PERFORM READ-RECORD.
*
 ERROR-PRINT.
     IF RECORD-HAS-BEEN-PRINTED
        NEXT SENTENCE
     ELSE
        MOVE 1 TO RECORD-PRINT-SWITCH
        MOVE EMPLOYEE-RECORD TO INPUT-RECORD
        WRITE PRINT-RECORD FROM INPUT-RECORD-OUT
              AFTER ADVANCING 3 LINES.
*
     WRITE PRINT-RECORD FROM ERROR-MESSAGE-RECORD
           AFTER ADVANCING 1 LINE.
```

FIGURE 7-6 (*continued*)

INPUT

```
BROWN,R.K.      12345156035
DAVIS,M.O.       5246H250603
GARCIA,L.A.     3345H000676
HARRISON,P.N.   21005000700
MARTIN,A.C.     5123512000
MARTINEZ,P.M.   44335800000
PETERSON,R.A.   6161H0001256
```

OUTPUT

```
                    INPUT DATA ERROR LISTING
                (RECORD PRECEDES ITS ERROR MESSAGES)


BROWN,R.K.      12345156035
                PAY CODE IS NEITHER S NOR H


DAVIS,M.O.       5246H250603
                EMPLOYEE NUMBER CONTAIN NON-NUMERIC CHARACTERS
                PAY CODE IS NEITHER S NOR H
                PAY RATE CONTAINS NON-NUMERIC CHARACTERS


HARRISON,P.N.   21005000700
                PAY CODE IS NEITHER S NOR H


MARTIN,A.C.     5123512000
                PAY CODE IS NEITHER S NOR H
                PAY RATE CONTAINS NON-NUMERIC CHARACTERS


MARTINEZ,P.M.   44335800000
                PAY CODE IS NEITHER S NOR H


PETERSON,R.A.   6161H0001256
                UNREASONABLE WAGE RATE FOR HOURLY EMPLOYEE
```

FIGURE 7-7   SAMPLE INPUT AND OUTPUT FOR THE PROGRAM TO CHECK INPUT DATA.

2   The purpose of a typical edit program is to test for the [accuracy / reasonableness] of input data.

reasonableness

3   For each apparent error detected by use of an edit program, it is good practice to [list only the item in error / list the entire record that contains an error].

*list the entire record that contains
an error*

SIGN CONDITIONS

The sign condition determines whether or not the algebraic value of an identifier or arithmetic expression is greater than, less than, or equal to, zero. The general format for the sign condition is:

The subject of the condition must be a numeric field or arithmetic expression. If the value contained in the field is greater than zero, it is POSITIVE; if the value is equal to zero, it is ZERO; and if it is less than zero, it is NEGATIVE.

As was true for the class condition test, the sign condition is used frequently as a check on the appropriateness of data. For example, if an inventory figure cannot be negative by definition, the presence of a negative value in such a field indicates some kind of error. In other circumstances, a zero or negative value in an inventory field might be indicative of an out-of-stock condition, and the test could be used to initiate a reordering procedure.

REVIEW

1   The sign condition can be used to test for three specific types of conditions in regard to the content held in a particular field: whether it is positive, _____, or _____.

negative; zero

2   The subject of the sign condition must be a _____ field.

numeric

CONDITION-NAME CONDITIONS

In Chapter 5: "DATA DIVISION Features," we described the use of condition-names, which are identified by level number 88. For completeness and later reference, we include such conditions here. For example, in the DATA DIVISION we have:

```
02  PAYROLL    PICTURE 9.
    88  HOURLY VALUE 1.
    88  SALARY VALUE 2.
```

Then in the PROCEDURE DIVISION we can test the condition-name by using a statement such as:

```
IF  HOURLY
    PERFORM HRLY-COMP
ELSE
    IF  SALARY
        PERFORM SALARY-COMP.
```

These condition-name tests are equivalent to the following relational conditions tests in terms of their results:

```
IF   PAYROLL = 1
     PERFORM HRLY-COMP
ELSE
     IF   PAYROLL = 2
          PERFORM SALARY-COMP.
```

The use of the condition-name test, however, generally is preferred, because it represents better documentation by more clearly describing what is being tested in the PROCEDURE DIVISION statement itself.

COMPLEX CONDITIONS

It is possible to combine the simple (individual) conditionals we have described into complex conditionals by the use of the logical operators OR, AND, and NOT. OR means either or both, and AND means both. Thus, consider the following statement:

```
IF BALANCE IS NEGATIVE AND DAYS-OVERDUE > 10
     PERFORM PAR-A.
```

The instruction indicates that the program should execute PAR-A when both the balance is negative and the number of overdue days exceeds 10.

On the other hand, consider the following statement:

```
IF INPUT-DATA IS NOT NUMERIC OR NAME-IS-MISSING
     MOVE 'CANT PROCESS, INCORRECT DATA' TO MESSAGE.
```

The program will move the indicated message to MESSAGE if either the input data are not numeric (perhaps because of a keying error) or the condition-name condition defined as NAME-IS-MISSING in the DATA DIVISION holds.

There is a rather complex set of rules associated with the writing and evaluation of complex conditionals. From the standpoint of the scope and orientation of this book, however, we shall limit our attention to the use of parentheses to clarify the meaning. For example, we can write:

```
IF (AGE IS GREATER THAN 28) OR (EXPERIENCE = 4)
     AND (EDUCATION IS GREATER THAN HS)) . . .
```

This condition holds either if age is greater than 28 or if both experience = 4 and education is greater than high school.

As another example, consider the following:

IF (KODE = 2) OR (KODE = 3)) AND (BALANCE-CODE = 1)
    MOVE SPACES TO ERROR-MESSAGE
    PERFORM OLD-ITEM-2.

In this example, the condition is true if BALANCE-CODE is equal to 1 and KODE is either equal to 2 *or* equal to 3.

    Thus, by the use of complex conditionals, we can write conditional tests that otherwise would require very long expressions consisting of several nested IF statements. Complex conditionals are useful particularly for selecting data from a file, since we can designate selective retrieval of records according to the presence or absence of complex conditions.

REVIEW

1 The conditional by which the type of record can be identified—for example, markup might vary according to the category of the item—is called the _____ test.

condition-name

2 Of course, the condition-name tested must be assigned in the DATA DIVISION as an 88 level statement, wherein it also is assigned a value. Although the condition also could be tested in the PROCEDURE DIVISION by testing the value, the condition-name test usually is preferred because it results in [greater programming accuracy / clearer documentation].

clearer documentation

3 In contrast to the use of simple conditionals, a combination of tests can be included in one statement by the use of _____ conditionals.

complex

4 The use of a complex conditional requires the use of one of the logical operators: _____, _____, or _____.

OR; NOT; AND

5 When the logical operator OR is used in a complex conditional test, the presence of [either / both / either or both] of the conditional states constitutes a YES condition.

either or both

6 When the logical operator AND is used in a complex conditional test, the presence of [either / both / either or both] of the conditional states constitutes a YES condition.

both

EXERCISES

7.1   Write PROCEDURE DIVISION statements to implement the logic included in the following flowchart.

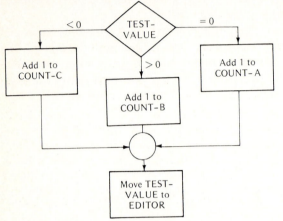

7.2   An input field has been defined as:

03   IN-FIELD   PICTURE X(10)

Two other fields in WORKING-STORAGE have been defined as:

01   AMOUNT   PICTURE 9(10).
01   NAME   PICTURE A(10).

We wish to test the content of IN-FIELD and, if it contains a number, to store it in AMOUNT; if it contains a name, to store it in NAME; and if a mixture of characters, to go to a paragraph called ERRORS.

   a   Write PROCEDURE DIVISION statements to accomplish this task.
   b   Suppose that, if the IN-FIELD contains a number, it is actually in dollars and cents. What would you do to make the number available in dollars and cents instead of as an integer? (*Hint:* Be careful!)

7.3   Using the 88 level number indicator in the DATA DIVISION and suitable condition-name clauses, the following obvious identifiers have been defined:

MALE

FEMALE

SINGLE-M

MARRIED-M

DIVORCED-M

WIDOWED-M

SINGLE-F

MARRIED-F

DIVORCED-F

WIDOWED-F

Assume we want to tabulate the number of individuals falling in the last eight classes, as, for example, the number of single males (SINGLE-M). We thus want to test the field containing the identifying code and ADD 1 TO the corresponding counter. Assume the following fields are to be used as counters: SM, MM, DM, WM, SF, MF, DF, WF (where SM stands for single males, etc.).

a   Draw a flowchart corresponding to your program logic.

b   Write *one* nested conditional expression to accomplish the required testing and tabulating.

7.4   Consider the following DATA DIVISION entries relating to a personnel record:

02	EDUCATION		PICTURE 99.
	88 H-S GRAD	VALUE 12.	
	88 COLLEGE-GRAD	VALUE 16.	
	88 MASTERS-GRAD	VALUE 17.	
	88 DOCTORATE-GRAD	VALUE 20.	
02	YEARS-OF-EXPERIENCE		PICTURE 99.
02	SEX		PICTURE 9.
	88 MALE	VALUE 1.	
	88 FEMALE	VALUE 2.	
02	GEOGRAPHIC-PREFERENCE		PICTURE 9.
	88 EAST	VALUE 1.	
	88 MIDWEST	VALUE 2.	
	88 WEST	VALUE 3.	
	88 SOUTH	VALUE 4.	
	88 WILLING-TO-TRAVEL	VALUE 5.	

Suppose that we want to find individuals who fulfill one of these three requirements:

a   Five years of experience, male, high school graduate, willing to travel

b   Male, one year of experience, master's degree, preferring the West or South

c   Three years of experience, female, doctorate, preferring the East

192

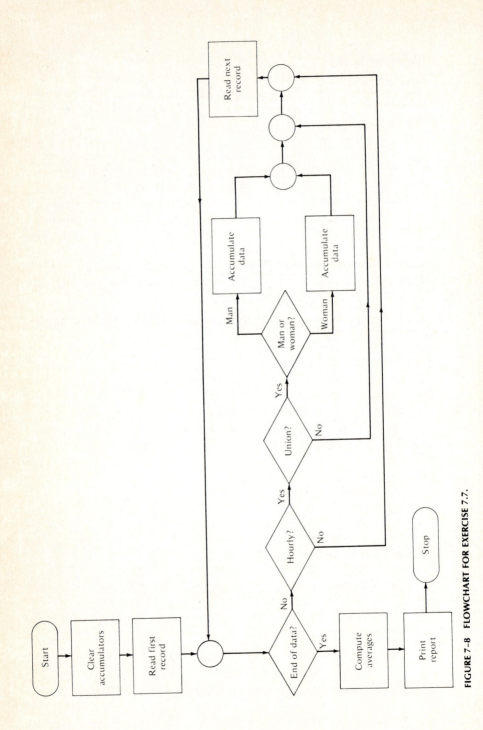

FIGURE 7-8 FLOWCHART FOR EXERCISE 7.7.

Write *one* compound conditional sentence by which we can check whether a record in question fulfills the first, second, or third of these requirements. If one of these requirements is met, we WRITE PRINTLINE FROM NAME. If the requirement is not met, we execute PAR-A.

7.5 Consider the following table of conditions:

QUANTITY	PRICE	RATING	DISCOUNT
>100	>10	<2	0.05
>100	>10	≥2	0.10
>100	≤10	<2	0.15
>100	≤10	≥2	0.20
≤100	$\left\{\begin{array}{c}< \\ =10 \\ >\end{array}\right\}$	$\left\{\begin{array}{c}< \\ =2 \\ >\end{array}\right\}$	0.25

a Write instructions—using nested IF—to MOVE to DISCOUNT the value shown depending on the conditions.

b Draw a structured flowchart corresponding to the data in the table.

7.6 Draw in flowchart form the following, where C1 stands for condition 1 and F1 stands for function (statement) 1.

```
IF  C1
        AND (C2 OR C3)
      F1
      F2
ELSE
     IF  C3
             OR (C6 AND C7)
          F3
     ELSE
             NEXT SENTENCE.
```

7.7 Write PROCEDURE DIVISION statements corresponding to the flowchart in Figure 7–8. Assume that each function block is a paragraph to be PERFORMED; for example, your first statement would be PERFORM CLEAR-ACCUMULATORS.

8

Additional DATA and PROCEDURE DIVISION statements

INTRODUCTION

This chapter presents a number of additional program statements. In general, these DATA and PROCEDURE DIVISION statements do certain things more easily than otherwise would be possible. As the chapter table of contents indicates, there is a great number of statements presented and described. It would be difficult for a beginning COBOL programmer to incorporate all of these options in one or even several programs. Thus, a realistic objective in studying this chapter is to become aware of these additional features and to understand their functions well enough so as to refer back to them if and when a programming occasion invites their use.

THE USAGE CLAUSE

Numeric data in a computer may be represented in one of two basic modes. They may be represented as character data or as numeric data. Both modes utilize binary characters (bits) of zero and one, but the meaning of a given bit depends on the coding method used.

In character mode, each decimal digit in a number is represented by a group of binary bits. Commonly, either six or eight bits comprise each digit; thus, in the six-bit Binary Coded Decimal (BCD) form, the decimal number 19 is represented as 000001001010. The first six bits represent the decimal digit 1, and the last six bits the digit 9. We also should mention two other commonly used coding schemes: the American Standard Code for Information Interchange (ASCII) and the Extended Binary Coded Decimal Interchange Code (EBCDIC), the latter used primarily by IBM.

Numeric data in numeric mode consists of binary bits that have positional values analogous to the decimal system. In the decimal system, the first digit in the number 111 has meaning (100), entirely different from that of the third digit (1), even though they look alike. The string of binary bits 000001001010 viewed as a binary number signifies a quantity of 74, not 19, as it would in the BCD code described above. Actually, a variety of numeric coding schemes are in use. We mention their names for reference and direct the interested reader to other sources for explanation (most introductory EDP texts contain descriptions of such codes). The common coding forms are: fixed-point binary, floating-point of single or double precision, packed-decimal, and zoned-decimal.

The arithmetic registers of computers perform arithmetic with numeric data that is in numeric, not character, mode. If numeric data is represented in character mode, it must first be converted to numeric mode before arithmetic computations can be performed.

In COBOL, data in character mode is described as being in DISPLAY mode, while data in numeric mode is described as being in COMPUTATIONAL mode. DISPLAY is the default condition: all data items are assumed to be in DISPLAY mode unless they are declared to be COMPUTATIONAL. The declaration is done in the DATA DIVISION with the USAGE clause. Consider the following examples:

02	AMOUNT-1		PIC 99.
02	AMOUNT-2		PIC 99 USAGE DISPLAY.
02	AMOUNT-3		PIC 99 USAGE COMPUTATIONAL.
02	AMOUNT-4		PIC 99 USAGE COMP.
02	AMOUNT-5	USAGE COMP	PIC 99 VALUE ZERO.

The first example omits the USAGE clause, and the item will be in DISPLAY mode by default. The second example makes the declaration explicit. The third and fourth examples illustrate the COMPUTATIONAL declaration in full and abbreviated form, respectively. The last example illustrates the point that the order of USAGE, PIC, and VALUE is immaterial.

From a programming standpoint, omission of the USAGE clause seems to be the easiest course of action. From the standpoint of program running efficiency, however, significant savings can be achieved by using the COMPUTATIONAL form. We therefore recommend that numeric fields in WORKING-STORAGE used for arithmetic be defined routinely as COMPUTATIONAL. Still, absence of the COMPUTATIONAL option does no harm in terms of the results. The compiler inserts the necessary instructions to convert a DISPLAY field into COMPUTATIONAL form prior to doing arithmetic and then converts the result back into DISPLAY form before storing it in a DISPLAY field.

Data punched onto cards or entered via an online keyboard terminal are in DISPLAY mode, and thus no COMPUTATIONAL fields should be used in the record descriptions of such an input file in the FILE SECTION. Similarly, printing COMPUTATIONAL data makes no sense. However, COMPUTATIONAL data may be read from or written onto magnetic media, such as tapes and disks.

Most compilers specify different forms of COMPUTATIONAL. For instance, IBM and UNIVAC use COMPUTATIONAL-1 (or COMP-1) to define a single precision floating-decimal field. ANSI COBOL recognizes only one form, COMPUTATIONAL (or COMP), and it is up to the implementor of the language to define the specific meaning of this standard term. Unless compelling reasons lead to the choice of nonstandard options, such as COMP-1 or the like, the programmer will find it advantageous in the long run to stick with the standard.

It should be noted that moving zeros to a group item whose elementary items contain USAGE COMPUTATIONAL clauses may result in nonzero data. Consider this group item:

```
01  GROUP-ITEM.
    02  AMOUNT-1    PIC 99V99 USAGE COMPUTATIONAL.
    02  AMOUNT-2    PIC 999V99 USAGE COMPUTATIONAL.
```

A statement such as MOVE ZEROS TO GROUP-ITEM will move "character" zeros into GROUP-ITEM. A zero in character mode is different from a zero in binary numeric mode. Therefore, if we subsequently write ADD TOTAL TO AMOUNT-1, erroneous results will be obtained from the arithmetic operation, since AMOUNT-1 does not contain a zero value. To avoid such problems, we should move zeros to each individual numeric field that has been defined as USAGE COMPUTATIONAL. Thus, MOVE ZERO TO AMOUNT-1, AMOUNT-2 would be the appropriate instruction for setting these two fields equal to zero. Of course, in the absence of the USAGE COMPUTATIONAL clauses, MOVE ZERO TO GROUP-ITEM would have been no problem in this case.

THE SYNCHRONIZED CLAUSE

The USAGE COMPUTATIONAL option increases program running efficiency, but it does not do the whole job. The SYNCHRONIZED clause is needed to achieve additional execution efficiency. The need for the SYNCHRONIZED clause derives from the fact that COBOL is a general language, but computers of different manufacturers differ in structure. Consider this example:

```
01   FIELD-A.
     02   FIELD-B      PIC 9 USAGE COMP.
     02   FIELD-C      PIC 99 USAGE COMP.
```

In a straightforward fashion, we defined two numeric computational fields of one- and two-decimal digits, respectively. In word-oriented computers, such as many UNIVAC, Honeywell, and CDC machines, both fields are stored in the same word, and arithmetic computations are not as efficient as when each field is stored in a separate word. In character-oriented computers, such as many IBM machines, arithmetic execution may not be as efficient as it could be because the fields are not in proper storage boundaries. The SYNCHRONIZED clause can be used to improve efficiency in this simple example.

Notice the SYNC abbreviation, which is an available alternative:

```
01   FIELD-A.
     02   FIELD-B      PIC 9 USAGE COMP SYNCHRONIZED.
     02   FIELD-B      PIC 99 USAGE COMP SYNC.
```

The use of this option is not always this simple. For other variations, one should consult the manufacturer's manual for the computer being used.

We hasten to add that the SYNCHRONIZED option should be used sparingly. In order to achieve efficiency, one must understand clearly the storage structure of a given computer and the compiler's implementation of the SYNCHRONIZED option. Because this storage structure differs among computers, program compatibility across different computers may be lost by use of the SYNCHRONIZED clause. The interested reader should study the manufacturer's manual for her or his own computer before using synchronization, and should consider use of the option only for programs that perform extensive numerical computation.

We digress for a moment to draw a brief comparison with the popular FORTRAN language. A user of that language may wonder why COBOL needs complications such as the SYNCHRONIZED clause, while FORTRAN does beautifully without any such considerations. FORTRAN achieves simplicity by limiting options and forcing uniformity. For instance, all numeric integer fields in FORTRAN occupy a full word (in a word-oriented machine), regardless of desired field size. In contrast, COBOL allows the programmer to define integer fields from 1 to 18 digits in size. In this case, the price of flexibility is complexity.

THE JUSTIFIED RIGHT CLAUSE

This option is used with elementary alphabetic or alphanumerica items only, and its effect is to override the convention of left-justifying non-numeric data. Suppose we have the record description 02 TITLE PICX(10). If we write MOVE "JONES" to TITLE, the effect in TITLE will be | J | O | N | E | S | | | | | | , with the name left-justified. However, if in the DATA DIVISION we had written 02 TITLE PICTURE X(10) JUSTIFIED RIGHT, execution of the above MOVE instruction would result in | | | | | | J | O | N | E | S | in TITLE.

As indicated by the previous example, the JUSTIFIED RIGHT clause always is used in conjunction with the PICTURE clause for elementary items; however, it cannot be used with level 66 or level 88 items. Level 66 is a special-purpose level explained later in this chapter. In addition to arranging right-justification, the JUSTIFIED RIGHT clause also affects truncation. Without the JUSTIFIED RIGHT clause, truncation takes place from the right for alphabetic and alphanumeric data. When the JUSTIFIED RIGHT clause is used, truncation takes place from the left, as for numeric data.

REVIEW

1 Numeric data stored in a computer may be represented in one of two basic modes: as _____ data or as _____ data.

character; numeric

2 In order to perform arithmetic computations, numeric data must be in _____ mode.

numeric

3 In COBOL, the two modes in which data can be represented are DISPLAY and COMPUTATIONAL. The appropriate form of the data can be indicated by use of the _____ clause in the DATA DIVISION.

USAGE

4 When the USAGE clause is not used, the field automatically is defined as being [DISPLAY / COMPUTATIONAL] in form.

DISPLAY

5 If zeros are moved into a group item, such zeros will always be in the [character / binary numeric] mode.

character

6 The option that can be used in the DATA DIVISION to improve the efficiency of arithmetic execution by the assignment of appropriate storage boundaries is the _____ clause.

SYNCHRONIZED

7 Elementary alphabetic or alphanumeric items can be positioned in the rightmost portion of the field by use of the _____ clause in the DATA DIVISION.

JUSTIFIED RIGHT

QUALIFICATION

Up to this point in the book, we always have indicated that every data-name must be unique in a given program. This requirement will be modified now by introducing the use of qualifiers, which retain the concept of unique data-names but expand the form to provide greater flexibility. A qualifier is a data-name of higher hierarchical level than the name it qualifies. The use of qualifiers results in having unique data-names for names that otherwise would not be unique, thus providing more flexibility in the assignment of data-names in the program. The following DATA DIVISION segment is an example of a case in which qualification would be necessary in the PROCEDURE DIVISION:

```
02   WEEKLY-TOTALS.
     03   HOURS            PICTURE 99V9.
     03   DEPARTMENT-NO    PICTURE 9(5).
02   MONTHLY-TOTALS.
     03   HOURS            PICTURE 999V9.
     03   (etc.)
```

Notice that HOURS seems to be used twice, but with respect to two different items, namely, the total hours for the week and the total hours for the month. If reference were made simply to HOURS, it would not be clear which storage field should be used; however, the use of qualifiers results in unique data-names and could be accomplished as follows in the PROCEDURE DIVISION instructions:

MOVE HOURS OF WEEKLY-TOTALS TO . . .
MOVE HOURS IN MONTHLY-TOTALS TO . . .

OF and IN in these program statements are equivalent, and use of either word after a data-name serves to signal the use of a qualifier. Since a data-name that is not unique in the program always must be qualified, the use of nonunique names always results in longer statements in the PROCEDURE DIVISION. Despite this disadvantage, qualifiers often are used because they improve documentation. For instance, the statements in the above example make it quite clear that we are working with weekly and monthly hours, respectively.

A common use of qualifiers is with records that have some fields in common, such as master and transaction records. If an employee has an assigned identification number that is included in a master record as well as in a transaction record, the following type of instruction can be included in the PROCEDURE DIVISION:

IF EMPLOY-NUMBER IN MASTER-RECORD EQUAL EMPLOY-NUMBER IN
    TRANSACTION-RECORD . . .

Again, the documentation aspect of the program is enhanced in this example in that it is quite clear what is being compared. A further use of the concept of nonunique data-names relates to the CORRESPONDING option, which is discussed in a subsequent section of this chapter.

At times, qualification requires several qualifiers. Consider the following example:

```
01  OLD-RECORD.                     01  NEW-RECORD.
    02  TODAYS-DATE...                  02  TODAYS-DATE...
        03  MONTH...                        03  MONTH...
        03  DAY...                           03  DAY...
        03  YEAR...                          03  YEAR...
    02  LAST-PERIODS-DATE...            02  LAST-PERIODS-DATE...
        03  MONTH...                        03  MONTH...
        03  DAY...                           03  DAY...
        03  YEAR...                          03  YEAR...
        03  TOTAL...                         03  TOTAL...
```

In this example, the OLD-RECORD and NEW-RECORD are assumed to be in the same program. Notice that there are four fields named MONTH. Thus, a qualifier such as MONTH OF LAST-PERIODS-DATE does not provide a unique reference because there are two such fields, one in the OLD-RECORD and one in the NEW-RECORD. Therefore, two qualifiers are needed in order to reference a unique field such as:

$$\text{MONTH} \left\{ \begin{matrix} \text{OF} \\ \text{IN} \end{matrix} \right\} \text{LAST-PERIODS-DATE} \left\{ \begin{matrix} \text{OF} \\ \text{IN} \end{matrix} \right\} \text{OLD-RECORD}$$

Since the TOTAL field in the preceding program example occurs only once in each record, only a single qualifier is required; therefore, TOTAL IN OLD-RECORD is an adequate reference in this case. The use of two qualifiers, such as TOTAL OF LAST-PERIODS-DATE IN OLD-RECORD is acceptable but unnecessary for the purpose of unique identification.

REVIEW

1 The use of qualifiers makes it possible to use the same data-name for variables that otherwise would have different data-names assigned to them. The main advantage of using qualifiers is that _____
_____ thereby is improved.

> *documentation (or interpretation*
> *of the program, etc.)*

2 When a qualifier is used, it always [precedes / follows] the referenced data-name, and its use is signaled by one of two words: _____ or
_____.

> *follows; OF; IN*

3 Qualifiers frequently are used when a master file record is updated, using data of individual transactions. Assume that the record-name for the master file is MASTER-RECORD and the record-name of the transactions file is TRANSACTION-RECORD. Both records contain a field called CUSTOMER-NUMBER. To determine that we are dealing with two records of the same customer, we say: IF CUSTOMER-NUMBER OF _____ EQUAL CUSTOMER-NUMBER OF

_____.

> MASTER-RECORD;
> TRANSACTION-RECORD (*either*
> *order*)

4 A sufficient number of qualifiers must be used to differentiate a particular data field from all other data fields in the program that are identified by

the same data-name. Suppose that a qualifier is used with a data-name that is unique and thus requires ι.ɔ qualifier. From the standpoint of programming requirements, the qualifier is unnecessary [and the program will terminate / but will not affect program execution].

> *but will not affect program*
> *execution (again, such a qualifier*
> *might be used to improve*
> *documentation)*

MULTIPLE DATA RECORDS

The following option is available in the file description to indicate the existence of more than one type of data record in the file:

```
FD file-name LABEL clause...

        ( RECORD IS    )
DATA    {              }   record-name-1 [record-name-2]...
        ( RECORDS ARE  )
```

Consider an example. Suppose that a bank's customers may make three kinds of transactions: deposits, withdrawals, and change of address. A record containing information about a deposit or withdrawal has a different format than one pertaining to a change of address. We assume that all records identify the account by a five-digit number in the first five columns and the type of transaction by a transaction code in column 6. Then, if it is a deposit or withdrawal record, the amount is recorded in columns 7–12, while if it is a change of address the new address is recorded in columns 7–50. We can write the following data entries:

```
FD TRANSACTION-FILE
    LABEL RECORDS OMITTED
    DATA RECORDS ARE FINANCIAL-REC
                     ADDRESS-REC.
01  FINANCIAL-REC.
    02   ACCOUNT      PIC 9(5).
    02   TRANS-CODE   PIC 9.
    02   AMOUNT       PIC 9(4)V99.
    02   FILLER       PIC X(38).
01  ADDRESS-REC.
    02   ACCOUNT      PIC 9(5).
    02   TRANS-CODE   PIC 9.
    02   NEW-ADDRESS  PIC X(44).
```

In this example, the FD entry has specified two types of data records, named FINANCIAL-REC and ADDRESS-REC. It is important to emphasize that, physically, a record in this file will consist of 50 characters of data (the sum of all PIC clauses in either record description). Use of two record descriptions simply allows us to reference that data by different names and in different ways.

Both record names reference the entire 50 columns of data. Thus, MOVE FINANCIAL-REC or MOVE ADDRESS-REC do exactly the same thing: they MOVE these 50 columns of data. Similarly, ACCOUNT of FINANCIAL-REC and ACCOUNT of ADDRESS-REC refer to the same first five columns of data, as do the TRANS-CODE names. However, AMOUNT refers to the data in columns 7–12 and, according to the PIC clause, it is assumed that the data are numeric. It should be recalled that a PICTURE clause simply specifies the storage allocation to data, and not the actual contents. The actual contents come about through input or MOVE type operations. Thus, if we were dealing with a change-of-address transaction and columns 7–12 contained the first six characters of the new address, a statement such as ADD 1 TO AMOUNT would produce unpredictable results, since we are performing arithmetic with nonnumeric data. More appropriately, we first would test to see what type of record we actually had before referencing the data in question. For this purpose, assume that we use a code of 1 for a deposit, 2 for withdrawal, and 3 for change of address. We could write:

```
IF TRANS-CODE OF FINANCIAL-REC = 1
   PERFORM PROCESS-DEPOSIT.
```

This statement checks to see if column 6 contains the value 1. Notice that, if we had used IF TRANS-CODE OF ADDRESS-REC = 1, it would be exactly the same thing, since both refer to column 6. To further clarify this point, we could have used this data description for ADDRESS-REC:

```
01  ADDRESS-REC.
    02  FILLER            PIC X(6).
    02  NEW-ADDRESS       PIC X(44).
```

ACCOUNT and TRANS-CODE need no qualification now, since they are unique names in FINANCIAL-REC. Use of TRANS-CODE still refers to column 6 of the data. Beginning students often equate the generic data-name FILLER with blank spaces. This should be a good point to discard any such misconception. In this example, the FILLER in ADDRESS-REC refers to the first six columns, which we know will contain data—the account number and the transaction code.

In general, a file may consist of more than one type of data record. As a rule, there should be a field that designates the type of record involved. In our example we used TRANS-CODE as a field that was in a fixed location no matter what the record type. Then we tested the value of that field to ascertain the type of record. In general, this identifying field should be common to all record types so that, no matter what the data are in other fields, this field can be tested.

REVIEW

1   When there is more than one type of data record in a file, the file description in the DATA DIVISION should identify [only one / more than one] file-name.

only one

2   When there is more than one type of data record in a file, the file description in the DATA DIVISION should identify [only one / more than one] record-name.

more than one

3   A coded entry in a specified field serves to differentiate the different input records when there is more than one data record. Particularly when the records are of variable length, the differentiating field should be located in the [left / right] part of the record field.

left

4   In the case of multiple-type record files, at any given time the internal storage can contain [only one / more than one] type of record.

only one

THE REDEFINES CLAUSE

The REDEFINES clause can be used to allow the same storage location to be referenced by different data-names or to allow a regrouping or different description of the data in a particular storage location. The general format associated with the use of this option is:

level-number   data-name-1 <u>REDEFINES</u> data-name-2

The following example illustrates the use of this option:

```
01  SAMPLE.
    02  RECEIVABLE.
        03  CUSTOMER-NUMBER            PICTURE 9(8).
        03  CUSTOMER-NAME              PICTURE X(11).
        03  AMOUNT                     PICTURE 9(4)V99.
    02  PAYABLE REDEFINES RECEIVABLE.
        03  VENDOR-NUMBER              PICTURE 9(6).
        03  VENDOR-NAME                PICTURE X(12).
        03  VENDOR-OWED-AMOUNT         PICTURE 9(5)V99.
```

In this example, use of the REDEFINES option allows the data-names RE-CEIVABLE and PAYABLE to refer to the same 25 positions in internal storage.

The format of these two data items in internal storage can be portrayed as follows:

RECEIVABLE

CUSTOMER-NUMBER	CUSTOMER-NAME	AMOUNT

PAYABLE

VENDOR-NUMBER	VENDOR-NAME	VENDOR-OWED-AMOUNT

In this example, notice that the format of the data items was also changed by the use of the REDEFINES option, but that the overall size of the item was not changed.

It should be made clear that the redefinition applies to the storage area involved and not to the data that may be stored in that area at any point in time. The programmer is responsible for providing the necessary program logic so that correct reference is made to the actual data stored. In the previous example program, if we write ADD VENDOR-OWED-AMOUNT TO . . . , the result will be to add the contents of the last seven storage positions, whatever these contents might be.

There are certain conditions under which the REDEFINES clause cannot be used. Two such conditions are:

1 The REDEFINES clause cannot be used at the 01 level in the FILE SEC-TION. Recall that the use of multiple data records in the FD entry has the same effect as use of the REDEFINES option, in that it permits use of the same storage location for different records.

2 The REDEFINES clause cannot be used when the levels of data-name-1 and data-name-2 are different. Further, the level number must not be at

the 66 or 88 level. The special-purpose 66 level is explained in the following section.

REVIEW

1 The same storage location can be used in conjunction with two different data-names by use of the _____ clause.

REDEFINES

2 When the REDEFINES option is used, the format of the data item [can / cannot] be changed as well.

can

3 Generally, the REDEFINES clause can be used when the two data items have the same level number. The exceptions are when the special-purpose 66 or 88 level numbers are used and when the level number is at 01 in the _____ SECTION, in which case the REDEFINES clause cannot be used.

FILE

THE RENAMES CLAUSE

The RENAMES clause provides the programmer with the capability of regrouping elementary data items. In a sense, it resembles the REDEFINES clause, except that it can form a new grouping of data items that combines several items. Use of the RENAMES clause always is signaled by the special 66 level number. The general format is:

```
66   data-name-1 RENAMES data-name-2 [THRU data-name-3]
```

Consider the following example, which includes use of the RENAMES clause.

```
01   TAX-RECORD.
       02   SOC-SEC-NUMBER          PICTURE X(9).
       02   NAME.
            03   FIRST-NAME          PICTURE X(10).
            03   INITIAL             PICTURE XX.
            03   LAST-NAME           PICTURE X(15).
       02   TOTALS-YEAR-TO-DATE.
            03   GROSS-PAY           PICTURE 9(8)V99.
            03   NET-PAY             PICTURE 9(8)V99.
            03   FED-TAX             PICTURE 9(6)V99.
            03   STATE-TAX           PICTURE 9(4)V99.
       66   LAST-GROSS RENAMES LAST-NAME THRU NET-PAY.
```

Schematically, the regrouping of data fields by use of the RENAMES clause in the last statement can be portrayed as follows:

NAME				TOTALS-YEAR-TO-DATE			
SOC-SEC-NUMBER	FIRST-NAME	INITIAL	LAST-NAME	GROSS-PAY	NET-PAY	FED-TAX	STATE-TAX
			LAST-GROSS				

In the example, LAST-GROSS is a storage field that consists of the LAST-NAME, GROSS-PAY, and NET-PAY fields. In this way, we can make reference to those three fields as one group, which would not be possible without use of the RENAMES clause.

There are other rules governing use of the RENAMES option, but they are beyond the scope of this text. The user should be aware that knowledge of additional rules may be necessary for the successful use of the RENAMES option in more complex situations.

REVIEW

1   Elementary data items that are part of different storage fields can be regrouped and formed into a new field by use of the _____ clause.

RENAMES

2   The DATA DIVISION statement in which the RENAMES clause is used is always assigned the level number _____ (number).

66

THE CURRENCY AND DECIMAL-POINT CLAUSES

COBOL has provisions for international usage. Changing the dollar sign and the convention of using a comma in lieu of a decimal point can be accommodated by means of two special clauses. These clauses are written in the SPECIAL-NAMES paragraph of the ENVIRONMENT DIVISION. It might seem inappropriate to introduce them at this point, but actually they are intrinsically related to the DATA DIVISION. The dollar sign of course is not the currency symbol for other nations. The programmer may specify the currency sign using the CURRENCY clause:

CURRENCY SIGN IS literal

For example, suppose that F is the currency sign. Then we would write CURRENCY SIGN IS 'F', and in PICTURE clauses we would use 'F' in place of $. The currency sign *cannot* be chosen from the following: 0 through 9, A, B, C, D, L, P, R, S, V, X, Z, space, *, +, −, comma, ., (,), ", /, or =.

In many countries outside the United States, the function of the decimal point and the comma are reversed. Thus, in Europe the numbers 1,35 and 2.534,99 are the equivalent of the American 1.35 and 2,534.99, respectively. To accommodate these different conventions we use the clause:

DECIMAL-POINT IS COMMA

Once this clause has been used, the function of comma and period are exchanged in the character string of the PICTURE clause and in numeric literals. For example, it is correct to write:

02   AMOUNT   PIC Z.ZZZ.ZZZ,ZZ

since the two decimal points have the same function as commas.

Thus, in a European COBOL program we might have:

ENVIRONMENT DIVISION.

.
.
.

SPECIAL-NAMES. CURRENCY SIGN IS 'F'
                DECIMAL-POINT IS COMMA.

REVIEW

1   The dollar sign can be changed to the appropriate symbol for another monetary system by use of the _____ clause.

CURRENCY

2   In monetary systems in which the decimal point and comma have functions opposite to those recognized in the United States, the interchange of these symbols can be achieved by use of the _____ _____ clause.

DECIMAL-POINT

WRITE WITH THE LINAGE CLAUSE

The following format represents an expanded form of the WRITE verb:

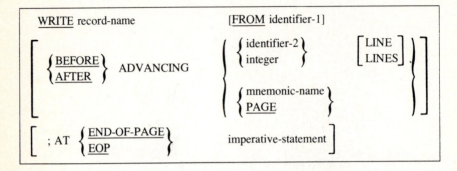

We see that the AT END-OF-PAGE clause is a new option not described previously. AT END-OF-PAGE is a conditional statement. When specified, a check is made to determine if the END-OF-PAGE (abbreviated EOP) condition is met. If it is, then the imperative statement is executed.

The END-OF-PAGE condition is defined by means of the LINAGE clause in the DATA DIVISION, which has the following format:

$$
\underline{\text{LINAGE}} \text{ IS } \left\{ \begin{array}{l} \text{data-name-1} \\ \text{integer-1} \end{array} \right\} \text{ LINES } \left[\text{, WITH } \underline{\text{FOOTING}} \text{ AT } \left\{ \begin{array}{l} \text{data-name-2} \\ \text{integer-2} \end{array} \right\} \right]
$$

$$
\left[\text{, LINES AT } \underline{\text{TOP}} \left\{ \begin{array}{l} \text{data-name-3} \\ \text{integer-3} \end{array} \right\} \right] \left[\text{, LINES AT } \underline{\text{BOTTOM}} \left\{ \begin{array}{l} \text{data-name-4} \\ \text{integer-4} \end{array} \right\} \right]
$$

Let us consider an example. We want to produce a report with the following format:

LINE NUMBER	CONTENTS
1–5	Not used
6	The page header
7–56	The body of the report
57–59	The page totals
60–66	Not used

We could proceed as follows:

DATA DIVISION.

.

.

.

FD   PRINT-FILE LABEL RECORD OMITTED
                DATA RECORD IS PRINT-REC
                LINAGE IS 54 LINES
                        WITH FOOTING AT 51
                        LINES AT TOP 5
                        LINES AT BOTTOM 7.

The page will consist of 66 lines, which is the sum of the values referenced in each phrase except for the FOOTING phrase. Five lines are unused at the top, and seven at the bottom.

   In the PROCEDURE DIVISION, the statement:

WRITE PRINT-REC FROM TOP-HEADER AFTER ADVANCING PAGE

will cause printing of the header on line 6 because now PAGE is associated with line 6, since LINES AT TOP 5 specifies that five lines be left blank at the top of the page. (TOP-HEADER in this example is assumed to contain the desired header.)

   Now consider these statements:

WRITE PRINT-REC FROM BODY-OF-REPORT-LINE
        AFTER ADVANCING 1 LINE
        AT END-OF-PAGE PERFORM TOTALS.
TOTALS.
        WRITE PRINT-REC FROM TOTALS-LINE
            AFTER ADVANCING 3 LINES
        WRITE PRINT-REC FROM TOP-HEADER
            AFTER ADVANCING PAGE.

We will keep printing data from BODY-OF-REPORT-LINE until we have reached line 56, (51 + 5), which is defined as the footing: WITH FOOTING AT 51. At that point, the END-OF-PAGE condition will hold and we will PERFORM TOTALS, in which we print data on line 59 (triple spacing) and then skip to the next page (line 6 of the next page) to print the page header, TOP-HEADER.

   A special counter is used whenever LINAGE is specified. It is called LINAGE-COUNTER, a COBOL reserved word. It is set to 1 when a print file is opened or when an ADVANCING PAGE is encountered. Afterward, the counter is automatically incremented the appropriate number of lines implied in each WRITE statement. When LINAGE-COUNTER is equal to the value of the FOOTING phrase, then an END-OF-PAGE condition occurs. The LINAGE-COUNTER may not be modified by the program, but it may be accessed. Thus, it is legitimate to write: IF LINAGE-COUNTER = 25 PERFORM MID-PAGE ROUTINE.

REVIEW

1   When an END-OF-PAGE (EOP) condition is specified in conjunction with a WRITE statement, then the description of the number of lines and their use has to be defined in a(n) _____ clause in the DATA DIVISION.

LINAGE

2   The special counter that is a reserved word and is used implicitly whenever the LINAGE option is specified is the _____.

LINAGE-COUNTER

3   Assume these entries:

LINAGE IS 25 LINES
WITH FOOTING AT 21
LINES AT TOP 2
LINES AT BOTTOM 3

Fill in the missing members:

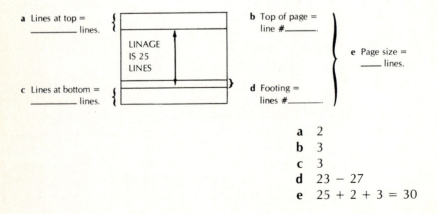

a Lines at top = _____ lines.

b Top of page = line #_____.

c Lines at bottom = _____ lines.

d Footing = lines #_____.

e Page size = _____ lines.

a   2
b   3
c   3
d   23 − 27
e   25 + 2 + 3 = 30

THE ACCEPT AND DISPLAY VERBS

Up to this point, we always have discussed input and output in connection with files. Such is the normal use of input and output verbs, but it also is possible to execute input and output in conjunction with storage fields that are not part of any files. This typically is done to permit the input and/or output of short data items to or from devices such as the console typewriter and the printer. The verbs that allow such input and output are ACCEPT and DISPLAY. The general formats associated with use of the ACCEPT verb are:

Format 1

ACCEPT identifier [FROM mnemonic-name]

Format 2

$$\text{ACCEPT identifier FROM} \left\{ \begin{array}{l} \text{DATE} \\ \text{DAY} \\ \text{TIME} \end{array} \right\}$$

The first format can be used as in this example: ACCEPT STARTING-CHECK-NO FROM CONSOLE-TYPE. As a result of executing this instruction, the computer will input data into the STARTING-CHECK-NO storage field from the device previously defined as CONSOLE-TYPE in the SPECIAL-NAMES paragraph of the ENVIRONMENT DIVISION. If this device is a typewriter, further program execution is delayed until the operator types in the appropriate input. If the device is a card reader, the next card will be read, and data will be input into STARTING-CHECK-NO.

Data input via ACCEPT is treated as if it were alphanumeric with respect to positioning. Suppose that STARTING-CHECK-NO has been defined with a PICTURE 99999. If ACCEPT is executed with reference to the console typewriter and the operator types in 12345, the receiving field will contain 12345. On the other hand, if the operator types 12, the 12 will be stored *left-justified* in STARTING-CHECK-NO, followed by three blanks. In general an entire record is moved from the input device to the identifier specified in ACCEPT. Thus when we typed 12 above, we were in effect transmitting a whole line from the console with blanks trailing the 12.

The second format of ACCEPT, given previously, can be used to move the contents of the COBOL predefined fields DATE, DAY, or TIME to a specified identifier. These latter three fields are not defined by the programmer but are made available by the compiler. Their *implicit* definition is:

```
DATE    999999
DAY     99999
TIME    99999999
```

The DATE field contains the year, month, and day. Assume that TODAY was defined:

```
02  TODAY.
      03  T-YEAR     PIC 99.
      03  T-MONTH    PIC 99.
      03  T-DAY      PIC 99.
```

The instruction ACCEPT TODAY FROM DATE issued on February 1, 1982, will cause the content of DATE, 820201, to be moved to TODAY.

The DAY field contains the year and the day of the year. Thus, July 1, 1982, will be stored as 82183.

TIME contains hours, minutes, seconds, and hundredths of a second, based on elapsed time after midnight on a 24-hour-clock. Thus, 8:30 P.M. is stored as 20300000. The smallest value of TIME is 00000000, and the largest is 23595999.

The general format associated with use of the DISPLAY verb is:

$$\underline{\text{DISPLAY}} \left\{ \begin{array}{l} \text{identifier-1} \\ \text{literal-1} \end{array} \right\} \left[\begin{array}{l} \text{, identifier-2} \\ \text{, literal-2} \end{array} \right] \ldots [\underline{\text{UPON}} \text{ mnemonic-name}]$$

Notice that DISPLAY can reference a series of identifiers or literals. Thus, we can write DISPLAY AMOUNT-A, 'IS A VALUE OUT OF RANGE' UPON CONSOLE-TYPE. Execution of this statement will result in the contents of the storage field AMOUNT-A being typed on the console typewriter, followed by the literal message in the quotation marks.

In some computer installations, ACCEPT and DISPLAY can be used only with devices predefined by the installation itself; thus, the device will not be named in the statement. For example, writing ACCEPT CODE-A may be valid and would refer to some specific device in the particular installation, such as the console typewriter or an alternate card reader. Similarly DISPLAY ERR-MESSAGE-1 may be valid in installations in which the DISPLAY verb is associated automatically with a particular device, such as the console typewriter or a printer.

Some installations also tend to use ACCEPT and DISPLAY as substitutes for READ and WRITE statements for card and printer files. For example, if the card reader is associated with ACCEPT and the printer is associated with DISPLAY, the programmer need not identify any files in the input and output statements. In an educational environment in which most input is from cards and most output is on the printer without any real "files" in use, the practice of using ACCEPT and DISPLAY may be expeditious. In a "real-world" environment, however, the verbs ACCEPT and DISPLAY have limited usage as input and output verbs because they lack the full power of READ and WRITE. A more common practice is to use DISPLAY for debugging purposes. For example, we can trace the contents of input records by the following approach:

READ INPUT-FILE RECORD AT END . . .
DISPLAY REC-IN UPON PRINTER.

In this case, REC-IN is assumed to be the name of the record read in, and we display its contents on a device called PRINTER.

REVIEW

1   The verb used to input short data items not usually part of any file as such is the _____ verb, whereas the verb similarly used for short output, usually on the console typewriter, is _____.

ACCEPT; DISPLAY

2   DATA input by use of the ACCEPT verb is always treated as being [alphabetic / numeric / alphanumeric].

alphanumeric

3   Because the DISPLAY verb can reference literals as well as identifiers, it can be used to convey certain _____ as well as data items.

messages

4   Although the DISPLAY verb has limited use in computer programs for regular data processing applications, it is used frequently in conjunction with the _____ of computer programs.

debugging

THE MOVE CORRESPONDING OPTION

Earlier in this chapter we described the concept of qualification. Defined briefly, this concept allows the programmer to use the same subordinate data-name in more than one place in the program, thus allowing nonunique data-names. The CORRESPONDING option, available for use with MOVE and with the arithmetic verbs, simplifies the program in cases in which the same operation is to be performed on one or several pairs of elementary, nonunique data-names. Let us take an example. Suppose we have the following two records:

```
01   PAY-RECORD.
     02   GROSS    PIC 9999V99.
     02   NET      PIC 9999V99.
     02   TAXES    PIC 999V99.
01   EDITED-RECORD.
     02   GROSS    PIC ZZZ9.99.
     02   TAXES    PIC ZZ9.99.
     02   NET      PIC ZZZ9.99.
```

If we want to move PAY-RECORD to EDITED-RECORD, we *cannot* do it in one statement. Writing MOVE PAY-RECORD to EDITED-RECORD would be incorrect, because the order of the fields NET and TAXES is not the same in the two records. Of course, the move could be accomplished by a separate MOVE statement for each of the three fields; however, the same result can be accomplished more easily by use of the CORRESPONDING option:

MOVE CORRESPONDING PAY-RECORD TO EDITED-RECORD.

The general format associated with the use of the CORRESPONDING option is:

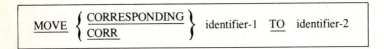

CORR is the abbreviated form of the option. Unlike the situation in the previous example, the two data-names may contain only some items that correspond, as in the following example:

```
02   INSPECTION.
     03   TOTAL-QUANTITY ...
     03   REJECTED ...
     03   ACCEPTED ...
     03   QUALITY-RATIO ...

01   QUALITY-REPORT.
     02   TOTAL-QUANTITY ...
     02   QUALITY-RATIO ...
```

Executing the statement MOVE CORR INSPECTION TO QUALITY-REPORT will result in the two items or fields, TOTAL-QUANTITY and QUALITY-RATIO, being moved.

In order for the CORRESPONDING option to be used, there must be pairs of items having the same name in two group items, and at least one of the items in each pair must be elementary. Another rule to remember is that any items that are subordinate to identifier-1 and identifier-2 and have RE-NAMES, REDEFINES, or OCCURS clauses are ignored in the move. Therefore, we cannot use the MOVE CORRESPONDING option to move a table of values, for example. However, the identifier-1 and identifier-2 items themselves may have REDEFINES or OCCURS clauses or may be subordinate to data items with such clauses. (These clauses are discussed in later chapters.)

The CORRESPONDING option also is available with ADD and SUB-TRACT, as can be observed in Appendix B: "Complete ANS COBOL Language Formats." In general, the option should be avoided or used sparingly with respect to both MOVE and the arithmetic verbs. Use of the CORRE-SPONDING option may result in errors when programs are modified subsequently, and therefore most programming managers tend to limit or forbid use of this option.

REVIEW

1   The abbreviated form of the CORRESPONDING option is _____.
Use of this option in conjunction with the MOVE instruction results in transfer of only the _____ items contained in two records.

CORR; *common (or*
corresponding)

2   When the MOVE CORRESPONDING option is used, an item will be moved if at least one of the items in each pair is at the _____ level and only if the receiving group item has an item with the same [storage capacity / name].

elementary; name

3   The MOVE CORRESPONDING option can be used to move elementary items [including / but not including] tables of values at the elementary level.

but not including

THE COMPUTE VERB

Use of the four arithmetic verbs we have studied thus far is particularly suitable for single arithmetic operations, but suppose it is required that an

TABLE 8-1   THE FIVE ARITHMETIC OPERATIONS IN COBOL

+	Addition
−	Subtraction
*	Multiplication
/	Division
**	Exponentiation (raising to a power)

answer be obtained by use of such a formula as $a = 3b - c + b(d - 2)$. If we were to use the four arithmetic verbs to solve this equation, a large number of statements would be required. However, use of the COMPUTE verb along with symbolic arithmetic operators makes it possible to write compact arithmetic statements for mathematical expressions.

Table 8-1 lists the symbols used for the arithmetic operations of addition, subtraction, multiplication, division, and exponentiation. Only the symbols for multiplication and exponentiation are different from the symbols commonly used in mathematics. In addition to the symbols, parentheses can be used to designate the order of operations; however, unlike their use in algebra, parentheses never are used to designate multiplication.

An arithmetic expression is formed by the use of arithmetic operators and data-names or literals. At least *one space must separate each operator symbol from the preceding and following data-names*, with parentheses used to designate or clarify the order of operations. Some examples of arithmetic expressions are:

ALGEBRAIC EXPRESSION	COBOL ARITHMETIC EXPRESSION
$a + b$	A + B
$a - b + (a - 5)c$	A − B + (A − 5) * C
$a^2 - \dfrac{b + c}{2}$	A**2 − (B + C) / 2

When parentheses are used, the operations within the parentheses are completed first, with order of priority given to the innermost sets, working from left to right in the arithmetic expression. In the absence of parentheses, the arithmetic operations are performed according to the following order of priority:

1 Exponentiation
2 Multiplication and division from left to right in the order written
3 Addition and subtraction from left to right in the order written

Consider the following COBOL examples:

COBOL ARITHMETIC EXPRESSION	ALGEBRAIC EXPRESSION
A + B / C	$a + \dfrac{b}{c}$
(A + B) / C	$\dfrac{a + b}{c}$
A + (B / C)	$a + \dfrac{b}{c}$

The first and third COBOL expressions represent the same algebraic expression. This is so because division takes priority over addition. Nevertheless, it is good programming practice to include the parentheses in such cases, since documentation thereby is improved.

In addition to the five arithmetic operations, COBOL defines a *unary* operation. Standard COBOL defines both a "+" and a "−" unary operator. The operator is simply an instruction to multiply a variable by +1 or −1, respectively. Thus, if we want to multiply variable B times the negative value of variable A, we could use the unary operator as follows:

$$B * (- A)$$

The − is the unary operator. In this example, parentheses are used to avoid having two consecutive arithmetic operators.

Returning to the COMPUTE verb, we note that the general format associated with the use of this verb is:

COMPUTE identifier-1 [ROUNDED] [, identifier-2 [ROUNDED]] . . . =
arithmetic-expression [; ON SIZE ERROR imperative-statement]

In its simplest form, the COMPUTE verb has the same effect as the MOVE verb. For example, COMPUTE AMOUNT = TOTAL is the same as MOVE TOTAL TO AMOUNT. In a more typical use, however, COMPUTE stores the result of an arithmetic expression in a data field. An example is:

COMPUTE GROSS = (REGULAR * WAGE) + 1.5 * (OVERTIME * WAGE).

Or, the COMPUTE verb can be used with the ROUNDED and ON SIZE ERROR options:

COMPUTE GROSS ROUNDED =
    (REGULAR * WAGE) + 1.5 * (OVERTIME * WAGE)
    ON SIZE ERROR
        PERFORM GROSS-TOO-BIG.

The arithmetic operators $+$, $-$, $*$, and $/$ correspond to the verbs ADD, SUBTRACT, MULTIPLY, and DIVIDE, respectively. The arithmetic operator $**$ has no corresponding verb and can be used only with the COMPUTE verb. Since exponentiation is a general mathematical process, it can be used to extract square roots as well as to raise numbers to various powers. Thus, $A**2$ means, a^2, but $AA**0.5$ means $\sqrt{A}$. This facility to extract roots increases the usefulness of the exponentiation operator. In general, however, COBOL has limited computational capabilities. COBOL programs are rarely written to accomplish tasks requiring complex computations. COBOL is used for data processing tasks rather than for computational tasks. Thus, logarithmic and trigonometric functions are not available in COBOL, although they commonly are available in other languages, such as FORTRAN and PL /1.

The identifier-1 in the COMPUTE format is the storage field that receives the results. It should be noted that it can be a numeric or numeric edited item. It really corresponds to the GIVING identifier clause in the other arithmetic verbs. All identifiers on the right-hand side, however, must be *elementary* numeric (nonedited) items.

REVIEW

1   As an alternative to the arithmetic verbs, arithmetic operators can be used in conjunction with the _____ verb.

COMPUTE

2   The arithmetic symbols used with the COMPUTE verb which indicate the operations addition, subtraction, multiplication, division, and exponentiation are _____, _____, _____, _____, and _____, respectively.

$+$, $-$, $*$, $/$, and $**$

3   The COBOL arithmetic expression corresponding to the algebraic expression $a^2 - 2ac + c^2$ is _____.

$(A**2) - (2 * A * C) + (C**2)$
(See further comment in the next review item.)

4   Suppose that all the parentheses included in the above answer were

omitted. The algebraic expression that corresponds to the resulting COBOL expression would be _____.

$$a^2 - 2ac + c^2 \text{ (Discussion continued in the next review item).}$$

5   Therefore, because of the order in which the arithmetic operations always are performed, no parentheses in fact are required in the COBOL expression just given. However, such parentheses usually are included to improve readability of the program. In the absence of parentheses, the order of priority for the arithmetic operations is such that _____ _____ always is performed first, followed by _____ and _____, and culminating with _____ and _____ _____.

exponentiation; multiplication; division; addition; subtraction

6   Typically, however, the use or nonuse of parentheses *does* make a difference in the way a COBOL arithmetic expression is evaluated. For each of the following COBOL expressions, indicate the equivalent algebraic expression:

COBOL ARITHMETIC EXPRESSION	ALGEBRAIC EXPRESSION
((A + (B * C)) / D)**2	
(A + (B * C)) / D**2	
A + (B * C) / D**2	
A + B * C / D**2	

$$\left(\frac{a + bc}{d} \right)^2$$

$$\frac{a + bc}{d^2}$$

$$a + \frac{bc}{d^2}$$

$$a + \frac{bc}{d^2}$$

7   An example of the use of the unary operator in a simple COBOL expression involving multiplication is _____.

$$A * (- B)$$

8   In the general format associated with the COMPUTE verb, the results of the arithmetic operation are stored in [identifier-1 / identifier-2].

identifier-1

THE STRING AND UNSTRING VERBS

These two verbs are designed to facilitate transfer of data from several sources into one destination and from one source to many destinations, respectively. In effect, use of these verbs allows one statement to be used in lieu of multiple uses of the MOVE verb and, possibly, in lieu of some DATA DIVISION entries.

We begin with two examples that illustrate uses of the STRING verb.

Suppose that EDIT-SOC-SEC contains a social security number, including hyphens after the third and fifth digits, as for instance '123-45-6789'. We wish to move the social security number to SOC-SEC while also removing the hyphens. The following data description entries are given:

```
01   SOC-SEC        PIC 9(9).
01   EDIT-SOC-SEC.
     02   PART-1     PIC 999.
     02   FILLER     PIC X   VALUE '-'.
     02   PART-2     PIC 99.
     02   FILLER     PIC X   VALUE '-'.
     02   PART-3     PIC 9999.
```

We now use the STRING statement:

```
STRING     PART-1 DELIMITED BY SIZE
           PART-2 DELIMITED BY SIZE
           PART-3 DELIMITED BY SIZE
   INTO     SOC-SEC.
```

The STRING here specifies moving the three fields, PART-1, PART-2, and PART-3, and positioning them adjacent to each other. The transfer of data can be thought of as taking place character by character. Thus, the data in PART-1 would be transferred into the first three positions of SOC-SEC, the data in PART-2 would be transferred into the next two positions of SOC-SEC, and so on. The DELIMITED BY SIZE clause specifies that the transfer of data from the associated field will stop (be delimited by) when as many characters have been transferred as the size of the source field. The next example illustrates the availability of other alternatives.

Assume that we want to print a report that lists a company name in columns 5–20, a city name starting with column 26, one blank space, and then the ZIP code. The source of data is VENDOR-RECORD:

```
01   VENDOR-RECORD.
     02   COMPANY-NAME     PIC X(15).
     02   STREET           PIC X(40).
     02   CITY-STATE       PIC X(20).
     02   ZIP              PIC 9(5).
```

The data in CITY-STATE are recorded so that the city name is followed by a comma, a space, and then the state code, e.g., LOS ANGELES, CA.

The output record is described as:

```
01   OUTPUT-REC   PIC X(132).
```

We use the STRING verb as follows:

```
MOVE SPACES TO OUTPUT-REC
MOVE 5 TO STARTING-PLACE.
STRING                 COMPANY-NAME              DELIMITED BY SIZE
                       '        '                DELIMITED BY SIZE
                       CITY-STATE                DELIMITED BY ','
                       SPACE, ZIP                DELIMITED BY SIZE
INTO OUTPUT-REC
WITH POINTER STARTING-PLACE.
```

The first MOVE statement clears the output record of any previous contents. The second MOVE sets STARTING-PLACE to a value of 5 so that the beginning of data transfer into OUTPUT-REC will begin in column 5 (WITH POINTER STARTING-PLACE). Of course, STARTING-PLACE is an arbitrary name chosen by the programmer; but it must be an integer field for obvious reasons.

The STRING statement specifies that, in effect, five fields will be transferred: COMPANY-NAME, the nonnumeric literal '   ', CITY-STATE, the figurative constant SPACE, and ZIP. Thus, starting with column 5 of OUTPUT-REC, the entire (DELIMITED BY SIZE) COMPANY-NAME is transferred and it is followed by the five-blank nonnumeric constant. The next data to be transferred come from CITY-STATE; the data are transferred character by character until a comma is encountered (DELIMITED BY ','). One blank follows (SPACE) and then the ZIP code. It should be pointed out that use of figurative constants, such as SPACE, ZEROS, or the like, always means one occurrence of the implied character. Thus, we would obtain one blank even if we had used SPACES instead of SPACE.

The general format of STRING is as follows:

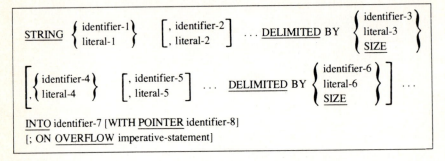

Our two examples have illustrated all but the OVERFLOW option. If the data specified to be transferred are greater than the size of the receiving item (identifier-7) during execution of a STRING statement, then the imperative statement of the OVERFLOW clause is executed. If the optional OVERFLOW is not used and the overflow condition arises, then the STRING operation is discontinued and the next program statement is executed. During execution, identifier-8, if used, is incremented by one as each character is transferred. It is the value of this identifier that is checked in determining an overflow condition. If identifier-8 is not used, an implied counter is used to fulfill the same function.

The UNSTRING verb, as its name implies, acts in the reverse direction of the STRING verb. We present two examples to illustrate use of this verb.

Suppose that data are recorded in free form (without predefined fields) as follows:

TED S BROWN,4,15,3.52
TINA LORI CHRISTIANSON,1,12,2.50

As we can see, name fields are separated by one or more blank spaces, then commas separate the remaining three fields. We would like to move these data fields to a fixed format record:

```
01   STUDENT-RECORD.
     02   FIRST-NAME         PIC X(15).
     02   MIDDLE-NAME        PIC X(15).
     02   LAST-NAME          PIC X(20).
     02   CLASSIFICATION     PIC 9.
     02   CREDIT-LOAD        PIC 99.
     02   GPA                PIC XXXX.
```

Assuming that the source data is in

```
01   FREE-FORM-RECORD       PIC X(57).
```

we can write:

```
UNSTRING   FREE-FORM-RECORD
           DELIMITED BY ALL SPACES OR ','
    INTO   FIRST-NAME
           MIDDLE-NAME
           LAST-NAME
           CLASSIFICATION
           CREDIT-LOAD
           GPA.
```

The DELIMITED clause specifies that fields in the source record are separated by one or more blank spaces (ALL SPACES), or single commas (OR ','). In essence, the source record is scanned character by character from left to right. When a blank or a comma appears, it is assumed that a new field begins. The delimiters in this case are blanks or commas, and they are not included in the data transfer, although the UNSTRING statement does include an option allowing the transfer of delimiters themselves.

Consider now a second example that expands on UNSTRING and illustrates combined use of STRING and UNSTRING.

Data records contain numbers in columns 1–6, followed by a name and a header separated from each other by a dollar sign. As in the previous example, a delimiter such as a dollar sign can be used to allow recording of data without adherence to predefined field positions. When data length is highly variable, such free-form data can save a lot of space. Two sample records are as follows:

```
349687INTERNATIONAL TOOLS, INC. $ BALANCE SHEET $
135002ACME CORP. $ INCOME STATEMENT $
```

We are interested in printing the company name, centered at column 40 on the top of a new page, followed by the name of the report on the third line, also centered at column 40. Solution of the problem involves separating the two fields, determining their size; and, on the basis of their size, centering the data in respect to column 40. We also assume that we wish to ascertain that there are indeed two fields available in the relevant part of the source record. First, we define some data fields:

```
01   FREE-FORM-RECORD     PIC X(46).
01   FIRST-LINE           PIC X(20).
01   SECOND-LINE          PIC X(20).
01   LENGTH-1             PIC 99.
01   LENGTH-2             PIC 99.
01   STARTING-POINT       PIC 99.
01   NO-OF-FIELDS         PIC 9.
01   OUTPUT-RECORD        PIC X(132).
```

Figure 8-1 presents a program segment written to accomplish the desired task. The NO-OF-FIELDS item is used to count the number of fields transferred. Notice its use in the TALLYING clause in the UNSTRING statement. The value 7 is moved to STARTING-POINT because the first six columns of FREE-FORM-RECORD contain a number that we wish to ignore. Notice the clause WITH POINTER STARTING-POINT. Using the $ as delimiter, we transfer data from the source record into two fields, FIRST-LINE and SECOND-LINE. In the process, we obtain a count of the characters moved into each receiving field in LENGTH-1 and LENGTH-2, respectively. The COUNT option provides this length count. Finally, use of the OVERFLOW specifies execution of PERFORM ERROR-ROUTINE-1 if the data being transferred exceeds the size of the receiving field. This could happen in our example if the delimiting dollar sign was missing, or if one field was longer than 20 characters—the size specified for FIRST-LINE and SECOND-LINE.

```
MOVE ZERO TO NO-OF-FIELDS
MOVE 7 TO STARTING-POINT
UNSTRING FREE-FORM-RECORD DELIMITED BY '$'
        INTO   FIRST-LINE
                    COUNT IN LENGTH-1
                 SECOND-LINE
                    COUNT IN LENGTH-2
        WITH POINTER STARTING-POINT
        TALLYING IN NO-OF-FIELDS
        ON OVERFLOW
             PERFORM ERROR-ROUTINE-1.
IF NO-OF-FIELDS NOT = 2
        PERFORM ERROR-ROUTINE-2
ELSE
        PERFORM PRINT-HEADERS.
        .
        .
        .

PRINT-HEADERS.
        COMPUTE LENGTH-1 = 40 − (LENGTH-1 / 2)
        COMPUTE LENGTH-2 = 40 − (LENGTH-2 / 2)
        MOVE SPACES TO OUTPUT-RECORD
        STRING FIRST-LINE DELIMITED BY SIZE
             INTO OUTPUT-RECORD
             WITH POINTER LENGTH-1
        WRITE OUTPUT-RECORD AFTER ADVANCING PAGE
        MOVE SPACES TO OUTPUT RECORD
        STRING SECOND-LINE DELIMITED BY SIZE
             INTO OUTPUT-RECORD
             WITH POINTER LENGTH-2
        WRITE OUTPUT-RECORD AFTER ADVANCING 2 LINES.
```

FIGURE 8-1   EXAMPLE PROGRAM INVOLVING THE USE OF UNSTRING AND STRING.

After the UNSTRING statement, we check to see that we indeed had two fields transferred; if not, we PERFORM ERROR-ROUTINE-2.

The PRINT-HEADERS paragraph computes the starting point of each line to the left of column 40. We divide the length of the field involved by 2 and we subtract this amount from 40. We then use the STRING verb to move the data, using LENGTH-1 as the pointer. Actually, it is the availability of the POINTER option in the STRING verb that makes it capable of achieving what the MOVE verb could not accomplish in this case. After the transfer of the data, we print the record and repeat the process for the next line of printed output. The general format of the UNSTRING verb is:

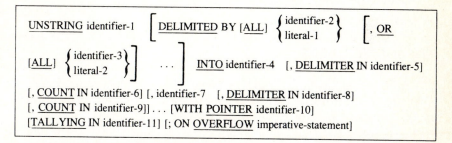

We have illustrated all the options except the DELIMITER IN clause. When used, the clause specifies the identifier to be used to receive the delimiter(s). This option is used if we wish to move the delimiters themselves.

REVIEW

1 The verb that is used to transfer data from several sources to one destination is the _____ verb.

STRING

2 The verb that is used to transfer data from one source to many destinations is the _____ verb.

UNSTRING

3 When the DELIMITED BY SIZE clause is used in conjunction with the STRING verb, transfer of data from the sending field stops when the number of characters which have been transferred equals the size of the [sending / receiving] field.

sending

4 If an OVERFLOW clause is not used in conjunction with a STRING verb and an overflow condition occurs, then [the STRING operation / program execution] is terminated.

the STRING *operation*

5   Used in conjunction with the UNSTRING verb, the DELIMITED BY clause specifies the basis used to signal the beginning of a new record in the [sending / receiving] field.

sending

6   The clause that is used if delimiters themselves, such as commas or spaces, are to be transferred to receiving fields during the UNSTRING operation is called the _____ clause.

DELIMITER IN

THE INSPECT VERB

At times we need to access and manipulate individual characters in a field. One very common use is to edit input data, such as replacing leading blanks by zeros. COBOL now provides the INSPECT verb to accomplish such character manipulations. This verb replaces the EXAMINE verb, which served a similar but more limited purpose in previous versions of the language.

The INSPECT verb is powerful but a bit complicated. Three formats are available, and these are presented in Appendix B: "Complete ANS COBOL Language Formats." Discussion of the complete set of options would exceed the intended scope of this text. We present some examples to illustrate the basic options.

EXAMPLE 1: Suppose we wanted to replace all *leading* blanks by leading zeros in a field called TEST. We would write:

INSPECT TEST REPLACING LEADING ' ' BY '0'.

EXAMPLE 2: Suppose we wanted to replace *all* blanks by zeros in a field called TEST. We would write:

INSPECT TEST REPLACING ALL ' ' BY '0'.

EXAMPLE 3: If we wanted to replace the first zero by a +, we would write:

INSPECT TEST REPLACING FIRST '0' BY '+'.

EXAMPLE 4: Suppose we wanted to ask the question: How many dollar signs are in TEST? We would write:

INSPECT TEST TALLYING COUNT-A FOR ALL '$'.

After this instruction is executed, the numeric field COUNT-A will contain a value equal to the number of $ in TEST. (COUNT-A would have been defined in the DATA DIVISION.)

EXAMPLE 5: Suppose we wanted to ask the question: How many zero characters are there to the left of the decimal and how many zeros are there to the right of the decimal point: We would write:

INSPECT TEST TALLYING COUNT-A FOR ALL '0' BEFORE INITIAL '.'
COUNT-B FOR ALL '0' AFTER '.'

This instruction would result in COUNT-A containing the number of zeros before the decimal point and COUNT-B containing the number of zeros after the decimal point.

EXAMPLE 6: We want to count the number of dollar signs in TEST and replace all dollar signs after the first one by asterisks. We write:

INSPECT TEST TALLYING COUNT-A FOR ALL '$'
REPLACING ALL '$' BY '*' AFTER INITIAL '$'.

EXAMPLE 7: We want to ask the question: assuming that TEST contains a name left-justified in TEST, how long is the name? (Unused positions are blank.) We write:

INSPECT TEST TALLYING COUNT-A FOR CHARACTERS BEFORE INITIAL ' '.

EXAMPLE 8: An untrained keypunch operator did not depress the numeric key; all numbers have been mispunched. For example, instead of a zero there is a /; instead of a 1 there is a U. To correct the data, we write:

INSPECT TEST REPLACING ALL '/' BY '0'
'U' BY '1'
'I' BY '2'
.
.
.
'.' BY '9'.

THE COPY VERB

COBOL provides for a library facility. By "library" we mean a collection of COBOL source program elements recorded on tape or disk and accessible by reference to *text-names*. A well-planned and maintained library can reduce the time needed to write routines common to several programs, and it can serve to standardize such common routines.

For example, suppose we include the following statement in the DATA DIVISION:

01   INVENTORY-RECORD COPY MATERIAL-RECORD.

We obtain the following source program listing at compilation time. The C characters on the left margin indicate that these entries were copied.

```
      01   INVENTORY-RECORD COPY MATERIAL-RECORD.
C         02   PART-NUMBER        PICTURE X(9).
C         02   PART-NAME          PICTURE X(15).
C         02   STOCK-QUANTITY     PICTURE 9(6).
```

We can use the copied items in the PROCEDURE DIVISION as if we had written their description in the DATA DIVISION of the current program. Notice that the record-name used in this program example, INVENTORY-RECORD, is not the same as the library-name for that record. Use of the same name is optional. It is good procedure, of course, to use the same name, so that comparison of different programs and communication between programmers are facilitated. The library simplifies program writing by standardizing records in different files so that programs can be maintained and revised easily.

Building the library commonly is done outside the COBOL language by means of JCL (Job Control Language) statements. Use of a library is a very *local* practice, and we direct the readers to their own computer system for details.

REVIEW

1   Individual characters in a field can be accessed and possibly changed by use of the _____ verb.

> INSPECT

2   Use of the TALLYING option in conjunction with the INSPECT verb makes it possible to _____ designated characters.

> count (etc.)

3   Use of the REPLACING option in conjunction with the INSPECT verb makes it possible to _____ designated characters.

> change

4   The verb that makes it possible to reference a precoded program segment from a library of such program segments is _____.

> COPY

5 When the COPY verb is used to obtain a record description from a library, the record-name used in the program and in the library [must / need not] be the same.

need not

EXERCISES

8.1 A large company has three subsidiaries that formerly were independent companies. Each subsidiary has a different product code, as follows:

> Subsidiary 1 uses a 4-character product code.
>
> Subsidiary 2 uses a 6-character product code.
>
> Subsidiary 3 uses a 7-character product code.

Apart from the difference in length, the product code can be used in a program that does some processing for all subsidiaries. The data in the program are contained in a field called PRODUCT-CODE, which has a size of seven characters.

a Write a DATA DIVISION description of PRODUCT-CODE so that PRODUCT-CODE can be tested to determine which subsidiary's product code it contains and so that the correct size product code can be MOVED. Assume that the data in PRODUCT-CODE is left-justified, with blanks filling the unused space. (*Hint:* REDEFINES or RENAMES may be useful.)

b Write PROCEDURE DIVISION statements to accomplish the processing objectives described in part **a**.

8.2 Assume the following DATA DIVISION entries:

```
01  A.
    02  X.
        03  Y.
    02  W.
        03  Y.

01  B.
    02  X.
        03  Y.
    02  W.
        03  Y.
```

Write PROCEDURE DIVISION statement(s) to move the last elementary item in A to the first elementary item in B.

8.3 A punched-card file contains name and address data for college students and their parents or guardians. The file is arranged so that for each student there are two cards. The first card contains the name and address of the student, and the second card contains the name and address of parent or guardian. The card formats are as follows:

STUDENT CARD		PARENT CARD	
FIELD	CARD COLUMNS	FIELD	CARD COLUMNS
Student number	1–9	Student number	1–9
Student name	10–30	Parent name	10–30
Street	31–60	Street	31–60
City	61–79	City	61–79
Card code = 1	80	Card code = 2	80

a Write ENVIRONMENT and DATA DIVISION file and record entries to describe this card file.

b Write PROCEDURE DIVISION statements to read two consecutive cards, testing to ascertain that they are student and parent cards, respectively. When the first card is read, if it is a student card, it is stored in CARD-WORK-AREA. If the first card is not a student card or if the second card is not a parent card for the same student, the program branches to a paragraph called ERROR-ROUTINE. If the cards are correct, the program branches to a paragraph called PROCESS.

8.4 In the following diagram there is a record called BIGFIELD. The numbers running from 1 to 13 indicate respective character positions. Thus, the record consists of 13 character positions. We want to be able to reference the following positions while also preserving the current structure of the record. Indicate how to accomplish this objective.

BIGFIELD						
GROUP-A			GROUP-B			
AA	AB	AC	BA	BB	BC	
1 2	3 4 5	6 7	8 9	10 11	12 13	

a Reference 1, 2, 3, 4 by one name
b Reference 5, 6, 7 by one name
c Reference 8, 9, 10 by one name

d Reference 11, 12, 13 by one name
e Reference 1, 2, 3, 4, 5, 6, 7 by one name
f Reference 8, 9, 10, 11, 12, 13 by one name
g Reference 3, 4, 5, 6, 7, 8, 9, 10 by one name

8.5 A file contains customer names in free form. The last name is written first, followed by a comma, followed by the first name or initial, followed by a comma, and finally followed by the middle name or initial. Write a program to read data from that file and print the data in the following fixed format:

Last name: columns 11–30

First name: columns 32–45

Middle name: columns 47–60

Print the data under suitable headings and use the following test data:

SIMON, AL, GEORGE
GARCIA, P., K.
LONGNAME, VALERIE, GEORGIA

8.6 Write a COBOL program to compute depreciation schedules, using the sum-of-the-digits method of depreciation. The sum-of-the-digits-method works as follows: Suppose that you have an asset of original value $1,000.00 to be depreciated over 3 years, using the sum-of-the-digits method. The following table shows the nature of the calculations involved:

YEAR	DEPRECIATION RATE	DEPRECIATION
1	$\dfrac{3}{1+2+3} = \dfrac{3}{6}$	$1,000 \times \dfrac{3}{6} = 500.00$
2	$\dfrac{2}{1+2+3} = \dfrac{2}{6}$	$1,000 \times \dfrac{2}{6} = 333.33$
3	$\dfrac{1}{1+2+3} = \dfrac{1}{6}$	$1,000 \times \dfrac{1}{6} = 166.67$

Notice that the depreciation rate varies from year to year, but that the rate is applied to the same (original) asset dollar value. The rate consists of a denominator that is the sum of the digits from 1 up to the number of years over which the asset is to be depreciated. To test your understanding of the concept, compute the denominator value for five years. The answer is 15. The numerator of the depreciation rate varies from the number of years to 1 in steps of 1. Thus, for a five-year depreciation schedule the numerator values are: 5, 4, 3, 2, 1.

Input: This is in the form of a deck of cards with the following data format:

CARD COLUMNS	CONTENT
1–5	Asset number
6–14	Original asset value in dollars and cents
15–16	Blank
17–18	Number of years over which the asset is to be depreciated
19–80	Blank

Output: This should be on a new page for each asset and should have approximately the following format:

ASSET 12345	ORIGINAL VALUE: $1,000.00		
YEAR	DEPRECIATION	ACCUMULATED DEPRECIATION	BOOK VALUE
1	$500.00	$ 500.00	$500.00
2	333.33	833.33	166.67
3	166.67	1,000.00	0.00

Note: In order always to show a final accumulated deprecation equal to the original value, as well as a final book value equal to zero, the depreciation of the last year is to be computed as follows:

Last year depreciation = original value − accumulated depreciation

Write and run a COBOL program to produce the desired output. Use as test data those shown in the preceding description.

8.7 A file contains data about the inventory of a company. Each inventory item is identified by a unique item number. The file is sorted on item number. There are three types of records in the file. A *balance* record contains the amount in inventory as of the last time the data were processed. A *receipt* record contains the amount of a shipment received. An *issue* record contains the amount sold. For each shipment received and each sale made, a separate record is created. We wish to read the records, process the data, produce an inventory report on the printer, and produce a set of new balance records.

Input is as follows:

COLUMN	CONTENT
1–5	Item number
6–20	Part name (on balance records only)
21	Type code
	1 = balance
	2 = receipt
	3 = issue
22–25	Quantity

Note: The records are sorted on item number. For each item, the balance record *precedes* the receipt and issue records.

Sample input is:

```
01212TRANSFORMER      12350
01212                 26000
01212                 30150
01212                 33050
01212                 31600
01515GEAR TRAIN       11000
01515                 30600
02010METAL PLATE      14000
```

Sample output: The printer output resulting from the previously given sample input is:

ITEM NUMBER	PART NAME	PREVIOUS BALANCE	NEW BALANCE
01212	TRANSFORMER	2350	3550
01515	GEAR TRAIN	1000	400
02010	METAL PLATE	4000	4000

The sample punched-card output resulting from the same sample input is:

```
01212TRANSFORMER      103550
01515GEAR TRAIN       100400
02010METAL PLATE      104000
```

These balance cards serve as input to the next program run, along with the receipt and issue records created between processing runs.

Write and run a COBOL program to accomplish the desired result. Assume all data are correct.

8.8 The data processing objective of this program is to compute and print the monthly schedule of payments resulting from a credit purchase. Given the amount of the credit purchase and the number of monthly payments planned, the amount of the monthly payment is computed as follows:

$$\text{Payment due} = \frac{\text{amount of credit purchase}}{\text{number of payments}} + 0.015 \text{ of unpaid balance}$$

Of course, this formula presumes an interest charge of 0.015 per month on the unpaid balance in the account. For example, suppose that a customer has purchased an item valued at $1,200.00 and is going to pay for it over a 12-month period. The payment due at the end of the first month is:

$$\text{Payment due} = \frac{\$1,200.00}{12} + 0.015 \ (\$1,200.00)$$

$$= \$100.00 + 0.015 \ (\$1,200.00) = \$100.00 + \$18.00 = \$118.00$$

Similarly, for the second month the payment is:

$$\text{Payment due} = \frac{\$1,200.00}{12} + 0.015 \ (\$1,100.00)$$

$$= \$100.00 + 0.015 \ (\$1,100.00) = \$100.00 + \$16.50 = \$116.50$$

The monthly payment consists of a constant element, which is the original amount of the credit purchase divided by the number of monthly payments, and a variable element, which is the monthly interest charge on the unpaid balance. With each monthly payment, the unpaid balance is decreased by the amount of the constant element.

The desired output for this program is illustrated in Figure 8–2. This case involves a credit transaction of $4,291.50. It is assumed that the letterhead is preprinted, but that the name and address, all column headings, and the numeric values will be printed as the result of program execution. Since the column headings are always the same, in practice these headings also would be preprinted on the form in order to conserve computer time. However, in our example we will print the headings in order to illustrate how this can be accomplished through the use of COBOL. For each monthly payment, the numeric information provided is the amount of the monthly interest charge, the total payment due that month, and the unpaid balance remaining after that month. Note also that the spacing of the computer printout is designed

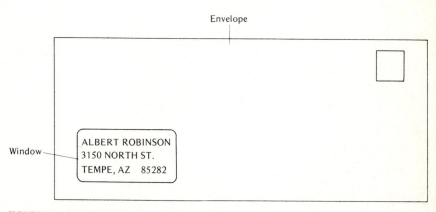

ABC COMPANY
5000 East Camelback Road
Phoenix, Arizona   85033

ALBERT ROBINSON
3150 NORTH ST.
TEMPE, AZ   85282

Fold here

SCHEDULE OF PAYMENTS

ORIGINAL AMOUNT $4,291.50

MONTH	INTEREST	TOTAL PAYMENT	UNPAID BALANCE
1	64.37	422.00	3,933.87
2	59.00	416.63	3,576.25
3	53.64	411.27	3,218.62
4	48.27	405.90	2,861.00
5	42.91	400.54	2,503.37
6	37.55	395.18	2,145.75
7	32.18	389.81	1,788.12
8	26.82	384.45	1,430.50
9	21.45	379.08	1,072.87
10	16.09	373.72	715.25
11	10.72	368.35	357.62
12	5.36	362.99	.00

Envelope

Window

ALBERT ROBINSON
3150 NORTH ST.
TEMPE, AZ   85282

FIGURE 8-2   DESIRED FORM OF OUTPUT FOR EXERCISE 8.8.

for use with a window envelope, thereby eliminating the need for separate addressing of envelopes.

Program input: This will consist of a file, with one record per customer. The record format and the layout of these data is as follows:

CARD COLUMNS	CONTENTS
1–20	Customer's name
21–45	Number and street
46–70	City, state, and ZIP code
71–78	Amount of credit purchase
79–80	Number of monthly payments

Write a COBOL program to accomplish the task we have described. Use the input for Figure 8-2 as test data for your program, and compare your output with the output in this figure.

9

Sequential file processing

FILE ORGANIZATION

The concept of *file organization* refers to the manner in which data records are arranged on a file-storage medium. There are three principal methods of file organization in COBOL: sequential, indexed sequential, and relative.

In a *sequential* file, the records are written in a serial order and are accessed (read) in the same order as written. The serial order need *not* be in any particular sequence, such as according to account number. Files assigned to the card reader, printer, and magnetic tape drive always are organized as sequential files. On the other hand, files stored on magnetic disk and other direct access storage devices may be sequential, indexed sequential, or relative files.

Although the language does not require it, sequential files on tape or disk most commonly are sorted so that the records are in some logical sequential order. For instance, if we have a customer file we might choose to sort the records on the basis of customer number. Then, if customer numbers are unique, each successive record read from the file should have a higher customer number than the one before. This practice of sorting the records is convenient when processing "batch" jobs, such as payroll. In such jobs, we sort the "transaction" data, such as time cards, in the same order as the employee payroll file. Then we need to go through that file only once, rather than go back and forth looking for employee records in random order.

Indexed sequential file organization means not only that the file is in sequential order, but that an index has been created so that records can be located directly without accessing them in sequence. We describe this file organization method in Chapter 13: "Indexed Sequential File Processing."

Relative file organization means that the file is stored in such a way that each record has an identifier by which it can be accessed directly. This method is covered in Chapter 14: "Relative File Processing."

REVIEW

1   The manner in which data records are arranged on a file storage medium is referred to as file _____.

organization

2   The type of file for which the records are written in a serial order and for which the records must be accessed in the same order as written is the _____ file organization.

sequential

3   The type of file for which the records have been read and stored in a serial order, but for which access can be direct, is the _____ _____ file organization.

indexed sequential

4   The type of file for which records are both stored and accessed directly according to the value of an identifier is the _____ file organization.

relative

5   If a file is assigned to a card reader, printer, or magnetic tape drive, it must be organized as a(n) _____ file.

sequential

6 A file that can be organized by any of the three methods described in this section is one for which the records are stored on magnetic _____.

disk

FILE STORAGE DEVICES

While the characteristics of the data processing task dictate which method of file organization is preferred, the storage device that is used determines which methods are possible. As related to file organization, it is useful to distinguish two main categories of storage devices: magnetic tape and mass-storage devices. The latter category refers mainly to magnetic disk, but it also includes other direct access storage devices, such as cartridge systems. As indicated in the preceding section, only the sequential file organization can be used for files stored on magnetic tape, whereas any method of file organization can be used for files stored on direct access storage devices.

The magnetic tape unit is the specialized input-output device used for reading and writing magnetic tapes. As illustrated in Figure 9-1, it includes two reels. The file reel contains the tape to be read or to be written on, and the machine reel contains the tape that already has been processed. The tape is threaded through a read-write head capable of performing the functions of reading and writing; thus, the tape transport unit works very much like a home tape recorder.

As the tape advances past the read-write head, the rated speed of reading or writing is a function of two factors: the recording density of the tape and the linear speed of the tape drive. Thus, if the recording density is 800 bytes per inch (bpi) and the speed is 100 inches per second, the rated read-write speed will be 80,000 bytes per second. Typical ranges are from 40,000 to over 300,000 bytes per second, but much higher speeds also are possible.

A magnetic disk is a magnetically sensitive circular surface resembling a phonograph record. Data are recorded on this disk surface in designated circular bands called tracks. Figure 9-2 portrays a magnetic disk storage device and includes a diagram of tracks on the surface of a disk. Typically, there are several hundred usable tracks on the surface of a magnetic disk. Each track can contain a few thousand characters around its circular length. Each track is separate from the others, and all tracks have the same capacity, even though the circles become smaller as we move away from the periphery. Tracks are referenced in numeric order from 0 up to the last.

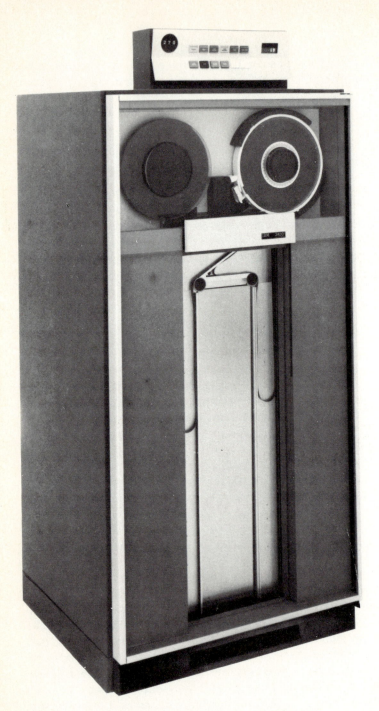

FIGURE 9-1   IBM 3420 MAGNETIC TAPE DRIVE. (IBM CORPORATION.)

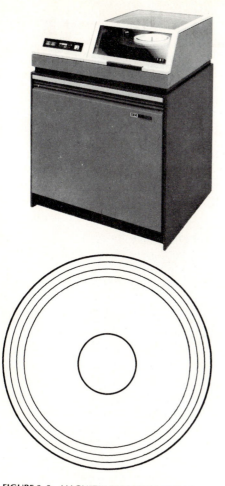

FIGURE 9-2 MAGNETIC DISK STORAGE DEVICE AND SCHEMATIC REPRESENTATION OF TRACKS ON A DISK SURFACE. (IBM CORPORATION.)

Thus, if we have 200 tracks, the first is designated track 000 and the last as track 199.

A disk pack refers to a group of disks stacked on a vertical spindle. The disks are parallel to each other but physically separated from one another. Such packs normally are removable as a unit, so that we can change disk packs for the same reasons that we change reels of magnetic tape. A disk pack of six disks has 10 usable surfaces, because the top and bottom surfaces of the two outer disks are not used since they are more exposed to handling and to the possibility of being "scratched."

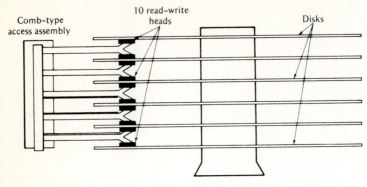

FIGURE 9-3   DISK ACCESS MECHANISM. (IBM CORPORATION.)

Typically, for each disk surface in a disk pack there is a read-write head—a device that can read data from or write data on the surface. These heads are fixed to a vertical column and can move as a unit toward or away from the center of the disk pack. Figure 9–3 illustrates the read-write head mechanism.

Data are recorded on any magnetic storage device in the form of *blocks*. Each block consists of a grouping of data written (or read) in one continuous operation. Several formats are possible for the data included in the block, as illustrated in Figures 9–4 and 9–5.

In addition to the number of records contained in each block, the size of each record is also of importance. In using magnetic storage, the record size is not restricted to the 80 characters associated with punched cards nor to any other particular limit. The records can be as long as is suitable for the applications involved. Furthermore, the records can be both fixed and variable in length. An example of a variable-length record is a record containing the transactions for the month for an individual checking account customer. The record for a customer who wrote 20 checks during the month is substantially shorter than the record of another customer who wrote 100 checks. Just as record size can be variable, so can the number of records per block. Overall, then, we can have fixed-length or variable-length records and

	1 block		1 block		1 block	
	RECORD	Gap	RECORD	Gap	RECORD	

FIGURE 9-4   TAPE RECORDING FORMAT CONTAINING ONE RECORD PER BLOCK.

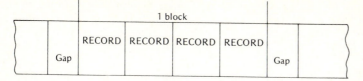

FIGURE 9-5   TAPE RECORDING FORMAT CONTAINING FOUR RECORDS PER BLOCK.

fixed-length or variable-length blocks. Even though the block size is variable, its size obviously cannot be unlimited. The programmer has to define the maximum limit on block size in each tape operation.

Perhaps one question remains to be answered. If variable-length records are written in a block, how can we distinguish between them? Typically, at the beginning of each record we have a control field that contains the length of the record. Thus, if we were forming a record that is to include the checks written by a bank customer, and if 15 characters were required to record the data of each check, we would increase the value of the record-length control field by 15 every time one more check was added to the record. Variable-length records are beyond the intended scope of this book; therefore, we will not elaborate on their use.

REVIEW

1   The magnetic tape unit requires the use of two reels when it is used: the machine reel and the file reel. The reel that contains the tape to be written on or read is the _____ reel; the reel that contains the tape that already has been processed is the _____ reel.

file; machine

2   The rated read-write speed of tape units typically varies between 40,000 to over 300,000 bytes per second and is a function of the recording _____ of the tape and the linear _____ of the tape drive.

density; speed

3   A group of magnetic disks stacked on a vertical shaft in a parallel fashion is called a(n) _____.

disk pack

4   Typically, a disk pack containing six disks has _____ (number) read-write heads.

10

5   A grouping of data that is written on a magnetic storage device in one continuous operation, and that may include one or more records, is called a _____.

block

6   In addition to the number of records contained in each block, block size also is determined by the length of each record. Although both the record size and the block size can be fixed, variable size is possible [only for records / only for blocks / for both records and blocks].

for both records and blocks

7   When variable record lengths are used in a block, the records are differentiated from one another by the use of a control field that indicates the _____ of each record.

length (or size, etc.)

FILE LABELS

Each magnetic file, such as a reel of tape or a disk pack, is identified by two means. Externally, an adhesive label is attached so that the operator can identify the contents of the file by reading this label. In addition, magnetic labels are included with the file itself. In general, two types of magnetic labels are used: the *header label* and the *trailer label*.

As implied by the name, a *header label* is located at the beginning of the file. This label contains such information as:

File identification: in terms of a file name or a file number

Retention period: the data prior to which the file cannot be overwritten

Creation date: the date the file was established

Sequence number: the sequence number for a multivolume file that consists of several columns (reels or disk packs).

The header label not only serves as a means of verifying the correct identity of an input file but also is used as a means of preventing inadvertent overwriting on a storage medium used as output. Prior to writing the first block, the header label of an output file is read in, and the retention period is checked against the current date. If the retention period date is later than the current date, a suitable error message will be generated for the operator.

The *trailer label* is a record written as the last record on the file. Typically, it contains the same information as the header label, but in addition it contains a block count, which is a count of the number of data blocks written on the file. This block count is used for control purposes. On a subsequent occasion when this file is input, the number of blocks read in by the program is accumulated and is compared with the block count recorded on the trailer label. If the two counts are not equal, there exists an indication of error.

The trailer label differs depending on whether a file is a single- or a multivolume file. If it is a single-volume file, the trailer is as described above. If it is a multivolume file, the trailer label of each volume indicates the volume (reel or disk pack) number as well.

Label processing is a specialized subject, and the methodology used often is specific to the standards of particular computer installations. In the next section of this chapter, we introduce label processing for sequential files at a simplified level. The reader should be aware that more information is available on the subject, and particularly that label processing is fundamental to preserving the security and integrity of the files for an organization.

REVIEW

1   Magnetic files are identified by two general types of labels: _____ labels for human use and _____ labels for machine use.

external; magnetic

2   Magnetic labels used with files are of two types. The label included at the beginning of a file is called the _____ label, while the label at the end of the file is called the _____ label.

header; trailer

3   For a multivolume file, both the header and trailer labels include a _____ number.

sequence

COBOL INSTRUCTIONS FOR SEQUENTIAL FILES

In the remaining sections of this chapter, we present a number of COBOL instructions and features pertaining to sequential files. In the preceding sections of this book, all of the files that were considered were also sequential, but they were oriented specifically toward use of the card reader and the printer. We now consider the instructions and features that are relevant with respect to magnetic tape and mass-storage files.

ENVIRONMENT DIVISION FEATURES

For sequential files, the SELECT and ASSIGN statements in the FILE-CONTROL paragraph of the INPUT-OUTPUT SECTION have the format:

SELECT   [OPTIONAL] file-name
    ASSIGN to implementor-name-1[,implementor-name-2] . . .
    [; ORGANIZATION IS SEQUENTIAL]
    [; ACCESS MODE IS SEQUENTIAL]

The instruction for each file must start with the key word SELECT. OPTIONAL can be used only with input files, and its inclusion signifies that a file may or may not be present. In a given program, we may have two input files: one containing current transactions, and the other containing corrected previous-error transactions. The second file may be declared OPTIONAL if we anticipate occasions of no previous-error transactions. (Of course, the program logic is responsible for handling the presence or absence of an optional file.)

In the ASSIGN statement, the "implementor-name" refers to the storage device designation. The designation may vary from such an example as ASSIGN TO SYS005-UT-3410-S-MAST for an IBM tape file to simpler forms, such as ASSIGN TO MASS-STORAGE A for a UNIVAC disk file. Obviously, each reader has to consult his or her local computer personnel for file designations.

If the file consists of more than one tape reel or disk unit, then the assignment is made to two or more "implementor-names," such as SELECT PAYROLL-FILE ASSIGN TO TAPE-UNIT-MR02, TAPE-UNIT-MR03.

The ORGANIZATION clause is optional, but when it is omitted the file is assumed to be SEQUENTIAL. For this reason, we have assumed sequential files in all previous examples in this book. The ACCESS MODE also is assumed to be SEQUENTIAL when not stated. We defer further discussion of these two clauses to Chapters 13 and 14, where we consider the options associated with indexed sequential and relative files.

The I/O-CONTROL paragraph of the INPUT-OUTPUT SECTION of the ENVIRONMENT DIVISION can be used to express some aspects particular to tape and disk files:

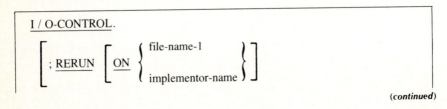

(continued)

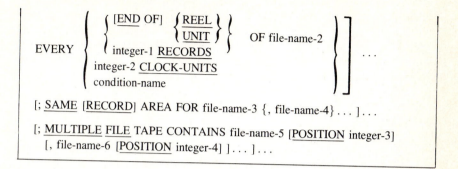

The RERUN clause can be used to instruct the computer to dump the program status, as it is in internal storage, onto a device—commonly a magnetic tape. Such a periodic recording of the program status permits restart of the program from the "middle," should an interruption become necessary. Such "checkpoints" are particularly useful in long program runs. For example, suppose a file update program has been running for 1 hour and there is a physical imperfection in the transactions tape, so that the last few transactions cannot be processed. Rather than correct the situation and rerun the entire program from its beginning, we could interrupt and restart it from the point where the last program status was recorded. The EVERY integer RECORDS clause specifies how often we record the program status. For example, we may have:

RERUN ON tape-unit-1 EVERY 1000 RECORDS OF TRANSACTION-FILE.

In this case, at most we would have to reprocess 1,000 TRANSACTION-FILE records should a program interruption occur. Additional options are available with the RERUN clause, which are self-explanatory for the most part. Their use is encountered in advanced applications, and therefore we do not deliberate on them.

The SAME RECORD AREA clause allows two or more files to share the same internal storage area. This option would be used if the internal storage available were insufficient, and two files were not in use at the same time. As an example we have:

SAME RECORD AREA FOR MONTHLY-FILE, QUARTERLY-FILE.

The MULTIPLE FILE clause can be used when more than one file is recorded on the same tape reel. The POSITION integer specifies the relative position of the file—in effect, whether the file is in the first position, the second, the third, etc. For example:

MULTIPLE FILE TAPE CONTAINS WEEKLY-FILE POSITION 2, MONTHLY-FILE
POSITION 4

could mean that WEEKLY-FILE is the second file in the reel and
MONTHLY-FILE is the fourth file in the reel.

REVIEW

1 In the FILE-CONTROL SECTION of the ENVIRONMENT DIVISION the
instruction for each file must start with the key word [SELECT / RESERVE],
followed by the file-name.

SELECT

2 The ASSIGN TO implementor-name clause identifies the _____
_____ to be used with each file.

storage device

3 When use of the optional ORGANIZATION clause is omitted, the file is
assumed to be a(n) _____ file.

sequential

4 When the ACCESS MODE clause is omitted, file access is assumed to be
_____.

sequential

5 In the I/O-CONTROL paragraph of the INPUT-OUTPUT SECTION, the
RERUN clause is used to record program status [at periodic points during
data processing / when an error condition is detected during the run].

at periodic points during data
processing

6 The SAME RECORD AREA clause generally is used in order to conserve
the number of _____ that need to be used.

storage areas

7 The MULTIPLE FILE clause is used in the INPUT-OUTPUT SECTION
when more than one file is recorded on the same tape reel. The POSI-
TION integer specifies the relative position of the _____ on the
reel.

file

DATA DIVISION FEATURES

Following is the general format for the DATA DIVISION, some options
of which are particularly meaningful for sequential files:

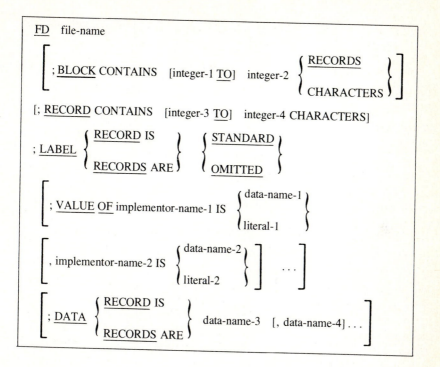

FD marks the beginning of a file description entry and is followed immediately by the name of the file. The name of the file already has been declared in the ENVIRONMENT DIVISION, where it was assigned to a hardware device.

If records are grouped together, the BLOCK CONTAINS clause is used. If each record constitutes one block, the clause may be omitted or the equivalent BLOCK CONTAINS 1 RECORD can be used. When a block contains several records, then the clause must be used. Typically, this clause is used with the RECORDS option indicated above. In such a case it references the number of records per block. For example, if we have:

FD PAYROLL-FILE BLOCK CONTAINS 10 RECORDS

each block will contain 10 records. However, if the records are of variable size, BLOCK CONTAINS 10 RECORDS will be interpreted to mean the maximum block size. Thus, if the records varied between 10 and 100 characters (this would be so identified in the record description), BLOCK CONTAINS 10 RECORDS would mean that blocks can be as short as 10 × 10 = 100 characters in length or as long as 10 × 100 = 1,000 characters in length. (Actually, the number of characters will be slightly different, depending on the *control fields* used by different compilers in recording variable-length blocks.)

If the option

FD PAYROLL-FILE BLOCK CONTAINS 5 TO 12 RECORDS

were used, it would imply that the number of records per block might be a number between 5 and 12, again giving variable block size.

The option BLOCK CONTAINS integer CHARACTERS is used when the block contains "padding"—the last part of the block may consist of unusable characters. This could be the case when it is desired that block size be fixed, but, because of variable record length, it is not possible to fill the entire block without splitting records across blocks.

RECORD CONTAINS [integer-1 TO] interger-2 CHARACTERS can be used for documentary purposes only. The record description will provide all such information to the compiler since, we recall, the record description specifies all the fields and their length. However, you may wonder how the record description is written for a variable-length record, such as corresponds to RECORD CONTAINS 20 TO 250 CHARACTERS. Up to now we have considered only fixed-length records. The subject will be covered in Chapter 11: "Basic Table Handling," in reference to the OCCURS clause with the DEPENDING ON option.

The LABEL RECORDS clause is required for all files. The OMITTED option indicates that the file has no beginning or ending label. If the STANDARD option is used, it is understood to be the standard labels for the particular computer installation. The natural question may be: Granted that they are "standard" for an installation, how do we communicate in the context of the program what the label should be? We said earlier that the label record contains data that identify the file, and obviously each file is identified uniquely. There are two basic ways of saying what the label contents should be. By the first approach (common in IBM computer systems), this information is communicated through program control cards submitted with the COBOL program. In other words, this information is not communicated, strictly speaking, in the COBOL program language. Another way of communicating the contents of label records is by use of the VALUE OF clause. For example, we could have for a particular case:

FD PAYROLL-FILE BLOCK CONTAINS 10 RECORDS
    LABEL RECORDS ARE STANDARD
    VALUE OF IDENTIFICATION IS "A2359"
    RETENTION-PERIOD IS 090
    DATA RECORD IS PAY-REC.

In this example, the words IDENTIFICATION and RETENTION-PERIOD are meaningful in a particular installation, and they indicate that the STANDARD label contains a field called IDENTIFICATION, whose content should be A2359. When the file is opened, the field is checked to ascertain that the A2359 data are there; in other words, that the correct file has been mounted. The RETENTION-PERIOD field implies that this file cannot be written on until 90 days have elapsed. Of course, other similar fields are used in the VALUE clause option.

The example DATA RECORDS ARE REC-1, REC-2 implies that the file contains two types of records.

As a way of summarizing the discussion in this section, the following are examples of file descriptions in the DATA DIVISION that are concerned with magnetic tape files:

```
FD  PAYROLL-FILE   BLOCK CONTAINS 10 RECORDS
                   RECORD CONTAINS 80 CHARACTERS
                   LABEL RECORDS ARE OMITTED
                   DATA RECORD IS SAMPLE-REC.


FD  FILE-A         BLOCK CONTAINS 600 CHARACTERS
                   LABEL RECORD IS STANDARD
                       VALUE OF IDENTIFICATION IS "A1-2B"
                   DATA RECORD IS REC.


FD  FILE-B         LABEL RECORDS OMITTED
                   DATA RECORD IS SIMPLE-REC.
```

REVIEW

1   With reference to the sample file descriptions just given, the names of the three files are _____, _____, and _____, respectively.

PAYROLL-FILE; FILE-A; FILE-B

2   The file description just given in which each block contains one record is the [first / second / third] description. The file description in which the record size can be variable is the [first / second / third] description.

third; second

3   The file description that includes a label record is the [first / second / third] description. The file description that includes the optional VALUE OF clause is the [first / second / third] description.

second; second

THE OPEN AND CLOSE VERBS

The OPEN verb initiates processing of a file and performs appropriate label processing. If the file is to be used as output, when the file is opened the existing label is checked to ascertain that the previous file can be "scratched." If so, the header label is written on the file. Similarly, if the file is opened for input, its label is read and checked for proper identification.

If an error condition arises as a result of such label processing, it either is reported by the operating system, which normally terminates the program, or it is handled by the program itself through use of the special USE verb in COBOL. Use of this verb is beyond the scope of this book, but we at least should be aware of this alternative.

The OPEN verb has the following format:

$$\underline{\text{OPEN}} \begin{Bmatrix} \underline{\text{INPUT}} & \text{file-name [with } \underline{\text{NO REWIND}}] \\ \underline{\text{OUTPUT}} & \text{file-name [with } \underline{\text{NO REWIND}}] \\ \underline{\text{I / O}} \\ \underline{\text{EXTEND}} \end{Bmatrix}$$

The INPUT and OUTPUT modes contain the NO REWIND option that can be used with magnetic tape files. Absence of the NO REWIND implies that the reel should be rewound, if necessary, so that it is at its beginning. If the NO REWIND is used, it is assumed that a previous CLOSE . . . WITH NO REWIND has resulted in the tape being positioned at the beginning of the desired file (by being at the end of the previous file that was just closed).

The I/O option can be used only for mass storage files. It allows the program to both input and output on the file. It is used if we want to change a record that we have just read. With tape files, however, we cannot rewrite a record that we have just read in.

The EXTEND option positions the file after its last record. It can be used to add new records at the end of the file and is really a special case of the OUTPUT mode option.

TABLE 9-1   PERMISSIBLE COMBINATIONS OF OPEN MODE OPTIONS AND INPUT-OUPUT VERBS

STATEMENT:	OPEN MODE			
	INPUT	OUTPUT	I / O	EXTEND
READ	X		X	
WRITE		X		X
REWRITE			X	

Correct use of input-output verbs depends on the option, or mode, used in the OPEN statement. Table 9–1 summarizes this relationship, with an X designating each permissible combination. For instance, if the INPUT mode option is used then the READ verb can be used, but the WRITE or REWRITE verbs cannot be used.

The CLOSE verb has the following expanded format:

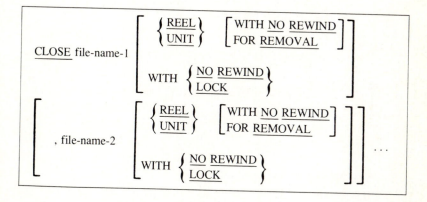

Prior to closing, a file must have been opened. "CLOSE file-name" results in end-of-file procedures. If label records have not been omitted, a trailer label is written and the tape is rewound automatically. If the option CLOSE file-name REEL is used, this results in closing that reel but not the file as such. Thus, the file itself still will be in an open status. The only circumstance under which the REEL option is used is in the case of multireel files, where the processing of a particular reel for a file may have been completed but other reels for the file still might remain to be processed. If we are using disk files, then the term UNIT is used instead of REEL. The NO REWIND option prevents the rewinding that otherwise is effected automatically by the CLOSE verb. One circumstance in which the user would not want to rewind the tape is when a second file subsequently is to be read from or written on the same tape reel. When the indicated LOCK option is used instead, the file is locked once the tape is rewound and can be reopened only by restarting the program. The LOCK option thereby serves as protection against accidentally opening and misusing a file whose data have already been processed. The FOR REMOVAL option is used to allow the operator to intervene, remove the reel (at least logically), and replace it with another reel. The specific procedure that should take place in conjunction with using the FOR REMOVAL option is not defined by COBOL; rather, it is determined by the user.

REVIEW

1   Processing of a file is initiated by the use of the _____ verb.
                                                                    OPEN

2   If the READ verb is to be used subsequent to a file being opened, then the INPUT mode option should be included in the OPEN statement. Similarly, if the WRITE verb is to be used then the _____ mode option should be included in the OPEN statement.
                                                        OUTPUT (or EXTEND)

3   End-of-file procedures are specified by use of the _____ verb.
                                                                    CLOSE

4   The option in the closing routine that serves to protect the file from use (and misuse) is the [NO REWIND / LOCK] option, whereas the option that permits further use of the reel is the [NO REWIND / LOCK] option.
                                                        LOCK; NO REWIND

THE READ, WRITE, AND REWRITE VERBS

The format for the READ verb remains the same as before:

```
READ   file-name RECORD [INTO identifier]
       [; AT END imperative statement]
```

However, if a file was designated as OPTIONAL in the SELECT statement and the file is not present, the AT END condition occurs when the first READ is executed. As Table 9-1 indicates, a READ is valid when a file has been opened as INPUT or I/O.

The relevant WRITE format is:

```
WRITE   record-name   [FROM   identifier]
```

As Table 9-1 indicates, the file must be opened as either OUTPUT or EXTEND if the WRITE verb is to be used.

If a BLOCK CONTAINS clause was used in the file description, the system will control automatically the operations needed to form an appropriate block prior to a physical write of the block itself. The programmer need not be concerned about the blocking operation.

The REWRITE statement is a specialized instruction for mass storage files. Its format is:

```
REWRITE   record-name   [FROM identifier]
```

In order to update a sequential file on disk we may use "OPEN I/O file-name." Then, after issuing a READ command that accesses the record to be updated, we use the REWRITE verb to replace the updated record in the same file instead of WRITE on a different file. With magnetic tape files, we must read a record from one file and MOVE and write the updated record on a new file.

It should be noted that REWRITE can be used only to update an existing file. If we are creating a file, we use the WRITE verb.

REVIEW

1   If the READ verb is to be used, the file must be opened in the _____ or _____ mode.

                                                                INPUT; I-O

2   If the WRITE verb is to be used, the file must be opened in the _____ or _____ mode.

                                                          OUTPUT; EXTEND

3   The verb that is used to update an existing file is the _____ verb. To use this verb, the file must be opened in the _____ mode.

                                                            REWRITE; I-O

SAMPLE PROGRAM TO CREATE A SEQUENTIAL FILE

Figure 9–6 illustrates the process of creating a sequential life on magnetic tape or disk. The source records are assumed to be in a card file. Each record is read in and it is checked for sequence on a field called CUST-NO in columns 1–6. If a record is not in ascending sequence, it is listed on the printer for visual review and correction.

SEQUENTIAL FILE UPDATING

Files on magnetic tape or disk are maintained or updated to reflect changes that take place. We speak of *master* and *transaction* files as being involved in the updating process.

A *master* file contains reference data that reflect the cumulative status as of a point in time. For example, a payroll master file would contain data on each employee, such as name, address, pay rate, year-to-date earnings, and so forth.

```
IDENTIFICATION DIVISION.
PROGRAM-ID.  CREATE-FILE.
*
ENVIRONMENT DIVISION.
*
CONFIGURATION SECTION.
SOURCE-COMPUTER.  ABC-480.
OBJECT-COMPUTER.  ABC-480.
INPUT-OUTPUT SECTION.
FILE-CONTROL.
    SELECT OLD-CUST-MAST-FILE ASSIGN TO DISK-DEVICE-A.
    SELECT CUST-SOURCE-FILE ASSIGN TO CARD-READER.
    SELECT SEQ-ERROR-FILE ASSIGN TO PRINTER.
*
DATA DIVISION.
*
FILE SECTION.
*
FD  OLD-CUST-MAST-FILE
    LABEL RECORDS ARE STANDARD
    BLOCK CONTAINS 5 RECORDS
    DATA RECORD IS CUST-MAST-REC.
01  CUST-MAST-REC               PIC X(75).
*
FD  CUST-SOURCE-FILE
    LABEL RECORDS OMITTED
    DATA RECORD IS CUST-SOURCE-REC.
01  CUST-SOURCE-REC.
    02 CUST-NO                  PIC 9(5).
    02 CUST-NAME                PIC X(20).
    02 CUST-ADDRESS             PIC X(50).
    02 FILLER                   PIC X(25).
*
FD  SEQ-ERROR-FILE
    LABEL RECORDS OMITTED
    DATA RECORD IS SEQ-ERROR-REC.
01  SEQ-ERROR-REC              PIC X(132).
*
WORKING-STORAGE SECTION.
*
01  END-OF-FILE-INDICATOR      PIC XXX VALUE 'NO'.
    88 END-OF-FILE             VALUE 'YES'.
*
01  PREVIOUS-CUST-NO           PIC 9(5) VALUE ZERO.
*
01  ERROR-MESSAGE.
    02 FILLER PIC X VALUE SPACE.
    02 FILLER                  PIC X(13) VALUE 'ERROR RECORD:'.
    02 RECORD-OUT              PIC X(75).
/
PROCEDURE DIVISION.
*
MAIN-ROUTINE.
    OPEN INPUT CUST-SOURCE-FILE
         OUTPUT OLD-CUST-MAST-FILE
                SEQ-ERROR-FILE.
*
    READ CUST-SOURCE-FILE RECORD
         AT END MOVE 'YES' TO END-OF-FILE-INDICATOR.
*
    PERFORM READ-CHECK-WRITE
            UNTIL END-OF-FILE
*
    CLOSE CUST-SOURCE-FILE
          OLD-CUST-MAST-FILE
          SEQ-ERROR-FILE
*
    STOP RUN.
*
READ-CHECK-WRITE.
    IF CUST-NO NOT > PREVIOUS-CUST-NO
        MOVE CUST-SOURCE-REC TO RECORD-OUT
        WRITE SEQ-ERROR-REC FROM ERROR-MESSAGE AFTER 1
    ELSE
        WRITE CUST-MAST-REC FROM CUST-SOURCE-REC
        MOVE CUST-NO TO PREVIOUS-CUST-NO.
*
    READ CUST-SOURCE-FILE RECORD
         AT END MOVE 'YES' TO END-OF-FILE-INDICATOR.
```

FIGURE 9-6 SAMPLE PROGRAM TO CREATE A SEQUENTIAL FILE.

A *transaction* file contains records that either reflect events or indicate changes to the master file. For example, a transaction record at a bank might be a deposit made or a check written. Other examples of transactions would be the addition of a new customer to the master file, deletion of a former customer's name, or a change of the customer's address.

Updating involves processing the transaction file against the master file. The process of updating varies a little, depending on whether we use magnetic tape or disk for storing the master file.

Figure 9-7 illustrates the general procedure involved in updating magnetic tape files. Beginning with the top of the figure, we assume that the transactions originally were recorded manually and then were punched onto cards and transferred onto magnetic tape on a card-to-tape computer run. The transactions are sorted after the card-to-tape conversion, rather than

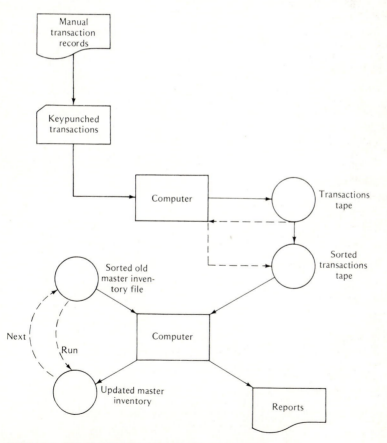

FIGURE 9-7   PROCEDURE USED FOR UPDATING A TAPE FILE.

before the conversion, because the transactions can be sorted faster and more reliably once the data are on tape. The old master file then is processed against the sorted transactions tape to produce the updated master tape. In addition, related reports might be produced on the printer.

As indicated by the dotted lines in Figure 9–7, what is now the updated master file becomes the old master file in the next update run, and the old master file from the first run will be used for entry of the updated master file on the next update run. This is known as a parent/child file relationship. However, the procedure we have described results in each case in destruction of the file for the week preceding the one being updated. If we want to have more historical backup, we could use a third file in this procedure, giving rise to a grandparent/parent/child relationship.

In order to update a master file, both the master file and the transaction file must be sorted on the same basis. Typically, they are sorted according to stock number, account number, employee number, or the like.

In the case of a master file stored on disk, we need not create a new file. We simply can REWRITE each updated record in its original location. Thus, it is not necessary to create a new master file each time; however, we should realize that doing so eliminates our backup capability. If something went wrong in the previous update run, we would not find it easy to reconstruct the file and rerun the update program. Thus, even with disk storage it often is preferrable to create a new master file.

REVIEW

1   The file that contains cumulative data as of a point in time is called the
    _____ file.

master

2   The file that contains records that reflect required changes to the master
    file is the _____ file.

transaction

3   In the process of updating, the updated master file becomes the _____
    master file in the next update run.

old

4   An existing master file can be updated directly, rather than by creating a
    new master file, when the existing file is stored on [tape / disk].

disk

SAMPLE SEQUENTIAL FILE UPDATE PROGRAM

We illustrate the general logic involved in a sequential file update by means of an example.

Master records consist of a customer number, a customer name, and an address. Transaction records consist of a customer number, a transaction code, a name field and an address field. The transactions are of three general types: changing the content of a specified customer's master record, adding a new customer record, and deleting a customer record. The "change" transactions are of two types: change name and change address. Although many types of changes can occur, in general the logic is the same. It should be noted, however, that often there may be many "change" transactions for a given master record; for example, the multiple purchases made by a customer during a given month.

A structure chart for the program is presented in Figure 9–8, a complete program listing is included in Figure 9–9, and sample input and output are shown in Figure 9–10.

The main function involved is to process a transaction record against a master record. To make sure that both files are in sequence, the READ-TRANS and READ-MASTER paragraphs perform appropriate sequence checking. When we compare a master record to a transaction record, there are three possibilities. If they are equal, we should have either a "change" or a "delete" type of transaction. If the master record is less than the transaction record, then we copy the old master record as-is onto the updated master file, since there are no transactions pertaining to that record. If the master record is higher than the transaction record, then it must be an "add" transaction in order to be valid.

At some point in the processing, one of the two files runs out of data (or both could run out at the same time). If no more transactions remain, we simply copy the rest of the old master onto the new master. If no more master records remain, then the remaining transactions should be add transactions and therefore should be higher than the last master record processed.

There are two kinds of error messages produced. The first one is generated if the files are found to be out of sequence. We then terminate the program, printing first the records involved and then the immediately preceding records, for reference. It is not always necessary to terminate the program, but in this case it seems the reasonable thing to do. The second type of error has to do with incorrect transaction codes. When such errors occur, we print an error message interspersed with the report output. A better procedure would be to save such error messages and list them after the main report is completed. Exercise 9.1 at the end of this chapter asks for such a modification to the program.

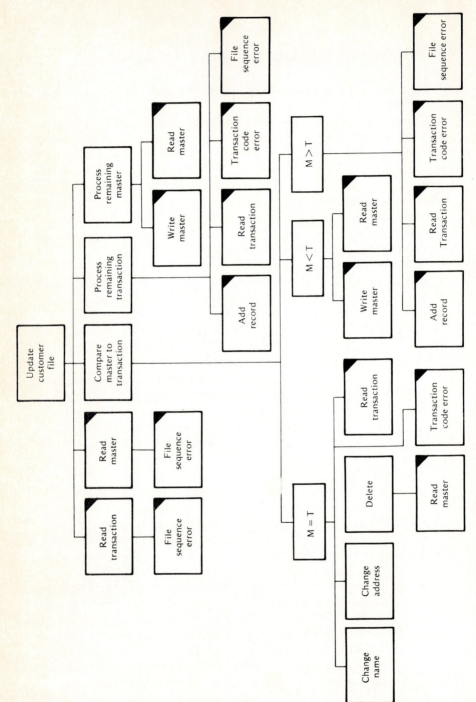

FIGURE 9-8 STRUCTURE CHART FOR THE UPDATE PROGRAM.

The printed output of this program is a simple listing of the updated file. Generally, there would be a list of updated, new, and deleted records printed, rather than the complete file. Exercise 9.2 at the end of this chapter asks for such a modification to the program.

The program is self-documenting and the reader should be able to follow it. This program can be used as the basis for all sequential updating programs because the basic logic of all such programs is the same.

```
IDENTIFICATION DIVISION.
PROGRAM-ID.  SIMPLEUPDATE.
*
ENVIRONMENT DIVISION.
*
CONFIGURATION SECTION.
SOURCE-COMPUTER:  ABC-480.
OBJECT-COMPUTER:  ABC-480.
*
INPUT-OUTPUT SECTION.
*
FILE-CONTROL.
      SELECT OLD-CUST-MASTER ASSIGN TO DISK-DEVICE-A;
            ORGANIZATION IS SEQUENTIAL;
            ACCESS MODE IS SEQUENTIAL.
      SELECT NEW-CUST-MASTER ASSIGN TO DISK-DEVICE-B;
            ORGANIZATION IS SEQUENTIAL;
            ACCESS MODE IS SEQUENTIAL.
      SELECT TRANS-FILE ASSIGN TO CARD-READER.
      SELECT REPORT-FILE ASSIGN TO PRINTER.
/
DATA DIVISION.
*
FILE SECTION.
*
FD   OLD-CUST-MASTER
     LABEL RECORDS ARE STANDARD
     BLOCK CONTAINS 5 RECORDS
     DATA RECORD IS OLD-MAST-REC.
*
01   OLD-MAST-REC.
     02 CUST-NO                      PIC 9(5).
     02 CUST-NAME                    PIC X(20).
     02 CUST-ADDRESS                 PIC X(50).
*
FD   NEW-CUST-MASTER
     LABEL RECORDS ARE STANDARD
     BLOCK CONTAINS 5 RECORDS
     DATA RECORD IS NEW-MAST-REC.
*
01   NEW-MAST-REC.
     02 CUST-NO                      PIC 9(5).
     02 CUST-NAME                    PIC X(20).
     02 CUST-ADDRESS                 PIC X(50).
*
FD   TRANS-FILE
     LABEL RECORDS OMITTED
     DATA RECORD IS TRANS-REC.
*
01   TRANS-REC.
     02 CUST-NO                      PIC 9(5).
     02 TRANS-CODE                   PIC 9.
        88 NEW-NAME                  VALUE 1.
        88 NEW-ADDRESS               VALUE 2.
        88 NEW-RECORD                VALUE 3.
        88 DELETE-RECORD             VALUE 4.
        88 ERROR-TRANSACTION         VALUES ZERO, 5 THRU 9.
     02 CUST-NAME                    PIC X(20).
     02 CUST-ADDRESS                 PIC X(50).
     02 FILLER                       PIC X(4).
*
FD   REPORT-FILE
     LABEL RECORDS OMITTED
     DATA RECORD REPORT-REC.
*
01   REPORT-REC                      PIC X(132).
```

FIGURE 9-9 LISTING OF THE UPDATE PROGRAM.   (*continued*)

```
/
 WORKING-STORAGE SECTION.
*
 01    END-OF-FILE-SWITCHES.
       02 END-OF-TRANS-SWITCH        PIC XXX VALUE 'NO'.
          88 TRANS-ENDED             VALUE 'YES'.
       02 END-OF-MASTER-SWITCH       PIC XXX VALUE 'NO'.
          88 MASTER-ENDED VALUE 'YES'.
*
 01    TERMINATION-SWITCH            PIC XXX VALUE 'NO'.
       88 TERMINAL-ERROR             VALUE 'YES'.
*
 01    PREVIOUS-REC-VALUES.
       02 PREVIOUS-TRANS-NO          PIC 9(5) VALUE ZERO.
       02 PREVIOUS-MAST-NO           PIC 9(5) VALUE ZERO.
*
 01    ERROR-MESSAGE-RECORD.
       02 FILLER                     PIC X VALUE SPACE.
       02 MESSAGE-FIELD              PIC X(75).
*
 01    PREVIOUS-VALUES-OUT.
       02 FILLER                     PIC X VALUE SPACE.
       02 FILLER                     PIC X(17)
                                     VALUE 'PREVIOUS TRANS NO'.
       02 TRANS-NO-OUT               PIC 9(5)
       02 FILLER                     PIC X(3) VALUE SPACES.
       02 FILLER                     PIC X(16)
                                     VALUE 'PREVIOUS MAST NO'.
       02 MAST-NO-OUT                PIC 9(5).
/
 PROCEDURE DIVISION.
*
 MAIN-LOGIC.
       OPEN INPUT   OLD-CUST-MASTER
                    TRANS-FILE
            OUTPUT  NEW-CUST-MASTER
                    REPORT-FILE.
*
       PERFORM READ-TRANS
       PERFORM READ-MASTER
*
       PERFORM COMPARE-M-TO-T
               UNTIL TRANS-ENDED
               OR    MASTER-ENDED
               OR    TERMINAL-ERROR.
*
       IF TRANS-ENDED
          PERFORM PROCESS-REMAINING-MASTER
                  UNTIL MASTER-ENDED
                     OR TERMINAL-ERROR
       ELSE
          IF MASTER-ENDED
             PERFORM PROCESS-REMAINING-TRANS
                     UNTIL TRANS-ENDED
                        OR TERMINAL-ERROR.
*
       CLOSE OLD-CUST-MASTER
             NEW-CUST-MASTER
             TRANS-FILE
             REPORT-FILE
*
       STOP RUN.
/
 COMPARE-M-TO-T.
       IF CUST-NO OF TRANS-REC = CUST-NO OF OLD-MAST-REC
          PERFORM M-EQUALS-T
       ELSE
          IF CUST-NO OF TRANS-REC < CUST-NO OF OLD-MAST-REC
             PERFORM M-LESS-THAN-T
          ELSE
             PERFORM M-GREATER-THAN-T.
*
 M-EQUALS-T.
       IF NEW-NAME
          PERFORM NAME-CHANGE
       ELSE
          IF NEW-ADDRESS
             PERFORM ADDRESS-CHANGE
          ELSE
             IF DELETE-RECORD
                PERFORM DELETION
             ELSE
                PERFORM TRANS-CODE-ERROR.
*
       PERFORM READ-TRANS.
```

FIGURE 9-9 (*continued*)

```
*
 M-LESS-THAN-T.
       PERFORM WRITE-MASTER
       PERFORM READ-MASTER.
*
 M-GREATER-THAN-T.
       IF NEW-RECORD
          PERFORM ADD-RECORD
          PERFORM READ-TRANS
       ELSE
          IF ERROR-TRANSACTION
             PERFORM TRANS-CODE-ERROR
             PERFORM READ-TRANS
          ELSE
             MOVE 'FILES OUT OF SEQUENCE' TO MESSAGE-FIELD
/            PERFORM FILE-SEQUENCE-ERROR.
 PROCESS-REMAINING-MASTER.
       PERFORM WRITE-MASTER
*
       PERFORM READ-MASTER.
*
 PROCESS-REMAINING-TRANS.
       IF NEW-RECORD
          AND CUST-NO OF TRANS-REC > PREVIOUS-MAST-NO
             PERFORM ADD-RECORD
             PERFORM READ-TRANS
       ELSE
          IF ERROR-TRANSACTION
             PERFORM TRANS-CODE-ERROR
             PERFORM READ-TRANS
          ELSE
             MOVE 'FILES OUT OF SEQUENCE' TO MESSAGE-FIELD
             PERFORM FILE-SEQUENCE-ERROR.
/
 READ-TRANS.
       READ TRANS-FILE RECORD
            AT END MOVE 'YES' TO END-OF-TRANS-SWITCH.
*
       IF TRANS-ENDED
          NEXT SENTENCE
       ELSE
          IF CUST-NO OF TRANS-REC < PREVIOUS-TRANS-NO
             MOVE 'TRANSACTION FILE OUT OF SEQUENCE'
                  TO MESSAGE-FIELD
             PERFORM FILE-SEQUENCE-ERROR
          ELSE
             MOVE CUST-NO OF TRANS-REC TO PREVIOUS-TRANS-NO.
*
 READ-MASTER.
       READ OLD-CUST-MASTER RECORD INTO NEW-MAST-REC
            AT END MOVE 'YES' TO END-OF-MASTER-SWITCH.
*
       IF MASTER-ENDED
          NEXT SENTENCE
       ELSE
          IF CUST-NO OF OLD-MAST-REC NOT > PREVIOUS-MAST-NO
             MOVE 'MASTER FILE OUT OF SEQUENCE' TO MESSAGE-FIELD
             PERFORM FILE-SEQUENCE-ERROR
          ELSE
             MOVE CUST-NO OF OLD-MAST-REC TO PREVIOUS-MAST-NO.
/
 NAME-CHANGE.
       MOVE CUST-NAME OF TRANS-REC TO CUST-NAME OF NEW-MAST-REC.
*
 ADDRESS-CHANGE.
       MOVE CUST-ADDRESS OF TRANS-REC
            TO CUST-ADDRESS OF NEW-MAST-REC.
*
 DELETION.
       PERFORM READ-MASTER.
*
 ADD-RECORD.
       MOVE CUST-NO OF TRANS-REC TO CUST-NO OF NEW-MAST-REC
       MOVE CUST-NAME OF TRANS-REC TO CUST-NAME OF NEW-MAST-REC
       MOVE CUST-ADDRESS OF TRANS-REC
            TO CUST-ADDRESS OF NEW-MAST-REC.
*
       PERFORM WRITE-MASTER
*
       MOVE OLD-MAST-REC TO NEW-MAST-REC.
*
*THE ABOVE MOVE RESTORES THE CONTENTS OF NEW-MAST-REC
*WHICH WERE DESTROYED BY THE NEW RECORD JUST ADDED.
*RECALL THAT IN READ-MASTER PARAGRAPH AS EACH OLD-MAST-REC
*IS READ IN IT IS MOVED INTO NEW-MAST-REC.
```

(continued)

```
*
 WRITE-MASTER.
      WRITE REPORT-REC FROM NEW-MAST-REC
              AFTER ADVANCING 1 LINE
*
      WRITE NEW-MAST-REC.
/
 FILE-SEQUENCE-ERROR.
      WRITE REPORT-REC FROM ERROR-MESSAGE-RECORD
              AFTER ADVANCING PAGE.
*
      MOVE 'TRANSACTION RECORD AT TIME OF ERROR'
              TO MESSAGE-FIELD
      WRITE REPORT-REC FROM ERROR-MESSAGE-RECORD
              AFTER ADVANCING 2 LINES
      MOVE TRANS-REC TO MESSAGE-FIELD
      WRITE REPORT-REC FROM ERROR-MESSAGE-RECORD
              AFTER ADVANCING 2 LINES
*
      MOVE 'MASTER RECORD AT TIME OF ERROR'
              TO MESSAGE-FIELD
      WRITE REPORT-REC FROM ERROR-MESSAGE-RECORD
              AFTER ADVANCING 2 LINES
      MOVE OLD-MAST-REC TO MESSAGE-FIELD
      WRITE REPORT-REC FROM ERROR-MESSAGE-RECORD
              AFTER ADVANCING 2 LINES
*
      MOVE 'MASTER RECORD AT TIME OF ERROR'
              TO MESSAGE-FIELD
      WRITE REPORT-REC FROM ERROR-MESSAGE-RECORD
              AFTER ADVANCING 2 LINES
      MOVE OLD-MAST-REC TO MESSAGE-FIELD
      WRITE REPORT-REC FROM ERROR-MESSAGE-RECORD
              AFTER ADVANCING 2 LINES
*
      MOVE PREVIOUS-TRANS-NO TO TRANS-NO-OUT
      MOVE PREVIOUS-MAST-NO TO MAST-NO-OUT
      WRITE REPORT-REC FROM PREVIOUS-VALUES-OUT
*
      MOVE 'YES' TO TERMINATION-SWITCH.
*
 TRANS-CODE-ERROR.
      MOVE SPACES TO REPORT-REC
      WRITE REPORT-REC
              AFTER ADVANCING 1 LINE
      MOVE 'THE FOLLOWING TRANSACTION RECORD CONTAINS A CODE ERROR'
              TO MESSAGE-FIELD
      WRITE REPORT-REC
              AFTER ADVANCING 1 LINE
      WRITE REPORT-REC FROM TRANS-REC
              AFTER ADVANCING 1 LINE
      MOVE SPACES TO REPORT-REC
      WRITE REPORT-REC
              AFTER ADVANCING 1 LINE.
```

FIGURE 9-9 (continued)

SAMPLE SEQUENTIAL REPORT-GENERATING PROGRAM

We conclude this chapter by presenting a sample report-generating program because sequential file processing often results in generating reports from such files. The reports that are generated will provide information about groups or classes of items.

Our sample program is an enhanced version of the simpler sample program for producing a sales report, described in Chapter 6. In addition to product categories, we now also categorize the data according to salesperson. Sample output from the report is presented in Figure 9-11. Sales totals are printed for each change in product and salesperson. It should be noted that when the salesperson changes, we print totals for the product even if the

Original Master-File Data

```
12345ADAMS              CUST-10 ADDRESS
14567BROWN              CUST-20 ADDRESS
20050PETERSON           CUST-30 ADDRESS
31020SMITH              CUST-50 ADDRESS
34250JONES              CUST-60 ADDRESS
40000THOMAS             CUST-70 ADDRESS
```

Transaction Data

```
145671XAVIER
300453MATHES            CUST-40 ADDRESS
310003PROVOST           CUST-45 ADDRESS
310204
330005WRONG CODE EXAMPLE
400002                  CUST-70 NEW-ADDRESS
320204
```

Output from Update Program

```
12345ADAMS              CUST-10 ADDRESS
14567XAVIER             CUST-20 ADDRESS
20050PETERSON           CUST-30 ADDRESS
30045MATHES             CUST-40 ADDRESS
31000PROVOST            CUST-45 ADDRESS


330005WRONG CODE EXAMPLE

34250JONES              CUST-60 ADDRESS

TRANSACTION FILE OUT OF SEQUENCE

TRANSACTION RECORD AT TIME OR ERROR

320204

MASTER RECORD AT TIME OF ERROR

40000THOMAS             CUST-70 ADDRESS
PREVIOUS TRANS NO40000   PREVIOUS MAST NO40000
```

FIGURE 9-10   SAMPLE INPUT AND OUTPUT FOR THE UPDATE PROGRAM.

SALESMAN NO.	PRODUCT NO.	SALES AMOUNT	TOTAL SALES
03	123	125.27	
		100.00	
			$225.27
	345	50.50	
		110.25	
		10.09	
			$170.84
			$396.11
05	123	4,000.00	
			$4,000.00
			$4,000.00
06	123	200.25	
			$200.25
			$200.25

FIGURE 9-11   SAMPLE OUTPUT FROM THE SEQUENTIAL REPORT PROGRAM.

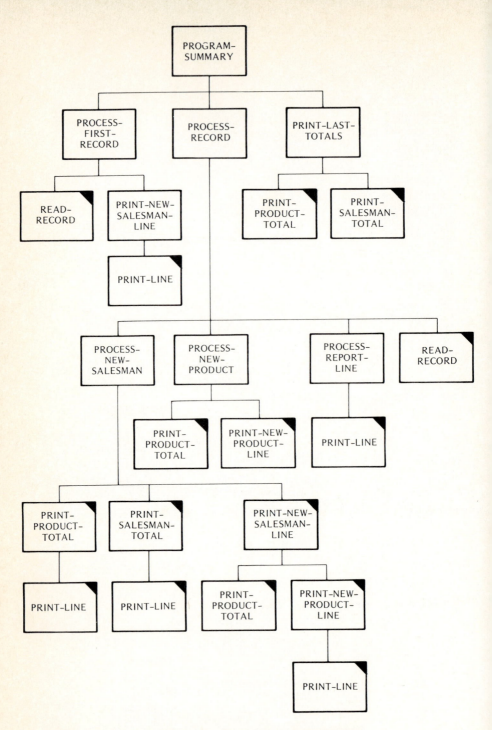

FIGURE 9-12 STRUCTURE CHART FOR THE SEQUENTIAL REPORT PROGRAM.

```
        IDENTIFICATION DIVISION.
        PROGRAM-ID.  SALESREPORT2.
*
        ENVIRONMENT DIVISION.
*
        CONFIGURATION SECTION.
        SOURCE-COMPUTER.  ABC-480.
        OBJECT-COMPUTER.  ABC-480.
*
        INPUT-OUTPUT SECTION.
*
        FILE-CONTROL.
            SELECT SALES-FILE ASSIGN TO CARD-READER.
            SELECT REPORT-FILE ASSIGN TO PRINTER.
/
        DATA DIVISION.
*
        FILE SECTION.
*
        FD  SALES-FILE
            LABEL RECORDS ARE OMITTED
            DATA RECORD IS SALES-RECORD.
        01  SALES-RECORD.
            02  SALESMAN-NO              PIC 99.
            02  PRODUCT-NO              PIC 999.
            02  SALES-AMOUNT           PIC 9(4)V99.
            02  FILLER                 PIC X(69).
*
        FD  REPORT-FILE
            LABEL RECORDS ARE OMITTED
            DATA RECORD IS REPORT-RECORD.
        01  REPORT-RECORD              PIC X(132).
*
        WORKING-STORAGE SECTION.
*
        01  END-OF-FILE-INDICATOR     PIC XXX VALUE 'NO'.
            88  END-OF-FILE    VALUE 'YES'.
            88  NOT-END-OF-FILE VALUE 'NO'.
*
        01  PREVIOUS-VALUES.
            02  PREVIOUS-SALESMAN-NO   PIC 99.
            02  PREVIOUS-PRODUCT-NO    PIC 999.
*
        01  PAGE-SIZE                  PIC 99 VALUE 25.
*
        01  LINE-COUNTER               PIC 99 VALUE 25.
*
        01  REPORT-TOTALS.
            02  SALESMAN-TOTAL         PIC 9(6)V99  VALUE ZERO.
            02  PRODUCT-TOTAL          PIC 9(5)V99  VALUE ZERO.
*
        01  REPORT-HEADING.
            02  FILLER                 PIC X(10) VALUE SPACES.
            02  FILLER                 PIC X(12) VALUE 'SALESMAN NO.'.
            02  FILLER                 PIC X(3) VALUE SPACES.
            02  FILLER                 PIC X(11) VALUE 'PRODUCT NO.'.
            02  FILLER                 PIC X(3) VALUE SPACES.
            02  FILLER                 PIC X(12) VALUE 'SALES AMOUNT'.
            02  FILLER                 PIC X(4) VALUE SPACES.
            02  FILLER                 PIC X(11) VALUE 'TOTAL SALES'.
*
        01  REPORT-LINE.
            02  FILLER                 PIC X(15) VALUE SPACES.
            02  SALESMAN-NO-OUT        PIC 99.
            02  FILLER                 PIC X(12) VALUE SPACES.
            02  PRODUCT-NO-OUT         PIC 999.
            02  FILLER                 PIC X(9) VALUE SPACES.
            02  SALES-AMOUNT-OUT       PIC Z,ZZ9.99.
            02  FILLER                 PIC X(6) VALUE SPACES.
            02  TOTAL-SALES-OUT        PIC $$$,$$9.99.
/
        PROCEDURE DIVISION.
*
        PROGRAM-SUMMARY.
*
            OPEN INPUT SALES-FILE
                 OUTPUT REPORT-FILE.
*
            PERFORM PROCESS-FIRST-RECORD
*
            PERFORM PROCESS-RECORD
                    UNTIL END-OF-FILE.
*
            PERFORM PRINT-LAST-TOTALS
*
            CLOSE SALES-FILE
                  REPORT-FILE.
*
            STOP RUN.
```

FIGURE 9-13 LISTING OF THE SEQUENTIAL REPORT PROGRAM.   (*continued*)

```
/
 PROCESS-FIRST-RECORD.
     PERFORM READ-RECORD.
     IF NOT-END-OF-FILE
         MOVE SALESMAN-NO TO PREVIOUS-SALESMAN-NO
         MOVE PRODUCT-NO TO PREVIOUS-PRODUCT-NO
         MOVE SALES-AMOUNT TO PRODUCT-TOTAL
         PERFORM PRINT-NEW-SALESMAN-LINE
         PERFORM READ-RECORD.
 *
 READ-RECORD.
     READ SALES-FILE
         AT END MOVE 'YES' TO END-OF-FILE-INDICATOR.
 *
 PRINT-NEW-SALESMAN-LINE.
     MOVE SPACES TO REPORT-LINE.
     MOVE SALESMAN-NO TO SALESMAN-NO-OUT.
     MOVE PRODUCT-NO TO PRODUCT-NO-OUT.
     MOVE SALES-AMOUNT TO SALES-AMOUNT-OUT.
     PERFORM PRINT-LINE.
 *
 PRINT-LINE.
     IF LINE-COUNTER = PAGE-SIZE
         WRITE REPORT-RECORD FROM REPORT-HEADING
             AFTER ADVANCING PAGE
         MOVE 1 TO LINE-COUNTER.
     WRITE REPORT-RECORD FROM REPORT-LINE
         AFTER ADVANCING 1 LINE.
     ADD 1 TO LINE-COUNTER.
/
 PROCESS-RECORD.
     IF SALESMAN-NO NOT = PREVIOUS-SALESMAN-NO
         PERFORM PROCESS-NEW-SALESMAN.
     IF SALESMAN-NO = PREVIOUS-SALESMAN-NO
         AND PRODUCT-NO NOT = PREVIOUS-PRODUCT-NO
         PERFORM PROCESS-NEW-PRODUCT.
     IF SALESMAN-NO = PREVIOUS-SALESMAN-NO
         AND PRODUCT-NO = PREVIOUS-PRODUCT-NO
         PERFORM PROCESS-REPORT-LINE.
     ADD SALES-AMOUNT TO PRODUCT-TOTAL.
 *
     PERFORM READ-RECORD.
 *
 PROCESS-NEW-SALESMAN.
     PERFORM PRINT-PRODUCT-TOTAL.
     PERFORM PRINT-SALESMAN-TOTAL.
     PERFORM PRINT-NEW-SALESMAN-LINE
     MOVE SALESMAN-NO TO PREVIOUS-SALESMAN-NO
     MOVE PRODUCT-NO TO PREVIOUS-PRODUCT-NO.
 *
 PRINT-PRODUCT-TOTAL.
     MOVE SPACES TO REPORT-LINE
     MOVE PRODUCT-TOTAL TO TOTAL-SALES-OUT
     PERFORM PRINT-LINE
     MOVE ZERO TO PRODUCT-TOTAL
     ADD PRODUCT-TOTAL TO SALESMAN-TOTAL.
 *
 PRINT-SALESMAN-TOTAL.
     MOVE SPACES TO REPORT-LINE
     MOVE SALESMAN-TOTAL TO TOTAL-SALES-OUT
     PERFORM PRINT-LINE
     MOVE ZERO TO SALESMAN-TOTAL.
 *
 PROCESS-NEW-PRODUCT.
     PERFORM PRINT-PRODUCT-TOTAL.
     PERFORM PRINT-NEW-PRODUCT-LINE.
     MOVE PRODUCT-NO TO PREVIOUS-PRODUCT-NO.
 *
 PRINT-NEW-PRODUCT-LINE.
     MOVE SPACES TO REPORT-LINE
     MOVE PRODUCT-NO TO PRODUCT-NO-OUT
     MOVE SALES-AMOUNT TO SALES-AMOUNT-OUT
     PERFORM PRINT-LINE.
 *
 PROCESS-REPORT-LINE.
     MOVE SPACES TO REPORT-LINE
     MOVE SALES-AMOUNT TO SALES-AMOUNT-OUT
     PERFORM PRINT-LINE.
 *
 PRINT-LAST-TOTALS.
     PERFORM PRINT-PRODUCT-TOTAL.
     PERFORM PRINT-SALESMAN-TOTAL.
```

FIGURE 9-13 (**continued**)

product might not change, since we assume the typical case where totals are desired for each product *within* a salesperson.

The kind of report logic illustrated here is referred to as involving *control breaks*. A change in report format occurs when we have a *break* in the sequence of products within a salesperson. This very common control break logic is described further in Chapter 16: "The Report Writer Feature." This deals explicitly with the topic of sequential report generation through the use of special instructions available in COBOL.

Figure 9–12 presents the structure chart for this sample program, while Figure 9–13 presents the listing of the program. Exercise 9.6 at the end of the chapter asks for a modification to the program.

EXERCISES

9.1 Modify the sample update program in Figure 9–9 so that transaction error records are saved on a tape (or disk) file and are printed after the update process has been completed. In a process chart form, we should have:

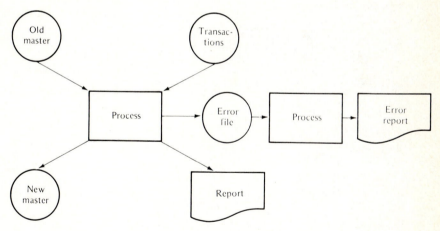

9.2 Modify the sample update program in Figure 9–9 so that during the update process only those master records that were in some way altered are output on the printer. Where appropriate, show both the old and the new record for visual reference and comparison. If a record is added or deleted, however, only one master record is relevant. The report should have the following format:

```
┌──────────────────────────────────────────────┐
│         CHANGES TO CUSTOMER MASTER             │
│                 MM/DD/YR                       │
│                                                │
│  RECORD                    ACTION              │
│  ─────────────────────────────────────────    │
│  OLD: xxxxxxxxxxxxxx       CHANGED ADDRESS     │
│  NEW: xxxxxxxxxxxxxx                            │
│                                                │
│  NEW: xxxxxxxxxxxxxx       NEW RECORD ADDED     │
│                                                │
│  OLD: xxxxxxxxxxxxxx       DELETED RECORD       │
│                                                │
│  OLD: xxxxxxxxxxxxxx       CHANGED NAME         │
│  NEW: xxxxxxxxxxxxxx                            │
└──────────────────────────────────────────────┘
```

9.3 Write a program to update a simplified payroll master file. The master is sequenced on employee number, and records have the following layout:

Employee number	PIC 9(5)
Employee name	PIC X(20)
Pay rate	PIC 9(2)V99
Witholding rate	PIC V99
Year-to-date gross pay	PIC 9(5)V99
Year-to-date net pay	PIC 9(5)V99

The transaction records are of two types. The first type contains changes to the master file and has the following layout:

Employee number	PIC 9(5)
Employee name	PIC X(20)
Transaction code	PIC 9
1 = Create new record	
2 = Delete record	
3 = Change pay rate	
Pay rate	PIC 9(2)V99
Withholding rate	PIC V99

The second type of transaction record is *daily* time cards that have the following layout:

Employee number	PIC 9(5)
Employee name	PIC X(20)
Transaction code	PIC 9
4 = Time card	
Hours worked	PIC 9(2)V99

In addition to the updated master file, the program should produce a printed report as follows:

EMPLOYEE NO.	EMPLOYEE NAME	THIS WEEK		YEAR-TO-DATE	
		GROSS	NET	GROSS	NET
.	.	.	.	.	.
.	.	.	.	.	.
.	.	.	.	.	.
TOTAL PAYROLL		XXXX	XXXX	XXXX	XXXX

For each employee, this week's gross pay is computed by multiplying pay-rate times the hours worked for the whole week (remember that time cards are daily records). If the hours worked exceed 40, time-and-a-half is paid for the hours over 40; however, no employee should work more than 10 hours in a given day nor more than 48 hours in a given week. Either condition would be an error, and the employee is not paid. Instead, an error message is printed.

Net pay is computed by multiplying gross pay by the withholding rate and subtracting this amount from the gross pay.

The year-to-date gross and net on the report include the addition of this week's gross and net pay to the previously accumulated amounts.

9.4 A company maintains inventory data on magnetic tape. The master file is sorted on part number and contains the following types of data for each item held in inventory:

FIELD	SIZE
Part number	5 numeric positions
Part name	15 alphanumeric positions
Quantity	5 numeric positions

For the sake of simplicity, there are two types of transactions: receipts and issues. Each transaction is recorded on a punched card of the following format:

FIELD	SIZE
Part number	5 numeric positions
Transaction code	1 numeric position
1 = receipt	
2 = issue	
Quantity	5 numeric positions

Batches of transaction cards are accumulated and then processed to update the master file and to print a report that lists each part number, name, previous quantity balance, and new balance. When the transaction code is 1, the quantity is added; if the code is 2, the quantity is subtracted.

a Write a program to create the master file, on tape, from data on punched cards. Sample input for the master tape is as follows:

```
035611/2 HP EL MOTOR02000
10513TRANSFORMER     08000
30561GEAR TRAIN-A    07890
30562GEAR TRAIN-B    10250
30564GEAR TRAIN-C    04650
30579GEAR TRAIN-G    08529
40100STEEL PLATE-1A  06099
40110STEEL PLATE-2A  00852
40120STEEL PLATE-3A  00996
40130STEEL PLATE-4A  01250
40140STEEL PLACE-5B  02899
40150STEEL PLATE-3C  08192
51000BRASS FTNGS-A   12695
51020BRASS FTNGS-B   08569
51030BRASS FTNGS-C   09992
60256BALL BEARING-A201695
60257BALL BEARING-A302561
60258BALL BEARING-A410883
60259BALL BEARING-A513429
60260BALL BEARING-A608866
60261BALL BEARING-A706219
```

b Write a program to update the master file, given a deck of transaction cards. The program should perform a sequence check to see that the cards are in the same sequence as the tape records. It is possible that some items may have no corresponding transactions, but no transactions are present for items not on the master tape. Sample input for transactions is as follows (the master tape input is the same as shown in part **a**):

```
10513200200
10513110000
30562200500
30562200800
30562200900
```

```
30564108000
40100112000
40100204000
40100203000
40140110000
51030200200
51030200965
60261200600
60261200500
60261200900
60261104000
```

Sample output is on the following page.

9.5 The county assessor's office maintains a tape file of property owners, in the following (simplified) format:

Lot number	9-digit code
Owner name	26 alphanumeric characters
Assessed valuation	8-digit field, including 2 decimal places

An update run involves reading card records and creating an updated tape file. The input cards have the following format:

Lot number	9-digit code
Code	1-digit code
1 = change owner name	
2 = change assessed valuation	
3 = change both owner and valuation	
4 = add to tax rolls	
9 = remove from tax rolls	
Owner name	26 characters
Assessed valuation	8 digits in dollars and cents

If a code of 1 is used, nothing is punched in the assessed valuation field. If a code of 2 is used, the owner field is blank. A code of 9 implies that the card is blank from column 11 on.

The printer report should have the following approximate layout:

LOT NUMBER	OWNER	ASSESSED VALUE	NEW OWNER	NEW ASSESSMENT	OFF ROLLS
XXXXXXXXX	XXXXXXXX	$ XXXXXX.XX	XXXXXXXXX	$ XXXXXX.XX	
XXXXXXXXX	XXXXXXXX	XXXX.XX			***

ITEM NUMBER	PART NAME	PREVIOUS BALANCE	NEW BALANCE
03561	1/2 HP EL MOTOR	2000	2000
10513	TRANSFORMER	8000	17800
30561	GEAR TRAIN—A	7890	7890
30562	GEAR TRAIN—B	10250	8050
30564	GEAR TRAIN—C	4650	12650
30579	GEAR TRAIN—G	8529	8529
40100	STEEL PLATE—1A	6099	11099
40110	STEEL PLATE—2A	0852	0852
40120	STEEL PLATE—3A	0996	0996
40130	STEEL PLATE—4A	1250	1250
40140	STEEL PLATE—5B	2899	12899
40150	STEEL PLATE—3C	8192	8192
51000	BRASS FTNGS—A	12695	12695
51020	BRASS FTNGS—B	8569	8569
51030	BRASS FTNGS—C	9992	8827
60256	BALL BEARING—A2	1695	1695
60257	BALL BEARING—A3	2561	2561
60258	BALL BEARING—A4	10883	10883
60259	BALL BEARING—A5	13429	13429
60260	BALL BEARING—A6	8866	8866
60261	BALL BEARING—A7	6219	8219

Whenever an item is eliminated, it is signaled by three asterisks in the OFF ROLLS column.

Write a program to update such a file. The program should check for correct sequence in the card and tape records and for possibly erroneous codes in the card.

The sample master file is as follows:

LOT NUMBER	OWNER NAME	ASSESSED VALUATION
000150000	JENKING, ANTHONY	10,872.00
000180000	ANDREWS, JULIA	256,237.00
000290000	THOMAS, THEODORE	162,116.00
000350000	MCDONALD, DONNA	769,276.00
000720000	MARTIN, JANE	99,998.00
001050000	RICHARDSON, PETER	820,600.00
001120000	SILVA, ROBIN	959,999.00

Sample card transaction records are:

LOT NUMBER	CODE	OWNER NAME	ASSESSED VALUATION
000180000	1	ANDREWS, THOMAS	
000290000	2		300,000.00
000720000	3	STEINMAN, WILLA	100,000.00
001050000	9		

Sample output is as follows: Lack of space prevents showing the first name on the same line as the last name in the OWNER and NEW OWNER columns; however, include this information on one line in your output.

LOT NUMBER	OWNER	ASSESSED VALUE	NEW OWNER	NEW ASSESSMENT	OFF ROLLS
00015000	JENKING, ANTHONY	$ 10,872.00			
000180000	ANDREWS, JULIA	$256,237.00	ANDREWS, THOMAS		
000290000	THOMAS, THEODORE	$162,116.00		$300,000.00	
000350000	MCDONALD, DONNA	$769,276.00			
000720000	MARTIN, JANE	$ 99,998.00	STEINMAN, WILLA	$100,000.00	
001050000	RICHARDSON, PETER	$820,600.00			***
001120000	SILVA, ROBIN	$959,999.00			

9.6   Modify the sample sequential report program in Figure 9-13 to include control breaks for a third category: Department. Assume that the department-name is an alphanumeric field in columns 1-10 of each input record.

The data are sorted in ascending sequence of product within salesperson and salesperson within department. A new page should be printed at the start of a new department.

Totals should be printed for each product, for each salesperson, and for each department.

10
Sorting and merging sequential files

COBOL SORT FEATURE

SORT STATEMENT FORMATS

FILE MERGING

EXERCISES

COBOL SORT FEATURE

In our description of sequential file maintenance in the preceding chapter, it was evident that sequential files must be sorted in sequence. The basis for the sequence is dictated by management needs. For example, in the processing of sales transactions, analysis may be required by product, by date, and by geographic area. In order to produce such a report, the data file has to be sorted so that the data are sequenced in the desired order.

Since file sorting frequently is required in maintaining an information system, the COBOL language incorporates a sort feature that makes it possible to accomplish this operation with minimal programming. The programmer need not be concerned with the details of any sort algorithm in using this feature, but may simply specify the files to be sorted, the sort key (or keys) to be used, and any special procedures for the handling of files before or after the sort. We illustrate here the COBOL sort feature by means of two examples.

EXAMPLE 1

Assume that we have a tape file with the following record description in the DATA DIVISION:

```
01  INTAPE-RECORD.
      02  ACCOUNT-NUMBER      PICTURE 9(8).
      02  NAME               PICTURE X(20).
      02  TRANSACTION-DATE.
          03  DAY-OF-YEAR     PICTURE 999.
          03  YEAR            PICTURE 99.
      02  OTHER-DATA          PICTURE X(71).
```

Suppose we wish to sort the file in ascending sequence according to ACCOUNT-NUMBER and in descending sequence according to YEAR. That is, for each account, all records are to be arranged from the most recent to the least recent YEAR. Also assume that the sorted file is called SORTED-FILE and is to be available on tape unit 3. The sorting process can be portrayed as involving three files, INPUT-FILE, SORT-FILE, and SORTED-FILE, as follows:

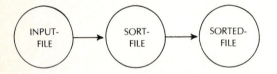

The sorting operation will create a need for more work tapes than the single SORT-FILE implied in the diagram above. Because the sorting procedure is preprogrammed, the programmer need not be concerned about the detail of the SORT-FILE; however, both the programmer and the computer operator should be aware that additional tape units should be assigned to the sorting task.

Figure 10-1 presents the COBOL program that can be used to sort the file described in this example problem. In the ENVIRONMENT DIVISION, notice that three files are identified in the SELECT statements. Tape files are involved in the present problem, but the files could have been stored just as well on disk, for example.

In the DATA DIVISION, the INPUT-FILE is described in the usual fashion. Notice, however, the SD (Sort Description) entry for the SORT-FILE. The level indicator SD indicates that this is the file to be used in conjunction with the sort routine. Notice also the absence of the LABEL RECORD clause. Some compilers permit the use of this clause, but ANS COBOL excludes the option. The record description in the DATA DIVISION is straightforward and follows the usual format. The SORTED-FILE is an ordinary file. Notice that we chose to simplify the record description for this file by defining one

```
     IDENTIFICATION DIVISION.
     PROGRAM-ID. SORT1.
*
     REMARKS.  THIS PROGRAM ILLUSTRATES SORTING A SEQUENTIAL
          FILE CALLED INPUT-FILE AND MAKING THE SORTED FILE
          AVAILABLE IN SORTED-FILE.
*
     ENVIRONMENT DIVISION.
*
     CONFIGURATION SECTION.
     SOURCE-COMPUTER. ABC-480.
     OBJECT-COMPUTER. ABC-480.
*
     INPUT-OUTPUT SECTION.
     FILE-CONTROL.
          SELECT INPUT-FILE ASSIGN           TO CARD-READER.
          SELECT SORT-FILE     ASSIGN TO SEQ-DEVICE-A.
          SELECT SORTED-FILE ASSIGN           TO PRINTER.
*
     DATA DIVISION.
*
     FILE SECTION.
     FD   INPUT-FILE LABEL RECORD OMITTED
                     DATA RECORD IS INTAPE-RECORD.
     01   INTAPE-RECORD.
          02   ACCOUNT-NUMBER        PICTURE 9(8).
          02   NAME                  PICTURE X(20).
          02   TRANSACTION-DATE.
               03   DAY-OF-YEAR      PICTURE 999.
               03   YEAR            PICTURE 99.
          02 OTHER-DATA              PICTURE X(71).
*
     SD   SORT-WORK-FILE DATA RECORD IS WORK-RECORD.
     01   WORK-RECORD.
          02   ACCOUNT-NUMBER-S      PICTURE 9(8).
          02   NAME-S                PICTURE X(20).
          02   TRANSACTION-DATE-S.
               03   DAY-OF-YEAR      PICTURE 999.
               03   YEAR-S          PICTURE 99.
          02   OTHER-DATA            PICTURE X(71).
*
     FD   SORTED-FILE LABEL RECORD OMITTED
                      DATA RECORD IS SORTED-RECORD.
     01   SORTED-RECORD             PICTURE X(104).
*
     PROCEDURE DIVISION.
     SORTING-PARAGRAPH.
          SORT SORT-WORK-FILE
               ON ASCENDING KEY ACCOUNT-NUMBER-S
               DESCENDING KEY YEAR-S
               USING INPUT-FILE
               GIVING SORTED-FILE.
*
          STOP RUN.
```

FIGURE 10-1   SAMPLE SORT PROGRAM FOR EXAMPLE 1.

overall PICTURE. Since the program is concerned only with sorting the file, there is no need to describe the parts of the records that constitute this file.

The relevant PROCEDURE DIVISION is simple and consists of just one paragraph. The SORT verb is very powerful in that the programmer need only specify the sort keys and the source and destination of the file records. The statement SORT SORT-FILE identifies the name of the file to be sorted—which should be the same file introduced by an SD entry in the DATA DIVISION. The ASCENDING KEY ACCOUNT-NUMBER-S clause specifies that the file is to be sorted in ascending ACCOUNT-NUMBER-S sequence. The DESCENDING KEY YEAR-S clause specifies that, within each ACCOUNT-NUMBER-S, we wish to sort in descending sequence with respect to the values contained in the YEAR-S field. Keep in mind that the key written first is the principal basis for the sort. Other keys are of decreasing sorting significance as we proceed from one to the next. For example, consider the following KEY clauses:

ASCENDING KEY STATE-NAME
ASCENDING KEY COUNTY-NAME
ASCENDING KEY CITY-NAME

The order of listing of these clauses indicates that STATE-NAME is the principal basis for the sort. Put another way, CITY-NAME will be sorted within COUNTY-NAME, and COUNTY-NAME will be sorted within STATE-NAME. Note that the sort keys are written according to the desired order of the sort, and not according to the order in which the keys appear in the record. For this example, it could very well be that the three fields used as sort keys are in the following physical order in the record: CITY-NAME, STATE-NAME, COUNTY-NAME.

The USING INPUT-FILE clause in Figure 10–1 specifies the file that is the source of the records, while the GIVING SORTED-FILE clause simply specifies the file on which the sort output is to be recorded. Finally, note that in the present example the programmer does *not* OPEN or CLOSE any of the three files involved. The use of the SORT verb automatically takes care of such procedures.

EXAMPLE 2

We now illustrate use of the COBOL sort feature with a more complex data processing task. Suppose we want to read a set of punched-card records, add a field to each record to indicate its sequential order, sort the file, store the sorted file on magnetic tape, and, finally, print the sorted tape as the output of the program. Figure 10–2 presents the COBOL program designed to accomplish this task. Notice that there are four files, called CARD-FILE, SORT-FILE, SORTED-FILE, and PRINT-FILE. DATA DIVISION entries follow the usual format, except for the use of SD to identify the SORT-FILE as the sort file, as was the case in the preceding example. In the present example, the WORKING-STORAGE SECTION is used to form the SEQUENCE-NUMBER.

In the PROCEDURE DIVISION, we first specify that we wish to sort the SORT-FILE on ASCENDING KEY NAME. Thus, the NAME field is the sort key. INPUT PROCEDURE IS READING-SEQUENCING indicates that records will become available to the SORT-FILE according to instructions contained in a section called READING-SEQUENCING. The first paragraph in the READING-SEQUENCING SECTION, called SET-UP, serves to open the

FIGURE 10-2   SAMPLE SORT PROGRAM FOR EXAMPLE 2.

```
       IDENTIFICATION DIVISION.
       PROGRAM-ID. SORT2.
*
 *ENVIRONMENT DIVISION.

       CONFIGURATION SECTION.
       SOURCE-COMPUTER. ABC-480.
       OBJECT-COMPUTER. ABC-480.

       INPUT-OUTPUT SECTION.
       FILE-CONTROL.
           SELECT  CARD-FILE ASSIGN    TO CARD-READER.
           SELECT SORT-FILE ASSIGN TO   DISK-DEVICE-A.
           SELECT SORTED-FILE  ASSIGN TO DISK-DEVICE-B.
           SELECT  PRINT-FILE ASSIGN   TO PRINTER.
*
       DATA DIVISION.
       FILE SECTION.
*
       FD  CARD-FILE LABEL RECORD OMITTED
           DATA RECORD IS CARD-RECORD.
       01  CARD-RECORD.
           02  FILLER
           02  CARD-NAME                 PICTURE X(10).
           02  FILLER                    PICTURE X(15).
           02  DATA-TO-BE-INSERTED       PICTURE X(51).
*                                        PICTURE 9999.
       SD  SORT-FILE DATA RECORD IS SORT-RECORD.
       01  SORT-RECORD.
           02  DATA-FROM-CARD.
               03 FILLER            PICTURE X(10).
               03 NAME              PICTURE X(15).
               03 FILLER            PICTURE X(55).
*
       FD  SORTED-FILE LABEL RECORD OMITTED
           DATA RECORD IS SORTED-RECORD.
       01  SORTED-RECORD                 PICTURE X(80).
*
       FD  PRINT-FILE LABEL RECORD OMITTED
           DATA RECORD IS PRINT-LINE.
       01  PRINT-LINE.
           02  OUT-LINE                  PICTURE X(132).
*
       WORKING-STORAGE SECTION.
       01  END-OF-DATA          PIC XXX.
       01  SEQUENCE-NUMBER      PIC 9(4).
/
       PROCEDURE DIVISION.
       MAIN-SORT-ROUTINE.
           MOVE ZERO TO SEQUENCE-NUMBER.
*
           SORT SORT-FILE ASCENDING KEY NAME
               INPUT   PROCEDURE IS READING-SEQUENCING
               OUTPUT  PROCEDURE IS RETURNING-PRINTING.

           STOP RUN.

       READING-SEQUENCING SECTION.
       SET-UP.
           OPEN INPUT CARD-FILE.
           MOVE 'NO' TO END-OF-DATA.
           PERFORM READ-DATA
           PERFORM SEQ-RELEASE
                   UNTIL END-OF-DATA = 'YES'
           CLOSE CARD-FILE
           GO TO END-OF-SECTION.

       READ-DATA.
           READ CARD-FILE RECORD
                AT END MOVE 'YES' TO END-OF-DATA.

       SEQ-RELEASE.
           ADD 1 TO SEQUENCE-NUMBER.
           MOVE SEQUENCE-NUMBER TO DATA-TO-BE-INSERTED.
           RELEASE SORT-RECORD FROM CARD-RECORD.
           PERFORM READ-DATA.

       END-OF-SECTION.
           EXIT.
```

(continued)

```
RETURNING-PRINTING SECTION.
SET-UP.
    OPEN OUTPUT SORTED-FILE
                PRINT-FILE
    MOVE "NO" TO END-OF-DATA
    PERFORM RETURN-DATA
    PERFORM WRITE-DATA
            UNTIL END-OF-DATA = "YES".
    CLOSE SORTED-FILE PRINT-FILE
    GO TO END-OF-SECTION.
RETURN-DATA.
    RETURN SORT-FILE RECORD INTO SORTED-RECORD
            AT END MOVE "YES" TO END-OF-DATA.
WRITE-DATA.
    WRITE PRINT-LINE FROM SORTED-RECORD
    WRITE SORTED-RECORD.
    PERFORM RETURN-DATA.
END-OF-SECTION.
    EXIT.
```

FIGURE 10-2 (Continued)

CARD-FILE as input. Then we enter a loop involving the SEQ-RELEASE paragraph. Each record is read, and in each case a four-digit sequence number is assigned to the field called DATA-TO-BE-INSERTED. Then we use the RELEASE SORT-RECORD FROM CARD-RECORD statement. This simply says to move the contents of CARD-RECORD to SORT-RECORD and then to write the SORT-RECORD on its file. The RELEASE command thus can be thought of as a specialized form of the WRITE instruction.

The loop terminates when the last record is read, at which point the program branches to END-OF-SECTION, after CARD-FILE is closed. The END-OF-SECTION paragraph is the last paragraph of the READING-SEQUENCING SECTION, and is indicated by the EXIT verb. Recall that the execution of the READING-SEQUENCING SECTION was initiated by execution of the INPUT PROCEDURE statement in the SORT statement. In fact, the INPUT PRO-CEDURE statement has the same effect as if we had written PERFORM READING-SEQUENCING. Program execution branches to that section, and, when it is completed, the next statement is executed. The next statement in the present example is OUTPUT PROCEDURE IS RETURNING-PRINTING, which indicates the name of another section; therefore, program execution then branches to the RETURNING-PRINTING SECTION.

The first paragraph of the RETURNING-PRINTING SECTION is the SET-UP, which opens the two output files. Then we PERFORM RETURN-DATA and enter a loop involving WRITE-DATA. The RETURN SORT-FILE RECORD INTO SORTED-RECORD statement is simply a special form of saying, "Read a record from the SORT-FILE and move it to the SORTED-RECORD." Notice the use of AT END, which parallels the same clause in the READ verb. After each record is RETURNed, we employ an implicit move (FROM SORTED-RECORD) and we WRITE PRINT-LINE. Finally, we WRITE SORTED-RECORD on tape. The process is repeated until the END-OF-DATA = 'YES' condition holds. The SET-UP paragraph closes the files and END-OF-SECTION is executed next. Program control then returns to the statement that follows the statement, OUTPUT PROCEDURE IS RETURNING-PRINTING, because this is where the branching occurred. The statement in question is STOP RUN and signifies the logical end of the program.

Thus, in this example we have demonstrated that, by using the INPUT PROCEDURE or the OUTPUT PROCEDURE option of the SORT verb, we can branch to another section of the program and perform any required data processing. By this approach, the sorting function can be combined with any other program processing task. Frequently, for instance, it may be desirable to perform a sort in the "middle" of a processing job. The sort does not have to be considered a separate job; rather, it can be embedded in the larger job.

REVIEW

1   The COBOL language feature by which a file can be sorted without having to write a sorting algorithm as such is called the _____ feature.

sort

2   In order to use the sort feature, the programmer must specify the _____ to be sorted and the _____ to be used as the basis for the sort.

file; key (or keys)

3   If a file is to be sorted on the basis of more than one key, the key that is written [first / last] is the principal basis for the sort.

first

4   In the second example problem in this section, two options of the SORT verb were used to branch to other parts of the program in order to perform required processing tasks. These were the _____ and _____ options of the SORT verb.

INPUT PROCEDURE; OUTPUT
PROCEDURE

SORT STATEMENT FORMATS

We now consider the COBOL format specifications that enable a programmer to use the sort feature. These format requirements are presented by division of the COBOL program.

IDENTIFICATION DIVISION

The usual format specifications are unaffected by the use of the SORT statement.

ENVIRONMENT DIVISION

In the FILE-CONTROL section we have the following:

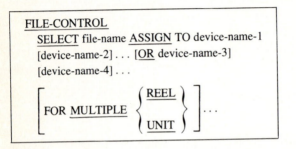

The difference from the FILE-CONTROL formats previously discussed is the presence of the OR option. This option allows the output of the sort procedure to be available on one of the devices either preceding or following the OR. The programmer does not know which device it will be at the time of writing the program. The compiler automatically inserts instructions such that at execution time the program keeps track of the hardware device on which the sorted file was written, and, when the program references the file, the correct device is addressed.

In the I-O-CONTROL paragraph, the format associated with use of the SORT option is:

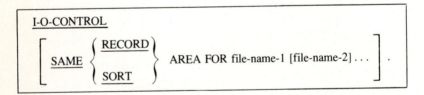

The SAME RECORD AREA option allows the sharing of the same storage location by several files, as indicated by the file-names that follow the clause. When this option is used, only one record is available at a given time, even though more than one file may have been opened. The reason for using this option is to save storage space. If the SAME SORT AREA clause is used, at least one of the files involved must be a sort file. Typically, this clause is used when more than one file is to be sorted. Some compilers treat this clause as a comment, since they provide their own space-saving routines.

DATA DIVISION
In the DATA DIVISION, the relevant format is:

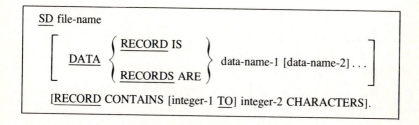

The level indicator SD identifies the beginning of a sort file sort description. Notice that, other than the SD, the file description has the usual format. Notice also that there is no BLOCK CONTAINS option. Whether or not any blocking is possible or desirable is determined automatically by the preprogrammed sort routine.

PROCEDURE DIVISION
The SORT verb is the basic verb in the SORT option. The format is as follows:

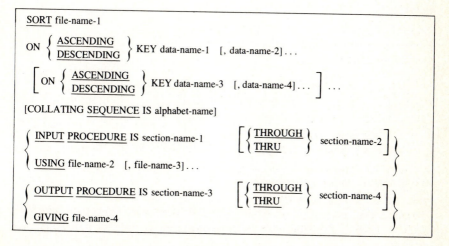

The verb SORT always is required. File-name-1 is the file designated in an SD entry in the DATA DIVISION. At least one KEY has to be specified. If more than one sort key is used and all are ascending (or all are descending), they can be written in the following form:

SORT file-name ON ASCENDING KEY ACCOUNT, NAME, YEAR.

Here we have specified an ascending sort by ACCOUNT, by NAME within ACCOUNT, and by YEAR within NAME. Or, we could have used the word ASCENDING (or DESCENDING) in conjunction with each KEY, as follows:

SORT file-name ON ASCENDING KEY ACCOUNT
    ON ASCENDING KEY NAME
    ON ASCENDING KEY YEAR.

The INPUT PROCEDURE and the OUTPUT PROCEDURE options refer to a section-name or a set of consecutive sections when the THRU option is exercised. The paragraphs in such sections specify the processing tasks to be performed prior to the sort (INPUT PROCEDURE) or after the sort (OUTPUT PROCEDURE). If the INPUT PROCEDURE is used, the verb RELEASE must be used somewhere in that procedure. If the OUTPUT PROCEDURE is used, the verb RETURN must be used somewhere in that procedure. The USING file-name-2 option is used when records are made available to the sort from file-name-2 without any processing. The GIVING file-name-4 option specifies that the sorted file is to be recorded on file-name-4.

The COLLATING SEQUENCE option allows the programmer to specify a particular collating sequence. In the SPECIAL-NAMES paragraph of the ENVIRONMENT DIVISION, one can specify an alphabet name. For instance, we could have written:

SPECIAL-NAMES.
    THEIR-SET IS STANDARD-1
    OUR-SET IS NATIVE.

In this case, the alphabet name THEIR-SET is associated with the ANSI standard character code set and therefore with that collating sequence. NATIVE is a COBOL word and specifies the computer's own set. Other options also are available but are uncommon in use.

The RELEASE verb just discussed has the following format:

<u>RELEASE</u> record-name [<u>FROM</u> identifier].

The RELEASE verb can be used only in a section referenced by the INPUT PROCEDURE of a SORT verb. The record-name in this format refers to a record in the sort file. If the FROM option is used, the effect is to move the contents of identifier to the record-name and then to RELEASE. In effect, RELEASE is a specialized form of the WRITE verb.

The RETURN verb, which is used in conjunction with the OUTPUT PROCEDURE of a SORT verb, has the following format:

> RETURN file-name RECORD [INTO identifier]
> AT END imperative statement.

The RETURN verb has the effect of a READ verb. The file-name is the name of the sort file. When the INTO option is used, the effect is the same as execution of the longer instruction RETURN file-name MOVE record-name TO identifier. The AT END clause is required. The imperative statement identifies the processing to be performed after all the records have been returned from the sort file.

REVIEW

1   In the ENVIRONMENT DIVISION, the option that allows the output of the sort procedure to be available on one of several possible output devices is the _____ option.

OR

2   In the DATA DIVISION, the file to be sorted is identified by the level indicator _____.

SD (standing for Sort Description)

3   If the INPUT PROCEDURE option is used in conjunction with the SORT verb, designated processing is performed [before / after] the sort, and the verb _____ must be used somewhere in the procedure.

before; RELEASE

4   If the OUTPUT PROCEDURE option is used in conjunction with the SORT verb, designated processing is performed [before / after] the sort, and the verb _____ must be used somewhere in the procedure.

after; RETURN

5   The RELEASE verb can be considered a specialized form of the _____ verb, while the RETURN verb can be considered, a form of the _____ verb.

WRITE; READ

FILE MERGING

A very common data processing procedure is that of merging two or more files. Merging simply means combining two or more files into one. For example, a bank may create a tape file containing the day's transactions in customer number order on a daily basis. Then, end-of-month processing

```
FD   FIRST-QUARTER LABEL RECORDS STANDARD
                     DATA RECORD    SALES-HISTORY.
01   SALES-HISTORY.
     02   DEPT-NO      PIC 999.
     02   PROD-NO      PIC 99999.
     .
     .
     .

FD   SECOND-QUARTER . . .
     .
     .
     .

FD   THIRD-QUARTER . . .
     .
     .
     .

FD   FOURTH-QUARTER . . .
     .
     .
     .

FD   YEARLY LABEL RECORDS STANDARD
                     DATA RECORD    CUMULATIVE-SALES.
01   CUMULATIVE-SALES
     02   DEPT-NO      PIC 999.
     02   PROD-NO      PIC 99999.
     .
     .
     .

SD   MERGE-FILE DATA RECORD    MERGE-RECORD.
01   MERGE-RECORD.
     02   DEPARTMENT   PIC 999.
     02   PRODUCT      PIC 99999.
     .
     .
     .

PROCEDURE DIVISION.
     .
     .
     .

     MERGE MERGE-FILE ON ASCENDING KEY DEPARTMENT
                       ON ASCENDING KEY PRODUCT
              USING FIRST-QUARTER, SECOND-QUARTER,
                     THIRD-QUARTER, FOURTH-QUARTER
              GIVING YEARLY.
```

FIGURE 10-3   OUTLINE FOR A MERGE PROGRAM.

requires that the daily tapes be combined into one, so that the entire month's transactions for each customer are accumulated.

Because it is frequently needed and of great importance, merging is implemented in COBOL as a very high-level language feature, in the form of the MERGE statement.

Let us consider an example. A business firm generates a sales history file at the end of the quarter. Each record in the file contains a department number and a product number, as well as many other fields. This quarterly file is sorted, with department number being the major sort key and product number being the minor sort key. At the end of the year we are interested in merging the four quarterly sales history files into one. Figure 10-3 presents an outline of the relevant parts of the program. Four files are introduced with an FD entry. Then the SD introduces the file to be used for the merge, which in this example is called MERGE-FILE. Notice that the data record description for this file corresponds to the record description of the four quarterly files. The merge statement in the PROCEDURE DIVISION references the SD file and specifies that the merge will proceed on the basis of DEPARTMENT being the major key and PRODUCT being the minor key. As is the case with the SORT verb, the keys decrease in significance in the order written. The ASCENDING option specifies that the next record of each of the four quarterly files will be examined, and the record sent to the output file next is the one that has the highest department number, or the highest product number if the department numbers are equal. If all four records have identical department and product values, then the records will be sent to the output file in the order in which the file names are written in the merge statement.

The USING clause specifies the files to be merged, which are the input files. These files must be closed at the time of merging. Opening is carried out by the MERGE statement in an implicit fashion.

The GIVING clause specifies the output file. This file will contain the combined set of the four quarterly files. This new file will be in the same sort order as the quarterly files. It should be emphasized that in order for the merge process to take place correctly the input files must be in the sort order indicated by the KEY specifications.

The general format of MERGE is as follows:

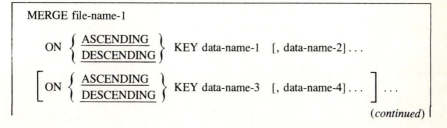

```
MERGE file-name-1

     ON  { ASCENDING  }  KEY data-name-1  [, data-name-2] ...
         { DESCENDING }

   [ ON  { ASCENDING  }  KEY data-name-3  [, data-name-4] ... ] ...
         { DESCENDING }
```
                                                              (continued)

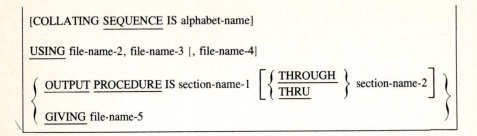

The OUTPUT PROCEDURE option parallels the one available with the SORT verb. A RETURN statement is used within the output procedure to make merged records available for processing, just as is the case with SORT. Unlike SORT, MERGE does not include any input procedure options; thus, the input files must be in proper form for merging before a MERGE instruction is executed.

REVIEW

1   The COBOL language feature by which monthly summaries of transactions can be combined to create an annual summary is the _____ statement.

MERGE

2   If 12 monthly summaries are to be combined to form an annual summary, then the number of FD entries required in the associated MERGE program is _____ (number).

13

3   In order for the merge process to take place correctly, it [is / is not] necessary that each input file be in the exact sort order indicated by the KEY specifications.

is

EXERCISES

10.1   A sort file has been defined as SORT-FILE, and, in part, its data division entries include:

```
02   COURSE-CODE    PIC XXX.
02   COLLEGE        PIC 99.
02   COURSE-NAME    PIC X(6).
```

Using the following data, write a SORT statement that could cause the sorted data shown. The original data come from CARD-FILE, and we want to have the sorted data in TAPE-FILE. Be sure to specify which are the major, intermediate, and minor sort keys.

ORIGINAL DATA	SORTED DATA
CIS20BILL	MGT10JILL
CIS30LINDA	QBA10BRENDA
QBA10BRENDA	CIS20MARY
CIS30XAVIER	CIS20JOHN
MGT10JILL	CIS20BILL
CIS20JOHN	CIS30XAVIER
CIS20MARY	CIS30LINDA

10.2 Using any data file available, write a program incorporating the COBOL sort feature to sort a file. For example, you could modify any of the exercises at the end of Chapter 9 to sort the master file or the transaction file in the required order.

10.3 Consider the following to be the contents of the four quarterly files discussed in the merging example in this chapter. Show the content of the output file.

FIRST QUARTER	SECOND QUARTER	THIRD QUARTER	FOURTH QUARTER
345 12345	123 00112	345 56111	931 00001
345 25936	987 56111		999 99999
619 01110			

10.4 Using any two sorted data files, write a program incorporating the MERGE feature to combine them into one file.

11

Basic table handling

INTRODUCTION

A table, like a file, is a collection of logically related entries. Examples are tax rates for different municipalities in a metropolitan area, commission rates for different product classes, and income tax rates for different levels of income and numbers of dependents. Such data are normally short enough to be placed in central storage and thus constitute a table. Table handling is fundamental to data processing. COBOL recognizes this fact and includes specialized instructions for table definition and manipulation.

This chapter is concerned with the basic concepts and methods for processing tables of data. The chapter that follows presents more advanced methods and language features for table handling.

SUBSCRIPTING AND THE OCCURS CLAUSE

A great deal of the documentation in COBOL derives from the use of appropriate data-names, that is, names that provide a direct clue to the type of data contained in the named storage location. There are situations, however, when practicality dictates that we dispense with the use of such names. For example, suppose we are processing data on the average income per household in each of the 50 states. If we chose to name the average income for each state uniquely, we could have such data names as ALABAMA-INCOME, ALASKA-INCOME, and so on, for a total of 50 names. It is easy to imagine the problems that this practice would cause in the PROCEDURE DIVISION. For example, 50 MOVE statements would be required before the results could be printed.

The use of tables and subscripts is a programming feature that is particularly useful in such situations. A table is simply a set of values stored in consecutive storage locations and assigned one data-name. Reference to specific entries in the table is made by the use of the one name along with a subscript that identifies the location of the particular entry. Entries in a one-dimensional table are numbered sequentially 1, 2, 3, . . . , on to the last. Thus, in our example of the average household income for the 50 states, imagine that we have a table of 50 entries. If the entries are arranged alphabetically and we wish to reference the average income for Arizona, the subscript will have a value of 3. Similarly, the subscripts for Washington and Wyoming will be 49 and 50, respectively. Use of the OCCURS clause in conjunction with the PICTURE clause enables the programmer to set up tables so that reference can be made to entire tables or individual values in tables by means of subscripts. A DATA DIVISION entry involving an OCCURS clause includes the data-name assigned to the table, the number of dimensions (up to three), the number of entries in each dimension, and the field characteristics of the entries. In this section, we consider one-dimensional tables only, such as the one for the average household income in the 50 states; in the next section we discuss two- and three-dimensional tables.

Assume that the data for average income is contained in a WORKING-STORAGE table, although it could be a FILE SECTION table just as well. Thus, we have:

```
WORKING-STORAGE SECTION.
01   . . .
01   . . .
01   STATE-INCOME-TABLE.
     02   AVERAGE-INCOME OCCURS 50 TIMES      PICTURE 9(6)V99.
```

The OCCURS 50 TIMES clause sets up a table in storage that has the following conceptual structure:

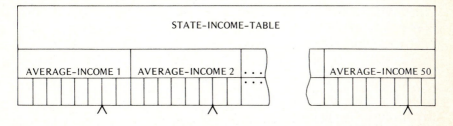

Execution of the PROCEDURE DIVISION statement MOVE STATE-INCOME-TABLE . . . will result in the entire table of 50 fields being moved. In order to move (or otherwise process) a single field or entry in the table, the subscript is included in parentheses and separated from the name by a space, as follows: MOVE AVERAGE-INCOME (12) TO . . . . This statement, of course, refers to the twelfth table entry.

The subscript may be a variable instead of a constant, but it always must be an integer (whole number). To understand the need for a subscript that is a variable, consider the following example. Suppose that some records have the following layout:

```
01   CARD.
     02   STATE-NUMBER      PICTURE 99.
     02   INCOME            PICTURE 9(6)V99.
```

Thus, the value in columns 1–2 is the number of the state when the states are listed alphabetically. The value in columns 3–10 is the average household income for that state. If the cards have not been arranged alphabetically, the following statement can be used to insert the income figure in the appropriate place in the table after the card has been read:

MOVE INCOME TO AVERAGE-INCOME (STATE-NUMBER)

As a result of this statement, if the state number were 49, the income value would be inserted in the forty-ninth entry of the average income table.

The OCCURS clause need not be used alone in a record; other reference entries may be included as well. For example, the record might have been structured as follows:

```
01   STATE-INCOME-TABLE.
     02   AVERAGE-INCOME OCCURS 50 TIMES      PICTURE 9(6)V99.
     02   NATIONAL-AVERAGE                    PICTURE 9(6)V99.
```

Notice, however, that STATE-INCOME-TABLE now refers to more than the table of 50 entries. If we want to make specific reference to the table of 50 entries, we will have to write something like this:

```
01  STATE-INCOME-TABLE.
    02  AV-TABLE.
        03  AVERAGE-INCOME OCCURS 50 TIMES    PICTURE 9(6)V99.
    02  NATIONAL-AVERAGE                      PICTURE 9(6)V99.
```

As a further illustration of a one-dimensional table, assume that we want to include the names of the states along with their corresponding average income figures:

```
01  STATE-INCOME-TABLE.
    02  NAME-INCOME OCCURS 50 TIMES.
        03  NAME      PICTURE X(12).
        03  INCOME    PICTURE 9(6)V99.
```

The OCCURS 50 TIMES clause sets up a table in storage that has the following structure:

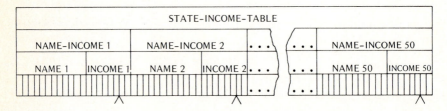

If we write NAME (1) we are referring to a storage field of 12 positions, whereas INCOME (1) refers to an 8-position field. If we write NAME-INCOME (1) we are referring to a storage field of 20 positions. Finally, STATE-INCOME-TABLE refers to the entire table of 100 fields.

REVIEW

1   The programmer can set up tables by using the _____ clause in the DATA DIVISION.

OCCURS

2   The OCCURS clause indicates the number of _____ in the table.

entries

3   Suppose a STATE-POPULATION-TABLE is to include the population figures for all 50 states in alphabetical order. Complete the description

below by writing the appropriate OCCURS clause. Assume that the PIC-
TURE for POPULATION is 9(8).

01   STATE-POPULATION-TABLE.

---

02   POPULATION OCCURS 50
            TIMES   PICTURE 9(8).

4   Suppose that both the state names and the population figures are read in
and we wish to set up a STATE-POPULATION-TABLE such that the 50
state names are located first in the table, followed by the 50 population
figures. Complete the following description, assuming that the PICTURE
for NAME is X(12).

01   STATE-POPULATION-TABLE.

---

02   NAME OCCURS 50
            TIMES   PICTURE X(12).
02   POPULATION OCCURS 50
            TIMES   PICTURE 9(8).

5   The table set up in the preceding question will have a total of 100 fields.
After all data are read in, the content of NAME (1) will be the state name
_____, and the content of POPULATION (50) will be the popula-
tion figure for the state of _____.

Alabama; Wyoming

AN EXAMPLE OF READING IN VALUES FOR A TABLE

Let us suppose that we have defined a tax table to contain 10 deduction
rates, thus:

01   TAX-TABLE.
        02   TAX-RATE OCCURS 10 TIMES   PICTURE V999.

We want to read in 10 values from punched cards. Assume that the
punched card file is called RATE-FILE, and that the specific field containing
the rate is called RATE. We will use a data-name, N, to specify the subscript
value. Initially, we want to read the first card and store the value of RATE in
the first cell of the TAX-TABLE. Then we want to increase the value of N and

repeat the process, storing each newly read value in the Nth place of TAX-TABLE. Notice that we account for the possibility of less than 10 cards in the input file, in which case we execute an error routine called NOT-ENOUGH-DATA. The following PROCEDURE DIVISION entries can accomplish the rate-reading objective:

```
MOVE 'NO' TO DATA-END
MOVE 1 TO N
PERFORM TABLE-READ UNTIL N > 10 OR DATA-END = 'YES'.
  .
  .
  .
```

```
TABLE-READ.
    READ RATE-FILE RECORD AT END MOVE 'YES' TO DATA-END.
    IF DATA-END = 'YES'
        PERFORM NOT-ENOUGH-DATA
    ELSE
        MOVE RATE TO TAX-RATE (N)
        ADD 1 TO N.
NOT-ENOUGH-DATA.
    (etc.)
```

AN EXAMPLE OF A TABLE OF CONSTANT VALUES

It often is desirable to build tables that contain specified constant values. One way to accomplish this objective is to define the table by using the OCCURS clause in the DATA DIVISION and then, through suitable PROCEDURE DIVISION instructions, to read in the desired values. There is yet another way of initializing a table with constant values; as the following example illustrates, the joint use of the OCCURS and REDEFINES clauses accomplishes this task.

Suppose that we want to have a table that contains the names of the 12 months of the year, so that we can reference these names by use of the table name and a subscript. For instance, we may want to reference the fifth month or the twelfth month, and so on. Using numeric values to reference the months is desirable, because arithmetic can be performed with numeric values. For instance, if we are on the sixth month and we want to reference the next month, we can simply add 1 to 6 and then make reference to the resulting month. The following example illustrates the common way of accomplishing this task:

```
01   MONTH-TABLE.
     02   FILLER     PICTURE X(9)  VALUE 'JANUARY   '.
     02   FILLER     PICTURE X(9)  VALUE 'FEBRUARY '.
     02   FILLER     PICTURE X(9)  VALUE 'MARCH     '.
     02   FILLER     PICTURE X(9)  VALUE 'APRIL     '.
     02   FILLER     PICTURE X(9)  VALUE 'MAY       '.
     02   FILLER     PICTURE X(9)  VALUE 'JUNE      '.
     02   FILLER     PICTURE X(9)  VALUE 'JULY      '.
     02   FILLER     PICTURE X(9)  VALUE 'AUGUST    '.
     02   FILLER     PICTURE X(9)  VALUE 'SEPTEMBER'.
     02   FILLER     PICTURE X(9)  VALUE 'OCTOBER   '.
     02   FILLER     PICTURE X(9)  VALUE 'NOVEMBER '.
     02   FILLER     PICTURE X(9)  VALUE 'DECEMBER '.
01   MONTHS REDEFINES MONTH-TABLE.
     02   MONTH      PICTURE X(9) OCCURS 12 TIMES.
```

Notice that the record MONTH-TABLE consists of 12 fields with each field conveniently named after each month. The VALUE clause is used to assign the constant (nonnumeric literal) values. The record called MONTHS is a table consisting of 12 entries. Each entry is referenced by the use of MONTH and a subscript. Thus, executing the instruction MOVE MONTH (3) TO PRINTAREA WRITE PRINTAREA results in the word MARCH being printed.

The procedure may seem unnecessarily roundabout. Let us justify the rationale. The VALUE clause cannot be used with the OCCURS clause. This makes sense, since the VALUE clause references *one* value and the OCCURS clause refers to several values. Thus, we use the REDEFINES clause with the OCCURS clause, after we have described each individual field. Of course, all entries in MONTH-TABLE must be of equal field size for the procedure to accomplish the correct result.

A practical example is given later in this chapter, using the table of months.

THE OCCURS . . . DEPENDING ON OPTION

Sometimes the number of entries in a table varies. The number of entries may be given by the value of a data-name. In such cases we may want to use the DEPENDING ON option of the OCCURS clause. In Chapter 9, we mentioned variable-sized tape records and deferred discussion until this point. We now illustrate the use of variable tape records with the OCCURS and DEPENDING ON clauses.

A bank utilizes magnetic tape to record the transactions of checking account customers. Some customers have a greater number of transactions than others; that is, they write more checks or make more deposits. It seems natural that tape records should be variable. Let us assume the following record layout:

FIELD	NUMBER OF POSITIONS
Customer number	6
Number of transactions	3
Transaction code	1
Date	5
Amount	7
Transaction code	1
Date	5
Amount	7
(etc. for up to 100 transactions)	

This is a case where a record may contain from 0 to 100 transactions. Notice that the minimum number of character positions is nine: six for the customer number and three for the number of transactions. The maximum size is 9 + (100 transactions × 13 characters per transaction) = 1,309. We then can have the following file description, assuming blocks of three records each:

```
FD   TAPE-FILE    BLOCK CONTAINS 3 RECORDS
                  RECORD CONTAINS 9 TO 1309 CHARACTERS
                  LABEL RECORD STANDARD
                  DATA RECORD IS CHECKING-ACCOUNT-RECORD.
01   CHECKING-ACCOUNT-RECORD.
     02   CUSTOMER-NUMBER           PICTURE 9(6).
     02   NUMBER-OF-TRANSACTIONS    PICTURE 999.
     02   TRANSACTION OCCURS 0 TO 100    TIMES DEPENDING ON
          NUMBER-OF-TRANSACTIONS.
          03   TRANSACTION-CODE     PICTURE 9.
          03   TRANSACTION-DATE     PICTURE 9(5).
          03   TRANSACTION-AMOUNT   PICTURE 9(5)V99.
```

Some comments are in order. First, the statement RECORD CONTAINS 9 TO 1309 CHARACTERS is optional, since the record description provides the same information. Notice also that it is possible in this case for TRANSACTION to occur *zero* times. It should be pointed out that NUMBER-OF-TRANSACTIONS does not automatically contain the number of transactions. It is the responsibility of the program logic to store the proper data in the data-name of the DEPENDING-ON clause.

The general form of the DEPENDING ON option is

... <u>OCCURS</u> integer-1 <u>TO</u> integer-2 TIMES <u>DEPENDING</u> ON data-name.

REVIEW

1 The OCCURS ... DEPENDING ON option can be used when the number of entries to be included in a table is [predetermined / variable].

variable

2 When the DEPENDING ON option is used, the word OCCURS in the program statement always is followed by a specified [value / range of values], and the phrase DEPENDING ON always is followed by a [data-name / specified value].

range of values; data-name

THE PERFORM VERB AND TABLE HANDLING

The PERFORM verb was introduced in Chapter 3, and its use was described further in Chapter 6. We now continue our study of the PERFORM verb by introducing additional formats and emphasizing the use of this verb for table handling applications.

Beginning with an example, suppose that we have monthly sales for the 12 months of the year, and we wish to compute the average monthly sales. The data has been stored in SALES-TABLE as follows:

```
01  SALES-TABLE.
    02  MONTHLY-SALES     PIC 9(6)V99 OCCURS 12 TIMES.
```

To compute the average monthly sales we now can write:

```
MOVE ZERO TO TOTAL-SALES
MOVE 1 TO N
PERFORM SUMMATION 12 TIMES
DIVIDE TOTAL-SALES BY 12 GIVING AVERAGE-SALES.
    .
    .
    .

SUMMATION.
    ADD MONTHLY-SALES (N) TO TOTAL-SALES
    ADD 1 TO N.
```

Instead of an explicit reference, such as PERFORM . . . 12 TIMES, we can use an identifier whose value is subject to change. For instance, we could change the previous example by using K as the identifier that contains the number of months for which we want to compute a sales average:

```
MOVE ZERO TO TOTAL-SALES
MOVE 1 TO N
PERFORM SUMMATION K TIMES
DIVIDE TOTAL-SALES BY K GIVING AVERAGE-SALES.
    .
    .
    .

SUMMATION.
    ADD MONTHLY-SALES (N) TO TOTAL-SALES
    ADD 1 TO N.
```

Note at this point, however, that if the integer or the identifier used with PERFORM has a value of zero or is negative, the effect is that the object of PERFORM is not executed. For example, if we say PERFORM ABC M TIMES and M happens to have a value of 0 or is negative, ABC will not be executed at all; rather, the program will go on to the next statement. In effect, this fact allows for conditional execution of a procedure, but in a confusing, implicit way.

There is available a format of the PERFORM verb that provides a convenient way of processing data in tables. This format is:

$$\underline{\text{PERFORM}} \text{ procedure-name-1 } [\underline{\text{THRU}} \text{ procedure-name-2}] \underline{\text{VARYING}}$$

$$\text{identifier-1 } \underline{\text{FROM}} \left\{ \begin{array}{l} \text{identifier-2} \\ \text{literal-1} \end{array} \right\} \underline{\text{BY}} \left\{ \begin{array}{l} \text{identifier-3} \\ \text{literal-2} \end{array} \right\} \underline{\text{UNTIL}} \text{ condition}$$

It will be easier to understand the components of this version of PERFORM if we first consider an example. Let us take the example that we have been describing and rewrite these instructions using the new format:

```
MOVE ZERO TO TOTAL-SALES
PERFORM SUMMATION VARYING N FROM 1 BY 1
    UNTIL N > 12
DIVIDE TOTAL-SALES BY 12 GIVING AVERAGE-SALES.
    .
    .
    .

SUMMATION.
    ADD MONTHLY-SALES (N) TO TOTAL-SALES.
```

The use of PERFORM . . . VARYING allows us to execute an object paragraph or paragraphs while systematically varying an identifier. Of course, this identifier (in the above example, N) must have been defined in the DATA DIVISION. Most often, the identifier varied is used as a subscript, as in this example; however, it could be used simply as a counter to control the number of executions of the object of the PERFORM verb. The flowchart in Figure 11-1 portrays the control logic involved in the execution of PER-FORM with the VARYING option.

It is worthwhile to consider some further examples in order to illustrate the potential of PERFORM . . . VARYING. Let us say a home mortgage company issues a set of payment coupons at the beginning of each year. There are 12 coupons, numbered 1 to 12, each containing the name of the month in which the payment is due and the amount. What is required in order to prepare the coupons, then, is a repetitive execution (12 times) of a task with two variable factors: the coupon number (01 to 12) and the month-name. Of course, the amount of payment due will be the same for each of the months, and our present example is not concerned with the determination of this amount.

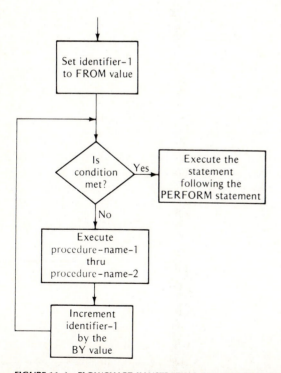

FIGURE 11-1   FLOWCHART ILLUSTRATING THE CONTROL LOGIC ASSOCIATED WITH USING THE VARYING OPTION WITH THE PERFORM VERB.

First, let us set up partial DATA DIVISION entries:

```
01   MONTH-NUMBER          PICTURE 99.
01   MONTHS-TABLE.
     02   MONTH             PICTURE X(9) OCCURS 12 TIMES.
01   COUPON. (fillers skipped)
     02   COUPON-NUMBER     PICTURE 99.
     02   MONTH-NAME        PICTURE X(9).
     02   EDITED-AMOUNT     PICTURE $$,$$9.99.
```

The MONTHS-TABLE will be filled with the names of the 12 months. Assume that the names are to be read from cards, the first card containing the name JANUARY and the twelfth card containing the name DECEMBER, in a field called CARD-MONTH. The following PROCEDURE DIVISION program segment can be used to accomplish this task:

```
PERFORM MONTH-READING
    VARYING MONTH-NUMBER FROM 1 BY 1
    UNTIL MONTH-NUMBER > 12.
    .
    .
    .

MONTH-READING.
    READ MONTH-CARD RECORD
        AT END MOVE 'YES' TO END-OF-DATA.
    IF END-OF-DATA = 'YES'
        NEXT SENTENCE
    ELSE
        MOVE CARD-MONTH TO MONTH (MONTH-NUMBER).
```

Once the 12 month-names have been entered in the MONTHS-TABLE by execution of the above program segment, the set of statements required to print the 12 coupons, each with a coupon number, month-name, and edited amount, can be written as:

```
PERFORM COUPON-PRINTING
    VARYING KOUNT FROM 1 BY 1
    UNTIL KOUNT > 12.
    .
    .
    .

COUPON-PRINTING.
    MOVE KOUNT TO COUPON-NUMBER.
    MOVE MONTH (KOUNT) TO MONTH-NAME.
    MOVE AMOUNT TO EDITED-AMOUNT.
    WRITE PRINT-LINE FROM COUPON.
```

Note that KOUNT, which is varied by PERFORM, is used in three ways:

1 To control the number of executions
2 As the coupon number
3 As the subscript to retrieve the corresponding month-name from MONTHS-TABLE

It now is appropriate to review the overall procedure by which the VARYING option is carried out, as already outlined in the flowchart in Figure 11–1. The procedure is as follows:

1 The identifier to be varied is set at its initial value, the value indicated by the clause:

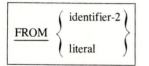

2 A test is made to determine if the condition specified by UNTIL is met. If it is met, PERFORM is skipped and control passes to the next statement. If the condition is not met, then the paragraph(s) specified is executed once.
3 The value of the varied identifier is incremented by the amount shown in the clause:

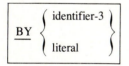

4 The procedure in steps 2 and 3 is repeated.

The condition need not refer to the value of the identifier-1, which is varied, even though the examples given illustrate only such cases. The condition can refer to other identifiers, but in all cases it must refer to identifiers that have their values altered by the paragraphs under PERFORM control. Otherwise, the loop will repeat indefinitely, as in the following example:

```
MOVE 10 TO AMOUNT
PERFORM ABC VARYING L FROM 1 BY 1
    UNTIL AMOUNT > 20.
ABC.
    WRITE REPORT LINE.
```

The problem with this segment is that, whereas the value of L is being incremented, the value of AMOUNT is being tested. Since AMOUNT never is altered by the ABC paragraph, there will be no end to the loop!

Now consider one more example that further illustrates use of the VARYING option and utilizes the STRING verb described in Chapter 8. Suppose that a header is to be centered in respect to column 40 of a printed page. The size of the header is variable, but it is always 20 or less characters long. The header is stored in the field called HEADER, and we wish to move it and print it from the output record called OUTPUT-RECORD.

Consider the following DATA and PROCEDURE DIVISION entries:

```
01   CHECK-FIELD        PIC X.
01   I                  PIC 99.
01   HEADER.
     02   INDIV-CHAR    PIC X OCCURS 20 TIMES.
.
.
.


MOVE SPACE TO CHECK-FIELD
PERFORM DETERMINE-SIZE VARYING I FROM 20 BY −1
         UNTIL CHECK-FIELD NOT = SPACE
             OR I = ZERO.
ADD 1 TO I
COMPUTE I = 40 − (I / 2)
MOVE SPACES TO OUTPUT-RECORD
STRING HEADER DELIMITED BY SIZE
    INTO OUTPUT-RECORD
    WITH POINTER I.
WRITE OUTPUT-RECORD. . . .
    .
    .
    .

DETERMINE-SIZE.
    IF INDIV-CHAR (I) NOT = SPACE
        MOVE 'X' TO CHECK-FIELD.
```

The PERFORM DETERMINE-SIZE statement searches the HEADER field, character by character, from the right end of the field. When a nonblank character is encountered or the entire field has been searched, we terminate the search. We then add 1 to I to restore it to the value that identifies the proper length. For example, if the data in HEADER consisted of ACME COMPANY, the Y character would cause X to be moved to CHECK-FIELD. Then, by nature of the PERFORM VARYING, I would be incremented by −1 and would become 11 before the UNTIL test was executed. Thus, the ADD 1 to I would restore I to the true length value of 12. Next, the procedure shows that we divide I by 2 and subtract this integer quotient from 40, which is the centering column. In this example, the data in HEADER is 12 characters long, thus, I would be I = 40 − 12/2 = 34. Then, use of the WITH POINTER I clause in the STRING verb would move the HEADER data into OUTPUT-RECORD, beginning with column 34.

REVIEW

1 In general, use of the PERFORM verb allows _____ execution of program modules.

repetitive

2 The object of PERFORM is not executed at all if the integer or the identifier used with PERFORM has a _____ or _____ value.

zero; negative

3 When using PERFORM . . . VARYING, control of PERFORM is associated with systematically incrementing the value of a(n) _____.

identifier

4 The key programming word that indicates that an identifier is to be systematically incremented in value is the COBOL reserved word _____.

VARYING

5 The test made to determine if the condition specified for terminating PERFORM control has been met is indicated by the COBOL reserved word _____.

UNTIL

6 If the identifier being incremented in a PERFORM . . . VARYING instruction is not the same as the identifier being tested, the result is that [the PERFORM is skipped / looping continues indefinitely].

looping continues indefinitely

SAMPLE FORECASTING PROGRAM

The example we will present in this section will illustrate the application of PERFORM, OCCURS, and REDEFINES, and the use of tables and subscripts. PERFORM often is used in conjunction with tables and subscripts; therefore, such a programming example is particularly appropriate.

The function of the program is to output a sales forecast based on punched-card input. The input values are:

NEXT-MONTH   A numeric value that designates the first month to be included in the forecast

HOW-MANY-MONTHS   A 2-digit number that designates the number of months to be included in the forecast

BASE   A dollar value used as the base for the forecast formula

COEFFICIENT   A numeric coefficient used in the forecast formula

The forecasting formula used is:

$$F_i = B + cN$$

The forecast for month i (F_i) is equal to the base (B) plus a coefficient (c) times the number of months (N) from the starting point. If the first month is 2 (February), then the forecast for April will be:

$$F_{April} = B + c(2)$$

Thus, $N = 2$ in this case, since April is 2 months after February, which is the starting month.

If the following input were used, the resulting output would be as shown in Figure 11–2.

NEXT-MONTH   05
HOW-MANY-MONTHS   09
BASE   0010000000
COEFFICIENT   0000025000

A sample forecast program listing is given in Figure 11–3. Notice that the setting up of the MONTH-TABLE in the WORKING-STORAGE SECTION is the same as presented in the earlier section of this chapter: "An Example of a Table of Constant Values."

PROJECTED SALES

MONTH	SALES
MAY	100250.00
JUNE	100500.00
JULY	100750.00
AUGUST	101000.00
SEPTEMBER	101250.00
OCTOBER	101500.00
NOVEMBER	101750.00
DECEMBER	102000.00
JANUARY	102250.00

FIGURE 11-2   ILLUSTRATIVE COMPUTER OUTPUT.

FIGURE 11-3   SAMPLE FORECAST PROGRAM.

```
IDENTIFICATION DIVISION.
PROGRAM-ID. FORECAST.
ENVIRONMENT DIVISION.
CONFIGURATION SECTION.
SOURCE-COMPUTER. ABC-480.
OBJECT-COMPUTER. ABC-480.
INPUT-OUTPUT SECTION.
FILE-CONTROL.
    SELECT INPUT-DATA ASSIGN TO CARD-READER.
    SELECT OUTPUT-FILE ASSIGN TO PRINTER.
*
DATA DIVISION.
FILE SECTION.
FD  INPUT-DATA LABEL RECORD OMITTED
              DATA RECORD IS INCARD.
01  INCARD.
    02 NEXT-MONTH      PICTURE 99.
    02 HOW-MANY-MONTHS PICTURE 99.
    02 BASE            PICTURE S9(8)V99.
    02 COEFFICIENT     PICTURE S9(8)V99.
    02 FILLER          PICTURE X(56).
FD  OUTPUT-FILE LABEL RECORD OMITTED
              DATA  RECORD OUT-LINE.
01  OUT-LINE PICTURE X(133).
*
WORKING-STORAGE SECTION.
01  WHICH-ONE        PIC 99.
01  MONTHS-FROM-NOW  PIC 99.
01  SALES            PIC S9(9)V99.
01  DATA-END         PIC XXX.
*
01  HEADER.
    02 FILLER              PICTURE X(15) VALUE SPACES.
    02 FILLER              PICTURE X(15) VALUE 'PROJECTED SALES'.
*
01  PRINT-RECORD.
    02 FILLER              PICTURE X VALUE SPACE.
    02 MONTH-NAME          PICTURE X(12).
    02 FILLER              PICTURE X(5) VALUE SPACES.
    02 EDIT-SALES          PICTURE -------99.99.
*
01  MONTH-TABLE.
    02 JANUARY             PICTURE X(12) VALUE 'JANUARY      '.
    02 FEBRUARY            PICTURE X(12) VALUE 'FEBRUARY     '.
    02 MARCH               PICTURE X(12) VALUE 'MARCH        '.
    02 APRIL               PICTURE X(12) VALUE 'APRIL        '.
    02 MAY                 PICTURE X(12) VALUE 'MAY          '.
    02 JUNE                PICTURE X(12) VALUE 'JUNE         '.
    02 JULY                PICTURE X(12) VALUE 'JULY         '.
    02 AUGUST              PICTURE X(12) VALUE 'AUGUST       '.
    02 SEPTEMBER           PICTURE X(12) VALUE 'SEPTEMBER    '.
    02 OCTOBER             PICTURE X(12) VALUE 'OCTOBER      '.
    02 NOVEMBER            PICTURE X(12) VALUE 'NOVEMBER     '.
    02 DECEMBER            PICTURE X(12) VALUE 'DECEMBER     '.
01  MONTHS REDEFINES MONTH-TABLE.
    02 MONTH               PICTURE X(12) OCCURS 12 TIMES.
/
PROCEDURE DIVISION.
MAIN-ROUTINE.
    OPEN INPUT INPUT-DATA
    OPEN OUTPUT OUTPUT-FILE
    MOVE 'NO' TO DATA-END
    READ INPUT-DATA RECORD
       AT END MOVE 'YES' TO DATA-END.
*
    IF DATA-END = 'NO'
       WRITE OUT-LINE FROM HEADER AFTER PAGE
       MOVE SPACES TO OUT-LINE
       WRITE OUT-LINE AFTER ADVANCING 1 LINE
       MOVE ZERO TO MONTHS-FROM-NOW
       MOVE NEXT-MONTH TO WHICH-ONE
       PERFORM CALCULATION-ROUTINE
              HOW-MANY-MONTHS TIMES
    ELSE
       MOVE 'NO DATA AVAILABLE' TO OUT-LINE
       WRITE OUT-LINE AFTER 1 LINE.
*
*
    CLOSE INPUT-DATA, OUTPUT-FILE.
    STOP RUN.
```

(continued)

```
*
 CALCULATION-ROUTINE.
     ADD 1 TO MONTHS-FROM-NOW
     IF WHICH-ONE IS GREATER THAN 12
         SUBTRACT 12 FROM WHICH-ONE.
     COMPUTE SALES =
             MONTHS-FROM-NOW * COEFFICIENT.
     ADD BASE TO SALES.
     MOVE MONTH (WHICH-ONE) TO MONTH-NAME.
     MOVE SALES TO EDIT-SALES.
     WRITE OUT-LINE FROM PRINT-RECORD
             AFTER ADVANCING 1 LINE.
     ADD 1 TO WHICH-ONE.
```

FIGURE 11-3 (*Continued*)

In the PROCEDURE DIVISION, the paragraph called CALCULATION-ROUTINE is performed HOW-MANY-MONTHS times. In this case, the input field, HOW-MANY-MONTHS, contains the number of desired executions of the forecasting computation.

The MONTH-FROM-NOW field corresponds to the N in the forecasting formula $F_i = B + cN$. Finally, the subscript WHICH-ONE is used to reference the name of the month relating to each successive line of output. Since we have only 12 months, we may need to "wraparound" the MONTH-TABLE entries. For instance, if NEXT-MONTH = 5 and HOW-MANY-MONTHS = 9, the last month is not the thirteenth (4 + 9); rather, it is the first month of the next year. Thus, when the month subscript called WHICH-ONE exceeds 12, we subtract 12 from it to "bend" it down around the table.

SAMPLE PROGRAM WITH GRAPHIC OUTPUT

We conclude the chapter with a sample program that utilizes table-handling concepts to produce graphic printer output in the form of a bar chart. The output format is illustrated in Figure 11-4. For each common stock, we print a bar whose length corresponds to the percent yield of the stock.

The yield is computed as the percent ratio of the dividend-per-share to the price-per-share. It is assumed that no yield can exceed 50 percent, but if the computed yield does exceed this percentage, an error message is printed.

The input consists of records containing the stock name, the stock price, and the dividend. Figure 11-5 presents the program listing. The graphic output is prepared in the two paragraphs named FILL-BAR and MOVE-X-TO-BAR. Essentially, we move as many X's to the output line as the percent yield of each stock.

```
                           PERCENT YIELD

                    0    5    10   15   20   25   30   35   40   45   50
         STOCK NAME  I....I....I....I....I....I....I....I....I....I....I
                     I
FORD MOTOR CO.       IXXXXXXXXXX
                     I
                     I
GENERAL MOTORS CORP. IXXXXXXXXXXX
                     I
                     I
CONTROL DATA CORP.   IX
                     I
                     I
IBM CORP.            IXXXXX
                     I
                     I
SPERRY RAND CORP.    IXXX
                     I
                     I
HONEYWELL CORP.      IXXXX
                     I
                     I
DIGITAL EQUIPMENT CO I
                     I
                     I
EXAMPLE ERROR-1      IINVALID INPUT DATA
                     I
                     I
EXAMPLE-ERROR-2      IINVALID INPUT DATA
                     I
                     I
JACK-POT             IYIELD HIGHER THAN 50%
                     I
```

FIGURE 11–4 SAMPLE GRAPHIC OUTPUT FOR THE STOCK-YIELD PROGRAM.

FIGURE 11–5 LISTING OF THE PROGRAM FOR GRAPHIC OUTPUT.

```
 IDENTIFICATION DIVISION.
 PROGRAM-ID. GRAPH.
*
 ENVIRONMENT DIVISION.
*
 CONFIGURATION SECTION.
 SOURCE-COMPUTER.  ABC-480.
 OBJECT-COMPUTER.  ABC-480.
*
 INPUT-OUTPUT SECTION.
 FILE-CONTROL.
     SELECT STOCK-FILE ASSIGN TO CARD-READER.
     SELECT REPORT-FILE ASSIGN TO PRINTER.
/
 DATA DIVISION.
*
 FILE SECTION.
*
 FD  STOCK-FILE
     LABEL RECORDS OMITTED
     DATA RECORD IS STOCK-REC.
 01  STOCK-REC.
     02 STOCK-NAME                 PIC X(20).
     02 STOCK-PRICE                PIC 9(3)V99.
     02 STOCK-DIVIDEND             PIC 9(2)V99.
     02 FILLER                     PIC X(51).
*
 FD  REPORT-FILE
     LABEL RECORDS OMITTED
     DATA RECORD IS REPORT-REC.
 01  REPORT-REC                    PIC X(132).
```

(continued)

```cobol
*
 WORKING-STORAGE SECTION.
*
 01  END-OF-FILE-SWITCH                  PIC XXX VALUE 'NO'.
     88 END-OF-FILE VALUE 'YES'.
*
 01  PERCENT-YIELD                       PIC 99.
*
 01  I                                   PIC 99.
*
 01  GRAPH-LINE.
     02 FILLER                           PIC X(5) VALUE SPACES.
     02 STOCK-NAME                       PIC X(20).
     02 FILLER                           PIC X(2) VALUE SPACES.
     02 FILLER                           PIC X VALUE 'I'.
     02 BAR-CHART.
        03 BAR-CELL OCCURS 50 TIMES PIC X.
*
 01  HEADING-1.
     02 FILLER                           PIC X(40) VALUE SPACES.
     02 FILLER                           PIC X(13) VALUE 'PERCENT YIELD'.
*
 01  HEADING-2.
     02 FILLER                           PIC X(27) VALUE SPACES.
     02 FILLER                           PIC X(51) VALUE
        '0    5   10   15   20   25   30   35   40   45   50'.
*
 01  HEADING-3.
     02 FILLER                           PIC X(10) VALUE SPACES.
     02 FILLER                           PIC X(10) VALUE 'STOCK NAME'.
     02 FILLER                           PIC X(7) VALUE SPACES.
     02 FILLER                           PIC X VALUE 'I'.
     02 FILLER                           PIC X(50) VALUE ALL '....I'.
*
 01  EMPTY-LINE.
     02 FILLER                           PIC X(27) VALUE SPACES.
     02 FILLER                           PIC X VALUE 'I'.
/
 PROCEDURE DIVISION.
 PROGRAM-SUMMARY.
     OPEN INPUT STOCK-FILE
          OUTPUT REPORT-FILE.
*
     PERFORM READ-STOCK-REC
*
     WRITE REPORT-REC FROM HEADING-1 AFTER PAGE.
     WRITE REPORT-REC FROM HEADING-2 AFTER 2.
     WRITE REPORT-REC FROM HEADING-3 AFTER 2.
*
     PERFORM PRINT-GRAPH
             UNTIL END-OF-FILE
*
     CLOSE STOCK-FILE
           REPORT-FILE
*
     STOP RUN.
*
 READ-STOCK-REC.
     READ STOCK-FILE RECORD
          AT END MOVE 'YES' TO END-OF-FILE-SWITCH.
*
*
 PRINT-GRAPH.
*
     WRITE REPORT-REC FROM EMPTY-LINE
*
     IF STOCK-PRICE NOT NUMERIC
        OR STOCK-DIVIDEND NOT NUMERIC
           OR STOCK-PRICE NOT > ZERO
           MOVE 'INVALID INPUT DATA' TO BAR-CHART
     ELSE
         COMPUTE PERCENT-YIELD ROUNDED
            = STOCK-DIVIDEND * 100.0 / STOCK-PRICE
         IF PERCENT-YIELD > 50
            MOVE 'YIELD HIGHER THAN 50%' TO BAR-CHART
     ELSE
         PERFORM FILL-BAR.
*
     MOVE STOCK-NAME OF STOCK-REC
          TO STOCK-NAME OF GRAPH-LINE
*
     WRITE REPORT-REC FROM GRAPH-LINE.
*
     WRITE REPORT-REC FROM EMPTY-LINE.
*
     PERFORM READ-STOCK-REC.
*
 FILL-BAR.
     MOVE SPACES TO BAR-CHART
     PERFORM MOVE-X-TO-BAR VARYING I FROM 1 BY 1
                     UNTIL I > PERCENT-YIELD.
*
 MOVE-X-TO-BAR.
     MOVE 'X' TO BAR-CELL (I).
```

FIGURE 11-5 (Continued)

EXERCISES

11.1   Write DATA DIVISION entries to set up a table that is to contain annual dollar sales for the years 1970–1982. No value will exceed $100,000,000.00.

11.2   Write DATA DIVISION entries to set up a table to contain dollar and unit sales for the years 1970–1982. We want to be able to reference the dollar sales or the unit sales individually for each year, as well as to reference as a group the dollar sales and unit sales pertaining to a given year. The general format of the table is as follows:

YEAR	DOLLAR SALES	UNIT SALES
1970		
1971		
.	.	.
.	.	.
.	.	.
1982		

11.3   Use DATA DIVISION entries to form a table containing the names of the days of the week so that the names are referenced by a subscript; thus, Monday would have a subscript 1 and Sunday would have a subscript 7.

11.4   Assume that TAX-TABLE contains 30 values (V999). Write the PROCEDURE and DATA DIVISION statements required to print the contents of the table in the following formats:

a   Print the 30 values in one column of 30 lines.
b   Print the 30 values at the rate of seven per line for as many lines as are needed.

11.5   For the following table, write the necessary program instructions to find the smallest value and to place it in SMALLEST. Disregard the possibility of ties.

02   TABLE OCCURS 50 TIMES   PICTURE X(12).

11.6   In the following two-dimensional table, we want to form the sum of each row and the sum of each column, as well as the grand total. The results of the summations are to be saved so that they can be printed later in the program. Write relevant DATA and PROCEDURE DIVISION entries.

```
01  SALES-DATA-TABLE.
    02  SALES-TERRITORY OCCURS 5 TIMES.
        03  QUARTER-SALES OCCURS 4 TIMES     PICTURE 9(6)V99.
```

11.7   A deck of up to 30 cards is in the following format:

Card columns 1–15: Name (alphanumeric)

Card columns 15–80: Other data (alphanumeric)

We wish to read the cards, sort the records in ascending order on the basis of the Name field, and print the sorted values on the printer in ascending order. Notice that there may be as many as 30 cards, but there may be fewer. Also notice that the sort key (the Name field) is alphanumeric, which implies that we may want to sort any mixture of characters; review your understanding of the idea of collating sequence, as discussed in Chapter 7 in the section called ''Relation Conditions.''

There are many ways to sort a set of data in storage. We now will describe one of these ''sorting algorithms.'' First, we must have a table of values in internal storage; therefore, as the cards are read, they must be stored in a table. Next, we must compare the first item to the second item in the table, and, if the second is smaller than the first, we must interchange them; that is, we must put the value of the second item in the first position and the value of the first item in the second position. We continue through the table, comparing the second to the third, the third to the fourth, and so on, until the table is completed. As each pair is compared, we interchange the items that are out of relative order.

This process of comparing pairs and interchanging is repeated over and over, each time going through the entire table. If the table to be sorted consists of N items, then we go through the table N − 1 times. As an example, suppose that we want to sort this table:

We know that we will need to go through the table N − 1 times, which is 4 − 1 = 3 times. In the following we show the comparisons and the interchanges for each pass through the table. When an interchange is made, it is indicated by an asterisk.

PAIR COMPARISONS		
PASS 1	PASS 2	PASS 3
10 − 8*	8 − 10	8 − 5*
10 − 16	10 − 5*	8 − 10
16 − 5*	10 − 16	10 − 16

TABLE OF CONTENTS AT THE END OF EACH PASS		
PASS 1	PASS 2	PASS 3
8	8	5
10	5	8
5	10	10
16	16	16

This method will result in a sorted table by the time the last pass is complete. The method does not recognize the possibility that the table may be in order either at the start or at the end of some pass. For example, if the original table contains the values 10, 5, 8, and 16, it will be sorted appropriately at the end of the first pass.

Write the required instructions to sort the deck of up to 30 cards in ascending order on the basis of the Name field. It is possible to modify the method to make it more efficient, as described in the next exercise; however, this makes the exercise a little more difficult.

11.8 The desired result is a sorted table, as described in the preceding exercise; however, the method is to be modified by the following additions.

Before we start each pass, we set a "switch" storage field equal to zero. Whenever we interchange a pair of values, we move a 1 to the switch. At the end of the pass, we test the switch. If it is equal to zero, the table is sorted and we need not proceed with the next pass. If the switch is equal to 1, we reset it to zero and make another pass through the table. In this way, we can recognize when the table is sorted and avoid unnecessary steps.

A second modification recognizes the fact that at the end of the first pass the largest value in the table is driven to the bottom cell, regardless of its original position. The second-largest value is driven to the second-from-the-bottom cell at the end of the second pass, and so on. In other words, the second pass need not consider the last cell, the third pass need not consider the second-from-the-last cell, and so on. The effective table length thus is shortened by one at the end of each pass, making the sorting considerably faster. To implement this technique, the subscript must be controlled so that each pass through the table uses a maximum subscript that is one less than the maximum subscript of the pass immediately preceding. Indicate how this can be done.

12

Additional table-handling features

TWO-DIMENSIONAL AND THREE-DIMENSIONAL TABLES

Two-dimensional tables require two subscripts to locate an individual entry, or field. As an example of a two-dimensional table, assume that a particular state has three state universities and we desire to set up a table that will contain the enrollment figures for each university according to class standing: freshman, sophomore, junior, senior, and graduate. Conceptually, the following type of table is required:

YEAR	ENROLLMENT BY UNIVERSITY		
	1	2	3
FR			
SO			
JR			
SR			
GR			

In order to set up the required storage locations, the following DATA DIVISION entries can be written:

```
01  ENROLLMENT-TABLE.
    02  UNIVERSITY-NUMBER
        OCCURS 3 TIMES.
        03  YEAR
            OCCURS 5 TIMES
            PICTURE 9(5).
```

Compilation of these DATA DIVISION statements results in the following conceptual storage layout:

ENROLLMENT-TABLE						
UNIVERSITY-NUMBER 1					UNIVERSITY-NUMBER-2	
YEAR 1	YEAR 2	YEAR 3	YEAR 4	YEAR 5	. . .	
					. . .	

Thus, for each of the three universities there are five fields, corresponding to the five class-standing classifications. Notice that the level number of YEAR is lower (03) than that of UNIVERSITY-NUMBER (02). If the level number of YEAR were the same as that of UNIVERSITY-NUMBER, then the table would not be two-dimensional. To illustrate the use of the table, consider the following examples.

UNIVERSITY-NUMBER (3) refers to all five fields associated with the third university.

YEAR (2, 4) refers to the senior (4) enrollment in the second (2) university. YEAR always must be used with double subscripts. The first subscript refers to the superior hierarchical level (in this case, UNIVERSITY-NUMBER), and the second subscript refers to the entry in the YEAR table.

YEAR (5, 2) is incorrect, since only three values have been defined for UNIVERSITY-NUMBER. However, YEAR (2, 5) is correct and identifies the graduate student enrollment in the second university.

Notice that, even though we have defined a two-dimensional table (YEAR), we also have defined a one-dimensional table (UNIVERSITY-NUMBER) and one field (ENROLLMENT-TABLE). This again exemplifies the power of COBOL to reference with great flexibility data at different hierarchical levels.

Three-dimensional tables involve the use of three subscripts. We can illustrate the statements required to set up a three-dimensional table by adding a further breakdown by male and female to our two-dimensional example, as follows:

```
01  ENROLLMENT-TABLE.
    02   UNIVERSITY-NUMBER
         OCCURS 3 TIMES.
         03   YEAR
              OCCURS 5 TIMES.
              04   SEX
                   OCCURS 2 TIMES
                   PICTURE 9(5).
```

Thus, SEX (2, 3, 1) refers to the enrollment of males (1) in the junior year (3) in the second university (2).

The following rules serve to summarize the requirements associated with the use of subscripted tables.

1 The OCCURS clause cannot apply to the 01 level. In other words, there cannot be a table of "records." However, this is a language rule and in no way prevents us from assigning a "record" to the 02 level and defining an 01 level name above it, as shown in the following example:

```
01  STATE-INCOME-TABLE.
    02   AVERAGE-INCOME
         OCCURS 50 TIMES
         PICTURE 9(6)V99.
```

2 The OCCURS clause cannot be used with level 77 items.
3 Subscripted tables may have one, two, or three dimensions.
4 The PICTURE clause applies to the elementary items only. Notice, for instance, the example of the three-dimensional table given previously.
5 Only one PICTURE description can be given for all like entries in a table, but there may be several entries that are not alike. The latter is exemplified by the example given earlier and reproduced here:

```
01  STATE-INCOME-TABLE.
    02   NAME-INCOME
         OCCURS 50 TIMES.
         03   NAME       PICTURE X(12).
         03   INCOME     PICTURE 9(6)V99.
```

The same PICTURE clause applies to all 50 Name fields above. Thus, OCCURS is used for homogeneous sets of data.

6   The subscripts may be integer constants, or they may be integer variables. Their values must be positive; they must not be zero or negative.

7   The subscript or subscripts are enclosed in one set of parentheses and are separated from the table-name by a space. Multiple subscripts are separated from each other by *commas* and *spaces*. Examples are:

A-TABLE (1)
A-TABLE (IDEN)
B-TABLE (3, COUNT)
C-TABLE (GRADE, CLASS, YEAR)
C-TABLE (GRADE, 3, YEAR)

REVIEW

1   In the two-dimensional ENROLLMENT-TABLE example, suppose we want UNIVERSITY-NUMBER to be at the lowest hierarchical level, instead of YEAR. Write the appropriate statements below, using a PICTURE of 9(5) for the elementary field.

01   ENROLLMENT-TABLE.
   02   _____
      03   _____

> YEAR OCCURS 5 TIMES.
> UNIVERSITY-NUMBER OCCURS
> 3 TIMES PICTURE 9(5).

2   For the example in the preceding question, the location of juniors in the first university is referenced by the subscripted variable _____ _____.

> UNIVERSITY-NUMBER (3, 1)

3   The PICTURE clause is used only at the [highest / lowest] hierarchical level of a table.

> *lowest*

4   The integer subscripts used in conjunction with subscripted variables [may / may not] be constant and [may / may not] be variables.

> *may; may*

5   A subscript used in conjunction with subscripted variables [may / may not] be zero and [may / may not] have a negative value.

> *may not; may not*

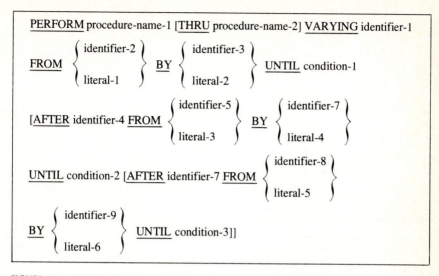

FIGURE 12–1   EXTENDED FORMAT OF THE PERFORM . . . VARYING STATEMENT.

THE PERFORM VERB AND TABLE HANDLING

In the preceding chapter, we described the use of the PERFORM verb for table handling. We will continue the description by presenting a format of the PERFORM verb that is particularly useful for processing two-dimensional and three-dimensional tables. The extended format of PER-FORM is presented in Figure 12–1. Consider the following example, which illustrates the use of two subscripts.

Assume that we have 20 punched cards, defined as:

```
FD  DATA-CARDS LABEL RECORD OMITTED DATA RECORD IS CARD.
01  CARD.
    02  CARD-VALUE     PICTURE 9(5)V99.
    02  FILLER         PICTURE X(73).
```

The data are sales values in each of the five sales territories in each of the last four quarters. The cards are ordered so that the first card contains the sales value for territory 1, quarter 1; the second card the value for territory 1, quarter 2, and so on. Therefore, the twentieth card contains the value for territory 5, quarter 4. We want to read the cards and store the values in a two-dimensional table of the following conceptual structure:

SALES TERRITORY	QUARTER			
	1	2	3	4
1				
2				
3				
4				
5				

The values in cards 1–4 are to be stored in row 1, columns 1–4 (according to card sequence). Card values 5–8 are to be stored in row 2, columns 1–4, and so on. Let us first define the table:

```
01  SALES-DATA-TABLE.
    02  SALES-TERRITORY
        OCCURS 5 TIMES.
        03  QUARTER-SALES
            OCCURS 4 TIMES
            PICTURE 9(5)V99.
```

Since the table is two-dimensional, we will use two subscripts. Let these be defined as:

```
01  TERRITORY    PICTURE 9.
01  QUARTER      PICTURE 9.
```

Now we can write PROCEDURE DIVISION statements to accomplish the desired input-storing task, as follows:

```
PERFORM READER
    VARYING TERRITORY FROM 1 BY 1
        UNTIL TERRITORY > 5
    AFTER QUARTER FROM 1 BY 1
        UNTIL QUARTER > 4.
    .
    .
    .

READER.
    READ DATA-CARDS
        AT END MOVE 'YES' TO END-OF-FILE-SWITCH.
    IF NOT END-OF-FILE
        MOVE CARD-VALUE
            TO QUARTER-SALES (TERRITORY, QUARTER).
```

Notice that TERRITORY is varied *after* varying QUARTER. Thus, the sequence of values contained in these two fields is:

TERRITORY	QUARTER
1	1
1	2
1	3
1	4
2	1
2	2
2	3
2	4
.	.
.	.
.	.
5	1
5	2
5	3
5	4

The paragraph called READER will be executed 20 times, as QUARTER and TERRITORY are varied through their specified ranges. Each time the READER paragraph is executed, the pair of values of the subscripts is unique, so that we store each card value in a new QUARTER-SALES cell of the table.

Next, consider an example involving three subscripts. Suppose that we have enrollment figures for six state colleges, each with four years of class levels that are subdivided into male and female students. We want to form the sum of enrollment for all colleges and all students, so we write:

```
01   ENROLLMENT-TABLE.
     02   COLLEGE
          OCCURS 6 TIMES.
          03   CLASS-LEVEL
               OCCURS 4 TIMES.
               04   STUDENTS
                    OCCURS 2 TIMES
                    PICTURE 9(5).
```

We now can write:

```
     MOVE ZERO TO TOTAL-ENROLLMENT
     PERFORM SUMMATION
          VARYING I FROM 1 BY 1
               UNTIL I > 6
          AFTER J FROM 1 BY 1
               UNTIL J > 4
          AFTER K FROM 1 BY 1
               UNTIL K > 2.
SUMMATION.
     ADD STUDENTS (I, J, K)
          TO TOTAL-ENROLLMENT.
```

The following table illustrates the values of the three subscripts, I, J, and K:

I	J	K
1	1	1
1	1	2
1	2	1
1	2	2
.	.	.
.	.	.
.	.	.
1	4	1
1	4	2
2	1	1
2	1	2
2	2	1
.	.	.
.	.	.
.	.	.
6	4	2

The identifier associated with the second AFTER varies the fastest, the identifier associated with the first AFTER varies the next fastest, and the identifier following the VARYING varies the slowest. Thus, SUMMATION will be executed a total of 48 times ($6 \times 4 \times 2$).

REVIEW

1   The enhanced format of the PERFORM verb described in this section extends the efficiency of COBOL by allowing the programmer systematically to vary up to _____ (number) identifiers in a nested fashion.

3

2   Each identifier may represent a subscript. For a two-dimensional table, for example, _____ (number) subscripts are involved.

2

3   If there are two categories in the first dimension of a table, three in the second, and two in the third, addition of all values in the table involves the summation of _____ (number) values.

$2 \times 3 \times 2 = 12$

SAMPLE PROGRAM WITH A TWO-DIMENSIONAL TABLE

Suppose that punched cards contain a quarter value in column 1, a region value in column 2, and a sales amount in columns 3–5. We want to read such a card file and produce a report that presents sales by quarter and region, as illustrated in the following table:

	REGION			
QUARTER	EAST	SOUTH	MIDWEST	WEST
1				
2				
3				
4				

Figure 12-2 presents a program to accomplish the task. The sales data are accumulated in a two-dimensional table, as indicated by the following description included in the WORKING-STORAGE SECTION of the DATA DIVISION:

```
01  SALES-TABLE.
    02  QUARTER-DATA
        OCCURS 4 TIMES.
        03  SALES
            OCCURS 4 TIMES
            PICTURE 9(5).
```

FIGURE 12-2   PROGRAM FOR A QUARTERLY REPORT.

```
IDENTIFICATION DIVISION.
PROGRAM-ID. TABLES.
*
ENVIRONMENT DIVISION.
CONFIGURATION SECTION.
SOURCE-COMPUTER. ABC-480.
OBJECT-COMPUTER. ABC-480.
INPUT-OUTPUT SECTION.
FILE-CONTROL.
    SELECT INPUT-FILE  ASSIGN TO CARD-READER.
    SELECT OUTPUT-FILE ASSIGN TO PRINTER.
*
DATA DIVISION.
FILE SECTION.
FD  INPUT-FILE LABEL RECORD OMITTED
                DATA RECORD IS INPUT-RECORD.
01  INPUT-RECORD.
    02 QUARTER        PIC 9.
    02 REGION         PIC 9.
    02 AMOUNT         PIC 999.
    02 FILLER         PIC X(75).
FD  OUTPUT-FILE LABEL RECORD OMITTED
                DATA RECORD IS OUTPUT-RECORD.
01  OUTPUT-RECORD  PIC X(132).
*
WORKING-STORAGE SECTION.
01  END-OF-DATA    PIC XXX.
*
01  SALES-TABLE.
    02 QUARTER-DATA
        OCCURS 4 TIMES.
        03 SALES
            OCCURS 4 TIMES
            PICTURE 9(5).
```

(continued)

```
*
 01  HEADER-1.
     02 FILLER PIC X(27) VALUE SPACES.
     02 FILLER PIC X(6)  VALUE 'REGION'.
 01  HEADER-2.
     02 FILLER PIC X(17) VALUE '  QUARTER      EAST'.
     02 FILLER PIC X(6)  VALUE SPACES.
     02 FILLER PIC X(9)  VALUE 'SOUTH     '.
     02 FILLER PIC X(15) VALUE 'MIDWEST    WEST'.
*
 01  OUTPUT-LINE.
     02 FILLER          PIC X(5).
     02 QUARTER-OUT      PIC 9.
     02 FILLER          PIC X(4).
     02 DATA-OUT OCCURS 4 TIMES.
        03 FILLER        PIC XX.
        03 REGION-OUT    PIC ZZ,ZZZ.
        03 FILLER        PIC XX.
/
 PROCEDURE DIVISION.
 MAIN-ROUTINE.
     OPEN INPUT  INPUT-FILE
          OUTPUT OUTPUT-FILE.
     MOVE 'NO' TO END-OF-DATA.
     MOVE ZERO TO SALES-TABLE.
*
     PERFORM READ-DATA.
     PERFORM READ-ACCUMULATE
        UNTIL END-OF-DATA = 'YES'.
*
     PERFORM HEADERS
*
     PERFORM PRINT-TABLE VARYING QUARTER FROM 1 BY 1
                 UNTIL QUARTER IS GREATER THAN 4.
*
     CLOSE INPUT-FILE, OUTPUT-FILE.
     STOP RUN.
*
 READ-DATA.
     READ INPUT-FILE AT END MOVE 'YES' TO END-OF-DATA.
*
 READ-ACCUMULATE.
     ADD AMOUNT TO SALES (QUARTER, REGION)
     PERFORM READ-DATA.
*
 HEADERS.
     WRITE OUTPUT-RECORD FROM HEADER-1 AFTER ADVANCING PAGE
     WRITE OUTPUT-RECORD FROM HEADER-2
        AFTER ADVANCING 3 LINES.
*
 PRINT-TABLE.
     MOVE SPACES TO OUTPUT-LINE.
     PERFORM MOVE-DATA VARYING REGION FROM 1 BY 1
                 UNTIL REGION IS GREATER THAN 4.
     MOVE QUARTER TO QUARTER-OUT.
     WRITE OUTPUT-RECORD FROM OUTPUT-LINE
        AFTER ADVANCING 2 LINES.
*
 MOVE-DATA.
     MOVE SALES (QUARTER, REGION) TO REGION-OUT (REGION).
```

FIGURE 12-2 (Continued)

TABLE SEARCHING WITH COBOL

The use of a dictionary to look up the meaning of words is perhaps the most common example of the need to search a table or file for particular entries. In the context of data processing, searching tables to find particular entries stored in them is a fundamental process. Because of the frequency with which table searching is used in computer programs, the COBOL language includes a specialized set of instructions to facilitate the programming task. Suppose, for example, that a company maintains a list of office employees in alphabetical order. There are 400 employees, and each is assigned a four-digit employee identification number. Because of coding requirements, such as having the departmental identification included in the code, there is no correspondence between the numeric order of the identification numbers and the alphabetic order of employee names. The DATA DIVISION statements that describe the table can be written as follows:

```
01  DATA-TABLE.
    02  NAME-NUMBER
        OCCURS 400 TIMES.
        03  NAME        PICTURE X(16).
        03  EMPL-NO      PICTURE 9999.
```

In this section, we consider two data processing tasks. First, given the name of an employee, determine his or her employee-number. Second, given the employee-number, determine his or her name. The procedures to be used with both sorted and unsorted tables also are described.

ONE METHOD FOR SEARCHING A SORTED TABLE

Assume that the table is sorted on the NAME field. Since the table will be searched by reference to the NAME field, the record description entry can be written in such a way as to indicate the fact that the table is sorted on NAME in ascending order. Further, the record description can be written so that reference to table entries can be made by use of a variant of the subscript concept, called an *index*. Thus, in place of the table description in the general DATA DIVISION statements cited above, the following statements can be written:

```
01  DATA-TABLE.
    02  NAME-NUMBER
        OCCURS 400 TIMES
        ASCENDING KEY IS NAME
        INDEXED BY WHICH-ONE.
        03  NAME        PICTURE X(16).
        03  EMPL-NO      PICTURE 9999.
```

Notice the ASCENDING KEY IS statement, which indicates that the item defined by the OCCURS clause is sorted in ascending sequence. The IN-DEXED BY WHICH-ONE clause defines WHICH-ONE as an index for NAME-NUMBER. Unlike a subscript, an index is *not* defined or described by a DATA DIVISION entry and PICTURE clause. It is a numeric field, normally binary, whose length is defined by the compiler used. If we write NAME (WHICH-ONE), we thus reference an entry in the table just as with the use of a regular subscript. Unlike a subscript, however, the value of WHICH-ONE is defined by one of three verbs: SET, SEARCH, or PERFORM. Rather than elaborating further on the use of WHICH-ONE as an index, the following example is used to provide additional understanding of this option.

Suppose that EMPL-NAME is a field that contains a name for which we want to determine the associated employee-number. In order to accomplish this task, we can execute the following PROCEDURE DIVISION statements:

```
SEARCH ALL NAME-NUMBER
    AT END PERFORM CANT-FIND
    WHEN NAME (WHICH-ONE) = EMPL-NAME
        MOVE EMPL-NO (WHICH-ONE) TO EDIT-NUMBER.
```

The instruction SEARCH ALL NAME-NUMBER indicates that all the entries in the NAME-NUMBER table should be searched. Recall that in the DATA DIVISION the OCCURS clause defined ASCENDING KEY IS NAME; therefore, the search is conducted with respect to the NAME field. If no match is found, the AT END clause is executed. As the table is searched, the procedure is to vary WHICH-ONE and to compare the resulting NAME (WHICH-ONE) to EMPL-NAME. If the two match, the MOVE statement that follows the WHEN is executed next and the search terminates. If no match is found, WHICH-ONE is changed to a new value and the procedure is repeated until the entire table has been searched. How is the value of WHICH-ONE varied? The instructions are included in the compiler. Since the table in the present example is sorted, it is likely that the compiler will provide instructions for a binary search. If a linear search were used, the values of WHICH-ONE in this example would be 1, 2, 3, . . . , 399, 400. Again, note that the search procedure is supplied automatically by the compiler, so that the programmer need not write any of the detailed instructions for this search. When a match is found, program execution is transferred to the instruction MOVE EMPL-NO (WHICH-ONE) TO EDIT-NUMBER following the WHEN. Notice that WHICH-ONE has the reference value of the record for which the match occurred; thus, it is used as a subscript, or index, to reference the corresponding EMPL-NO.

AN ALTERNATIVE APPROACH FOR SORTED TABLES

We now demonstrate some options, with respect to the preceding search procedure, by using an alternate approach to the task. First, we rewrite the DATA DIVISION entries as follows:

```
01  DATA-TABLE.
    02  NAME
        OCCURS 400 TIMES
        ASCENDING KEY IS NAME
        INDEXED BY NAME-INDEX
        PICTURE IS X(16).
    02  EMPL-NO
        OCCURS 400 TIMES
        INDEXED BY NO-INDEX
        PICTURE 9999.
```

In effect, two tables are defined, one called NAME and the other called EMPL-NO. The NAME table is sorted on ascending sequence and is indexed by NAME-INDEX, while the EMPL-NO table is indexed by NO-INDEX. Of course, the two PICTURE descriptions refer to the NAME and EMPL-NO fields, respectively, and *not* to the index names.

In relation to these DATA DIVISION statements, the following PROCEDURE DIVISION statements then can be written:

```
SET NAME-INDEX TO 1.
SET NO-INDEX TO 1.
SEARCH NAME VARYING NO-INDEX
    AT END PERFORM NO-MATCH
    WHEN EMPL-NAME = NAME(NAME-INDEX)
        MOVE EMPL-NO(NO-INDEX) TO EDIT-FIELD.
```

The SEARCH statement contains the VARYING option, which in effect indicates that NO-INDEX is to be varied in the same way as the index of the table being searched (in this case NAME-INDEX). Thus, for example, when NAME-INDEX equals 10, NO-INDEX also is equal to 10. As a result, the EMPL-NO (NO-INDEX) referred to in the MOVE statement corresponds to the NAME for which a match was found. If a match occurred in the thirty-fourth position of the NAME table, for example, NAME-INDEX and NO-INDEX both would have a value of 34. Thus, the employee-number that is output corresponds to the name of the employee for which a match was found. Since the ALL option is not used with the SEARCH verb, the search procedure involves accessing every entry in the table in sequence until a match is found or the entire table is searched. In effect, then, we do not take advantage of the fact that the table was sorted.

SEARCHING AN UNSORTED TABLE

We now consider the search procedure that can be used with an unsorted table. Further, though it makes no difference in the general procedure used, we now shall assume that we have an employee-number and we wish to find the corresponding name, rather than vice versa. The relevant DATA DIVISION entries can be written as follows:

```
01  DATA-TABLE.
    02  NAME-NUMBER
        OCCURS 400 TIMES
        INDEXED BY N.
        03  NAME      PICTURE X(16).
        03  EMPL-NO   PICTURE 9999.
```

The NAME-NUMBER table is indexed by N, which is an index-name of our choice. Assume that the employee-number in question is stored in EMPLOYEE-NUMBER. In the PROCEDURE DIVISION, we can write:

```
SET N TO 1.
SEARCH NAME-NUMBER
    AT END PERFORM NO-MATCH
    WHEN EMPLOYEE-NUMBER = EMPL-NO (N)
        MOVE NAME (N) TO EDIT-NAME.
```

The value of N is initialized at 1 by the statement SET N TO 1. Since the table has not been sorted (and particularly, since it has not been sorted with respect to EMPL-NO), a linear search will be performed beginning with the first entry of the table. If we have a reason to begin the search at another point, either constant or variable, such statements as SET N TO 52 or SET N TO FIRST-VALUE can be written. Notice that the SEARCH verb does not include use of the ALL option. The ALL option can be used only with tables that have the KEY option in OCCURS; that is, it can be used only with sorted tables. The search procedure followed is to vary N from its first value of 1, by increments of 1, up to the last value (in this case 400), each time testing to determine if EMPLOYEE-NUMBER equals EMPL-NO(N). If a match is found, NAME(N) is moved to EDIT-NAME so that it can be output. If no match is found in the entire table, AT END is executed.

REVIEW

1 The variant of the subscript concept, which can be used to reference table entries, is called a(n) _____.

index

2 The value of an index used to reference table entries is defined by one of three verbs: SET, SEARCH, or PERFORM. If a SEARCH instruction is

executed and no match is found in the data table, the _____
clause always is executed.

AT END

3   By the alternative approach for determining the employee-number, given the name of the employee, two tables were defined, one for NAME and the other for EMPL-NO. The index number associated with EMPL-NO was set equal to the index of the NAME table being searched by the use of the _____ option.

VARYING

4   When an unsorted table is searched, the method always used is _____ search.

linear

COBOL LANGUAGE OPTIONS IN TABLE SEARCHING

Now that we have explored the basic ideas associated with table searching by means of examples, we can turn our attention to a formal consideration of the language options. We do not consider all the possible options that could be used; rather, we describe the basic ones.

THE OCCURS CLAUSE

First, let us consider the format associated with the OCCURS clause:

```
OCCURS integer TIMES

   [ { ASCENDING  }  KEY IS data-name-1 [data-name-2] ... ]
   [ { DESCENDING }                                       ]

       [INDEXED BY index-name-1 [index-name-2] ... ]
```

Some examples may help illustrate the available forms of the OCCURS option. Let us consider this one first:

```
02   SAMPLE OCCURS 100 TIMES
     ASCENDING KEY IS YEAR MONTH.
     03   OTHER-DATA     PICTURE X(20).
     03   MONTH          PICTURE 99.
     03   YEAR           PICTURE 99.
     03   REST-OF-IT     PICTURE X(40).
```

In this example there are two keys, YEAR and MONTH. Keys are listed in decreasing order of significance. Thus, the months are sorted in ascending sequence within the years, which are also in ascending sequence. As the example illustrates, the order in which the keys appear in the KEY clause is *not* related to their physical order in the record.

Here is a second example:

```
02  SAMPLE PICTURE 9(8) OCCURS 100 TIMES
    INDEXED BY N.
```

In this case we specify an index called N, presumably for the purpose of later using this index in a SEARCH statement.

THE USAGE CLAUSE

Consider now the USAGE clause. We can specify that the USAGE of a data item is INDEX, so that the item can be used in conjunction with SET, SEARCH, or PERFORM statements. You may recall that USAGE IS DISPLAY and USAGE IS COMPUTATIONAL are the other available options; as shown in the following format:

As an example of implementing the USAGE clause, consider the following program segment:

```
01  SAMPLE.
    02  FIRST-PART    PICTURE X(10).
    02  K USAGE IS INDEX.
```

The item called K is an INDEX item; therefore, no PICTURE clause is given. All index items are handled according to the rules associated with particular computer systems. Normally, index items are in binary form.

THE SEARCH VERB

Consider now the SEARCH verb, which is the cornerstone of a search instruction. Two principal formats are available, as follows:

FORMAT 1

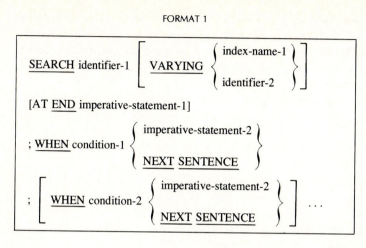

FORMAT 2

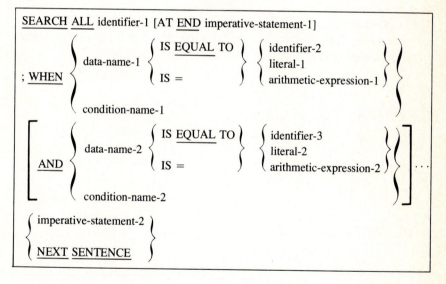

In Format 1, identifier-1 is an item whose description in the DATA DIVISION contains an OCCURS and an INDEXED BY clause. When the VARYING option is used, index-name-2 or identifier-2 is varied in the same way as the index specified in the relevant INDEXED BY clause. Identifier-2 must be specified as USAGE IS INDEX, or it must be an elementary integer item. The AT END clause is optional. If it is omitted, program control will pass to the next sentence when the table has been searched and no match has been found. If AT END is included and imperative-statement-1 does not terminate with GO TO, a branch to the next sentence will be made (in effect bypassing the WHEN clauses). WHEN introduces another form of conditional expression.

Format 2 is used with sorted tables, that is, tables for which the OCCURS clause contains a KEY in addition to the INDEXED BY option. The search may be a binary search, or any other method included in a particular compiler; however, as far as the programmer is concerned, only the instructions included in Format 2 are required.

Notice that in Format 2 only one WHEN option is available, but multiple AND conditions are allowed. Thus, all the conditions must be true in order for the search to be satisfied. In contrast, whenever multiple WHEN statements are used in Format 1, any one of these conditions being true constitutes a sufficient reason for search termination.

THE SET VERB

Basically, the SET verb is a variation of MOVE and provides a way of handling index items. Two formats are available, as follows:

FORMAT 1

$$\underline{SET} \left\{ \begin{array}{l} \text{index-name-1 [index-name-2]} \dots \\ \\ \text{identifier-1 [identifier-2]} \dots \end{array} \right\} \underline{TO} \left\{ \begin{array}{l} \text{index-name-3} \\ \text{identifier-3} \\ \text{integer-1} \end{array} \right\}$$

FORMAT 2

$$\underline{SET} \text{ index-name-1 [index-name-2]} \dots \left\{ \begin{array}{l} \underline{UP}\ \underline{BY} \\ \underline{DOWN}\ \underline{BY} \end{array} \right\} \left\{ \begin{array}{l} \text{identifier-1} \\ \text{integer-1} \end{array} \right\}$$

In Format 1, if we use index-name-1, we can set it equal to index-name-3, identifier-3, or literal-1. If identifier-3 is used, it must be defined as an elementary integer item; if integer-1 is used, it must be a positive integer. If we set identifier-1 and it has not been defined by a USAGE IS INDEX clause, it can be set only to index-name-3.

If we write SET A TO B, we basically are moving the value of B to A. In this way, we can transfer data to an index item or an identifier, for use either in a SEARCH or after a SEARCH. For instance, we may have two tables, one INDEXED BY A and the other INDEXED BY B. After performing a search and finding a match on the first table, we may want to reference the corresponding entry in the second table. We then SET B TO A so that B can be used as a subscript or index in the second table.

In FORMAT 2, we can increase or decrease the value of index-name-1 either by a positive integer (literal-1) or by the value of identifier-1, which must be a field that has not been defined as USAGE IS INDEX. The effect of UP BY is to increase the value of index-name-1, while the effect of DOWN BY is to change index-name-1 by the indicated decrement.

REVIEW

1 The COBOL language option used to indicate the total number of table entries and to identify the key or keys associated with the records is the _____ clause.

OCCURS

2 The COBOL option used to identify a particular data item as being an index is the _____ clause.

USAGE

3 The COBOL verb that identifies the table to be searched and also includes options to indicate what should be done when a match is found as well as when it is not found is _____.

SEARCH

4 The COBOL verb that is a variation of the MOVE verb and provides the basis for designating the value to be assigned to an INDEX is _____.

SET

SAMPLE PROGRAM WITH INDEXING AND SEARCHING

An input file consists of records containing a student name and the numeric score for each of eight parts of a standardized test. Our objective is to store the data in a table and then to illustrate use of SEARCH to identify those students who either scored 100.0 on any part of the test, or who scored less than 50.0 on any part of the test.

The program is presented in Figure 12–3. Notice that S is designated in the WORKING-STORAGE in INDEXED BY S, and then it is used in the PERFORM . . . VARYING of the PROGRAM-SUMMARY paragraph. Then observe that, after the PERFORM statement, we write SET S DOWN BY 1, which means to subtract 1 from S. After so adjusting S, it represents the

number of student records that were read in. We then save the value of S in
M (SET M TO S) to be used to control the printing task. Notice that M is a
WORKING-STORAGE USAGE INDEX item.

After the table has been stored, we search it in the CHECK-SCORES-
AND-PRINT paragraph. Notice that we did not include the AT END option

FIGURE 12-3   LISTING FOR PROGRAM WITH INDEXING AND SEARCHING.

```
IDENTIFICATION DIVISION.
PROGRAM-ID.  GRADES.
*
ENVIRONMENT DIVISION.
*
CONFIGURATION SECTION.
SOURCE-COMPUTER.  ABC-480.
OBJECT-COMPUTER.  ABC-480.
*
INPUT-OUTPUT SECTION.
FILE-CONTROL.
    SELECT EXAM-FILE ASSIGN TO CARD-READER.
    SELECT REPORT-FILE ASSIGN TO PRINTER.
/
DATA DIVISION.
*
FILE SECTION.
*
FD   EXAM-FILE
     LABEL RECORDS OMITTED
     DATA RECORD IS EXAM-REC.
01   EXAM-REC.
     02  STUDENT-NAME               PIC X(20).
     02  EXAM-SCORES.
         03  SCORES-IN
             OCCURS 8 TIMES         PIC 9(3)V9.
     02  FILLER                     PIC X(28).
*
FD   REPORT-FILE
     LABEL RECORDS OMITTED
     DATA RECORD REPORT-REC.
01   REPORT-REC                     PIC X(132).
*
WORKING-STORAGE SECTION.
*
01   END-OF-FILE-SWITCH             PIC XXX VALUE 'NO'.
     88  END-OF-FILE                VALUE 'YES'.
*
01   M   USAGE INDEX.
*
*
01   EXAM-TABLE.
     02  STUDENT-DATA
         OCCURS 50 TIMES
         INDEXED BY S.
         03  STUDENT-NAME           PIC X(20).
         03  EXAM-SCORES.
             04  SCORE              PIC 9(3)V9
                 OCCURS 8 TIMES
                 INDEXED BY Q.
*
*
*
01   HEADING-1.
     02  FILLER                     PIC X(50) VALUE SPACES.
     02  FILLER                     PIC X(9) VALUE 'EXAM PART'.
*
01   HEADING-2.
     02  FILLER                     PIC X(8) VALUE SPACES.
     02  FILLER                     PIC X(12) VALUE 'STUDENT-NAME'.
     02  FILLER                     PIC X(12) VALUE SPACES.
     02  FILLER                     PIC X(50) VALUE
         '1      2      3      4      5      6      7      8'.
*
01   REPORT-LINE.
     02  FILLER                     PIC X(5) VALUE SPACES.
     02  STUDENT-NAME               PIC X(20).
     02  FILLER                     PIC X(2) VALUE SPACES.
     02  SCORE-OUT
         OCCURS 8 TIMES
         INDEXED BY R
         PICTURE ZZZ99.9.
```

(continued)

```
/
 PROCEDURE DIVISION.
*
 PROGRAM-SUMMARY.
     OPEN INPUT EXAM-FILE
          OUTPUT REPORT-FILE.
*
     PERFORM READ-EXAM-REC
*
     PERFORM STORE-RECORD
             VARYING S FROM 1 BY 1
                     UNTIL S > 50
                     OR END-OF-FILE.
*
     SET S DOWN BY 1.
     SET M TO S.
*
     WRITE REPORT-REC FROM HEADING-1 AFTER PAGE.
     WRITE REPORT-REC FROM HEADING-2 AFTER 2.
*
     PERFORM CHECK-SCORES-AND-PRINT
             VARYING S FROM 1 BY 1
                     UNTIL S > M.
*
     CLOSE EXAM-FILE
           REPORT-FILE.
*
     STOP RUN.
/
 CHECK-SCORES-AND-PRINT.
     SET Q TO 1
     SEARCH SCORE
            WHEN SCORE (S, Q) = 100.0
                 PERFORM PRINT-SCORES;
            WHEN SCORE (S, Q) < 50.0
                 PERFORM PRINT-SCORES.
*
 PRINT-SCORES.
     PERFORM MOVE-SCORES
             VARYING Q FROM 1 BY 1
                     UNTIL Q > 8.
     MOVE STUDENT-NAME OF EXAM-TABLE (S)
          TO STUDENT-NAME OF REPORT-LINE
     WRITE REPORT-REC FROM REPORT-LINE
           AFTER ADVANCING 2 LINES.
*
 MOVE-SCORES.
     SET R TO Q
     MOVE SCORE (S, Q) TO SCORE-OUT (R).
*
 READ-EXAM-REC.
     READ EXAM-FILE RECORD
          AT END MOVE 'YES' TO END-OF-FILE-SWITCH.
*
 STORE-RECORD.
     MOVE STUDENT-NAME OF EXAM-REC
          TO STUDENT-NAME OF EXAM-TABLE (S).
     MOVE EXAM-SCORES OF EXAM-REC
          TO EXAM-SCORES OF EXAM-TABLE (S).
*
     PERFORM READ-EXAM-REC.
```

FIGURE 12-3 (*Continued*)

in this use of Format 1 of the SEARCH, since it was not needed. If neither a score of 100 nor a score of less than 50 is found for a given student, we simply want to continue with the next student without doing anything AT END.

When either one of the two search conditions is true, we PERFORM PRINT-SCORES and the search for that student record terminates. Then, because of the PERFORM CHECK-SCORES-AND-PRINT in the PROGRAM-SUMMARY, we repeat the search for the next student.

The MOVE-SCORES paragraph illustrates again the use of SET. Since SCORE-OUT was indexed by R, we SET R TO Q so that in the MOVE statement we reference the corresponding scores.

Sample Input

STUDENT-1	09051000082306000900089909770777
STUDENT-2	02000732066605920812085503000600
STUDENT-3	09000820100008320777075306890920
STUDENT-4	07450789082306950765074806780802
STUDENT-5	04500720073010000235024506250213

Sample Output

	EXAM PART							
STUDENT NAME	1	2	3	4	5	6	7	8
STUDENT-1	90.5	100.0	82.3	60.0	90.0	89.9	87.7	77.7
STUDENT-2	20.0	73.2	66.6	59.2	81.2	85.5	30.0	60.0
STUDENT-3	90.5	82.0	100.0	83.2	77.7	75.3	68.9	92.0
STUDENT-5	45.0	72.0	73.0	100.0	23.5	24.5	62.5	21.3

FIGURE 12-4   SAMPLE INPUT AND OUTPUT FOR THE PROGRAM WITH INDEXING AND SEARCH-ING.

Figure 12-4 illustrates sample input and output for the program. The program provides a somewhat contrived set of cases to illustrate the options. Exercise 12.4 at the end of the chapter asks the student to modify the example in order to incorporate other features of searching.

EXERCISES

12.1   A marketing survey conducted by a company involved administering a questionnaire of 25 questions. The responses to each question have been coded by a 1-digit code, ranging from 0 to 9. We want to

Question	Response Code									
	0	1	2	3	4	5	6	7	8	9
1										
2										
⋮										
24										
25										

accumulate a table of the responses to each of the 25 questions, as shown in the diagram on page 340. Write DATA DIVISION entries to form such a table. It should be possible to make reference to each individual cell in the table, as well as each row (question).

12.2 Suppose that the table described in the following contains 20 values:

```
01  SALES-DATA-TABLE.
    02   SALES-TERRITORY
         OCCURS 5 TIMES.
         03   QUARTER-SALES
              OCCURS 4 TIMES
              PICTURE 9(6)V99.
```

We wish to print the table values with the rows representing quarters and the columns representing sales territories. Write the necessary program instructions.

12.3 Card records contain sales data as follows:

COLUMNS	DATA
1–5	Amount (whole dollar)
6	Region code: 1 = West, 2 = Midwest 3 = South, 4 = East
7–8	Month code (numeric)

We want to be able to read in the data and produce the sales analysis report on page 342. Input records that contain error region codes, error month codes, or nonnumeric amounts should be excluded from the tabulation and are to be printed with a suitable error message. Data are shown below. Write a program to produce such a report.

00133412	00197308	00152201	00160108	00060412
00096410	00142409	00118408	00152109	00030411
00085201	00356407	00190406	00202100	0015412
00099101	00428407	00150309	00200312	00018311
00110202	00234202	00160110	00145311	00072312
00100303	00152103	00213211	20200410	00035211
00050405	00123101	00115112	00900309	00150303
00040004	01100205	00118109	00100106	00160202
00030704	01200307	00219208	00500206	00110101
00018103	00142211	00300402	/ 560507	00200204
00025302	00156208	00200203	70082 01	00220308
00020401	00171307	00145302	00233102	00183407
00010106	00145405	00142304	00422109	00157301
00123102	00201403	00140205	00150212	00085409
00185303	00300302	00150207	00050211	00096110

ACME CORPORATION
SALES ANALYSIS REPORT

MONTH	WEST	MIDWEST	SOUTH	EAST	MONTHLY TOTAL	PERCENT OF YEAR TOTAL
JANUARY						
FEBRUARY						
MARCH						
APRIL						
MAY						
JUNE						
JULY						
AUGUST						
SEPTEMBER						
OCTOBER						
NOVEMBER						
DECEMBER						
TOTAL						
PERCENT OF TOTAL						

12.4 Modify the sample searching program in the last section of the chapter as follows. Assume that the student names are sorted in ascending sequence. After the table is created, read records, each of which contains a student name. Search the table and print the test score data for that student. If the name of the student cannot be found, print a suitable error message.

12.5 Write a COBOL program segment to perform a search in a sorted table called TABLE, searching for an entry that matches THIS-RECORD. If a match is found, the program goes to the paragraph MATCHED; otherwise, it goes to the paragraph NO-MATCH. Use I to hold the position of the matching table entry, if there is a match. Assume the following data descriptions:

```
01  THIS-RECORD      PICTURE X(12).
01  I                PICTURE 999.
01  TABLE.
    02  CELL         PICTURE X(12) OCCURS 100 TIMES
                     INDEXED BY N.
```

12.6 How does COBOL differentiate between searching sorted and unsorted tables?

12.7 What is the difference between an index and a subscript in COBOL?

12.8 Review the meaning of the following search-related COBOL features, explaining the use of each feature:

    a OCCURS accompanied by the ASCENDING, (DESCENDING) KEY options
    b INDEXED BY
    c USAGE IS INDEX
    d SEARCH and its several optional forms
    e SET TO and SET UP BY or SET DOWN BY

12.9 Incorporate the indexing capability of COBOL into a program that you have written previously, and use the SEARCH verb in conjunction with any required search.

13

Indexed sequential file processing

INTRODUCTION

In Chapter 9, we introduced the three common methods of file organization: sequential, indexed sequential, and relative or direct. We also described programming concepts relating to the first of these organizational methods. In this chapter, we will describe the Indexed Sequential Access Method (ISAM), while in the following chapter we shall study the processing of relative files.

INDEXED SEQUENTIAL FILE ORGANIZATION

This form of file organization represents something of a balance between sequential file organization and relative file organization. It allows sequential storage but facilitates random accessing or processing. The method utilizes an index table that indicates the approximate storage location for a given record. An indexed sequential file consists of two principal components: the *main file* and the *index*.

The *main file* is the storage area that includes the records in sequential order. It consists of two segments, namely, the *prime* area and the *overflow* area. The prime area is loaded with the records in sequential order when the file is first created, whereas the overflow area is designed to accommodate additions to the file.

The *index* (or index file) is designed to facilitate random access to records in the main file. Its function is similar to the labels attached to the outside of each card drawer in a typical library card catalog. If we are trying to locate the card reference to an author, say, C. A. Johnson, we consult the labels on the fronts of the card drawers. We start from the beginning until we find the drawer that indicates that the last card in that drawer exceeds "Johnson" or, by coincidence, that it is "Johnson." In a somewhat similar way, the index file consists of records referencing the last record in each group of records in the main file. When we want to access a record identified by a key, such as "Johnson," the index is searched until we find a record that equals or exceeds "Johnson." At that point, we have identified the group of records that includes the "Johnson" record.

Because disks are subdivided naturally into cylinders and tracks within cylinders, the index file often consists of two levels of indexes, as illustrated in Figure 13-1. In the figure, we have assumed a simplified case of a file written on three cylinders, each cylinder consisting of 10 tracks (numbered 0 through 9). The first record in the cylinder index shows that the last record in that cylinder has a key of DAN, and that the track index for that cylinder is in cylinder 0, track 0. Turning to the track index for that cylinder, we see that the last record on the first track (cylinder 0, track 0) is 'ANDY,' the last record on the second track is CHRIS, and the last record on the tenth track is DAN. Suppose we are trying to locate the record for "GIGI." The process is as follows. First, the cylinder index is searched until LINDA is encountered. Since LINDA is higher than GIGI, the GIGI record must be in the second cylinder (cylinder 1). Next, we find that the first record on the track index for cylinder 1 is GEORGE; so we read the second record —HELEN. Now we know that GIGI is in the second track (track 1) of the second cylinder. At this point, the identified track is read sequentially to locate the record itself (or perhaps to discover that there is no record identified as GIGI).

This illustration highlights the structure and use of the index file in an indexed sequential file. Creation of the index is done by the operating system, not by the applications programmer; nevertheless, it is useful to understand the rudiments of the indexing method. When a file is created initially as an indexed file, the records must be in ascending order with respect to their key, and the operating system creates the main file and the index.

CYLINDER INDEX

CYLINDER NUMBER	HIGHEST KEY IN CYLINDER	ADDRESS OF TRACK INDEX FOR CYLINDER
0	DAN	00
1	LINDA	10
2	WILLIE	20

TRACK INDEXES FOR EACH CYLINDER

TRACK ADDRESS OF TRACK INDEX	HIGHEST KEY IN TRACK	ADDRESS OF TRACK	
00	ANDY	00	
00	CHRIS	01	
.	.		Cylinder 0
.	.		
.	.		
00	DAN	09	
10	GEORGE	10	
10	HELEN	11	
.	.		Cylinder 1
.	.		
10	LINDA	19	
20	MARIAN	20	
20	PAT	21	
.	.		Cylinder 2
.	.		
20	WILLIE	29	

FIGURE 13-1   **ILLUSTRATION OF CYLINDER AND TRACK INDEXES.**

The area on which the main file is written during its creation is called the *prime* area. After the file is created initially, we may want to add records to it. This is permissible, but it introduces some complications. The added records result in creation of *overflow,* which is an area separate from the prime area. Thus, *physically,* the main file no longer is sequential; however, from the point of view of the programmer, the file is *logically* sequential. The records in the prime tracks are linked to the records in the overflow tracks, so that the file is accessible as if it were in physical sequential order. We also should point out that, just as the main file is subdivided into prime and overflow areas, so is the index file enhanced to include index records in prime and in overflow tracks. The details of overflow concepts and implementation go beyond the scope of this book; still, the user of COBOL should be aware of the fact that the presence of overflow slows down the processing of an indexed file. As a result, when "enough" records have been added to degrade performance sufficiently, the file is re-created to organize it physically as one file in prime areas and to eliminate the overflow.

When records are deleted from the file, they normally are "tagged" as deleted, but they are not physically erased. Again, from the viewpoint of the applications programmer, the records are not there, since the operating system "skips" over them as the result of reading the deletion code written on the record.

REVIEW

1   The type of disk file organization that allows sequential storage but facilitates random accessing or processing is called _____ _____ file organization.

indexed sequential

2   The *main file* in an indexed sequential file includes two types of file storage areas referred to as the _____ area and the _____ area.

prime; overflow

3   The index file used in conjunction with an indexed sequential file often consists of two levels of indexes: a _____ index and a _____ index.

cylinder; track

4   Suppose that a file is written on five cylinders of 10 tracks each and that the cylinder index indicates that a particular record is in cylinder 3. The track location for this record then is determined by reference to track _____ of cylinder _____.

0; 3 (because the track index is commonly written in the first track of the designated cylinder)

5   After records are added to an indexed sequential file, the added records are stored in the [prime / overflow] area.

overflow

6   After records are added to an indexed sequential file, the file no longer is sequential [logically / physically] but is sequential [logically / physically].

physically; logically

7   Records that are deleted from an indexed sequential file normally [are /
    are not] physically erased from the file.

are not

AN EXAMPLE OF THE CREATION OF AN INDEXED FILE

An indexed file may be created with minimal effort on the part of the
programmer. The source records first must be sorted in ascending sequence
on a data field that will serve as a sort key for the file. It should be kept in
mind that an indexed file is a sequential file; therefore, the records are
positioned in ascending order. We should consider an example to illustrate
the process.

Suppose that source records that contain data about vendors are available on punched cards. Columns 1–8 contain an identifier that is unique for
each vendor, columns 9–68 contain other relevant data, and columns 69–80
are unused. We want to copy these records on disk, forming an indexed file
sorted on the basis of the data in columns 1–8. Each disk record will consist
of 68 characters.

First, we sort the source records on columns 1–8. In the following
sample data, the records already are sorted, except for the fourth record
(37654310), which is placed out of order purposely to illustrate the effects of
such a condition:

```
12345678ACME-10
22345678ACME-20
35120001ACME-30
37654310ACME-40
35290001ACME-50
45678912ACME-60
49678912ACME-70
54371203ACME-80
58120000ACME-90
60000000ACME-92
70000000ACME-93
80000000ACME-94
99999999ACME-99
```

Figure 13–2 presents a COBOL program written to create an indexed file.
Notice the SELECT statement. ACCESS IS SEQUENTIAL specifies that the
access mode for this file is sequential. ORGANIZATION IS INDEXED
specifies that this is an indexed file. RECORD KEY IS VENDOR-NUMBER

```
IDENTIFICATION DIVISION.
PROGRAM-ID. INDEXFILE.
ENVIRONMENT DIVISION.
CONFIGURATION SECTION.
SOURCE-COMPUTER. ABC-480.
OBJECT-COMPUTER. ABC-480.
INPUT-OUTPUT SECTION.
FILE-CONTROL.
     SELECT DISKFILE    ASSIGN TO  DISK-DEVICE
                        ACCESS IS SEQUENTIAL
                        ORGANIZATION IS INDEXED
                        RECORD KEY IS VENDOR-NUMBER.
     SELECT  CARDFILE   ASSIGN TO CARD-READER.
     SELECT  PRINTFILE  ASSIGN TO PRINTER.
DATA DIVISION.
FILE SECTION.
FD  DISKFILE LABEL RECORDS ARE STANDARD
             DATA RECORD IS DISK-RECORD.
01  DISK-RECORD.
     02 VENDOR-NUMBER       PIC X(8).
     02 VENDOR-DATA         PIC X(60).
*
FD  CARDFILE LABEL RECORD OMITTED
             DATA  RECORD IS CARD.
01  CARD.
     02 VENDOR-IDENT        PIC 9(8).
     02 VENDOR-DATA         PIC X(60).
     02 FILLER             PIC X(12).
FD  PRINTFILE LABEL RECORDS OMITTED
             DATA RECORD IS PRINT-RECORD.
01  PRINT-RECORD           PIC X(132).
*
WORKING-STORAGE SECTION.
01  END-OF-DATA-INDICATOR  PIC 9 VALUE ZERO.
     88 INPUT-ENDED VALUE 1.
/
PROCEDURE DIVISION.
MAIN-ROUTINE.
     OPEN INPUT CARDFILE
          OUTPUT DISKFILE, PRINTFILE.
     PERFORM READ-CARD.
     PERFORM FILE-CREATE
          UNTIL INPUT-ENDED.
     CLOSE CARDFILE DISKFILE
     STOP RUN.
*
READ-CARD.
     READ CARDFILE RECORD
          AT END MOVE 1 TO END-OF-DATA-INDICATOR.
*
FILE-CREATE.
     MOVE VENDOR-IDENT TO VENDOR-NUMBER
     MOVE VENDOR-DATA OF CARD TO VENDOR-DATA OF DISK-RECORD
     WRITE DISK-RECORD
          INVALID KEY  PERFORM ERROR-CASE.
     PERFORM READ-CARD.
*
ERROR-CASE.
     MOVE ' INVALID KEY CONDITION FOR THIS RECORD' TO PRINT-RECORD
     WRITE PRINT-RECORD AFTER ADVANCING 1 LINE
     WRITE PRINT-RECORD FROM CARD AFTER ADVANCING 1 LINE.
```

FIGURE 13-2   A COBOL PROGRAM TO CREATE AN INDEXED FILE.

specifies that there is a field called VENDOR-NUMBER that is a field in the file record and that serves as the sort key for the file. In other words, the file will be in ascending order of VENDOR-NUMBER values.

In the DATA DIVISION in Figure 13-2, observe that VENDOR-NUMBER is a field in the record description of the indexed file (DISKFILE). The current ANS COBOL standard specifies that RECORD KEY must be a field in the file record and that it must be alphanumeric. At the time of this writing, different compilers handle the process differently. For example, IBM compilers require that the first field in the record be a deletion code set to LOW-VALUES by the programmer to indicate that a record exists (that is, that it has not been deleted—which could happen in subsequent processing of the file). Therefore, if you are using such a compiler, VENDOR-NUMBER cannot be the first field in the record. As another example of variable practice, some UNIVAC compilers use the term ACTUAL KEY instead of REC-ORD KEY and allow that key to be a field in WORKING-STORAGE. We anticipate that such variations from the standard will have been removed from current practice by the time this book is published. Still, many programs have been written under the old guidelines, and one can expect to continue seeing these variations in existing programs.

In the PROCEDURE DIVISION of Figure 13–2, the relevant part is:

```
FILE-CREATE.
    MOVE VENDOR-INDENT TO VENDOR-NUMBER
    MOVE VENDOR-DATA OF CARD TO VENDOR-DATA OF DISK-RECORD
    WRITE DISK-RECORD
        INVALID KEY PERFORM ERROR-CASE.
    PERFORM READ-CARD.
```

We move VENDOR-INDENT, a field in the input card, to VENDOR-NUMBER, which was declared to be the RECORD KEY in the SELECT statement. The move of VENDOR-DATA simply transfers the other fields of the source record to the output record. The WRITE statement now includes the INVALID KEY condition. This condition is true whenever the record key of the record about to be written is not greater than the key of the preceding record in the file. If the INVALID KEY condition is true, we execute the imperative statement that follows—in this case, PERFORM ERROR-CASE. Reviewing ERROR-CASE in Figure 13–2, we observe that we print an error message and list the error record. Using the sample input data presented earlier, we would receive one error message and the fourth record would be printed, since it is the one record out of sequence.

Creation of an indexed file is a complex task; yet the language is very high level with respect to this task. The programmer need write very few instructions to invoke the procedure necessary for the task. In review, these instructions involve a few clauses in the SELECT statement, provision for a record key in the record description of the file, and moving data to the output record in the PROCEDURE DIVISION. In the following section, we study these specialized instructions in a more thorough and comprehensive framework.

REVIEW

1   An indexed file essentially is a [sequential / direct] file.

sequential

2   In the ENVIRONMENT DIVISION, after the file is described as being SEQUENTIAL and INDEXED, the basis on which the file is sorted is identified by the COBOL reserved words _____.

RECORD KEY

3   The current ANS COBOL standard specifies that RECORD KEY must be alphanumeric and that it [must / need not] be a field in the file record.

must

4   The fact that one or more records to be written in an indexed file are not in the appropriate sequence is detected and identified by using the _____ option in conjunction with the WRITE statement.

INVALID KEY

COBOL LANGUAGE INSTRUCTIONS FOR INDEXED FILES

Indexed files are in very wide use. Even though the early standard version of COBOL had no provision for them, the use of such files increased substantially in the early 1970s. As a consequence, each manufacturer developed its own program instructions and procedures. The current version of ANS COBOL does contain language formats for indexed files; we present these here. It should be noted that many programs were written in the prestandard era, and it will be natural to find continued adherence to manufacturer-dependent versions for some years to come. Fortunately, the current variations among manufacturers and the standard are not great, and the reader of this text should need only minimal changes to adopt the standard to a local version, if it is necessary to do so.

There are two divisions that involve special instructions—the ENVIRONMENT DIVISION and the PROCEDURE DIVISION.

ENVIRONMENT DIVISION

In the ENVIRONMENT DIVISION, we encounter some new options based on the following format:

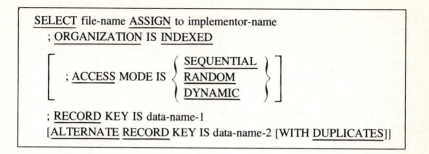

The ORGANIZATION statement specifies that this will be an indexed file and ultimately will invoke the program routines that will create or use the index. COBOL is a very high-level language in this option. Creation and use of the index is a complex procedure, yet the programmer needs to write one statement only.

The ACCESS MODE clause specifies the way records in the file will be accessed. ACCESS MODE IS SEQUENTIAL specifies that records will be accessed in ascending order of the record key. Omission of the ACCESS clause defaults to the SEQUENTIAL option. Thus, up to now, our omission of this clause from programming considerations in this book has implied the sequential access mode. The RANDOM option specifies that the order in which records are accessed will be controlled by the programmer. This control is accomplished by moving the value of the key of the desired record into the RECORD KEY field and then issuing an input-output command (READ, WRITE, REWRITE, DELETE).

The DYNAMIC option allows the programmer to change at will from sequential access to random access, using appropriate forms of input-output statements. This option is not implemented in some compilers. In its absence, the file for a given program must be declared to be either in SEQUENTIAL or in RANDOM access mode, but not in both modes in the same program.

We repeat here a point made in the previous section on creating an indexed file. When the file is first being created, it *must* be in sequential access mode. In subsequent uses, it may be in any of the three options, SEQUENTIAL, RANDOM, or DYNAMIC.

RECORD KEY references a data-name that must be a field within the record description of the file. In case of multiple records, a field from any record description may be given. RECORD KEY specifies the field, on the basis of which the file is sorted. The ALTERNATE RECORD option specifies a record key that is an alternate record key for the file. When alternate keys are used, we can access records either on the basis of the *prime* key specified in the RECORD KEY clause or on the basis of another ALTERNATE RECORD KEY. The file, of course, always is sorted on the basis of the prime record key. The DUPLICATES phrase specifies that the value of the associated alternate record key may be duplicated within any of the records in the file. In the absence of this phrase, the presence of duplicate key values is an error condition. Notice that duplicate key values are permitted for alternate keys. Each record must have a unique prime key. An example of alternate key values that are duplicates may be the ZIP code in a record where the ZIP code was specified as an alternate record key. Such a key allows the accessing of a record with a specified ZIP code—with recognition that the record so accessed will not be unique with respect to this (alternate) key value.

REVIEW

1   In the SELECT statement in the ENVIRONMENT DIVISION, the fact that a file is to be set up as an indexed file is specified by the _____ statement.

ORGANIZATION

2   A file organized as an indexed file [can / cannot] be accessed in a sequential manner.

can

3   Omission of the ACCESS clause in the SELECT statement for an indexed file results in the file having to be accessed by the [sequential / random] mode.

sequential

4   The ACCESS MODE option that allows the programmer to change at will from sequential access to random access is called the _____ mode.

DYNAMIC

5   When the ALTERNATE RECORD KEY is used to access a record in a file, the file has to be sorted on the basis of the [prime / alternate] key.

prime

6   The ALTERNATE KEY associated with a record [must / need not] be a unique key value in the file.

need not

PROCEDURE DIVISION

An indexed file can be opened as INPUT, OUTPUT, or I/O (input-output). Table 13–1 summarizes the permissible input-output statements for each of these options, depending on the access mode specified.

Reading records from an indexed file is accomplished by using one of the two following formats:

Format 1

```
READ file-name [NEXT] RECORD [INTO identifier]
    [; AT END imperative-statement]
```

Format 2

```
READ file-name RECORD [INTO identifier]
    [; KEY IS data-name]
    [; INVALID KEY imperative-statement]
```

The first format must be used if the SEQUENTIAL access mode has been specified either explicitly or implicitly (by default). The NEXT phrase must be specified when a file is declared to be in the DYNAMIC access mode and

TABLE 13–1   PERMISSIBLE INPUT-OUTPUT STATEMENTS

FILE ACCESS MODE	STATEMENT	OPEN MODE		
		INPUT	OUTPUT	I/O
Sequential	READ	X		X
	WRITE		X	
	REWRITE			X
	START	X		X
	DELETE			X
Random	READ	X		X
	WRITE		X	X
	REWRITE			X
	START			
	DELETE			X
Dynamic	READ	X		X
	WRITE		X	X
	REWRITE			X
	START	X		X
	DELETE			X

records are to be retrieved sequentially. Execution of READ . . . NEXT REC-ORD retrieves from the file the next record whose record key is higher than the one accessed previously. From a logical standpoint, READ . . . NEXT operates identically to READ in a sequential magnetic tape file. We use the qualification "from a logical standpoint" because in an indexed file the physical and logical order may not be in direct correspondence. This happens when an indexed file has new records added to it. Instead of being "squeezed" in between existing records, they are put in a physically separate location (overflow) and connected by address pointers to the records that logically precede and follow them. The AT END clause has the same meaning as in a sequential file.

Format 2 is used for files in RANDOM access mode; it also is used when records are to be retrieved randomly from a file in DYNAMIC access mode. The KEY clause references the data-name specified as a key either in the RECORD KEY or the ALTERNATE RECORD KEY clauses. If the KEY clause is omitted in the Format 2 READ statement, the prime key (RECORD KEY) of the file is assumed by default. The INVALID KEY condition holds when no record can be located whose record key matches the value of the data-name specified or implied by the KEY IS clause. For instance, we may have:

MOVE 123456789 TO SOC-SEC-NO.
READ STUDENT-MASTER RECORD
    KEY IS SOC-SEC-NO
    INVALID KEY PERFORM ERROR-READ.

In this example, ERROR-READ will be executed if no record in the file has a SOC-SEC-NO key equal to 123456789.

Records are recorded in the file by use of the following WRITE statement format:

<u>WRITE</u> record-name [<u>FROM</u> identifier] [; <u>INVALID</u> KEY imperative-statement]

When a file is being created, WRITE is used as illustrated in the previous section. After a file has been created, WRITE is used to add new records to the file. As always, the proper value is moved to the prime record key, and the execution of WRITE causes the new record to be inserted in the correct logical position within the file. The INVALID KEY condition is true under the following circumstances: (1) when the file has been opened as OUTPUT, and the value of the prime record key is not greater than the value of the prime record key of the previous record; (2) when the file has been opened as I/O, and the value of the prime record key is equal to the value of the prime record key of a record already existing in the file; (3) when an attempt is being made to write more records than can be accommodated by the available disk storage.

The INVALID KEY clause appears as an option in the general format. From the viewpoint of this text, it is required. It is *not* required whenever the programmer provides for the same effect as the INVALID KEY clause by use of the USE verb. However, a discussion of the USE verb is beyond the scope of this book, since it is employed in more advanced applications than the ones reasonable for student environments. Therefore, WRITE should include the INVALID KEY clause.

In updating tasks, REWRITE is used to replace a record existing in the file. The format is as follows:

REWRITE record-name [FROM identifier] [; INVALID KEY
imperative-statement]

At the time of execution of REWRITE, the file must be open in the I/O mode. The record being replaced is the one whose key matches the value of the prime record key. The INVALID KEY holds when the value of the record key in the record to be replaced does not match the value of the record key of the last record read, or the value of the record key does not equal the record key of any record existing in the file.

The DELETE statement logically removes a record from an indexed file. The format is:

DELETE file-name RECORD [;INVALID KEY imperative-statement]

A DELETE command can be executed only if the file has been opened in I/O mode. If the file was declared to be in a SEQUENTIAL access mode, the INVALID KEY must *not* be specified, because a DELETE statement must have been preceded by a successful READ statement, which precludes the possibility of any INVALID KEY condition. The AT END associated with READ serves in lieu of the INVALID KEY in such a case.

If the file has been declared to be in RANDOM or DYNAMIC access mode, INVALID KEY is true when the file does not contain a record whose prime record key value matches the value of the record key. Thus, the programmer is responsible for moving the key value of the record to be deleted to RECORD KEY.

The START verb allows sequential retrieval of records from a point other than the beginning of the file. Thus, it is possible to retrieve records sequentially starting with some record in the "middle" of the file, as shown in the following:

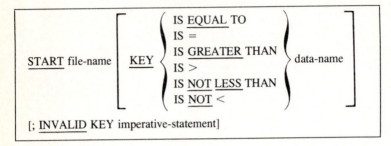

The file must be in SEQUENTIAL or DYNAMIC access mode and must be open in the INPUT or I/O mode at the time START is executed. The KEY phrase may be omitted, in which case EQUAL is implied. In essence, the START statement means to position the file to that record whose record key satisfies the explicit or implicit KEY condition. For example, if CUSTOMER-NAME is a record key and we want to retrieve the records of customers whose names begin with M or higher, we can write:

```
MOVE 'M' TO CUSTOMER-NAME
START CUSTOMER-FILE
    KEY IS NOT LESS THAN CUSTOMER-NAME
    INVALID KEY PERFORM ERROR-START.
```

In this program segment, MOVE is an alphanumeric move resulting in CUSTOMER-NAME containing the letter M and blanks to the right of M. The KEY IS NOT LESS condition specifies that we want to position the file to the first record whose key is not less than the letter M; in other words, it will be the first name that begins with the letter M. A READ statement then retrieves that record, and subsequent READ statement execution retrieves the following records sequentially.

The data-name in the KEY phrase can be either a record key (specified as RECORD KEY, or ALTERNATE RECORD KEY) or a data item subordinate to a record key, provided that the data item is the first (leftmost) field in the record key. In other words we can specify the "first part" of a record key.

The INVALID condition is true if the KEY condition cannot be met. For example, consider the following program segment:

```
MOVE 'MICHNER' TO CUSTOMER-NAME.
START CUSTOMER-FILE
    KEY IS EQUAL TO CUSTOMER-NAME
    INVALID KEY PERFORM ERROR-START.
```

ERROR-START will be executed if there is no customer in the file whose record key is equal to 'MICHNER'.

REVIEW

1   In the PROCEDURE DIVISION, reading records from an indexed file is accomplished by using the _____ verb.

READ

2   Whenever records in an indexed file are to be retrieved randomly, the _____ clause indicates the data-name to be used to identify each record.

KEY

3   If the KEY clause is omitted in conjunction with random retrieval of records, the basis for identifying each record is the [RECORD KEY / ALTERNATE RECORD KEY].

RECORD KEY

4   In the PROCEDURE DIVISION, records are added to an indexed file by using the _____ verb.

WRITE

5   Execution of a WRITE statement to add a record to an indexed file results in the record being added [at the end of the file / in the correct logical position within the file].

in the correct logical position within the file

6   The verb that is used to modify a record held in an indexed file is _____.

REWRITE

7   In order for a REWRITE instruction to be executed, the file must be open in _____ mode.

I/O

8   The verb used to remove a record from an indexed file is _____.

DELETE

9   A DELETE command can be executed only if the file has been opened in _____ mode.

I/O

10   The verb that makes possible the sequential retrieval of records from a point other than the beginning of the file is ——————.

START

11   In conjunction with executing a START statement, the data-name used as the key [must / need not] have been specified previously as RECORD KEY or ALTERNATE RECORD KEY.

need not

AN EXAMPLE OF PROCESSING AN INDEXED FILE

We present an example here that illustrates the use of most of the language statements and options presented in the preceding section. The example involves processing the vendor file created by the example program in Figure 13-2. We now give the following record description to the file:

```
FD  DISKFILE LABEL RECORDS ARE STANDARD
              DATA RECORD IS DISK-RECORD.
01  DISK-RECORD.
    02  VENDOR-NUMBER    PIC X(8).
    02  VENDOR-NAME      PIC X(15).
    02  VENDOR-ADDRESS   PIC X(45).
```

Transaction records are submitted through a CARDFILE and have the following record description:

```
01  CARD.
    02  TRANS-CODE                              PIC 9.
        88  CHANGE-ADDRESS                      VALUE 1.
        88  ADD-VENDOR                          VALUE 2.
        88  DELETE-VENDOR                       VALUE 3.
        88  ERROR-CODE VALUES ARE ZERO, 4 THRU 9.
    02  VENDOR-IDENT                            PIC 9(8).
    02  VENDOR-NAME                             PIC X(15).
    02  VENDOR-ADDRESS                          PIC X(45).
    02  FILLER                                  PIC X(11).
```

It is apparent from the self-documenting nature of this record description that we are interested in changing the address of a vendor, and in adding or deleting vendors.

Figure 13-3 presents the complete program. Notice in the ENVIRON-MENT DIVISION that DISKFILE is in DYNAMIC access mode and that

FIGURE 13-3 SAMPLE PROGRAM TO ILLUSTRATE PROCESSING OF AN INDEXED FILE.

```
IDENTIFICATION DIVISION.
PROGRAM-ID. UPDATEISAM.
ENVIRONMENT DIVISION.
CONFIGURATION SECTION.
SOURCE-COMPUTER. ABC-480.
OBJECT-COMPUTER. ABC-480.
INPUT-OUTPUT SECTION.
FILE-CONTROL.
    SELECT DISKFILE ASSIGN TO MASS-STORAGE-ISAMFILE
                    ORGANIZATION IS INDEXED
                    ACCESS MODE IS DYNAMIC
                    RECORD KEY IS VENDOR-NUMBER.
*
    SELECT CARDFILE ASSIGN TO CARD-READER.
    SELECT PRINTFILE ASSIGN TO PRINTER.
DATA DIVISION.
FILE SECTION.
FD  DISKFILE LABEL RECORDS ARE STANDARD
             DATA RECORD IS DISK-RECORD.
01  DISK-RECORD.
    02 VENDOR-NUMBER       PIC X(8).
    02 VENDOR-NAME         PIC X(15).
    02 VENDOR-ADDRESS      PIC X(45).
FD  CARDFILE LABEL RECORDS ARE OMITTED
             DATA RECORD IS CARD.
01  CARD.
    02 TRANS-CODE          PIC 9.
       88 CHANGE-ADDRESS   VALUE 1.
       88 ADD-VENDOR       VALUE 2.
       88 DELETE-VENDOR    VALUE 3.
       88 ERROR-CODE       VALUES ARE ZERO, 4 THRU 9.
    02 VENDOR-IDENT        PIC 9(8).
    02 VENDOR-NAME         PIC X(15).
    02 VENDOR-ADDRESS      PIC X(45).
    02 FILLER              PIC X(11).
FD  PRINTFILE LABEL RECORD OMITTED
              DATA RECORD PRINTLINE.
01  PRINTLINE             PIC X(132).
*
WORKING-STORAGE SECTION.
01  END-OF-DATA-INDICATOR  PIC 9 VALUE ZERO.
    88 INPUT-ENDED VALUE 1.

PROCEDURE DIVISION.
MAIN-ROUTINE.
*
* THIS PORTION ILLUSTRATES RANDOM UPDATING OF INDEXED FILE
*
    OPEN INPUT  CARDFILE
         OUTPUT PRINTFILE
         I-O    DISKFILE.
    MOVE ' LISTING FROM UPDATE PORTION' TO PRINTLINE
    WRITE PRINTLINE AFTER ADVANCING PAGE.
    PERFORM READ-CARD.
    PERFORM UPDATE
        UNTIL INPUT-ENDED.
    CLOSE DISKFILE.
*
* THIS PORTION ILLUSTRATES SEQUENTIAL RETRIEVAL.
*
    MOVE ZERO TO END-OF-DATA-INDICATOR.
    MOVE ' LISTING FROM SEQUENTIAL RETRIEVAL' TO PRINTLINE
    WRITE PRINTLINE AFTER ADVANCING 5 LINES.
    OPEN INPUT DISKFILE
    PERFORM READ-DISK.
    PERFORM LISTING
        UNTIL INPUT-ENDED.
    CLOSE DISKFILE.
*
* THIS PORTION ILLUSTRATES USE OF THE START VERB.
*
    MOVE ZERO TO END-OF-DATA-INDICATOR
    MOVE 35290001 TO VENDOR-NUMBER
    OPEN INPUT DISKFILE
    START DISKFILE KEY IS GREATER THAN VENDOR-NUMBER
          INVALID KEY MOVE 1 TO END-OF-DATA-INDICATOR.
    MOVE   ' LISTING FROM USE OF START VERB' TO PRINTLINE
    WRITE PRINTLINE AFTER ADVANCING 5 LINES
    PERFORM READ-DISK
    PERFORM LISTING
        UNTIL INPUT-ENDED
    CLOSE DISKFILE.
*
    STOP RUN.
```

(continued)

```
READ-CARD.
     READ CARDFILE RECORD
           AT END MOVE 1 TO END-OF-DATA-INDICATOR.
*
 UPDATE.
     MOVE VENDOR-IDENT OF CARD TO VENDOR-NUMBER.
     IF CHANGE-ADDRESS
        PERFORM ADDRESS-1 THRU ADDRESS-3
     ELSE
        IF ADD-VENDOR
           PERFORM ADDITION-1 THRU ADDITION-3
        ELSE
           IF DELETE-VENDOR
              PERFORM DELETION-1 THRU DELETION-3
           ELSE
              PERFORM ERROR-CARD.
     PERFORM READ-CARD.
*
 ADDRESS-1.
     READ DISKFILE RECORD
           INVALID KEY GO TO ADDRESS-2-0.
     MOVE VENDOR-ADDRESS OF CARD TO VENDOR-ADDRESS OF DISK-RECORD.
     REWRITE DISK-RECORD
           INVALID KEY GO TO ADDRESS-2-1.
     GO TO ADDRESS-3.
 ADDRESS-2-0.
     MOVE ' CANNOT FIND DISK RECORD FOR THIS CARD ' TO PRINTLINE
     WRITE PRINTLINE AFTER ADVANCING 1 LINE.
     WRITE PRINTLINE FROM CARD AFTER ADVANCING 1 LINE.
     GO TO ADDRESS-3.
 ADDRESS-2-1.
     MOVE ' CANNOT REWRITE THIS RECORD' TO PRINTLINE
     WRITE PRINTLINE AFTER ADVANCING 1 LINE.
     WRITE PRINTLINE FROM DISK-RECORD AFTER ADVANCING 1 LINE.
     GO TO ADDRESS-3.
 ADDRESS-3.
     EXIT.
*
 ADDITION-1.
     MOVE VENDOR-NAME    OF CARD TO VENDOR-NAME   OF DISK-RECORD
     MOVE VENDOR-ADDRESS OF CARD TO VENDOR-ADDRESS OF DISK-RECORD
     WRITE DISK-RECORD
           INVALID KEY GO TO ADDITION-2.
     GO TO ADDITION-3.
 ADDITION-2.
     MOVE ' CANNOT CREATE A RECORD FROM THIS CARD' TO PRINTLINE
     WRITE PRINTLINE AFTER ADVANCING 1 LINE
     WRITE PRINTLINE FROM CARD AFTER ADVANCING 1 LINE.
     GO TO ADDITION-3.
 ADDITION-3.
     EXIT.
*
 DELETION-1.
     DELETE DISK-RECORD
           INVALID KEY GO TO DELETION-2.
     GO TO DELETION-3.
 DELETION-2.
     MOVE ' CANNOT DELETE RECORD SPECIFIED BY THIS CARD'
         TO PRINTLINE
     WRITE PRINTLINE AFTER ADVANCING 1 LINE
     WRITE PRINTLINE FROM CARD AFTER ADVANCING 1 LINE
     GO TO DELETION-3.
 DELETION-3.
     EXIT.
*
 ERROR-CARD.
     MOVE ' WRONG TRANSACTION CODE IN CARD' TO PRINTLINE
     WRITE PRINTLINE AFTER ADVANCING 1 LINE
     WRITE PRINTLINE FROM CARD AFTER ADVANCING 1 LINE.
*
 READ-DISK.
     READ DISKFILE NEXT RECORD
           AT END MOVE 1 TO END-OF-DATA-INDICATOR.
*
 LISTING.
     WRITE PRINTLINE FROM DISK-RECORD AFTER ADVANCING 1 LINE.
     PERFORM READ-DISK.
```

FIGURE 13-3 (Continued)

VENDOR-NUMBER is the record key. The PROCEDURE DIVISION is self-documenting and consists of three control portions that illustrate random updating, sequential retrieval, and use of the START verb, respectively. The first portion illustrates random access and updating. The following sample input records were used:

211111111ACME-01	ADDED RECORD
135120001	NEW ADDRESS
497654310	ERROR CODE TEST = 4
349678912	DELETE
160000000	NEW ADDRESS
349678912	DELETE PREVIOUSLY DELETED
169743210	CHANGE NONEXISTING

We have written comments instead of data to simplify debugging. For instance, the first record has a code of 2 (column 1), which means to add a new vendor whose number is 11111111. Instead of address, we have written the comment ADDED RECORD.

The first portion of the MAIN-ROUTINE illustrates random updating of an indexed sequential file. By studying Figure 13-3, we can see that the UPDATE paragraph analyzes the transaction code. Then we execute the ADDRESS, ADDITION, DELETION, or ERROR-CARD paragraph. Each of these paragraphs illustrates, respectively: the replacing of a record (RE-WRITE), the addition of a record (WRITE), the deletion of a record (DELETE), and the handling of INVALID KEY conditions.

In the second portion of the MAIN-ROUTINE procedure, we illustrate sequential retrieval. When OPEN INPUT DISKFILE is executed, the open instruction causes the file to be positioned at the beginning, so that when the first READ DISKFILE NEXT RECORD is executed, the first record is retrieved.

The third portion of the MAIN-ROUTINE illustrates use of the START verb:

```
MOVE 35290001 TO VENDOR-NUMBER.
START DISKFILE KEY IS GREATER THAN VENDOR-NUMBER
    INVALID KEY MOVE 1 TO END-OF-DATA-INDICATOR.
```

In this illustration, we want to retrieve sequentially all records whose key is greater than 35290001. The record whose key equals 35290001 will not be retrieved, since the GREATER THAN option is used.

Figure 13-4 shows the output resulting from executing the program in Figure 13-3. The reader will find it useful to run the programs in Figures 13-2 and 13-3 and obtain the results shown in Figure 13-4. Since compilers differ, some changes to "localize" the programs may be necessary, and the task may prove well worth the effort. Of course, the small volume of data involved allows easy desk-checking of the program.

```
LISTING FROM UPDATE PORTION
WRONG TRANSACTION CODE IN CARD
497654310              ERROR CODE TEST = 4
CANNOT DELETE RECORD SPECIFIED BY THIS CARD
349678912              DELETE PREVIOUSLY DELETED
CANNOT FIND DISK RECORD FOR THIS CARD
169743210              CHANGE NON-EXISTING


LISTING FROM SEQUENTIAL RETRIEVAL
11111111ACME-01        ADDED RECORD
12345678ACME-10
22345678ACME-20
35120001ACME-30        NEW ADDRESS
37654310ACME-40
45678912ACME-60
54371203ACME-80
58120000ACME-90
60000000ACME-92        NEW ADDRESS
70000000ACME-93
80000000ACME-94
99999999ACME-99


LISTING FROM USE OF START VERB
37654310ACME-40
45678912ACME-60
54371203ACME-80
58120000ACME-90
60000000ACME-92        NEW ADDRESS
70000000ACME-93
80000000ACME-94
99999999ACME-99
```

FIGURE 13-4 SAMPLE OUTPUT FROM THE PROGRAM IN FIGURE 13-3.

EXERCISES

13.1 In updating a sequential file, all records in the master file are read, but only those records for which there are transactions are updated. Therefore, if in reading a master record it is determined that the record has no corresponding transactions, we will want to bypass that record. On the other hand, if transactions have been processed, we will want to rewrite the updated record in its place on the disk. Outline the programming logic that will accomplish this selective rewriting of master records.

13.2 Outline a program to re-create an indexed sequential file. Assume that the original file has too many overflow records and that we therefore want to create a new version of the file to eliminate all overflow. Include in your outline the FILE-CONTROL paragraph of the ENVIRONMENT DIVISION and the complete PROCEDURE DIVISION. Assume that OLD-FILE, OLD-REC, NEW-FILE, and NEW-REC are the corresponding file- and record-names.

13.3   Refer to Exercise 9.4 for the program description.
  a   Create the master file as an indexed file, using the part number as the RECORD KEY.
  b   Update the master file on a random basis, using the part number as the RECORD KEY.

13.4   Refer to Exercise 9.5 for the program description.

  a   Create the master file as an indexed sequential file, using the lot number as the RECORD KEY.
  b   Update the master file on a random basis, using the lot number as the RECORD KEY.

14

Relative file processing

RELATIVE FILE ORGANIZATION

A relative file is one in which records are accessed by reference to their relative position in the file. If we think of a file that can hold 100 records, the first record has a *relative key* of 1, while the last one has a relative key of 100. Access to records in a file organized as relative is by reference to the relative key of each record. For instance, we may use the following two types of commands:

1 Write this record as the 20th record in the file.
2 Read the 68th record in the file.

As this shows, reference is made to the relative location of a record. We say "relative" as distinguished from the *absolute* location of a given record. An absolute location would be specified in terms of the address of the record within a specific disk volume, within a specific cylinder, within a specific track, and the record number in that track.

Relative file organization is ideal for a case where records are identified by consecutive numbers. For instance, suppose that invoice records are numbered 0001, 0002, 0003. . . . We can use relative organization and store the records in the order of the invoice number. If we want to access invoice number 0050, we can do so simply by accessing the record whose relative key is 50. It is rare, however, that records can be numbered exactly consecutively as in this example, and relative file organization requires some specific techniques in order to utilize this method of file organization.

There are several key-to-address transformation methods that can be used to transform record keys (identifiers) to relative location addresses. All such methods have one common property: they enable us to transform record identifiers, such as social security numbers, product numbers, and customer names, to relative key values. Thus, if we want the record of product number 1234, we would apply a key-to-address transformation procedure that would transform product number 1234 into a relative key value, say 371. Then we would retrieve the 371st record in the relative file, with the expectation that it would be the record of product number 1234.

As the preceding example illustrates, a relative file can be a high-performance file. We can compute the address of a record without having to use index structures, as is required with indexed sequential files. It generally is true that relative files can provide fast, direct access to records, but it should be added that the level of performance depends on the specific file and the specific method chosen. Good performance in a relative file often requires some analysis and experimentation. The main reason for variability in performance is that all known key-to-address methods produce *synonyms,* which are said to occur when the key-to-address method generates the same relative key for two or more data records. For instance, it may be that product numbers 1234 and 4965 both generate the same relative key; therefore, we need additional processing beyond the key-to-address methods.

There are many ways to handle the occurrence of synonyms, but we illustrate here one procedure that is successful. At file creation time, go through the file and mark each record as a vacant record, using a special field in the record for this purpose. Then, as each data record is being stored in the file, we apply the chosen key-to-address method and compute a *home-address* relative key value. We now read that record space, and, if it is marked as vacant, we record the data in the space and then mark it as occupied. If we previously stored a data record in the home-address space, we look at the next record space to see if it is vacant and, if it is, we write the data record there. If it is occupied, we continue looking for a vacancy in consecutive record spaces, and either we find a vacancy or we come full circle in the case of a file that is completely filled. For example, suppose that V = vacant, and O = occupied. Let us assume that we want to store a product record for product number 2645 in the file. Further, let us assume that the chosen key-to-address method computes a relative key of 132. As illustrated in the following, the product record would be stored in relative record location 134, which is the first available vacancy.

RECORD RELATIVE KEY		130		131		132		133		134		135
Content	V		O	7391	O	0935	O	5383	V		V	

If we wanted to retrieve the record of product number 2645 after it had been loaded into the file, we would compute its home address as 132 as before. We would attempt to retrieve the record at location 132 by comparing the record key of 2645 to the record key at location 132, which happens to be 0935. This comparison indicates that record 2645 is a synonym, and we would continue searching sequentially until the record was found at location 134. Notice that, if we were trying to retrieve a record that in fact did not exist in the file, we would know that the record did not exist as soon as we came upon the first vacancy. We could conclude that the record did not exist because if a record is a synonym it is stored in the *first* available vacancy past the home address.

This procedure needs to be expanded to take account of deletion of records from the file. If we desire to free up the record space when a record is deleted, we recommend that the space be marked as deleted. If we want to add a new record, a deleted record then constitutes a vacancy. If we are retrieving a record and it is not at its home addres, however, we should continue looking for it until we encounter the first vacancy, *not* counting deleted records as vacancies. In the preceding example of record 2645, whose home address was 132 but which was written at 134 due to synonyms, suppose that the record at location 133 was later deleted. To retrieve record 2645 from location 134, we would have to continue looking past the deleted record at location 133. Of course, if the record at location 133 were deleted *before* record 2645 was added to the file, then record 2645 would have been written at location 133.

This procedure for handling synonyms is incorporated into the program illustration in Figure 14-1, later in this chapter.

REVIEW

1 In a relative file, the location of a record is described relative to the other _____ in the file.

records

2 Any key-to-address transformation method is concerned with converting a record key (identifier) into a relative _____.

location address

3 When two different record keys result in the same relative location address, it is said that a _____ has been produced.

synonym

4 When a synonym has occurred, a common solution is to store the synonym in the first vacant record space [preceding / following] the home-address space.

following

5 When records are deleted from a relative file and are marked as deleted, such record spaces then [are / are not] available for the storage of new records.

are

6 If a record is neither at its home address nor at the first vacancy after that address (not counting deleted records), then we can conclude that _____.

the record does not exist

THE DIVISION REMAINDER METHOD

In the preceding section, we saw that use of relative file organization is predicated on a key-to-address transformation capability. There are several key-to-address methods available. One that is in wide use is the division remainder method.

In order to apply the division remainder method, we first must choose the file size. A rule of thumb to determine the file size is to divide the number of records in the file by 0.80, so that 80 percent of the file will be filled and 20 percent of the file will be unused.* This unused space serves two pur-

*Where X = file size

If No. Records = $.80X$

Then $X = \dfrac{\text{No. Records}}{.80}$

poses: it cuts down the incidence of synonyms and it also allows for file expansion. The term *packing factor* or *file density* is used to denote the percent of filled space in a relative file. If we divide the number of data records by 0.80, the result is an 80 percent packing factor, or density. In general, the lower the packing factor the fewer the synonyms but the greater the unused file space. We can see now why relative files require analysis and experimentation. For instance, record size and frequency of access are factors that would be considered in the analysis for choosing a suitable packing factor.

Once the file size has been chosen, we select a prime number closest to the file size. A prime number is divisible only by itself and the number 1. For instance, the numbers 3 and 7 are prime numbers. There are tables of prime numbers available in mathematical handbooks. Use of a prime number is not critical, however. We also can use the file size instead of the prime number closest to it, and in most cases there is little difference in the number of synonyms generated. In general, however, the use of a prime number is likely to result in fewer synonyms.

Suppose a customer file contains 9,600 records. We decide on a packing factor of 80 percent; therefore, the allocated file size is $9,600 \div 0.80 = 12,000$ record spaces. The prime number closest to 12,000 is 11,987. The customers are identified by a six-digit customer number. The first step in the division remainder method is to divide the record identifier by the prime number (or the file size itself). Thus, if we want to compute the location address of customer 123456, we divide this record identifier by the prime number 11987, obtaining a whole-number quotient of 10 and a remainder of 3586. By the division remainder method, the remainder plus 1 is the computed home address. For our example, the address is thus $3586 + 1 = 3587$. If we had used the file size instead of the prime number as the divisor, we would have divided 123456 by 12000, giving a whole-number quotient of 10 and a remainder of 3456. The home address in this case would have been $3456 + 1 = 3457$.

It should be noted that, when we divide a number by any divisor, the remainder from the division can range from zero to the value of the divisor minus one. Thus, if we are dividing by 12000, the smallest possible remainder is zero and the largest possible remainder is 11999. Since we add one to the remainder in the division remainder method, we can see that division by the file size results in the smallest computed value being one and the largest value being the file size itself. Thus, by taking the remainder plus one, we generate addresses that correspond to the relative addresses in the file. In the case where a prime number is used that is smaller than the file size itself, a few addresses would be impossible to generate. For example, with a prime number of 11987 as a divisor and a file size of 12000, we would never generate addresses 11988, 11989, 11990, . . . 12000. Still, those addresses could be occupied by records if we happened to have enough synonyms in the addresses 11987 and before.

As indicated by this example, the division remainder method is rather easy to apply. In the sample program given later in the chapter (Figure 14-1), the procedure is implemented as follows:

MOVE ITEM-NUMBER OF CARD-RECORD TO WORKFIELD
DIVIDE PRIME-NUMBER INTO WORKFIELD GIVING QUOTIENT
COMPUTE LOCATION-ADDRESS =
    WORKFIELD − (PRIME-NUMBER ∗ QUOTIENT) + 1.

The QUOTIENT field must be defined as an integer field, of course. Then the remainder is computed by multiplying the divisor by the integer quotient and then subtracting the result from the dividend. The address is stored in LOCATION-ADDRESS as the remainder plus one.

The division remainder method, as well as other methods for transforming record identifiers into file addresses, has the property of giving about an equal chance to every possible file address. The general relationship between the record identifier and the address computed is random, and this is the reason that key-to-address methods are referred to as *randomizing* methods. The term *hashing* also is used very widely to describe such randomizing key-to-address methods.

REVIEW

1   A key-to-address transformation is required for relative files in order to convert a record key (identifier) into a relative file address. The widely used method described in this section is called the _____ method.

division remainder

2   The percent of filled space in a relative file is identified by the term

_____.

packing factor (or file density)

3   Suppose an accounts payable file includes 2,100 records. If a 70 percent packing factor is to be used, the allocated file size would be _____ record spaces.

$$2,100 \div 0.70 = 3,000$$

4 Given a file size of 3,000, transform Account No. 4211 into a file address by using the file size as the divisor. _____

Integer quotient: 1
Remainder: 1211
File Address: 1211 + 1 = 1212

5 Given a file size of 3,000, transform Account No. 911 into a file address by using the file size as the divisor. _____

Integer quotient: 0
Remainder: 911
File Address: 911 + 1 = 912

6 Key-to-address methods are called randomizing methods because the possible [record identifiers / file addresses] have about an equal chance of occurring.

file addresses

OTHER KEY-TO-ADDRESS TRANSFORMATION METHODS

DIGIT ANALYSIS METHOD

By this method a frequency count is performed in regard to the number of times each of the 10 digits occurs in each of the positions included in the record key. For example, Table 14-1 presents a frequency count for the

TABLE 14-1   FREQUENCY OF OCCURRENCE OF THE DIGITS 1-9 FOR 2,800 FIVE-POSITION KEYS

| DIGIT | KEY POSITION | | | | |
	1	2	3	4	5
0	2026				
1	618	250	218	1012	260
2	128	395	391	185	382
3	23	263	389	299	271
4	5	298	330	52	302
5		335	299	101	387
6		303	339	18	299
7		289	308	134	301
8		267	267	999	245
9		400	259		353

number of times each digit occurred in a five-position numeric key for 2,800 records. In this tabulation we can observe that digits 0–9 occur with approximately uniform distribution in key positions 2, 3, and 5; therefore, if a three-digit address were required, the digits in these three positions in the record keys could be used. Given that there are 2,800 records, however, a four-digit address would be required. Suppose we desire the first digit to be a 0, 1, 2, or 3 only. Such assignment can be made with about equal frequency for each digit by using a rule such as the following: assign a "0" when digits in positions 2 and 3 both contain odd numbers, a "1" if position 2 is odd and position 3 is even, a "2" if position 2 is even and position 3 is odd, or a "3" if positions 2 and 3 both contain even numbers. Thus, the address for key 16258 would be 3628: the "3" from the fact that positions 2 and 3 both contain even numbers and the "628" from key positions 2, 3, and 5. Other rules for prefixing additional digits can be formulated for different circumstances. In any event, the digit analysis method relies on the digits in some of the key positions being approximately equally distributed. If such is not the case, the method cannot be used with good results.

MID-SQUARE METHOD

The record key is multiplied by itself, and the product is truncated from both left and right so as to form a number equal to the desired address length. Thus, key 36258 would be squared to give 1314642564. To form a four-digit address, this number would be truncated from both the left and right, resulting in the address 4642.

FOLDING

The key is separated into two parts which then are added together to form the address. For example, suppose key 1234567 is to be transformed into a four-digit address. We can add the first four positions to the last three positions to form the address; in this case: $1234 + 567 = 1801$. As another possibility, we can begin with the middle four digits and add the other digits as follows:

1 2 | 3 4 5 6 | 7
    Address

In general, the concept of folding does not refer to one standard method but to a general class of possibilities.

ALPHABETIC KEYS

It is possible and sometimes common that the key is alphabetic, as in the case of a student file that utilizes an alphabetic key. In order to determine a numeric address, a procedure is defined by which letters are transformed into numbers. These numbers then might be used as addresses or, more likely, might be used in conjunction with one of the randomizing techniques discussed previously. Thus, if the transformation rule is that A = 00, B = 01, ... Z = 25, then ADAM would become 00030012. Of course, other transformation rules are possible, such as A = 11, B = 12, ... Z = 36.

The key-to-address transformation methods that have been discussed are not the only ones that can be used, but they do represent the principal techniques. As indicated previously, the division remainder technique is used most frequently and generally works at least as well as other methods, but special circumstances may make some other method desirable for a given file.

REVIEW

1   The transformation method for which the digits in at least some of the key positions must be dispersed about equally in terms of value is the _____ method.

digit analysis

2   The transformation method in which the key is multiplied by itself as part of the procedure for determining the address for the record is the _____ _____ method.

mid-square

3   The transformation method in which one part of a key number is added to another part of the number to form the address is the _____ method.

folding

4   Alphabetic keys generally are transformed [directly into a numeric address / into a numeric code for subsequent determination of an address].

into a numeric code for subsequent determination of an address

5   The transformation technique most frequently used in conjunction with relative file organization is the _____ method.

division remainder

COBOL STATEMENTS FOR RELATIVE FILES

Matters such as key-to-address transformations and handling of synonyms are not acknowledged by the language. COBOL assumes that the programmer handles these. The language provides only the basic mechanism by which relative files can be created and processed.

The relevant ENVIRONMENT DIVISION format for relative files is as follows:

```
SELECT file-name ASSIGN TO implementor-name
  ; ORGANIZATION IS RELATIVE

  ⎡                      ⎧ SEQUENTIAL    [, RELATIVE KEY IS data-name] ⎫ ⎤
  ⎢ ; ACCESS MODE IS     ⎨ RANDOM  ⎬                                   ⎬ ⎥
  ⎣                      ⎩ DYNAMIC ⎭    , RELATIVE KEY IS data-name    ⎭ ⎦
```

ORGANIZATION IS RELATIVE has the obvious meaning. The ACCESS MODE clause has the same meaning as discussed for indexed files. Notice, however, RELATIVE KEY as contrasted to RECORD KEY. The data-name specified as RELATIVE KEY *must* be a WORKING-STORAGE unsigned integer item. Its function is to contain the location address for the record about to be accessed, or the location of the record that was just accessed.

The reader should understand clearly the role of RELATIVE KEY, which is different from the RECORD KEY of indexed files. RECORD KEY is part of the file record. RELATIVE KEY is an item apart from the record. Given a record, the value of its identifier field is taken by the programmer and transformed through a key-to-address routine to give a location address stored in the RELATIVE KEY field, as portrayed in the following:

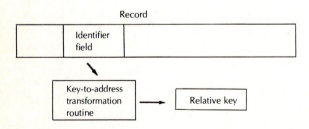

A relative file may be created either sequentially or randomly. If it is to be created sequentially, we may omit the RELATIVE KEY clause—an option shown in the previous ENVIRONMENT DIVISION format. In the format, observe that the RELATIVE KEY clause is required if the access mode is RANDOM or DYNAMIC. To create the file sequentially, we can write:

SELECT file-name ASSIGN TO device
    ORGANIZATION IS RELATIVE
    ACCESS MODE IS SEQUENTIAL.

In the PROCEDURE DIVISION, we then open the file as OUTPUT and we WRITE record-name. The first execution of WRITE records in the first record location, the second execution records in the second location, and so on.

The WRITE verb has the same format as presented for indexed files. The INVALID KEY clause applies when we try to write more records than can be accommodated in the allocated space, or when we try to write on a space already written on (synonym). Of course, file space is allocated using job control language (JCL) statements.

A relative file also may be created randomly, in which case we use ACCESS MODE IS RANDOM RELATIVE KEY IS. . . . In a later section we present an example illustrating the process.

Records are read from a relative file using one of two formats:

Format 1

```
READ file-name [NEXT] RECORD [INTO identifier]
     [; AT END imperative-statement]
```

Format 2

```
READ file-name RECORD [INTO identifier]
     [, INVALID KEY imperative statement]
```

Format 1 must be used if records are retrieved in sequential mode. NEXT must be used if DYNAMIC access mode is specified and records are retrieved sequentially.

Format 2 is used when the access mode is RANDOM, or when the access mode is DYNAMIC and records are retrieved in random order. The INVALID KEY condition occurs when RELATIVE KEY contains an address pointing to a record that was deleted previously (see DELETE verb, following), or to an address beyond the boundaries of the file.

A record may be updated using REWRITE, which has the same format as for indexed files. This verb functions in the same way as discussed for indexed files, with the exception that RELATIVE KEY contains the address of the record to be replaced.

Records may be deleted from the file using DELETE, just as is done with indexed sequential files. The file must be opened I/O at the time a DELETE is executed.

Sequential retrieval of records may be accomplished using the SE-

QUENTIAL or DYNAMIC access mode, the issuance of an OPEN INPUT instruction, and repetitive execution of READ or READ NEXT. Whenever sequential retrieval is desired from a point other than the beginning of a file, then the START command can be used. The same format applies as for indexed files, except that the starting record location is placed in the RELATIVE KEY field.

REVIEW

1 The location address determined by a key-to-address routine is stored in the _____ field.

RELATIVE KEY

2 For an indexed file, the RECORD KEY [is / is not] part of the original file record. For a relative file, the RELATIVE KEY [is / is not] part of the original file record.

is; is not

3 In the SELECT statement of the ENVIRONMENT DIVISION, the RELATIVE KEY clause is not needed and may be omitted if the file is to be created [sequentially / randomly].

sequentially

4 One particular adverse consequence associated with creating a relative file sequentially is the absence of any vacant _____ locations between the stored file records.

storage

5 Records stored sequentially in a relative file [can / cannot] be accessed randomly.

can

6 Records stored randomly in a relative file [can / cannot] be accessed sequentially.

can

AN EXAMPLE OF CREATING A RELATIVE FILE

A punched-card file is to be transferred to disk, organized as a relative file. For simplicity, we assume that there will be no more than 50 records. Each card contains an ITEM-NUMBER in columns 1–5 and an ITEM-NAME in columns 6–25. We shall use ITEM-NUMBER as the identifier for each record and we shall compute disk addresses using this identifier and the prime number 47. We assume that our operating system takes care of cylin-

der, track, and record references (indeed, this is typically the case). Therefore, by using the division remainder technique, we convert each ITEM-
NUMBER value to a (relative) disk address in the range 1–50.

Figure 14–1 presents a program written to create such a relative file.
Notice that, for the reason explained in the first section of this chapter, the
first field in the disk record is used to identify whether the record is vacant or
occupied:

```
01   DISK-RECORD.
      02   REC-STATUS-CODE      PIC 9.
           88   VACANT-RECORD    VALUE ZERO.
           88   USED-RECORD      VALUE 1.
```

In the MAIN-ROUTINE we perform ZERO-DISK as many times as the
value of MAX-NO-OF-LOCATIONS, which was set to 50 in the DATA DIVI-
SION. The function of ZERO-DISK is to initialize to zero the REC-STATUS-
CODE of each record space, thereby indicating a vacant record space.

The main task in the MAIN-ROUTINE is the repeated execution of
READ-PROCESS-CARD, whose function can be outlined as follows: We
read each card record and compute its home-address (LOCATION-
ADDRESS) in the RANDOMIZE-READ paragraph. We then access (READ)
the contents of the record specified by LOCATION-ADDRESS. If the space is
vacant (IF VACANT-RECORD), we indicate that it no longer is vacant and
we write the record there:

```
MOVE 1   TO REC-STATUS-CODE
MOVE ITEM-NUMBER OF CARD-RECORD
      TO ITEM-NUMBER OF DISK-RECORD
(etc.)
```

If the home address computed in RANDOMIZE-READ is not vacant, we
proceed to search for a vacant space in the following consecutive locations.
In order to present infinite looping, we use LOOP-FLAG and STARTING-
ADDRESS. Let us consider an example. Suppose that a record transforms to
location 40. We set LOOP-FLAG to "NO" and STARTING-ADDRESS to 40.
If location 40 is occupied already, we increment LOCATION-ADDRESS to
41 and check to determine if that location is vacant. If it is not vacant, we
continue searching for a vacant location by increments of 1. Notice that we
avoid going beyond the file size (50) in HANDLE-SYNONYMS by subtracting MAX-NO-OF-LOCATIONS FROM LOCATION-ADDRESS. This subtraction brings us to the beginning of the file, and we continue searching for a
vacancy. In the event that the entire file is full, LOCATION-ADDRESS eventually would become equal to the STARTING-ADDRESS, indicating that we
have come full circle. At that point, we set LOOP-FLAG to "YES" and we
print an error message. The program would terminate because a "YES" in

FIGURE 14-1   SAMPLE PROGRAM FOR CREATING A RELATIVE FILE.

```
IDENTIFICATION DIVISION.
PROGRAM-ID. RELATIVE-FILE.
*
ENVIRONMENT DIVISION.
CONFIGURATION SECTION.
SOURCE-COMPUTER. ABC-480.
OBJECT-COMPUTER. ABC-480.
INPUT-OUTPUT SECTION.
FILE-CONTROL.
        SELECT DISK-FILE     ASSIGN TO  DISK-DEVICE-A
                             ORGANIZATION IS RELATIVE
                             ACCESS MODE IS RANDOM
                             RELATIVE KEY IS LOCATION-ADDRESS.
*
        SELECT CARD-FILE   ASSIGN TO CARD-READER.
        SELECT PRINT-FILE  ASSIGN TO PRINTER.
*
*
DATA DIVISION.
FILE SECTION.
FD  DISK-FILE         LABEL RECORDS OMITTED
                      DATA RECORD IS DISK-RECORD
                      RECORD CONTAINS 25 CHARACTERS.

01  DISK-RECORD.
    02 REC-STATUS-CODE  PIC 9.
        88 VACANT-RECORD        VALUE ZERO.
        88 USED-RECORD          VALUE 1.

    02 ITEM-NUMBER      PIC 9(5).
    02 ITEM-NAME        PIC X(20).
*
FD  CARD-FILE      LABEL RECORDS OMITTED
                   DATA RECORD IS CARD-RECORD.

01  CARD-RECORD.
    02 ITEM-NUMBER      PIC 9(5).
    02 ITEM-NAME        PIC X(20).
    02 FILLER           PIC X(55).
*
FD  PRINT-FILE     LABEL RECORDS OMITTED
                   DATA RECORD IS PRINT-RECORD.
01  PRINT-RECORD         PIC X(132).
*
*
WORKING-STORAGE SECTION.
01  END-OF-DATA-FLAG    PIC XXX        VALUE 'NO'.
    88 END-OF-CARDS                    VALUE 'YES'.
01  LOOP-FLAG           PIC XXX.
    88 FILE-IS-FULL                    VALUE 'YES'.
01  LOCATION-ADDRESS    PIC 999.
01  STARTING-ADDRESS    PIC 999.
01  PRIME-NUMBER        PIC 99         VALUE 47.
01  WORKFIELD           PIC S99999 USAGE COMP.
01  QUOTIENT            PIC S999   USAGE COMP.
01  MAX-NO-OF-LOCATIONS PIC 999 VALUE 50.
01  I                   PIC 999.
01  ERROR-RECORD.
    02 FILLER           PIC X VALUE SPACE.
    02 ERROR-LOCATION   PIC ZZ999.
    02 FILLER           PIC XX VALUE SPACE.
    02 ERR-MESSAGE      PIC X(50).
/
PROCEDURE DIVISION.
MAIN-ROUTINE.
        OPEN INPUT  CARD-FILE
        OPEN OUTPUT DISK-FILE
                    PRINT-FILE.
*
        PERFORM ZERO-DISK
            VARYING I FROM 1 BY 1 UNTIL I > MAX-NO-OF-LOCATIONS.
*
        CLOSE DISK-FILE.
*
        OPEN I-O DISK-FILE
*
        PERFORM READ-PROCESS-CARD
            UNTIL END-OF-CARDS
               OR FILE-IS-FULL.
*
        CLOSE CARD-FILE
              PRINT-FILE
              DISK-FILE.
        STOP RUN.
*
```

(continued)

```
*
 ZERO-DISK.
      MOVE 1 TO LOCATION-ADDRESS
      MOVE ZERO TO REC-STATUS-CODE
      WRITE DISK-RECORD
          INVALID KEY PERFORM CANT-ACCESS.
*
 READ-PROCESS-CARD.
      READ CARD-FILE RECORD
            AT END MOVE 'YES' TO END-OF-DATA-FLAG.
      IF NOT END-OF-CARDS
         PERFORM LOAD-RECORD.
*
 LOAD-RECORD.
      PERFORM RANDOMIZE-READ
      IF VACANT-RECORD
         NEXT SENTENCE
      ELSE
         MOVE LOCATION-ADDRESS TO STARTING-ADDRESS
         MOVE 'NO' TO LOOP-FLAG
         PERFORM HANDLE-SYNONYMS
            UNTIL VACANT-RECORD
                  OR FILE-IS-FULL.
*
      IF FILE-IS-FULL
         NEXT SENTENCE
      ELSE
         MOVE 1 TO REC-STATUS-CODE
         MOVE ITEM-NUMBER OF CARD-RECORD
            TO ITEM-NUMBER OF DISK-RECORD
         MOVE ITEM-NAME OF CARD-RECORD
            TO ITEM-NAME OF DISK-RECORD
         WRITE DISK-RECORD
             INVALID KEY PERFORM CANT-ACCESS.
*
 RANDOMIZE-READ.
      MOVE ITEM-NUMBER OF CARD-RECORD TO WORKFIELD
      DIVIDE PRIME-NUMBER INTO WORKFIELD GIVING QUOTIENT
      COMPUTE LOCATION-ADDRESS =
          WORKFIELD - (PRIME-NUMBER * QUOTIENT) + 1
*COULD ALSO WRITE THE FOLLOWING INSTEAD OF COMPUTE
* DIVIDE PRIME-NUMBER INTO WORKFIELD GIVING QUOTIENT
*        REMAINDER LOCATION-ADDRESS
* ADD 1 TO LOCATION-ADDRESS
*
*
      PERFORM READ-DISK-REC.
*
 HANDLE-SYNONYMS.
      ADD 1 TO LOCATION-ADDRESS
      IF LOCATION-ADDRESS > MAX-NO-OF-LOCATIONS
         SUBTRACT MAX-NO-OF-LOCATIONS FROM LOCATION-ADDRESS.
*
      IF LOCATION-ADDRESS = STARTING-ADDRESS
         MOVE ITEM-NUMBER OF DISK-RECORD TO ERROR-LOCATION
         MOVE 'FILE IS FULL, NEW RECORD IS' TO ERR-MESSAGE
         WRITE PRINT-RECORD FROM ERROR-RECORD AFTER 2 LINES
         MOVE 'YES' TO LOOP-FLAG
      ELSE
         PERFORM READ-DISK-REC.
*
 READ-DISK-REC.
      READ DISK-FILE RECORD
          INVALID KEY PERFORM CANT-ACCESS.
*
 CANT-ACCESS.
      MOVE LOCATION-ADDRESS TO ERROR-LOCATION
      MOVE 'THIS RECORD LOCATION CAUSED INVALID KEY'
          TO ERR-MESSAGE
      WRITE PRINT-RECORD FROM ERROR-RECORD AFTER 2 LINES.
```

FIGURE 14–1 (*Continued*)

LOOP-FLAG is the condition-name FILE-IS-FULL, which causes termination in the MAIN-ROUTINE as shown:

PERFORM READ-PROCESS-CARD
    UNTIL END-OF-CARDS
        OR FILE-IS-FULL.

AN EXAMPLE OF UPDATING A RELATIVE FILE

We illustrate the use of relative file organization by a sample program that updates the file created by the program in Figure 14–1. Figures 14–2 and 14–3 present the hierarchy chart and the corresponding program for the update task.

Transaction records are submitted through a TRANS-FILE assigned to the card reader. In each transaction record, there is a code indicating the type of transaction:

```
01  TRANS-REC.
    02  TRANS-CODE          PIC 9.
        88  ADD-TRANS       VALUE ZERO.
        88  DELETE-TRANS    VALUE 1.
        88  MODIFY-TRANS    VALUE 2.
        88  ERROR-TRANS     VALUES 3 THRU 9.
    02  ITEM-NUMBER         PIC 9(5).
    02  ITEM-NAME           PIC X(20).
    02  FILLER              PIC X(54).
```

An ADD-TRANS indicates the addition of a new record to the disk file, a DELETE-TRANS indicates the deletion of a record existing in the file, while a MODIFY-TRANS represents a change in the ITEM-NAME of the disk record.

It should be noted that disk records are specified by the following description:

```
01  DISK-RECORD.
    02  REC-STATUS-CODE     PIC 9.
        88  VACANT-RECORD   VALUE ZERO.
        88  USED-RECORD     VALUE 1.
        88  DELETED-RECORD  VALUE 2.
    02  ITEM-NUMBER         PIC 9(5).
    02  ITEM-NAME           PIC X(20).
```

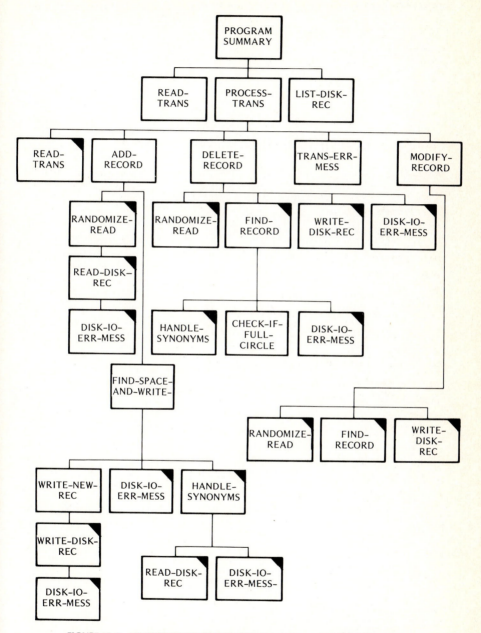

FIGURE 14–2   HIERARCHY CHART FOR THE RELATIVE FILE UPDATE PROGRAM.

FIGURE 14-3 SAMPLE PROGRAM FOR UPDATING A RELATIVE FILE

```
IDENTIFICATION DIVISION.
PROGRAM-ID. REL-UPDATE.
*
ENVIRONMENT DIVISION.
CONFIGURATION SECTION.
SOURCE-COMPUTER. ABC-480.
OBJECT-COMPUTER. ABC-480.
*
INPUT-OUTPUT SECTION.
FILE-CONTROL.
    SELECT DISK-FILE      ASSIGN TO DISK-DEVICE-A
                          ORGANIZATION IS RELATIVE
                          ACCESS MODE IS RANDOM
                          RELATIVE KEY IS LOCATION-ADDRESS.
    SELECT TRANS-FILE     ASSIGN TO CARD-READER.
    SELECT PRINT-FILE     ASSIGN TO PRINTER.
*
DATA DIVISION.
FILE SECTION.
*
FD  DISK-FILE     LABEL RECORDS OMITTED
                  DATA RECORD IS DISK-RECORD
                  RECORD CONTAINS 25 CHARACTERS.
01  DISK-RECORD.
    02  REC-STATUS-CODE PIC 9.
        88  VACANT-RECORD   VALUE ZERO.
        88  USED-RECORD     VALUE 1.
        88  DELETED-RECORD VALUE 2.
    02  ITEM-NUMBER       PIC 9(5).
    02  ITEM-NAME         PIC X(20).
*
FD  TRANS-FILE    LABEL RECORDS OMITTED
                  DATA RECORD IS TRANS-REC.
01  TRANS-REC.
    02  TRANS-CODE        PIC 9.
        88  ADD-TRANS     VALUE ZERO.
        88  DELETE-TRANS VALUE 1.
        88  MODIFY-TRANS VALUE 2.
        88  ERROR-TRANS   VALUES 3 THRU 9.
    02  ITEM-NUMBER       PIC 9(5).
    02  ITEM-NAME         PIC X(20).
    02  FILLER            PIC X(54).
*
FD  PRINT-FILE    LABEL RECORDS OMITTED
                  DATA RECORD IS PRINT-REC.
01  PRINT-REC             PIC X(132).
*
WORKING-STORAGE SECTION.
*
01  FLAGS.
    02  END-OF-TRANS-FLAG     PIC XXX VALUE 'NO '.
        88  END-OF-TRANS      VALUE 'YES'.
*
    02  SYNONYM-LOOP-FLAG     PIC XXX VALUE 'NO '.
        88  FILE-IS-FULL      VALUE 'YES'.
*
    02  READ-VALIDITY-FLAG    PIC 9.
        88  VALID-READ        VALUE ZERO.
        88  INVALID-READ      VALUE 1.
*
    02  WRITE-VALIDITY-FLAG   PIC 9.
        88  VALID-WRITE       VALUE ZERO.
        88  INVALID-WRITE     VALUE 1.
*
    02  RECORD-FOUND-FLAG     PIC 9.
        88  RECORD-FOUND      VALUE ZERO.
        88  RECORD-NOT-FOUND VALUE 1.
        88  STILL-LOOKING     VALUE 2.
*
    02  ADD-REC-FLAG         PIC 9.
        88  RECORD-ADDED      VALUE ZERO.
        88  RECORD-NOT-ADDED  VALUE 1.
*
*
01  LOCATION-ADDRESS     PIC 9(3).
01  MAX-NO-OF-LOCATIONS PIC 9(3) VALUE 50.
01  STARTING-ADDRESS    PIC 9(3).
01  PRIME-NUMBER        PIC 99 VALUE 47.
01  WORKFIELD           PIC S9(5).
01  QUOTIENT            PIC S9(3).
*
01  ERROR-RECORD.
    02  FILLER          PIC X VALUE SPACE.
    02  ERROR-LOCATION PIC ZZ999.
    02  ERR-MESSAGE     PIC X(50).
```

(continued)

```
/
 PROCEDURE DIVISION.
 PROGRAM-SUMMARY.
     OPEN INPUT  TRANS-FILE
     OPEN OUTPUT PRINT-FILE
     OPEN I-O    DISK-FILE.
*
     PERFORM READ-TRANS
*
     PERFORM PROCESS-TRANS
             UNTIL END-OF-TRANS OR FILE-IS-FULL.
*
*
*   FOLLOWING IS SEQUENTIAL LISTING OF DIRECT FILE
*
     MOVE ZERO TO READ-VALIDITY-FLAG
     PERFORM LIST-DISK-FILE
             VARYING LOCATION-ADDRESS FROM 1 BY 1
                     UNTIL LOCATION-ADDRESS >
                       MAX-NO-OF-LOCATIONS
                     OR READ-VALIDITY-FLAG = 1.
*
     CLOSE DISK-FILE
           PRINT-FILE
           TRANS-FILE.
*
     STOP RUN.
*
 READ-TRANS.
     READ TRANS-FILE RECORD
          AT END MOVE 'YES' TO END-OF-TRANS-FLAG.
*
 PROCESS-TRANS.
     IF ADD-TRANS
         PERFORM ADD-RECORD
     ELSE
         IF DELETE-TRANS
             PERFORM DELETE-RECORD
         ELSE
             IF MODIFY-TRANS
                 PERFORM MODIFY-RECORD
             ELSE
                 PERFORM TRANS-ERR-MESS.
*
     PERFORM READ-TRANS.
*
 ADD-RECORD.
     PERFORM RANDOMIZE-READ
     MOVE 1 TO ADD-REC-FLAG
     MOVE ZERO TO READ-VALIDITY-FLAG.
*
     PERFORM FIND-SPACE-AND-WRITE
             UNTIL RECORD-ADDED OR INVALID-READ OR FILE-IS-FULL.
*
 FIND-SPACE-AND-WRITE.
     IF VACANT-RECORD OR DELETED-RECORD
         PERFORM WRITE-NEW-REC
         MOVE ZERO TO ADD-REC-FLAG
     ELSE
         IF ITEM-NUMBER OF TRANS-REC
            = ITEM-NUMBER OF DISK-RECORD
             MOVE 'ATTEMPT TO ADD DUPLICATE RECORD' TO ERR-MESSAGE
             PERFORM DISK-IO-ERR-MESS
         ELSE
             PERFORM HANDLE-SYNONYMS.
*
 RANDOMIZE-READ.
     MOVE ITEM-NUMBER OF TRANS-REC TO WORKFIELD
     DIVIDE PRIME-NUMBER INTO WORKFIELD GIVING QUOTIENT
     COMPUTE LOCATION-ADDRESS =
             WORKFIELD - (QUOTIENT * PRIME-NUMBER) + 1
*
*COULD ALSO WRITE THE FOLLOWING INSTEAD OF COMPUTE
* DIVIDE PRIME-NUMBER INTO WORKFIELD GIVING QUOTIENT
*        REMAINDER LOCATION-ADDRESS
* ADD 1 TO LOCATION-ADDRESS
*
*
*
     MOVE 'NO' TO SYNONYM-LOOP-FLAG
     MOVE LOCATION-ADDRESS TO STARTING-ADDRESS
*
     PERFORM READ-DISK-REC.
```

FIGURE 14-3 (*Continued*)

```
*
 READ-DISK-REC.
     MOVE ZERO TO READ-VALIDITY-FLAG
     READ DISK-FILE RECORD
          INVALID KEY MOVE 1 TO READ-VALIDITY-FLAG.
*
     IF INVALID-READ
        MOVE 'THIS RECORD LOCATION CANNOT BE READ'
             TO ERR-MESSAGE
        PERFORM DISK-IO-ERR-MESS.
*
*
 DISK-IO-ERR-MESS.
     MOVE LOCATION-ADDRESS TO ERROR-LOCATION
     WRITE PRINT-REC FROM ERROR-RECORD AFTER 2 LINES
     MOVE SPACES TO ERROR-RECORD
     MOVE 'TRANSACTION RECORD IS' TO ERR-MESSAGE
     WRITE PRINT-REC FROM ERROR-RECORD AFTER 2 LINES
     MOVE TRANS-REC TO ERR-MESSAGE
     WRITE PRINT-REC FROM ERROR-RECORD AFTER 2 LINES.
*
*
 HANDLE-SYNONYMS.
     MOVE 'NO' TO SYNONYM-LOOP-FLAG
     ADD 1 TO LOCATION-ADDRESS
     IF LOCATION-ADDRESS GREATER THAN MAX-NO-OF-LOCATIONS
        MOVE 1 TO LOCATION-ADDRESS.
*
     IF LOCATION-ADDRESS = STARTING-ADDRESS
        MOVE 'ENTIRE FILE READ FULL CIRCLE' TO ERR-MESSAGE
        PERFORM DISK-IO-ERR-MESS
*
        MOVE 'YES' TO SYNONYM-LOOP-FLAG
     ELSE
        PERFORM READ-DISK-REC.
*
 WRITE-NEW-REC.
     MOVE 1 TO REC-STATUS-CODE
     MOVE ITEM-NUMBER OF TRANS-REC
          TO ITEM-NUMBER OF DISK-RECORD
     MOVE ITEM-NAME OF TRANS-REC
          TO ITEM-NAME OF DISK-RECORD

     PERFORM WRITE-DISK-REC.
*
 WRITE-DISK-REC.
     MOVE ZERO TO WRITE-VALIDITY-FLAG
     REWRITE DISK-RECORD
          INVALID KEY MOVE 1 TO WRITE-VALIDITY-FLAG.
     IF INVALID-WRITE
        MOVE 'THIS RECORD LOCATION CANNOT BE WRITTEN'
             TO ERR-MESSAGE
        PERFORM DISK-IO-ERR-MESS.
*
/
 DELETE-RECORD.
     MOVE 2 TO RECORD-FOUND-FLAG
     MOVE ZERO TO READ-VALIDITY-FLAG
     PERFORM RANDOMIZE-READ
     PERFORM FIND-RECORD
             UNTIL RECORD-FOUND
                OR RECORD-NOT-FOUND
                OR INVALID-READ.
     IF RECORD-FOUND
        MOVE 1 TO REC-STATUS-CODE
        PERFORM WRITE-DISK-REC
     ELSE
        IF RECORD-NOT-FOUND
           MOVE 'ATTEMPT TO DELETE NONEXISTENT RECORD'
                TO ERR-MESSAGE
           PERFORM DISK-IO-ERR-MESS.
*
 FIND-RECORD.
     IF USED-RECORD
        IF ITEM-NUMBER OF TRANS-REC = ITEM-NUMBER OF DISK-RECORD
           MOVE ZERO TO RECORD-FOUND-FLAG
        ELSE
           PERFORM HANDLE-SYNONYMS
           PERFORM CHECK-IF-FULL-CIRCLE
     ELSE
        IF DELETED-RECORD
           PERFORM HANDLE-SYNONYMS
           PERFORM CHECK-IF-FULL-CIRCLE
        ELSE
           IF VACANT-RECORD
              MOVE 1 TO RECORD-FOUND-FLAG
           ELSE
              MOVE 1 TO RECORD-FOUND-FLAG
              MOVE 'STATUS CODE OF DISK-REC IS INVALID'
                   TO ERR-MESSAGE
              PERFORM DISK-IO-ERR-MESS.
```

FIGURE 14-3 (Continued)

```
*
 CHECK-IF-FULL-CIRCLE.
     IF FILE-IS-FULL
         MOVE 'CAME FULL CIRCLE' TO ERR-MESSAGE
         PERFORM DISK-IO-ERR-MESS
         MOVE 1 TO RECORD-FOUND-FLAG.
*
*
*
 MODIFY-RECORD.
     MOVE 2 TO RECORD-FOUND-FLAG
     MOVE ZERO TO READ-VALIDITY-FLAG
     PERFORM RANDOMIZE-READ.
*
     PERFORM FIND-RECORD
         UNTIL RECORD-FOUND
             OR RECORD-NOT-FOUND
             OR INVALID-READ.
*
     IF RECORD-FOUND
         MOVE ITEM-NAME OF TRANS-REC TO ITEM-NAME OF DISK-RECORD
         PERFORM WRITE-DISK-REC
     ELSE
         IF RECORD-NOT-FOUND
             MOVE 'ATTEMPT TO MODIFY NONEXISTENT RECORD'
                 TO ERR-MESSAGE
             PERFORM DISK-IO-ERR-MESS.
*
 TRANS-ERR-MESS.
     MOVE SPACES TO ERROR-RECORD
     MOVE 'THIS TRANSACTION HAS INVALID-CODE' TO ERR-MESSAGE
     WRITE PRINT-REC FROM ERROR-RECORD AFTER 2 LINES
     MOVE TRANS-REC TO ERR-MESSAGE
     WRITE PRINT-REC FROM ERROR-RECORD AFTER 2 LINES.
*
*
 LIST-DISK-FILE.
     READ DISK-FILE  RECORD
         INVALID KEY MOVE 1 TO READ-VALIDITY-FLAG.
     IF READ-VALIDITY-FLAG = ZERO
         WRITE PRINT-REC FROM DISK-RECORD AFTER 1.
 MAP,NI
 XQT
034567NEW ITEM-1
093398NEW ITEM-2
123456DELETE-1
342564ERR TRANS
000281SYNONYM-1
000375SYNONYM-2
000422SYNONYM-3
000469SYNONYM-4
000516SYNONYM-5
000610SYNONYM-6
 EOF
 RUN,/R ASP,RYLDK877,3QBA007R,S30
 SYM PRINT$,,BUSN01
 COB, STFYTR
```

FIGURE 14-3 (*Continued*)

When a record is deleted, the REC-STATUS-CODE for that record space is set equal to 2. On any subsequent occasion, we can identify the fact that the record space is available for a new record, and we ignore it when looking for synonyms, as explained in the first section of this chapter. For instance, suppose that a transaction record specifies deletion of an item-number. In the DELETED-RECORD paragraph of Figure 14-3, we see that we PERFORM RANDOMIZE-READ to compute the home address of the item record and then read the record at the home address. Then we say:

PERFORM FIND-RECORD

    UNTIL RECORD-FOUND OR RECORD-NOT-FOUND

    OR INVALID-READ.

In the FIND-RECORD paragraph, we first check to determine if the record space at the home address is occupied (IF USED-RECORD). If it is occupied, we check to determine if the ITEM-NUMBER in the transaction record matches the one in the disk record, in which case that is the record to be deleted. If the record space is occupied but does not contain the record that we want, then the FIND-RECORD paragraph PERFORMs HANDLE-SYNONYMS. As a result, the next disk record is read and we repeat the process under control of the PERFORM FIND-RECORD UNTIL . . . loop in the DELETED-RECORD paragraph.

Continuing our analysis of the FIND-RECORD paragraph, note that we say IF DELETED-RECORD PERFORM HANDLE-SYNONYMS PERFORM CHECK-IF-FULL-CIRCLE. If there is a deleted record, we simply PERFORM HANDLE-SYNONYMS in order to move to the next disk record space on the relative file. The CHECK-IF-FULL-CIRCLE procedure prevents us from searching the entire file repeatedly for a nonexisting record, in the case where all records are occupied or vacant from deletions only. Notice that the FIND-RECORD terminates (MOVE 1 TO RECORD-FOUND-FLAG) when a vacant record is encountered (IF VACANT-RECORD), since such an occurrence indicates that the record does not exist.

The program is substantially self-documenting, and the student should be able to review it and follow the details. The overall task is typical of most update programs, and the sample program can be used as the basic structure for most of them.

EXERCISES

14.1   Do a digit analysis of the following set of customer account numbers: 8023, 9178, 9034, 8187, 8056, 9162, 9019.

14.2   Based on the digit analysis in Exercise 14.1, describe a key-to-address transformation method for a file that consists of 100 customer accounts. Demonstrate the procedure by computing the address for account numbers 8023 and 3456.

14.3   Outline what changes would be needed in the sample program for creating a relative file in Figure 14–1 to guarantee that there will be no duplicate records in the file. A duplicate record is one that has the same key as another record in the file.

14.4   Outline what changes would be needed in the sample program for creating a relative file in Figure 14–3 to guarantee that there will be no duplicate records in the file. A duplicate record is one that has the same key as another record in the file.

14.5 Refer to Exercise 9.4 for the program description.

   a Create the master file as a relative file, using the part number as the RELATIVE KEY.

   b Update the master file on a random basis, using the part number as the RELATIVE KEY.

14.6 A manufacturer of three product classes has a sales force consisting of 100 salespeople, each person assigned a unique salesperson number of five digits. Salespeople are paid on commission, receiving monthly commission benefits as well as an annual bonus based on monthly performance. We want to maintain commission data for each salesperson, by product class and by month, on a disk file.

   a Create a relative file that will contain a record of the commission data for each salesperson in the following form. Salesperson number will serve for the RELATIVE KEY.

FIELD	FIELD SIZE
Salesperson number	5 digits
Salesperson-name	
Last name	15 characters
First name	10 characters
Middle initial	1 character
Commission totals by product class (3 classes) and by month (12 months).	Each total can be as large as 999,999.99. Note: There will be 36 totals.

The file is created by reading one card per salesperson, containing the salesperson-number and salesperson-name fields. After the randomizing technique has been employed to determine the disk location, all commission totals (36 fields) are set to zero. Then the record is written on the disk.

   b Update this file, using sales transaction data punched on cards. Use the salesperson number as the RELATIVE KEY.

The transaction cards have the following layout:

CARD COLUMNS	FIELD
1–5	Salesperson number
6	Commission code (based on product class)
	1 = 0.02 of sales
	2 = 0.03 of sales
	3 = 0.05 of sales
7–8	Month code (from 01 to 12)
9–14	Sales value in dollars and cents

Assume that the transaction cards are sorted by salesperson number; therefore, we need to access the relevant master record only once for each set of cards corresponding to one salesperson. Of course, we may have transactions for only *some* of the salespeople.

As each salesperson is processed, we want to print on the printer a report, as follows:

CURRENT COMMISSION DATA			
		TOTALS	
SALESPERSON NUMBER	SALESPERSON-NAME	THIS MONTH	YEAR-TO-DATE
12345	LAST, FIRST, M.	$ 870.35	$18,562.40
24966	LAST, FIRST, M.	1020.20	12,112.96
.	.	.	.
.	.	.	.
.	.	.	.

In other words, we want to accumulate the commissions, regardless of product class, for the current month; as well as the year-to-date totals for all months through the present one.

15

Modular programs and subroutines

PROGRAM MODULARITY

In Chapter 4: "Program Structure and Design," we discussed the concept of *partitioning,* in relation to good program design. Partitioning is extremely important as a design tool because it gives us the ability to subdivide a large, complex task into smaller, simpler tasks or modules that the human mind can manage more easily. The human mind can handle complexity only up to a point, and we always are forced to break down complex tasks into smaller subtasks. No programmer really has the choice of working on a one-thousand-line PROCEDURE DIVISION as one task; at any given time the programmer must focus on only a small part of the entire program task. Thus, partitioning is a necessary act. There are good ways and bad ways of partitioning a program task, and they correspond to whether we approach the partitioning task systematically or let it develop haphazardly.

Good program design relies on the *top-down approach* to partitioning a program into hierarchically interdependent modules. We begin with an all-inclusive statement of the program task, which corresponds to the *one* main module that summarizes the program description and controls the execution of the entire program. Next, we proceed to partition the main module into subordinate modules, each corresponding to one *cohesive* function. Each such function is a program module that has the *black box* characteristic: we describe *what* it does, but we are not concerned with the detail of *how* it does its function. Treatment of modules as black boxes allows us to comprehend the overall structure and interdependencies of program functions or modules, without attempting to deal with the detail associated with each module.

As described in Chapter 4, we continue the top-down design process by taking each subordinate module and concentrating on it as if it were the main module. As a result, we break each subordinate module into "subsubordinate" modules, and we continue the process until we have reached a level of detail that requires no further partitioning. This top-down design process results in a generalized structure such as that illustrated in Figure 15-1. Each block in such a structure, or hierarchy, chart refers to a module

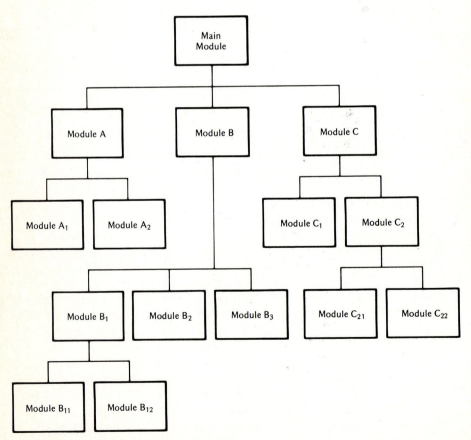

FIGURE 15-1 GENERALIZED STRUCTURE CHART.

that represents a cohesive function. The modules are interrelated, being subordinate to their respective immediate superiors; however, they also are independent from other modules, so that a given module requires no assumptions
about the function of other modules that are not subordinate to it. Thus, we
need concentrate only on the vertical dimension associated with a given

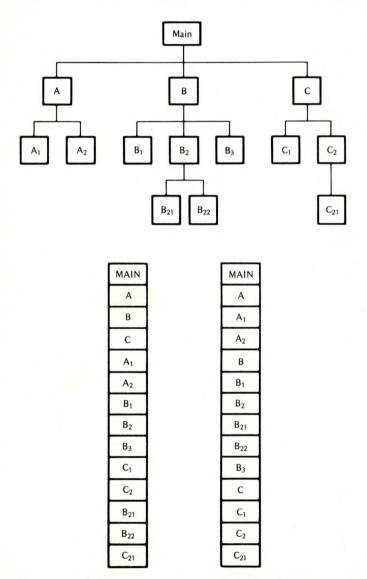

A. Horizontal layout   B. Vertical layout

FIGURE 15–2   MODULE LAYOUT AS RELATED TO A STRUCTURE CHART.

module, and we can, at a given time, ignore the horizontal dimension at the level of the module under consideration.

This top-down design allows us to approach in a systematic, tested way the process of partitioning a large task, so that we attain a completely designed program without undue complexity. The resulting design structure is highly modular and at the same time logically and systematically coordinated. We stress the point that modularity as such is not very useful. Anybody can chop up a program into "modules" having random and confusing interrelationships, but a good top-down designer can create a modular structure that is the best known answer to program complexity.

The structure chart is a visual aid to program design, but it is not a program structure. Eventually, each module on the chart will have to be represented on a program structure. In simple programs, such as the majority of programs in this book, each module represents a paragraph or a group of paragraphs in the program. In large programs, each module represents a section or an independent subroutine, as described in the remainder of this chapter.

There are two basic ways to arrange the overall program layout as it relates to a corresponding structure chart. As illustrated in Figure 15–2, the modules can be positioned in either a horizontal or vertical arrangement. Neither approach is perfect for all purposes. If we are interested in reviewing the overall program structure, the horizontal layout representation is better. On the other hand, if we want to associate the program structure with the vertical relationships in the structure chart, then the vertical layout representation is better. In any case, cross referencing of modules most often is accomplished by using a numerical prefix or suffix with each module. Such a prefix or suffix denotes the physical position of the module in the program. For example, suppose that the following eight module names have been numbered with a three-digit prefix denoting their order:

010-EDIT-INPUT
.
.
.

020-READ-RECORD
.
.
.

030-COMPUTE-EARNINGS
.
.
.

040-COMPUTE-TAX

.

.

.

050-COMPUTE-DEDUCTIONS

.

.

.

060-EDIT-OUTPUT

.

.

.

070-PRINT-HEADINGS

.

.

.

080-PRINT-REPORT.

If in the course of the program we were to encounter the statement PER-FORM 050-COMPUTE-DEDUCTIONS, we could locate the object of the PERFORM by noting the 050 prefix and referring to that general location in the program.

In this book, we have not numbered paragraphs because the length of the sample programs has not warranted such systematic numbering; still, one can see easily that programs that consist of many paragraphs or sections can be rather difficult to read if we have no systematic way to identify their general location. In complex programs, the numbering scheme can be fairly elaborate. For instance, section-names could be numbered in the hundreds and paragraph-names in the tens. Thus, if we encountered the statement PERFORM 230-CHECK-EMPL-NO, we would know that CHECK-EMPL-NO is paragraph 30 in section 200.

REVIEW

1 The process of subdividing a complex programming task into simpler tasks or modules is called _____.

partitioning

2 The approach to partitioning by which one begins by focusing on the one main module that summarizes the program task is the _____ approach.

top-down

3 The *black box* orientation toward identifying program modules implies that we [are / are not] concerned about *what* a modules does, and we [are / are not] concerned about *how* that function is performed.

are; are not

4 In a structure chart, modules are related to one another in the [horizontal / vertical] dimension.

vertical

5 In large programs, numerical prefixes or suffixes often are used to denote the physical position of _____ in the program.

modules

PROGRAM SUBROUTINES

Throughout this book, we have utilized the PERFORM verb as the basic control mechanism for implementing modular program structure. Still, it often is desirable to program a task in terms of one *main* program and one or more *subroutines* or *subprograms*. In such a structure, the main program is the executable program. Subprograms can be written and compiled independently, but they can be executed only in conjunction with a main program. There are three basic reasons why subprograms are desirable.

1 Whenever a task is either too large for one person or the time available requires the formation of a project team, subroutines are a natural way of partitioning one task among several persons. Because subprograms can be compiled independently, each team member can work individually to develop and test a portion of the total task. Communication among the team members is limited to brief coordinative activities assigned to a *chief programmer* who is responsible for the overall project design and for effective and efficient interfacing *between* subtasks partitioned out as subroutines.

2 There is a frequent need to incorporate the same task into more than one program. In such a case, a subroutine that is written and tested once can be recorded in a program library and can be used by several programs, thus avoiding the "reinvention-of-the-wheel" syndrome that often plagues ill-managed data processing staffs.

3 When using subroutines, we can identify the data items specifically involved with the functions performed by each individual subroutine. In contrast, there is only one DATA DIVISION in each program, and it contains a description of the data for all modules in the program, as a group.

When using subroutines, there is one *main program* and one or more subroutines. The main program initiates and controls execution involving the execution of subroutines and, eventually, termination of the job. A given subroutine may be called into execution by the main program, or it may be called by another subroutine; however, in a given program there must be at least one call issued by the main program, and that must be the first call. After that point, subroutines may call each other—although they cannot call themselves (recursion is not allowed). You may have noticed the use of the word "call." It is standard terminology in reference to subroutine execution, and it is implemented in COBOL through the verb CALL.

We will explain the implementation of program subroutines using an example.

REVIEW

1 In lieu of using the PERFORM verb, modular program structure can be implemented by writing separate _____.

subroutines (or *subprograms*)

2 The use of subroutines makes the partitioning of a programming task among several individuals [easier / more difficult].

easier

3 A subroutine [can / cannot] be used easily in conjunction with different programs.

can

4 When a subroutine is written, the data involved in that subroutine are described specifically in the DATA DIVISION of the [main program / subroutine].

subroutine

AN EXAMPLE OF MAIN AND SUBROUTINE STRUCTURE

This example task is concerned with checking for errors in punched-card data pertaining to an inventory. The data items have the following format:

CARD COLUMNS	FIELD-NAME
1–5	ITEM-NUMBER
6–20	ITEM-NAME
21	ITEM-CODE
22–26	QUANTITY

The basic checking procedure is concerned with the value of ITEM-CODE, because this signifies the type of record. The number "1" means that the QUANTITY field contains the previous balance for the item specified by ITEM-NUMBER; the number "2" indicates the receipt of goods; and "3" indicates the issue of goods from inventory. Any other code is an error. We assume that the cards are sorted so that all cards of the same item number are grouped together and the card with a "1" in column 21 leads the group. We recognize four types of error conditions:

DUPLICATE BALANCE CARD: This condition arises whenever more than one card in a group of the same item number has a code of 1.

MISPLACED BALANCE CARD: A card with a code of 1 exists, but it is not the first in the group.

BALANCE CARD MISSING: The first card in a group is not a code 1 card.

INCORRECT CODE: A code other than 1, 2, or 3 exists.

On detection of a card meeting one of these conditions, the card is printed with the corresponding explanatory error message so that it can be corrected.

In addition to the error messages, we also desire a summary of totals, as shown in Figure 15–3, which illustrates a set of sample input records and the resulting sample output.

We decide to use a subroutine to check for data validity. Our immediate reason for using a subroutine is to illustrate the process. In general, it is desirable to use a subroutine if changes in the type of data checking are possible, so that such changes can be made in the subroutine independently of the main program. We proceed to define the function of the main program and the subprograms as follows:

MAIN PROGRAM: This reads each data card and gives each card to the subroutine to check if it contains valid data. If execution of the subroutine indicates that the data are not valid, the card is printed along with an error message. If execution of the subroutine indicates that the data are valid, then we accumulate the proper totals. We then proceed to read another card. When all the cards have been read, we print a summary of the accumulated totals and terminate the program.

SUBROUTINE: The subprogram receives a data card from the main program. It checks for errors. If an error is found, an appropriate error message is supplied to the main program. If no error is found, a blank error message is supplied to the main program. Then the subroutine terminates. The four error messages are:

DUPLICATE BALANCE CARD
MISPLACED BALANCE CARD
BALANCE CARD MISSING
INCORRECT CODE

From this discussion, we can see that in order for the process to be completed the main program must make available to the subroutine the data that have been read, and the subroutine must make an appropriate error message available to the main program. The need to pass data to and from a called program almost always is present when using subroutines. We refer to such data items as the *arguments* in a call statement.

In our example, we need the value of ITEM-CODE as one argument. We also need to provide the subroutine with the value of ITEM-NUMBER; however, the values of ITEM-NAME and QUANTITY are not needed by the subroutine, and therefore are not specified as arguments. As we have stated

Sample input

```
12345TEST-ITEM-1     100100
12345TEST-ITEM-1     200100
12345TEST-ITEM-1     300200
23456TEST-ITEM-2     300010
34567TEST-ITEM-3     100020
34567TEST-ITEM-3     200100
34567TEST-ITEM-3     300050
45678TEST-ITEM-4     200100
45678TEST-ITEM-4     100100
45678TEST-ITEM-4     300100
45678TEST-ITEM-4     100200
56789TEST-ITEM-5     100100
56789TEST-ITEM-5     40050
56789TEST-ITEM-5     300020
67890TEST-ITEM-6     100300
67890TEST-ITEM-6     300100
78901TEST-ITEM-7     100400
78901TEST-ITEM-7     100300
89012TEST-ITEM-8     100200
```

Sample output

```
23456TEST-ITEM-2     300010     BALANCE CARD MISSING
45678TEST-ITEM-4     200100     BALANCE CARD MISSING
45678TEST-ITEM-4     100100     MISPLACED BALANCE CARD
45678TEST-ITEM-4     300100     BALANCE CARD MISSING
45678TEST-ITEM-4     100200     MISPLACED BALANCE CARD
56789TEST-ITEM-5     40050      INCORRECT CODE
78901TEST-ITEM-7     100300     DUPLICATE BALANCE CARD
```

```
VALID RECORDS   =              012
INVALID RECORDS =              007
BALANCE TOTAL   =              1120
RECEIPTS TOTAL  =              200
ISSUES TOTAL    =              370
```

FIGURE 15-3   SAMPLE INPUT AND OUTPUT FOR THE INVENTORY EXAMPLE.

already, another argument is an error message; but we need to specify some additional arguments. Suppose that we have item number 12345 with a code of 1. If the previous card was also item number 12345 with a code of 1, we have the case of a duplicate balance card, but with the data otherwise being correct. Therefore, the item number of the previous item must be known, and we specify an argument to contain that value. In addition, we need to know whether a correctly placed balance card has been encountered or not, in order to differentiate between a misplaced balance card and a duplicate balance card. We set up a field as an argument to serve in this capacity. When a new item number is encountered, we place a 1 in this argument if the code is 1; otherwise we use a 2. For example, when we encounter a code of 1 on the third card of a given item, it is a case of a misplaced balance card if the indicator argument has a value of 2.

The two arguments just discussed, the value of the previous item number and the indicator for a correctly placed balance card, are needed only by the subroutine. The question can be raised as to why they are designated as arguments rather than just as data-names in the subroutine. We designate them as arguments in order to adhere to a very important rule of good modular programming practice: *a subroutine should be like a black box; its output should be dependent strictly on the input, and not on any "remembered" state of the subroutine that resulted from a previous call.* This rule is imperative when a subroutine is called by several other subroutines in the same program, and it is a good rule to follow even for a simple case, as in our example. Therefore, if the content of a data field used by a subroutine changes from call to call, it is a good procedure to include such a data field in the argument list.

In a subroutine, the arguments are specified in a special section of the DATA DIVISION, called the LINKAGE SECTION. For our example, the section can be written as follows:

```
LINKAGE SECTION.
01   ERROR-MESSAGE        PIC X(25).
01   OTHER-DATA.
     02   PREVIOUS-ITEM   PIC 99999.
     02   CURRENT-ITEM    PIC 99999.
     02   KODE            PIC 9.
     02   BALANCE-CODE    PIC 9.
```

In this case, there are two arguments, one an elementary-level 01 field, and the other a group 01 field. We have made these choices to illustrate the available options. Equally acceptable is the incorporation of ERROR-MESSAGE as an 02 field in OTHER-DATA, or designation of the four 02-level items as level-77 items.

Figure 15-4 presents a complete listing of the subroutine we have just discussed, including the LINKAGE SECTION. It will be noticed that a WORKING-STORAGE SECTION also is used, and in this case it consists of the four error-messages. The absence of a FILE SECTION is explained by the fact that in this example the subroutine is not involved in input or output operations. The PROCEDURE DIVISION requires some explanation. First, note that the division heading is followed by the word USING, which is followed by the list of arguments written in the LINKAGE SECTION. We have written the two arguments on separate lines for better visibility. This is especially useful if the argument list is long. Another characteristic of a subroutine is that there should be no STOP RUN statement. Instead, we use

```
IDENTIFICATION DIVISION.
PROGRAM-ID. EDIT-PROGRAM.
ENVIRONMENT DIVISION.
CONFIGURATION SECTION.
SOURCE-COMPUTER. ABC-480.
OBJECT-COMPUTER. ABC-480.
DATA DIVISION.

WORKING-STORAGE SECTION.
01   MESSAGE-1   PIC X(22) VALUE 'DUPLICATE BALANCE CARD'.
01   MESSAGE-2   PIC X(22) VALUE 'MISPLACED BALANCE CARD'.
01   MESSAGE-3   PIC X(20) VALUE 'BALANCE CARD MISSING'.
01   MESSAGE-4   PIC X(14) VALUE 'INCORRECT CODE'.

LINKAGE SECTION.
01   ERROR-MESSAGE           PIC X(25).
01   OTHER-DATA.
     02 PREVIOUS-ITEM         PIC 99999.
     02 CURRENT-ITEM          PIC 99999.
     02 KODE                  PIC 9.
     02 BALANCE-CODE          PIC 9.

PROCEDURE DIVISION  USING   ERROR-MESSAGE
                            OTHER-DATA.

MAIN-CHECK.
    IF PREVIOUS-ITEM = CURRENT-ITEM
        PERFORM OLD-ITEM-1 THRU OLD-ITEM-2
    ELSE
        PERFORM NEW-ITEM-1.
GO-BACK.
    EXIT PROGRAM.
OLD-ITEM-1.
    IF ((KODE = 2) OR (KODE = 3)) AND (BALANCE-CODE = 1)
        MOVE SPACES TO ERROR-MESSAGE
        GO TO OLD-ITEM-2.
    IF (KODE = 1) AND (BALANCE-CODE = 1)
        MOVE MESSAGE-1 TO ERROR-MESSAGE
        GO TO OLD-ITEM-2.
    IF (KODE = 1) AND (BALANCE-CODE = 2)
        MOVE MESSAGE-2 TO ERROR-MESSAGE
        GO TO OLD-ITEM-2.
    IF ((KODE = 2) OR (KODE = 3)) AND (BALANCE-CODE = 2)
        MOVE MESSAGE-3 TO ERROR-MESSAGE
        GO TO OLD-ITEM-2.
    IF (KODE = ZERO) OR (KODE > 3)
        MOVE MESSAGE-4 TO ERROR-MESSAGE
        GO TO OLD-ITEM-2.
OLD-ITEM-2.
    EXIT.
NEW-ITEM-1.
    MOVE CURRENT-ITEM TO PREVIOUS-ITEM.
    IF KODE = 1
        MOVE SPACES TO ERROR-MESSAGE
        MOVE 1 TO BALANCE-CODE
    ELSE
        MOVE MESSAGE-3 TO ERROR-MESSAGE
        MOVE 2 TO BALANCE-CODE.
```

FIGURE 15-4   LISTING OF THE SUBROUTINE FOR THE INVENTORY-DATA-CHECKING EXAMPLE.

the EXIT PROGRAM statement to indicate termination of the subroutine. The use of this statement can be seen in the GO-BACK paragraph. Recall that termination of a subroutine does not mean termination of the program. It simply denotes that we return to the program that called the subroutine and continue with the next instruction of that calling program.

To review, then, there are three special aspects of a subroutine: (1) the presence of a LINKAGE SECTION, (2) the USING clause in the PROCEDURE DIVISION heading, and (3) the use of EXIT PROGRAM in place of STOP RUN. A subroutine may use no arguments; in such a case, neither LINKAGE nor USING will be required, but such a situation is infrequent.

Figure 15-5 presents a complete listing of the main program. First, we direct our attention to the CHECK-ROUTINE paragraph in the PROCEDURE DIVISION. Notice the sentence:

CALL 'EDIT-PROGRAM' USING ERROR-MESSAGE
                                 CALL-ARGUMENTS.

CALL is very similar to PERFORM, except that the object of CALL is a *separately compiled* subroutine instead of a paragraph in the program. A

FIGURE 15-5 LISTING OF THE MAIN PROGRAM FOR THE INVENTORY-DATA-CHECKING EXAMPLE.

```
IDENTIFICATION DIVISION.
PROGRAM-ID. MAIN-PROGRAM.
ENVIRONMENT DIVISION.
CONFIGURATION SECTION.
SOURCE-COMPUTER. ABC-480.
OBJECT-COMPUTER. ABC-480.
INPUT-OUTPUT SECTION.
FILE-CONTROL.
    SELECT CARD-FILE    ASSIGN TO CARD-READER.
    SELECT PRINT-FILE ASSIGN TO PRINTER.
DATA DIVISION.

FILE SECTION.
FD  CARD-FILE
        LABEL RECORDS ARE OMITTED
        DATA RECORD IS CARD-RECORD.
01  CARD-RECORD.
    02  ITEM-NUMBER     PIC  99999.
    02  ITEM-NAME       PIC  X(15).
    02  ITEM-CODE       PIC  9.
    02  QUANTITY        PIC  99999.
    02  FILLER          PIC  X(54).
FD  PRINT-FILE
        LABEL RECORD OMITTED
        DATA RECORD IS PRINT-LINE.
01  PRINT-LINE.
    02  FILLER          PIC  X.
    02  PART-1          PIC  X(26).
    02  FILLER          PIC  XXXX.
    02  PART-2          PIC  X(25).
    02  FILLER          PIC  X(79).

WORKING-STORAGE SECTION.
01  VALID-RECORDS       PIC  999999 USAGE COMP VALUE ZEROS.
01  INVALID-RECORDS     PIC  999999 USAGE COMP VALUE ZEROS.
01  ERROR-MESSAGE       PIC  X(25).
01  END-OF-DATA         PIC  9.
01  EDIT-FIELD          PIC  ZZZZZ999.
01  BALANCE-TOTAL       PIC  9(8) USAGE COMP VALUE ZEROS.
01  RECEIPTS-TOTAL      PIC  9(8) USAGE COMP VALUE ZEROS.
01  ISSUES-TOTAL        PIC  9(8) USAGE COMP VALUE ZEROS.
01  CALL-ARGUMENTS.
    02  OLD-ITEM        PIC  99999.
    02  NEW-ITEM        PIC  99999.
    02  KODE            PIC  9.
    02  BALANCE-CODE    PIC  9.
```

(continued)

```
PROCEDURE DIVISION.
SET-UP.
      OPEN INPUT CARD-FILE
           OUTPUT PRINT-FILE.
      MOVE ZEROS TO OLD-ITEM.
      MOVE ZERO TO END-OF-DATA.
      PERFORM READ-CARD.
MAIN-LOGIC.
      PERFORM CHECK-ROUTINE
           UNTIL END-OF-DATA = 1
      PERFORM PRINT-SUMMARY.
      CLOSE CARD-FILE  PRINT-FILE.
JOB-END.
      STOP RUN.
READ-CARD.
      READ CARD-FILE
           AT END
                MOVE 1 TO END-OF-DATA.
      MOVE ITEM-NUMBER TO NEW-ITEM.
      MOVE ITEM-CODE TO KODE.

CHECK-ROUTINE.
      CALL 'EDIT-PROGRAM' USING ERROR-MESSAGE
                                CALL-ARGUMENTS.

      IF ERROR-MESSAGE = SPACES
         ADD 1 TO VALID-RECORDS
         PERFORM ACCUMULATE-ROUTINE
      ELSE
         MOVE SPACES TO PRINT-LINE
         MOVE CARD-RECORD TO PART-1
         MOVE ERROR-MESSAGE TO PART-2
         WRITE PRINT-LINE BEFORE ADVANCING 1 LINE
         ADD 1 TO INVALID-RECORDS.
      PERFORM READ-CARD.
ACCUMULATE-ROUTINE.
      IF KODE = 1
         ADD QUANTITY TO BALANCE-TOTAL.
      IF KODE = 2
         ADD QUANTITY TO RECEIPTS-TOTAL.
      IF KODE = 3
         ADD QUANTITY TO ISSUES-TOTAL.

PRINT-SUMMARY.
      MOVE SPACES TO PRINT-LINE
      MOVE VALID-RECORDS TO EDIT-FIELD
      MOVE EDIT-FIELD TO PART-2
      MOVE 'VALID RECORDS = ' TO PART-1
      WRITE PRINT-LINE AFTER ADVANCING PAGE.
      MOVE SPACES TO PRINT-LINE
      MOVE INVALID-RECORDS TO EDIT-FIELD
      MOVE EDIT-FIELD TO PART-2
      MOVE 'INVALID RECORDS = ' TO PART-1
      WRITE PRINT-LINE AFTER ADVANCING 2 LINES
      MOVE SPACES TO PRINT-LINE
      MOVE BALANCE-TOTAL TO EDIT-FIELD
      MOVE EDIT-FIELD TO PART-2
      MOVE 'BALANCE TOTAL = ' TO PART-1
      WRITE PRINT-LINE AFTER ADVANCING 2 LINES
      MOVE SPACES TO PRINT-LINE
      MOVE RECEIPTS-TOTAL TO EDIT-FIELD
      MOVE EDIT-FIELD TO PART-2
      MOVE 'RECEIPTS TOTAL = ' TO PART-1
      WRITE PRINT-LINE AFTER ADVANCING 2 LINES
      MOVE SPACES TO PRINT-LINE
      MOVE ISSUES-TOTAL TO EDIT-FIELD
      MOVE EDIT-FIELD TO PART-2
      MOVE 'ISSUES TOTAL    =' TO PART-1
      WRITE PRINT-LINE AFTER ADVANCING 2 LINES.
```

FIGURE 15-5 (*Continued*)

CALL statement in essence is an instruction to execute the specified subroutine-name, which is the program-name given in the PROGRAM-ID paragraph of the subroutine. The USING clause introduces the argument list. In this case, the first argument is ERROR-MESSAGE, which is a level-01 WORKING-STORAGE field. The PICTURE associated with this field is X(25), which is identical to the one in the subroutine. The second argument is called CALL-ARGUMENTS, and it is a level-01 WORKING-STORAGE field. Table 15–1 contrasts the arguments in the subroutine with the arguments in the main program.

The program in Figures 15–4 and 15–5 are substantially self-documenting; however, it may be worthwhile to comment on some of the programming features and logic incorporated in the subprogram in Figure 15–4. The OLD-ITEM-1 paragraph incorporates the use of complex conditions using the AND and OR operators along with parentheses. Parentheses are used to clarify the condition specified. For instance, the condition "(KODE = 2) or (KODE = 3) AND (BALANCE-CODE = 1)" can be described in the following table:

CONDITION VALUE	KODE	BALANCE-CODE
True	2	1
True	3	1
False	All other combinations	

The use of compound conditions facilitates logical testing, which otherwise is difficult to do with simple conditions. Incidentally, the task of checking the data in this program is rather difficult conceptually, because it is hard to determine clearly all the possibilities. A good tool for such applica-

TABLE 15–1 ARGUMENTS IN THE MAIN PROGRAM AND THE SUBROUTINE.

MAIN PROGRAM		SUBROUTINE	
.			
.			
.			
WORKING-STORAGE SECTION.		LINKAGE SECTION.	
.			
.			
.			
01 ERROR-MESSAGE	PIC X(25).	01 ERROR-MESSAGE	PIC X(25).
.			
.			
.			
01 CALL-ARGUMENTS.		01 OTHER-DATA.	
02 OLD-ITEM	PIC 99999.	02 PREVIOUS-ITEM	PIC 999999.
02 NEW-ITEM	PIC 99999.	02 CURRENT-ITEM	PIC 99999.
02 KODE	PIC 9.	02 KODE	PIC 9.
02 BALANCE-CODE	PIC 9.	02 BALANCE-CODE	PIC 9.
.			
.			
.			
CALL 'EDIT-PROGRAM' USING		PROCEDURE DIVISION USING ERROR-MESSAGE	
ERROR-MESSAGE CALL-ARGUMENTS.		OTHER DATA.	

TABLE 15-2   DECISION TABLE FOR THE INVENTORY EXAMPLE

CONDITION	POSSIBILITY							
	1	2	3	4	5	6	7	8
PREVIOUS-ITEM = CURRENT-ITEM	X	X	X					
PREVIOUS-ITEM NOT = CURRENT-ITEM				X	X	X	X	X
KODE = 1	X			X	X			
KODE = 2 OR 3		X		X	X			X
KODE NOT = 1 OR 2 OR 3			X			X	X	
BALANCE-CODE = 1				X		X		
BALANCE-CODE = 2					X			X
ACTION	1	2	3	4	5	6	7	8
BLANK ERROR MESSAGE	X					X		
DUPLICATE BALANCE CARD				X				
MISPLACED BALANCE CARD					X			
BALANCE CARD MISSING		X	X					X
INCORRECT CODE							X	

tions is a *decision table,* which facilitates complete enumeration of all the possibilities. Table 15-2 is a decision table that was constructed to facilitate writing the subroutine. Without its use, the programming task is rather difficult.

A few words on the use of GO TO in the subroutine are warranted. First, notice that each GO TO refers to a paragraph further down in the program, so that we are causing no backtracking. Then notice that we can replace each GO TO by a period. Since the conditions are mutually exclusive, if one of the first three conditions is true, then the subsequent ones must be false. Correct logic will be preserved, but we will be testing conditions unnecessarily. We have positioned the first condition in that particular position because that is the condition that we expect to prevail most of the time. Omission of GO TO would cause all four conditions to be tested, when in fact the first one is the only one needed in most instances.

REVIEW

1   When using subroutines, there is one _____ and one or more _____.

main program; subroutines

2   The data items passed to and from a called program (subroutine) are referred to as the _____ in the CALL statement.

arguments

3   The COBOL verb that is similar to PERFORM, except that the object is a separately compiled subroutine instead of a paragraph in the program, is _____.

CALL

4   The item-name assigned to an argument in the main program and assigned to that argument in the subroutine [must / need not] be the same.

need not

5   The PICTURE description of an argument in the main program and the description in the subroutine [must / need not] be the same.

must

6   The type of analytical table that is useful for portraying all the possible combinations of results that can be encountered in a checking procedure is a(n) _____.

decision table

DATA COMMUNICATION ACROSS SUBROUTINES

As the preceding example illustrated, data are communicated from the calling to the called program and back through the arguments. In the example, there were two arguments: ERROR-MESSAGE and OTHER-DATA in the subroutine, and ERROR-MESSAGE and CALL-ARGUMENTS in the main program. The choice of the data-names OTHER-DATA and CALL-ARGUMENTS can be questioned. In themselves, the names provide no clue as to what data are being passed to and from the subroutine. In contrast, ERROR-MESSAGE is self-documenting. In the example, we used a group-level data item to illustrate that arguments can be group data. In general, however, it is preferable to use many single arguments, so that the reader can be clear as to the data involved. Thus, the call could have been written:

```
CALL 'EDIT-PROGRAM' USING   ERROR-MESSAGE
                            OLD-ITEM
                            NEW-ITEM
                            KODE
                            BALANCE-CODE
```

Each argument would have been an 01-level item in both the main program and in the subroutine.

In general, the data communicated across subroutines as arguments are a very important program feature. These arguments should be presented explicitly, so that the program reader does not have to hunt back through the

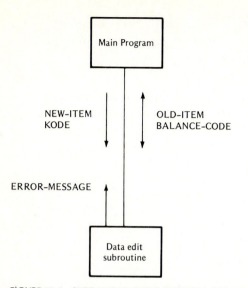

FIGURE 15-6   SUBROUTINE ARGUMENTS IN A STRUCTURE CHART.

DATA DIVISION to determine the list of arguments. As a matter of fact, the argument list is such an integral part of the specification of a module's function that it is recommended that the arguments be included in the structure chart during program design. Such a chart for the sample program in this chapter is presented in Figure 15-6. The argument names are shown along with an arrow indicating the direction of data flow. The main program sends two arguments to the subroutine: NEW-ITEM and KODE. The subroutine returns one item, ERROR-MESSAGE. Then there are two items, OLD-ITEM and BALANCE-CODE, that are shared by both programs; this is depicted by the arrows pointing in both directions.

EXERCISES

15.1   Discuss the concept of modularity in program design.

15.2   Discuss three main reasons for using externally compiled subroutines rather than using PERFORM structures within a large program.

15.3   Employees pay FICA-RATE percent of their first FICA-LIMIT annual earnings as F.I.C.A. tax. We wish to write a subroutine that will compute the F.I.C.A. tax for each employee. Outline a skeleton program structure for a main program and the subroutine. The main program calls the subroutine to compute the F.I.C.A. tax. Be sure to include argument definition and PROCEDURE DIVISION statements for both the main program and the subroutine.

15.4 Write Exercise 8.6, dealing with a depreciation schedule, as a main program and subroutine. The main program should read in the data and print the headers. Then it should call a subroutine that computes and prints the depreciation schedule. The main program should read new data and repeat the cycle until all input data have been read and processed.

Under the preceding requirement, a printer file has to be available for both the main program and the subroutine. Some help will be needed from someone who knows your installation in order to avoid erroneous use of OPEN, CLOSE, and WRITE sequences. If you find this to be a problem, try completing this assignment by doing all the printing, including the header, in the subroutine.

16

The report writer feature

INTRODUCTION

The report writer module provides the facility for producing reports by specifying the physical appearance of a report rather than by requiring specification of the detailed procedures necessary to produce the report. For most reports, the report writer facility will prove an advantage by reducing program logic requirements and by reducing errors. The report writer is part of the COBOL language, and it can be incorporated into any program except in cases of small system compilers which do not include this feature.

Our description of the report writer begins with a basic example, in an attempt to impart an overall view of the use of this language feature. Then additional capabilities are discussed in the context of a more advanced example and some modifications of that example. Finally, the formal language skeleton is presented along with explanations. Full treatment of the report writer is beyond the scope of this text and would require considerable additional space. Still, this discussion will provide information sufficient to enable the programmer to produce most of the kinds of reports generated in practice.

A BASIC EXAMPLE

The report writer focuses the attention of the programmer on the format of the desired report. It is for this reason that it is almost imperative that one begin with a layout of the report. Most professionals utilize special printer chart forms, such as shown in Figure 16-1, to lay out the report format. Students may utilize 80-column COBOL coding forms or simply use plain paper with suitable annotations.

Figure 16-1 presents the desired report format for the basic example. In this case, there are five parts to the report. The first one is a *report heading,* a title for the report. Such a heading will appear only once in a report, and, in this example, we desire it to be on a separate page. Then there is the *page heading.* This is a heading that we want to have printed at the beginning of each page of the report. The report *detail* consists of the actual data of the report. In this case, we require four fields for each line of report detail. The first field includes 18 alphanumerics in columns 4-21, the second field includes two numerics in columns 27-28, the third field includes four alphanumerics in columns 39-42, and the fourth field is a numeric edited field in columns 52-61. A *page footing* is desired that consists of the literal, PAGE, and a Z9 field to print the page number. Finally, corresponding to the report heading, we desire a *report footing,* which will be printed at the very end of the report. In the report writer terminology, the report heading, the page heading, the detail, the page footing and the report footing are called *report groups.* Additional report groups will be described later.

Now that we have described the horizontal format for each report group, we turn our attention to the vertical format of the report. Most reports consist of pages. For this example, we assume that a page consists of 25 lines. Within the per-page limit of 25 lines, we define the desired vertical layout, as shown in Figure 16-1. Notice that the report heading will start on line 12 of the first page and will end on line 18. No other data will be presented on that page. The page heading will appear on line 5, and, since in this case it consists of only one line, it will also end on line 5. The first detail line will start on line 7 (we double space between it and the page heading), while the last detail line will be printed on line 19. Then the page footing will appear on line 23, while the report footing will appear on line 25 of the last page only.

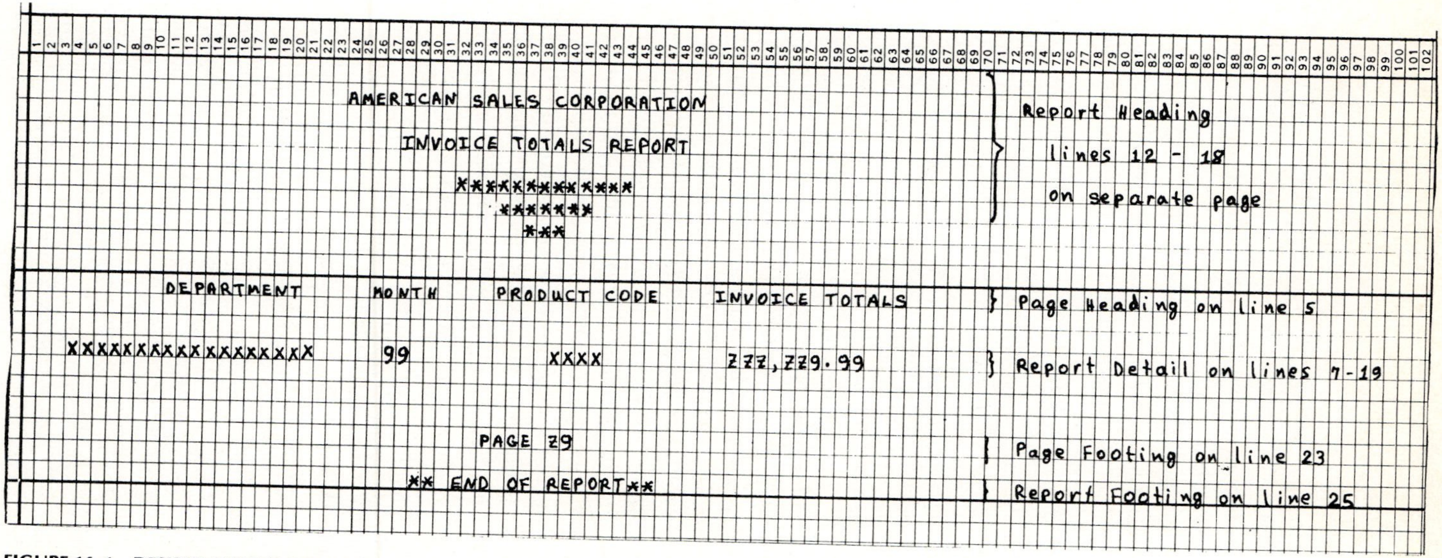

FIGURE 16-1 DESIRED REPORT FORMAT.

Figure 16–2 presents the header page, the second page, and the last page of the report. The design of the report format constitutes the major conceptual effort in report writing. The next step consists of translating the two-dimensional layout to COBOL instructions.

Let us assume that our task is defined as follows. We desire to read data from a card file and to produce a report with the format presented in Figure 16–1. The card file records have the following record description:

CARD COLUMN	DATA-NAME	PICTURE
1–18	DEPARTMENT-IN	X(18)
19–20	MONTH-IN	99
21–24	PRODUCT-CODE-IN	X(4)
25–32	INVOICE-TOTALS-IN	9(6)V99
33–80	FILLER	X(48)

Our task will involve printing a report with appropriate page headings, specified horizontal and vertical spacing, and page and report footings. The data for the report will be provided from a card file. For each card read in there will be a report line printed. Figure 16–3 presents the first part of a program written to accomplish this task. It will be noted that it is just like any COBOL program so far, with one file assigned to CARD-READER and another file assigned to the PRINTER. The FD entry and the record description for CARD-IN are typical of COBOL programs in general.

We want to produce the report on the device called PRINTER (as indicated by the SELECT statement in the ENVIRONMENT DIVISION). Since this will be a report produced by the report writer, the FD for REPORTFILE is as follows:

```
FD  REPORTFILE
        LABEL RECORDS ARE OMITTED
        REPORT IS INVOICE-REPORT.
```

The terms REPORTFILE and INVOICE-REPORT are arbitrary choices of the program author. That the LABEL RECORDS ARE OMITTED is no surprise, since this is a printer file, but they could have been STANDARD if, for example, the report were to be produced on tape (for eventual transmission to printer or display terminal). What is new is the REPORT IS clause. Instead of saying DATA RECORD IS, as is the case for other files, we now use the reserved word REPORT IS.

Figure 16–4 presents the complete COBOL program. Notice that, following the FILE SECTION of the DATA DIVISION and the WORKING-STORAGE SECTION, we write the REPORT SECTION.

```
                    AMERICAN SALES CORPORATION
                      INVOICE TOTALS REPORT
                       ***************
                          *******
                            ***

        DEPARTMENT        MONTH      PRODUCT CODE      INVOICE-TOTALS
    APPLIANCES            01            A-10               100.25
    APPLIANCES            01            A-11                25.25
    APPLIANCES            01            A-15               250.00
    APPLIANCES            01            B-13                83.00
    APPLIANCES            01            B-20             9,008.30
    APPLIANCES            01            B-21               150.50
    APPLIANCES            01            B-22               326.60
    APPLIANCES            01            C-10                 8.90
    APPLIANCES            02            A-10                90.20
    APPLIANCES            02            A-15                85.37
    APPLIANCES            02            A-25               654.92
    APPLIANCES            02            B-18               870.00
    APPLIANCES            02            B-20                50.00

                         PAGE    2

        DEPARTMENT        MONTH      PRODUCT CODE      INVOICE-TOTALS
    CHILDRENS CLOTHING    03            1-16               118.42
    CHILDRENS CLOTHING    03            1-17               100.00
    CHILDRENS CLOTHING    03            1-18                20.00
    CHILDRENS CLOTHING    03            1-19                70.00
    CHILDRENS CLOTHING    03            1-20                79.85
    CHILDRENS CLOTHING    03            1-21                85.42
    CHILDRENS CLOTHING    03            1-22               160.66
    CHILDRENS CLOTHING    03            1-23               158.18
    CHILDRENS CLOTHING    03            1-24               750.00

                         PAGE    6
                      **END OF REPORT**
```

FIGURE 16-2   HEADER PAGE, PAGE 2, AND LAST PAGE OF THE REQUIRED REPORT.

```
IDENTIFICATION DIVISION.
PROGRAM-ID. REPGEN1.

ENVIRONMENT DIVISION.
CONFIGURATION SECTION.
SOURCE-COMPUTER. ABC-480.
OBJECT-COMPUTER. ABC-480.
INPUT-OUTPUT SECTION.
FILE-CONTROL.
    SELECT CARDFILE    ASSIGN TO CARD-READER.
    SELECT REPORTFILE ASSIGN TO PRINTER.

DATA DIVISION.
FILE SECTION.
FD  CARDFILE
        LABEL RECORDS ARE OMITTED
        DATA RECORD IS CARD-IN.
01   CARD-IN.
     02 DEPARTMENT-IN        PIC X(18).
     02 MONTH-IN             PIC 99.
     02 PRODUCT-CODE-IN      PIC X(4).
     02 INVOICE-TOTALS-IN    PIC 9(6)V99.
     02 FILLER              PIC X(48).
```

FIGURE 16-3   FIRST PART OF THE COBOL PROGRAM FOR THE BASIC EXAMPLE.

The Report Description (RD) entry parallels the File Description (FD) entry of an ordinary file. The report-name in RD INVOICE-REPORT must be the same as in the FD entry of the report file, where the REPORT IS clause gives the report-name. The PAGE clause is optional, but it is commonly used unless we simply desire a report that is continuous and not broken into pages (in other words, a report consisting of one long page). In the example, we have:

```
RD  INVOICE-REPORT
        PAGE LIMIT IS 25 LINES
        HEADING 5
        FIRST DETAIL 7
        LAST DETAIL 19.
```

The indentations and the separate lines are used here for visual clarity. The RD must appear in columns 8–9, and the other clauses must be in column 12 or to the right of 12. PAGE LIMIT IS 25 LINES defines the page size in terms of vertical lines. This page size has nothing to do with the physical size of the paper, which is defined by the crease. It should be kept in mind that the space between pages is controlled by the printer carriage control tape, which is designated by the operator or reflects the convention of each computer installation.

FIGURE 16-4   THE COMPLETE COBOL PROGRAM FOR THE BASIC EXAMPLE.

```
IDENTIFICATION DIVISION.
PROGRAM-ID. REPGEN1.

ENVIRONMENT DIVISION.
CONFIGURATION SECTION.
SOURCE-COMPUTER. ABC-480.
OBJECT-COMPUTER. ABC-480.
INPUT-OUTPUT SECTION.
FILE-CONTROL.
        SELECT CARDFILE    ASSIGN TO CARD-READER.
        SELECT REPORTFILE ASSIGN TO PRINTER.

DATA DIVISION.
FILE SECTION.
FD  CARDFILE
        LABEL RECORDS ARE OMITTED
        DATA RECORD IS CARD-IN.
01  CARD-IN.
        02 DEPARTMENT-IN         PIC X(18).
        02 MONTH-IN              PIC 99.
        02 PRODUCT-CODE-IN       PIC X(4).
        02 INVOICE-TOTALS-IN     PIC 9(6)V99.
        02 FILLER                PIC X(48).

FD  REPORTFILE
        LABEL RECORDS ARE OMITTED
        REPORT IS INVOICE-REPORT.

WORKING-STORAGE SECTION.
01  END-OF-DATA              PIC XXX.

REPORT SECTION.
RD  INVOICE-REPORT
        PAGE LIMIT IS 25 LINES
        HEADING 5
        FIRST DETAIL 7
        LAST  DETAIL 19.
```

(continued)

```
01    TYPE IS REPORT HEADING
          NEXT GROUP NEXT PAGE.
      02 LINE NUMBER IS 12
          COLUMN NUMBER IS 24
          PICTURE IS A(26)
          VALUE IS 'AMERICAN SALES CORPORATION'.
      02 LINE NUMBER IS PLUS 2
          COLUMN NUMBER IS 28
          PICTURE IS X(21)
          VALUE IS 'INVOICE TOTALS REPORT'.
      02 LINE NUMBER IS PLUS 2
          COLUMN NUMBER IS 32
          PICTURE IS X(13)
          VALUE IS ALL '*'.
      02 LINE NUMBER IS PLUS 1
          COLUMN NUMBER IS 35
          PICTURE IS X(7)
          VALUE ALL '*'.
      02 LINE NUMBER IS PLUS 1
          COLUMN NUMBER IS 37
          PICTURE IS XXX
          VALUE '***'.

01    TYPE PAGE HEADING
      LINE NUMBER IS 5.
      02 COLUMN NUMBER IS 11
          PICTURE IS X(20)
          VALUE IS 'DEPARTMENT        MONTH'.
      02 COLUMN NUMBER IS 35
          PICTURE IS X(30)
          VALUE IS 'PRODUCT CODE        INVOICE-TOTALS'.

01    INVOICE-DATA
          TYPE IS DETAIL
          LINE NUMBER IS PLUS 1.
      02 COLUMN NUMBER IS 4
          PICTURE IS X(18)
          SOURCE IS DEPARTMENT-IN.
      02 COLUMN NUMBER IS 27
          PICTURE IS 99
          SOURCE IS MONTH-IN.
      02 COLUMN NUMBER IS 39
          SOURCE IS PRODUCT-CODE-IN
          PICTURE IS X(4).
      02 COLUMN NUMBER IS 52
          PICTURE IS ZZZ,ZZ9.99
          SOURCE IS INVOICE-TOTALS-IN.

01    TYPE PAGE FOOTING.
      02 LINE 23.
          03 COLUMN 34
              PIC AAAA
              VALUE 'PAGE'.
          03 COLUMN 40
              PIC Z9
              SOURCE IS PAGE-COUNTER.
01    TYPE REPORT FOOTING
      LINE 25.
      02 COLUMN 30
      VALUE '**END OF REPORT**'
      PIC X(17).


PROCEDURE DIVISION.
SET-UP.
      OPEN INPUT   CARDFILE
          OUTPUT REPORTFILE.
      MOVE 'NO' TO END-OF-DATA
      READ CARDFILE RECORD
          AT END MOVE 'YES' TO END-OF-DATA.
      INITIATE INVOICE-REPORT.
      PERFORM READ-PRINT
          UNTIL END-OF-DATA = 'YES'.
      TERMINATE INVOICE-REPORT
      CLOSE CARDFILE REPORTFILE
      STOP RUN.
READ-PRINT.
      GENERATE INVOICE-DATA.
      READ CARDFILE RECORD
          AT END MOVE 'YES' TO END-OF-DATA.
```

FIGURE 16-4 (*Continued*)

The HEADING 5 entry in Figure 16–4 means that page or report headings will start on line 5. In our example, the report heading is on a separate page; therefore, line 5 is relevant for the page heading only. The entries for FIRST DETAIL and LAST DETAIL define the inclusive range of lines on which detail report lines can be written.

It will be noted that in this example no mention is made in the PAGE entry about the page and report footing. The omission is intentional, so that the example can provide an illustration of defining vertical positioning apart from the PAGE option. A later example will include another option (FOOTING) in the PAGE description.

After the RD entry, it will be noted that there are five report groups described, each at the 01 level:

```
01   TYPE IS REPORT HEADING. . . .
     .
     .
     .

01   TYPE PAGE HEADING. . . .
     .
     .
     .

01   INVOICE-DATA TYPE IS DETAIL. . . .
     .
     .
     .

01   TYPE PAGE FOOTING. . . .
     .
     .
     .

01   TYPE REPORT FOOTING. . . .
```

Each 01 level in Figure 16–4 introduces a report group in a fashion analogous to the record descriptions in an ordinary file. A report group may consist of one or several lines of output, and within each line there may be one or several fields. Following is a description of each report group and an explanation of the options used.

The first report group is:

```
01   TYPE IS REPORT HEADING
       NEXT GROUP NEXT PAGE.
     02   LINE NUMBER IS 12
          COLUMN NUMBER IS 24
          PICTURE IS A(26)
          VALUE IS 'AMERICAN SALES CORPORATION'.
```

```
02   LINE NUMBER IS PLUS 2
     COLUMN NUMBER IS 28
     PICTURE IS X(21)
     VALUE IS 'INVOICE TOTALS REPORT'.
02   LINE NUMBER IS PLUS 2
     COLUMN NUMBER IS 32
     PICTURE IS X(13)
     VALUE ALL '*'.
02   LINE NUMBER IS PLUS 1
     COLUMN NUMBER IS 35
     PICTURE IS X(7)
     VALUE ALL '*'.
02   LINE NUMBER IS PLUS 1
     COLUMN NUMBER IS 37
     PICTURE IS XXX
     VALUE '***'.
```

The 01 level number introduces a new report group. The reserved words TYPE IS REPORT HEADING declare the type of report group about to be described. The NEXT GROUP specifies the positioning of the next group, and NEXT PAGE specifies that it should be on the next page. It will be recalled that the report heading was to be on a page by itself.

At the 02 level, there are five entries. In this case each represents one line. The level numbers used are in the range 01–49, as usual. The first level-02 entry reads:

```
02   LINE NUMBER IS 12
     COLUMN NUMBER IS 24
     PICTURE IS A(26)
     VALUE IS 'AMERICAN SALES CORPORATION'.
```

The LINE NUMBER IS 12 specifies that we want this item to be printed on line 12. Then, in column 24 (COLUMN NUMBER IS 24), we want to print a field whose PICTURE IS A(26) and whose content is supplied by the VALUE clause.

The second level-02 entry illustrates what is called *relative* line spacing with the option LINE NUMBER IS PLUS 2, meaning to double space from the previous line. In our example, the previous line was number 12, which was specified by *absolute* line spacing; therefore, the PLUS 2 in this case has the same effect as having said LINE NUMBER IS 14.

The remaining three level-02 entries of this report group are similar to the first two and have the purpose of printing three lines of asterisks for visual effect.

The second report group in Figure 16–4—remember, a report group is introduced by an 01 level—is TYPE PAGE HEADING, which implies that this information will be printed once for each page as a heading on the page. The LINE NUMBER IS 5 specifies that the page heading will be printed on line 5. Notice that, for this report group, the LINE clause is not given at the 02 level, unlike the previous report group (the REPORT HEADING). The reason for the difference is that the PAGE HEADING will consist of one line only and so the LINE clause can be included in the 01 level.

Two level-02 entries now introduce two fields, one starting in column 11, the other starting in column 35. They both contain literals specified by VALUE clauses. The presence of two fields is simply for illustration. One longer field would have the same effect as two shorter ones, since the intent is simply to print a heading.

The third report group described is given a data-name (INVOICE-DATA) and is TYPE DETAIL. The data-name is optional for the other report groups but is required for this one because later on, in the PROCEDURE DIVISION, we will want to make direct reference to this report group. The first field of this group is:

```
02   COLUMN NUMBER IS 4
     PICTURE IS X(18)
     SOURCE IS DEPARTMENT-IN.
```

The SOURCE clause specifies the source of the contents of this field. It is analogous in effect to a MOVE DEPARTMENT-IN TO the X(18) field starting in column 4. Whenever this report group is to be printed, the data contained in the field DEPARTMENT-IN will be moved to the current field. (It will be recalled that DEPARTMENT-IN was a field in the card input file, in this example.)

The remaining three fields of the INVOICE-DATA report group specify the location and source for the remainder of the line.

The next level-01 entry in Figure 16–4 introduces a TYPE PAGE FOOT-ING, which will be printed once for each page. The page footing will consist of one line of output as specified by 02 LINE 23. Notice that, for illustration of the available options, the LINE clause has been given its own 02 level and that the IS has been omitted, being optional in all cases. There are two fields in that line, each introduced at the 03 level (it could have been 04 or higher just as well). The first field starts at column 34 and has the VALUE clause, the second field is in columns 40–41 and has the SOURCE IS PAGE-COUNTER clause. The PAGE-COUNTER is a COBOL reserved word. It is a counter that contains an integer value indicating the page number of the current page. The counter is updated automatically each time a new page is to be printed, and so no special instructions along this line are required. However, the programmer may access (but not alter) the content of PAGE-COUNTER both in the REPORT SECTION and in the PROCEDURE DIVISION. The effect of this page footing report group will be to print the page number at the bottom of each page, as can be observed in Figure 16-2.

The final report group described in Figure 16-4 is TYPE REPORT FOOT-ING, which indicates that the report footing will be printed at the end of the report at the bottom of the last page, on line 25.

Completion of the REPORT SECTION constitutes the end of the major task in the use of the report writer. The PROCEDURE DIVISION for this example is rather simple:

```
PROCEDURE DIVISION.
SET-UP.
     OPEN INPUT CARDFILE
          OUTPUT REPORTFILE.
     MOVE 'NO' TO END-OF-DATA
     READ CARDFILE RECORD
          AT END MOVE 'YES' TO END-OF-DATA.
     INITIATE INVOICE-REPORT.
     PERFORM READ-PRINT
          UNTIL END-OF-DATA = 'YES'
     TERMINATE INVOICE-REPORT
     CLOSE CARDFILE REPORTFILE
     STOP RUN.
READ-PRINT.
     GENERATE INVOICE-DATA.
     READ CARDFILE RECORD
          AT END MOVE 'YES' TO END-OF-DATA.
```

First the files are opened and the first input record is read. Then comes the INITIATE INVOICE-REPORT which is an instruction that is analogous to OPEN for files. For instance, the INITIATE will cause the PAGE-COUNTER to be set to zero. Other actions resulting from the INITIATE will be described later. For now, it will suffice to say that before a report can be written the INITIATE command must be issued once—and only once.

In the READ-PRINT paragraph, the procedure consists of reading a record from the CARDFILE and then GENERATING INVOICE-DATA. It will be recalled that INVOICE-DATA was the data-name that we gave to the TYPE IS DETAIL report group. As a result of executing the GENERATE instruction, the report writer will control the printing of all other report groups (REPORT HEADING, PAGE HEADING, PAGE FOOTING) used in this example. Thus, the report writer is concerned mainly with report format specifications, not with procedure specifications.

When all the records from CARDFILE have been processed, we TER-MINATE INVOICE-REPORT in the JOB-END paragraph. As a result of the TERMINATE, the report footing will be printed. The TERMINATE is analogous to CLOSE.

REVIEW

1   The report writer module of COBOL makes it possible for the programmer to arrange production of a report by specifying the [programming procedures / format] associated with the report.

format

2   In the terminology of the report writer, such parts of the report as the report heading, page heading, and page footing are called report _____.

groups

3   Typically, the first step associated with using the report writer is to lay out the desired format of the report on a _____ chart.

printer

4   When the report writer module is used, the format of the report is described in the _____ DIVISION of the COBOL program.

DATA

5   In the DATA DIVISION of the COBOL program, the section in which the report format is described, and which typically follows the FILE SECTION and the WORKING-STORAGE SECTION, is the _____ _____.

REPORT SECTION

6   In the REPORT SECTION of the DATA DIVISION, each of the report groups associated with the report is assigned the level number _____.

01

7   Within each report group in the REPORT SECTION, each item of output typically is described at the level number _____ when several items (usually lines) are included.

02

8   If the report writer module is used, then in the PROCEDURE DIVISION the _____ command must be executed, both after the OPEN command for the files and before the report can be printed.

INITIATE

9 In the PROCEDURE DIVISION, the printed output for all of the report groups is achieved by execution of the _____ command.

GENERATE

10 When the report writer module is used, the PROCEDURE DIVISION command that is analogous to the CLOSE and also results in the report footing being printed is the _____ command.

TERMINATE

CONTROL BREAKS IN REPORT WRITING

Most reports pertain to data that are associated with categories which bear a hierarchical relation to each other. Very often, the categories correspond to organizational departments or groupings. For instance, suppose that we are producing a report listing alphabetically the enrollment for a college. We have students enrolled in a section, sections belonging to a course, courses belonging to a department, and departments belonging to a college. Suppose that we are interested in having the enrollment reported in a way that makes these relationships meaningful. To achieve this objective, we designate that each section begin on a new page with a header, that there be a header for each course, and that there be a header for each department. Further, we designate that total enrollment be reported for each section, for each course, for each department, and for the entire college.

In the context of the recurring control breaks in this example, we would say that we have three control breaks: section, course, and department. We speak of department as the *major* control, course as the *intermediate,* and section as the *minor* control. Of course, we may have more than three control levels, each subordinate to its superior and all subordinate to one— the major control.

As the report is being produced we want to *break* the routine whenever a new section, a new course, or a new department begins. The *control* is based on the content of the fields that designate the section, course, and department. We would expect that the report writer would check the section, for instance; and, if it changed, we would want to print the total enrollment for the section just listed. But it may be that the section did not change (say section 1 of a one-section course), but the course number changed from CIS-302 to CIS-402. The report writer then also must be checking the course designation to capture the change. A similar checking procedure is required for department designation.

The highest level of control break is called the *final* control, which is of course nonrecurring. In essence, it is a means of controlling the report writer action when all the detail data have been processed. In the registration example, a final control break would occur when the last department in the college had been processed and we were ready to report the enrollment for the entire college.

A point that relates to the control breaks is the fact that the report writer enables the user to present report groups that are called *control headings* and *control footings*. A *control heading* is a report group (one or more lines of output) that is presented when a control break occurs. For example, a control heading specified for the department field could be used to print the department-name and start a new page. As the name implies, a *control footing* is a report group that is presented at the end of a group and before the next category begins. In our example, at the end of each course we might desire a control footing to write the accumulated total enrollment of all the sections in that course. Typically, control footings are used for accumulating and reporting totals, while control headings are used for printing headers.

It should be noted that the control fields and the sort order of the input file are related. In our example, we would expect that the data have been sorted by student within section, by section within course, by course within department, and by department within the college. This sorting would be appropriate to establishing control breaks that treat department as a more inclusive control than course, course as more inclusive than section, and so forth.

The desire to designate hierarchically related control fields and to take actions dependent on the contents of these fields is very common in report production, and is implemented in the report writer module of COBOL.

REVIEW

1 When control breaks are used in conjunction with the report writer, the category that is at the highest hierarchical level compared with the other categories is termed the _____ control.

major

2 In addition to the major control break, other levels of such breaks are _____ and _____ controls.

intermediate; minor

3 When all data have been processed, the last break is associated with the output of grand totals for all of the categories and is called the _____ control break.

final

4   A heading (or footing) that is printed just before (or just after) a data group
that is associated with a control break is called a _____ heading
(or footing).

control

AN EXAMPLE WITH CONTROL BREAKS

The basic purpose of the example that follows is to introduce the concept
of control breaks. In addition, other features of the report writer will be
illustrated.

We begin with a description of the desired report, in terms of the format
of the layout and in terms of the content. In discussing the basic example
earlier, we illustrated the process of developing the report specifications. At
this point we assume that the task specification stage has been completed,
and we proceed to illustrate the desired report by presenting three sample
pages in Figure 16-5. Notice that this report essentially is a revised version of
the first example in this chapter.

Figure 16-5 presents the first page of the report in part *(a)*. The report
header is now on the same page as the first page header and the first page
detail. The page header has been modified by dropping the column DE-
PARTMENT and adding two new columns, MONTH TOTAL and DEPT.
TOTAL.

A new report group appears that consists of the fixed header, DEPART-
MENT: and the department name (in the case of the first page it is
APPLIANCES). This type of header is absent from the second page, part *(b)*,
because we want department name to be printed only at the start of a new
department listing.

The page footing remains the same as in the previous example.

Part *(b)* of Figure 16-5 presents the second page of the report and serves
to illustrate the accumulation of month and department totals. The page is
short because the end of the first department (APPLIANCES) occurs on this
page and we want to start each department at the top of a new page. The line
of asterisks is used for visual effect.

Part *(c)* of Figure 16-5 presents the last page of the report. One item
deserves special attention: the line GRAND TOTAL FOR INVOICE REPORT.
The purpose is to show the grand total of all invoice totals processed in this
report. It is, therefore, produced as a *final* control footing.

Now that we have a clear visualization of the desired report, let us
consider the programming aspects. Figure 6-6 presents the entire program

AMERICAN SALES CORPORATION
INVOICE TOTALS REPORT

DEPARTMENT: APPLIANCES

MONTH	PRODUCT CODE	INVOICE-TOTALS	MONTH TOTAL	DEPT. TOTAL
01	A-10	100.25		
	A-11	25.25		
	A-15	250.00		
	B-13	83.00		
	B-20	9,008.30		
	B-21	150.50		
	B-22	326.60		
	C-10	8.90		
			9,952.80	

PAGE 1

(a)

MONTH	PRODUCT CODE	INVOICE-TOTALS	MONTH TOTAL	DEPT. TOTAL
02	A-10	90.20		
	A-15	85.37		
	A-25	654.92		
	B-18	870.00		
	B-20	850.00		
			1,750.49	
03	A-15	15.00		
	B-20	182.18		
			197.18	11,900.47

****

PAGE 2

(b)

```
MONTH     PRODUCT CODE    INVOICE-TOTALS      MONTH TOTAL    DEPT. TOTAL

03           1-19            70.00
             1-20            79.85
             1-21            85.42
             1-22           160.66
             1-23           158.18
             1-24           750.00

                                               2,041.16        5,157.10

****************************************************************************
****************************************************************************

          GRAND TOTAL FOR INVOICE REPORT      19,289.69


                        PAGE     7

                   **END OF REPORT**

                         (c)
```

FIGURE 16-5 (a) FIRST PAGE OF THE REPORT. (b) SECOND PAGE OF THE REPORT. (c) LAST PAGE OF THE REPORT.

from which the sample report pages were produced. Up to the REPORT SECTION, the program is identical to the one used in the basic example.

The Report Descrption (RD) entry specifies the fields that will be used for control break purposes:

```
RD  INVOICE-REPORT
        CONTROLS ARE FINAL
                    DEPARTMENT-IN
                    MONTH-IN
```

There are three control breaks specified. One is declared with the reserved word FINAL. This is always the most inclusive control in the hierarchy. The next control field is DEPARTMENT-IN, which is a field in the input record. The minor control is MONTH-IN, which is also a field in the input record. The order of writeup establishes the hierarchy. The FINAL must be the first control (if used); then the remaining order is established. Thus, if instead of having written MONTH-IN as the last item we had written it as the second, we would have established DEPARTMENT-IN as the minor control.

In the present example, we want control footings for month and department. Referring back to Figure 16–5, it should be noted that the data presented to the report writer were sorted by month within department. If the data were sorted by department within month and given the hierarchy of FINAL, DEPARTMENT-IN, MONTH-IN, then the report would be different. The difference would be that department totals would be produced for all departments for each month. Thus, it is important to relate the input file sort order with the control breaks desired and, when required, sort the input file in a different order or change the format of the report.

The PAGE clause in the RD entry in Figure 16–6 is similar in form to the basic example. The FOOTING 20 clause specifies that line 20 will be the last line number on which a CONTROL FOOTING report group may be presented. PAGE FOOTING and REPORT FOOTING report groups must follow line 20.

The REPORT HEADING group is specified to begin on LINE 2. The absence of NEXT GROUP NEXT PAGE (as contrasted to Figure 16–4) implies that this heading will be on the first page of the report, along with the page heading.

The next report group is:

```
01  PAGE-TOP TYPE IS PAGE HEADING
        LINE NUMBER IS PLUS 2.
        (etc.)
```

For illustration, a data-name (PAGE-TOP) has been assigned to this TYPE PAGE HEADING report group, and this heading begins two lines below the

FIGURE 16-6 COBOL PROGRAM FOR THE EXAMPLE WITH CONTROL BREAKS.

```
IDENTIFICATION DIVISION.
PROGRAM-ID. REPGEN2.

ENVIRONMENT DIVISION.
CONFIGURATION SECTION.
SOURCE-COMPUTER. ABC-480.
OBJECT-COMPUTER. ABC-480.
INPUT-OUTPUT SECTION.
FILE-CONTROL.
    SELECT CARDFILE   ASSIGN TO CARD-READER.
    SELECT REPORTFILE ASSIGN TO PRINTER.


DATA DIVISION.
FILE SECTION.
FD  CARDFILE
        LABEL RECORDS ARE OMITTED
        DATA RECORD IS CARD-IN.
01  CARD-IN.
    02 DEPARTMENT-IN        PIC X(18).
    02 MONTH-IN             PIC 99.
    02 PRODUCT-CODE-IN      PIC X(4).
    02 INVOICE-TOTALS-IN    PIC 9(6)V99.
    02 FILLER               PIC X(48).

FD  REPORTFILE
        LABEL RECORDS ARE OMITTED
        REPORT IS INVOICE-REPORT.
WORKING-STORAGE SECTION.
01  END-OF-DATA         PIC XXX.

REPORT SECTION.
RD  INVOICE-REPORT
        CONTROLS ARE FINAL
                     DEPARTMENT-IN
                     MONTH-IN
        PAGE LIMIT IS 25 LINES
            HEADING 2
            FIRST DETAIL 5
            LAST DETAIL 18
            FOOTING 20.

01 TYPE IS REPORT HEADING.
    02 LINE IS 2
       COLUMN NUMBER IS 35
       PICTURE IS A(26)
       VALUE IS 'AMERICAN SALES CORPORATION'.
    02 LINE NUMBER IS PLUS 2
       COLUMN NUMBER IS 38
       PICTURE IS X(21)
       VALUE IS 'INVOICE TOTALS REPORT'.

01  PAGE-TOP TYPE IS PAGE HEADING
        LINE NUMBER IS PLUS 2.
    02 COLUMN NUMBER IS 25
       PICTURE IS XXXXX
       VALUE IS 'MONTH'.
    02 COLUMN NUMBER IS 35
       PICTURE IS X(30)
       VALUE IS 'PRODUCT CODE    INVOICE-TOTALS'.
    03 COLUMN NUMBER IS 72
       VALUE IS 'MONTH TOTAL    DEPT. TOTAL'
       PICTURE IS X(25).

01 TYPE IS CONTROL HEADING DEPARTMENT-IN
        LINE NUMBER IS PLUS 2
        NEXT GROUP IS PLUS 2.
    02 COLUMN 6
       PICTURE X(11)
       VALUE 'DEPARTMENT:'.
    02 COLUMN 18
       PICTURE X(18)
       SOURCE DEPARTMENT-IN.

01  INVOICE-DATA
        TYPE IS DETAIL
        LINE NUMBER IS PLUS 1.
```

(continued)

```
        02  COLUMN NUMBER IS 4
            PIC IS X(18)
            SOURCE IS DEPARTMENT-IN
            GROUP INDICATE.
        02  COLUMN NUMBER IS 27
            PICTURE IS 99
            SOURCE IS MONTH-IN
            GROUP INDICATE.
        02  COLUMN NUMBER IS 39
            SOURCE IS PRODUCT-CODE-IN
            PIC X(4).
        02  COLUMN NUMBER IS 52
            PIC IS ZZZ,ZZ9.99
            SOURCE IS INVOICE-TOTALS-IN.

    01  TYPE IS CONTROL FOOTING MONTH-IN
            LINE NUMBER IS PLUS 1.
        02  MONTH-TOTAL
            COLUMN NUMBER IS 69
            PICTURE IS Z,ZZZ,ZZ9.99
            SUM INVOICE-TOTALS-IN.

    01  DEPT-TOTAL  TYPE IS CONTROL FOOTING DEPARTMENT-IN
            NEXT GROUP NEXT PAGE.
        02  LINE NUMBER PLUS 1
            COLUMN NUMBER IS 82
            PICTURE IS ZZ,ZZZZ,ZZ9.99
            SUM MONTH-TOTAL.
        02  LINE NUMBER IS PLUS 2
            PICTURE IS X(95)
            VALUE ALL '*'
            COLUMN NUMBER IS 2.

    01  TYPE IS CONTROL FOOTING FINAL.
        02  LINE NUMBER IS PLUS 2
            COLUMN NUMBER 2
            PICTURE X(95)
            VALUE ALL '*'.
        02  LINE NUMBER PLUS 2.
            03  COLUMN NUMBER 36
                PIC X(30)
                VALUE 'GRAND TOTAL FOR INVOICE REPORT'.
            03  COLUMN NUMBER 66
                PIC ZZZ,ZZZ,ZZ9.99
                SUM INVOICE-TOTALS-IN.

    01  TYPE PAGE FOOTING.
        02  LINE 23.
            03  COLUMN 46
                PIC AAAA
                VALUE 'PAGE'.
            03  COLUMN 54
                PIC Z9
                SOURCE IS PAGE-COUNTER.
    01  TYPE REPORT FOOTING
            LINE NUMBER IS PLUS 2.
        02  COLUMN NUMBER IS 41
            PICTURE X(17)
            VALUE '**END OF REPORT**'.


PROCEDURE DIVISION.
SET-UP.
    OPEN INPUT  CARDFILE
         OUTPUT REPORTFILE.
    MOVE 'NO' TO END-OF-DATA
    INITIATE INVOICE-REPORT
    READ CARDFILE RECORD
        AT END MOVE 'YES' TO END-OF-DATA.
    PERFORM READ-PRINT
        UNTIL END-OF-DATA = 'YES'.
    TERMINATE INVOICE-REPORT
    CLOSE CARDFILE REPORTFILE
    STOP RUN.
READ-PRINT.
    GENERATE INVOICE-DATA.
    READ CARDFILE RECORD
        AT END MOVE 'YES' TO END-OF-DATA.
```

FIGURE 16–6 (*Continued*)

previous line printed. Referring back to the REPORT HEADING description, it will be observed that the report heading begins on line 2 and consists of two lines with double spacing (PLUS 2). Thus, the report heading will be printed on lines 2–4, and the page heading will begin on line 6 of the first page. On subsequent pages, however, the report heading will not be printed. Then the page heading will start on line 4, which is determined as follows: the PAGE clause established line 2 as the first line on which a heading (HEADING 2) can be printed. Since the PAGE HEADING has relative spacing (LINE NUMBER IS PLUS 2), it follows that the page heading will start on line 4 of the second and subsequent pages.

The next report group in Figure 16–6 is:

```
01   TYPE IS CONTROL HEADING DEPARTMENT-IN
         LINE NUMBER IS PLUS 2
         NEXT GROUP IS PLUS 2.
     02   COLUMN 6
         PICTURE X(11)
         VALUE 'DEPARTMENT:'.
     02   COLUMN 18
         PICTURE X(18)
         SOURCE DEPARTMENT-IN.
```

This is a CONTROL HEADING group, and it will be printed every time that the DEPARTMENT-IN field changes value. Referring to Figure 16–5, the header DEPARTMENT: XXXXXXXXXXXXXXXXXX (where the X's stand for the department name) is printed only when a new department is introduced in the input stream. (The fact that the DEPARTMENT-IN field is used both as a control heading break and as a source field is just a coincidence in this example.)

The clauses LINE NUMBER IS PLUS 2, and NEXT GROUP IS PLUS 2 specify that this report group will be printed two lines after the previous report group (the page header) and that the next group (which is a detail report group in this example) will be presented two lines below, thus double spacing before and after. The two 02 fields are similar to the type we have discussed already in the basic example.

Reviewing Figure 16–5, you will notice that DEPARTMENT: APPLIANCES is single spaced after the page header, seemingly contradicting the LINE NUMBER PLUS 2 clause. The explanation for this lies in the complicated rules by which the report writer operates. If no previous report body group has been presented on the page, then the single spacing prevails; otherwise, the relative spacing specified in the CONTROL HEADING takes effect. Thus, in this case, single spacing resulted from DEPARTMENT: APPLIANCES being the first report body group. If we had another control break based on DEPART-MENT-IN, there would have been double spacing.

The next report group specified in Figure 16-6 is 01 INVOICE-DATA TYPE IS DETAIL LINE NUMBER IS PLUS 1. As in the previous example, this will be the report group referenced in the GENERATE statement in the PROCEDURE DIVISION. The only difference between this and the corresponding group in the basic example is the use of the GROUP INDICATE clause. Specifically, we have:

02   COLUMN NUMBER IS 27
     PIC IS X(99)
     SOURCE IS MONTH-IN
     GROUP INDICATE.

The effect of the GROUP INDICATE is to print the data only at the beginning of a report, at the beginning of each page, and after each control break. A glance at the sample report output in Figure 16-5 will show the effect of the GROUP INDICATE. A good contrast is provided by the absence of this clause in the description of the detail group of the basic example.

The next report group in Figure 16-6 is:

01   TYPE IS CONTROL FOOTING MONTH-IN
         LINE NUMBER IS PLUS 1.
     02   MONTH-TOTAL
          COLUMN NUMBER IS 69
          PICTURE IS Z,ZZZ,ZZ9.99
          SUM INVOICE-TOTALS-IN.

The TYPE clause specifies this to be a CONTROL FOOTING associated with the data-name MONTH-IN, which is a data-name in the input file record. The meaning of this control footing is that whenever the value of the data-name MONTH-IN changes, a control break will occur which will, in turn, result in printing the edited sum of the values of the data-name INVOICE-TOTALS-IN in column 69 of the next line. As each detail group is presented, the sum of the INVOICE-TOTALS-IN fields is formed in the MONTH-TOTAL field.

The ability to specify summation fields whose data are printed as a result of control breaks is a fundamental capability of the report writer. A sum counter is set initially to zero by the report writer. Then, as each detail line is presented, the specified data are added to this sum counter. When a control break occurs, the value of the sum counter is printed and then it is reset to zero. In the present example, a name has been given to the accumulator: MONTH-TOTAL. As each input card is read and a detail report line is printed, MONTH-TOTAL is incremented by the value of INVOICE-TOTALS-IN. Then, when MONTH-IN changes value, the edited value of MONTH-TOTAL will be printed, starting in column 69. Referring to part *(a)* of Figure 16–5, it will be observed that when the month changed from 01 to 02 a month total of 9,952.80 was printed.

The next report group introduced in Figure 16–6 is:

01   DEPT-TOTAL TYPE IS CONTROL FOOTING DEPARTMENT-IN
        NEXT GROUP NEXT PAGE.

The effect of this control footing is to sum the values of the MONTH-TOTAL sum counter (SUM MONTH-TOTAL) and to print the edited sum, starting in column 82 of the next line. Reference to Figure 16–5 reveals that this sum counter is printed only when the department changes; thus, all the month totals for a given department are printed before the department total. Referring back to CONTROLS ARE FINAL DEPARTMENT-IN MONTH-IN serves to remind us that in this hierarchy of control breaks the MONTH-IN is subordinate to DEPARTMENT-IN. Thus, the expected order of control footings is that several MONTH-TOTALS will be printed for each DEPT-TOTAL.

Incidentally, the order in which the control footing report groups are written is immaterial. The logic of report presentation is not related to the order in which the report groups are specified in the program.

Two additional features of the DEPT-TOTAL report group deserve attention. The NEXT GROUP NEXT PAGE clause specifies that, after this group, we want to start a new page. The second feature is that this group consists of two lines. The first one prints the value of the sum counter while the second line consists of asterisks.

The next group is:

01   TYPE IS CONTROL FOOTING FINAL.

No name is given to this report group (names are optional). This kind of control footing will be printed after all control breaks have occurred, since it is the highest in the control hierarchy. Thus, after the last detail group has been presented and after all the control footings have been presented, the final control footing is presented in the report. In a sense it resembles a report footing, except that SUM clauses can appear only in control footing groups; therefore, a CONTROL FOOTING FINAL is necessary.

The SUM INVOICE-TOTALS-IN specifies that this sum counter (and we have given it no name) will accumulate the sums of the INVOICE-TOTALS-IN values. Actually, it would be advisable to have said SUM DEPT-TOTAL to reduce the required number of additions, in a fashion similar to the SUM MONTH-TOTAL specified for the DEPT-TOTAL group. This inadvisable variation is shown here to illustrate the options available. If the report consisted of thousands of lines the extra additions might be considered somewhat inefficient.

One point needs clarification. Referring to part *(c)* of Figure 16-5, the question may be raised: Why is the final control footing not printed on a new page, since the previous control footing (DEPT-TOTAL) contained the NEXT GROUP NEXT PAGE clause? The reason is that the NEXT GROUP clause is ignored when it is specified on a control footing report group that is at a level other than the highest level at which a control break is detected. In this case, a final control footing is at a higher level; therefore, the NEXT GROUP clause associated with the DEPT-TOTAL control footing group is ignored.

The PAGE FOOTING and REPORT FOOTING groups in Figure 16-6 are similar to the ones in the basic example in Figure 16-4.

The PROCEDURE DIVISION is identical to the one in the basic example, illustrating that the differences in the resulting report are attributable to the differences in the report description, rather than in the procedures specified.

REVIEW

1 In the RD entry in the REPORT SECTION of the DATA DIVISION, if the FINAL control break is used then it must be the [first one / last one] listed.

first one

2 When the major report groups are described at the 01 level in the DATA DIVISION, then the CONTROL HEADING and CONTROL FOOTING groups are described at the [01 / 02] level.

01

3 The effect of the GROUP INDICATE clause in the description of a report group is to print the associated information only at the beginning of the report, at the beginning of each _____, and after each _____ _____.

page; control break

4 The data-name that is associated with either a CONTROL HEADING or a CONTROL FOOTING must be a data-name in the _____ file record.

input

5 A CONTROL HEADING report group typically involves the specification of descriptive _____ headings.

column (or report)

6   A CONTROL FOOTING report group typically involves the specification of various _____ which are to be reported.

sums (or totals)

7   Even though a report footing has been specified, it also is necessary to specify a FINAL control footing if the output of a _____ clause is desired at the end of the report

SUM

AN EXAMPLE USING DECLARATIVES

Figure 16–7 illustrates the output of what appears similar to the report discussed in the more advanced example, with one main exception: The line PAGE TOTAL = 10,783.29 is new. Suppose then that we are interested in showing a PAGE TOTAL for the INVOICE-TOTALS printed on that page. This example will serve as a vehicle to illustrate how the programmer can specify procedures other than those made possible by the standard report groups.

What we desire is to have the INVOICE-TOTALS summarized and printed at the bottom of the page above the page footing. In a sense, we desire a control break associated with the end of a page, but the rules of the CONTROLS clause specify that we must not use control breaks associated with data-names defined in the REPORT SECTION. Further, a SUM counter cannot be used except with CONTROL FOOTING report groups.

In order to proceed directly to the illustration, consider the modification to the more advanced example in Figure 16–8. A WORKING-STORAGE field has been added, called PAGE-ACCUMULATOR. Then, in the PROCE-DURE DIVISION, the reserved word DECLARATIVES introduces a special-purpose section; in this example, it is the PAGE-END SECTION. The USE verb specifies the condition under which the procedures in the DECLAR-ATIVES portion will be executed; in this case, it is BEFORE REPORTING PAGE-TOP. It will be recalled that PAGE-TOP was the name given to the page heading report group. Thus, the procedures specified in this section will be executed before printing the page header. Now, looking at PAR-A, the simple task of MOVE ZEROS TO PAGE-ACCUMULATOR is the only procedure specified in this section (PAR-B simply contains an EXIT com-mand). In essence, then, we have said: before printing the heading on each page, zero out the WORKING-STORAGE field called PAGE-ACCUMULA-TOR. The END DECLARATIVES marks the end of the declarative part of the PROCEDURE DIVISION.

```
                    AMERICAN SALES CORPORATION
                      INVOICE TOTALS REPORT

DEPARTMENT       MONTH      PRODUCT CODE     INVOICE-TOTALS     MONTH TOTAL     DEPT. TOTAL
APPLIANCES        01           A-10             100.25
                               A-11              25.26
                               A-15             250.00
                               B-13             283.00
                               B-20           9,008.30
                               B-21             150.50
                               B-22             326.60
                               C-10               8.90

                  02           A-10              90.20
                               A-15              85.37
                               A-25             654.92                             9,952.80


                            PAGE TOTAL =    10,783.29

                                  PAGE      1
```

FIGURE 16-7   OUTPUT RESULTING FROM THE MODIFIED PROGRAM USING DECLARATIVES.

434

FIGURE 16-8   REVISED PROGRAM FOR THE MORE ADVANCED EXAMPLE USING DECLARATIVES.

```
IDENTIFICATION DIVISION.
PROGRAM-ID. REPGEN3.

ENVIRONMENT DIVISION.
CONFIGURATION SECTION.
SOURCE-COMPUTER. ABC-480.
OBJECT-COMPUTER. ABC-480.
INPUT-OUTPUT SECTION.
FILE-CONTROL.
    SELECT CARDFILE   ASSIGN TO CARD-READER.
    SELECT REPORTFILE ASSIGN TO PRINTER.

DATA DIVISION.
FILE SECTION.
FD  CARDFILE
        LABEL RECORDS ARE OMITTED
        DATA RECORD IS CARD-IN.
01  CARD-IN.
    02 DEPARTMENT-IN       PIC X(18).
    02 MONTH-IN            PIC 99.
    02 PRODUCT-CODE-IN     PIC X(4).
    02 INVOICE-TOTALS-IN   PIC 9(6)V99.
    02 FILLER             PIC X(48).

FD  REPORTFILE
        LABEL RECORDS ARE OMITTED
        REPORT IS INVOICE-REPORT.

WORKING-STORAGE SECTION.
01  END-OF-DATA        PIC XXX.
01  PAGE-ACCUMULATOR  PIC 9(7)V99.

REPORT SECTION.
RD  INVOICE-REPORT
        CONTROLS ARE FINAL
                     DEPARTMENT-IN
                     MONTH-IN
        PAGE LIMIT IS 25 LINES
             HEADING 2
             FIRST DETAIL 5
             LAST DETAIL 18
             FOOTING 20.

01 TYPE IS REPORT HEADING.
    02 LINE IS 2
       COLUMN NUMBER IS 35
       PICTURE IS A(26)
       VALUE IS 'AMERICAN SALES CORPORATION'.
    02 LINE NUMBER IS PLUS 2
       COLUMN NUMBER IS 38
       PICTURE IS X(21)
       VALUE IS 'INVOICE TOTALS REPORT'.

01 PAGE-TOP TYPE IS PAGE HEADING
        LINE NUMBER IS PLUS 2.
    02 COLUMN NUMBER IS 6
       PICTURE IS X(24)
       VALUE IS 'DEPARTMENT          MONTH'.
    02 COLUMN NUMBER IS 35
       PICTURE IS X(30)
       VALUE IS 'PRODUCT CODE      INVOICE-TOTALS'.
    03 COLUMN NUMBER IS 72
       VALUE IS 'MONTH TOTAL    DEPT. TOTAL'
       PICTURE IS X(25).

01 INVOICE-DATA
       TYPE IS DETAIL
       LINE NUMBER IS PLUS 1.
    02 COLUMN NUMBER IS 4
       PIC IS X(18)
       SOURCE IS DEPARTMENT-IN
       GROUP INDICATE.
    02 COLUMN NUMBER IS 27
       PICTURE IS 99
       SOURCE IS MONTH-IN
       GROUP INDICATE.
       02 COLUMN NUMBER IS 39
       SOURCE IS PRODUCT-CODE-IN
       PIC X(4).
    02 COLUMN NUMBER IS 52
       PIC IS ZZZ,ZZ9.99
       SOURCE IS INVOICE-TOTALS-IN.
```

(continued)

```
01   TYPE IS CONTROL FOOTING MONTH-IN
         LINE NUMBER IS PLUS 1.
     02 MONTH-TOTAL
         COLUMN NUMBER IS 69
         PICTURE IS Z,ZZZ,ZZ9.99
         SUM INVOICE-TOTALS-IN.

01   DEPT-TOTAL  TYPE IS CONTROL FOOTING DEPARTMENT-IN
         NEXT GROUP NEXT PAGE.
     02 LINE NUMBER PLUS 1
         COLUMN NUMBER IS 82
         PICTURE IS ZZ,ZZZZ,ZZ9.99
         SUM MONTH-TOTAL.
     02 LINE NUMBER IS PLUS 2
             PICTURE IS X(95)
         VALUE ALL '*'
         COLUMN NUMBER IS 2.

01   TYPE IS CONTROL FOOTING FINAL.
     02 LINE NUMBER IS PLUS 2
         COLUMN NUMBER 2
         PICTURE X(95)
         VALUE ALL '*'.
     02 LINE NUMBER PLUS 2:
         03 COLUMN NUMBER 32
             PIC X(30)
             VALUE 'GRAND TOTAL FOR INVOICE REPORT'.
         03 COLUMN NUMBER 66
             PIC ZZZ,ZZZ,ZZ9.99
         SUM INVOICE-TOTALS-IN.

01   TYPE PAGE FOOTING.
     02 LINE 21.
         03 COLUMN 34
             PIC A(12)
             VALUE 'PAGE TOTAL ='.
         03 COLUMN 49
             PIC ZZ,ZZZ,ZZ9.99
             SOURCE PAGE-ACCUMULATOR.
     02 LINE 23.
         03 COLUMN 46
             PIC AAAA
             VALUE 'PAGE'.
         03 COLUMN 52
             PIC Z9
             SOURCE IS PAGE-COUNTER.

01   TYPE REPORT FOOTING
         LINE NUMBER IS PLUS 2:
     02 COLUMN NUMBER IS 41
         PICTURE X(17)
         VALUE '**END OF REPORT**'.


PROCEDURE DIVISION.

DECLARATIVES.
PAGE-END SECTION.
     USE BEFORE REPORTING PAGE-TOP.

PAR-A.
     MOVE ZEROS TO PAGE-ACCUMULATOR.
PAR-B.
     EXIT.
END DECLARATIVES.

PROCEDURAL SECTION.
SET-UP.
     OPEN INPUT  CARDFILE
             OUTPUT REPORTFILE.
     MOVE 'NO' TO END-OF-DATA
     INITIATE INVOICE-REPORT
     READ CARDFILE RECORD
             AT END MOVE 'YES' TO END-OF-DATA.
     PERFORM READ-PRINT
         UNTIL END-OF-DATA = 'YES'.
     TERMINATE INVOICE-REPORT
     CLOSE CARDFILE REPORTFILE
     STOP RUN.
READ-PRINT.
     GENERATE INVOICE-DATA.
     ADD INVOICE-TOTALS-IN TO PAGE-ACCUMULATOR
     READ CARDFILE RECORD
             AT END MOVE 'YES' TO END-OF-DATA.
```

FIGURE 16–8 (*Continued*)

In the READ-PRINT paragraph, observe the two statements:

GENERATE INVOICE-DATA.
ADD INVOICE-TOTALS-IN TO PAGE-ACCUMULATOR.

After each report detail group is generated, the value of PAGE-ACCUMULATOR is incremented by the amount of INVOICE-TOTALS-IN. When a page footing is printed, the value of PAGE-ACCUMULATOR serves as the SOURCE. Then, the declarative portion takes effect, before the next page heading is printed, and the PAGE-ACCUMULATOR is set to zero to begin again the new page accumulation.

REVIEW

1   The reserved word DECLARATIVES is used to introduce special purpose sections in the _____ DIVISION of a COBOL program.

PROCEDURE

2   The verb that specifies the condition under which the procedures under DECLARATIVES are to be executed is the _____ verb.

USE

3   When presentation of the DECLARATIVES in the PROCEDURE DIVISION has been completed, this is indicated by the command _____ _____.

END DECLARATIVES

LANGUAGE SPECIFICATIONS FOR THE COBOL REPORT WRITER

A complete language specification description is beyond the scope of the present discussion; however, a full list of the language options is included in Appendix B of this book. In the following description, only a few of the options are highlighted.

One option looks like this:

$\left\{ \begin{array}{l} \text{CONTROL IS} \\ \text{CONTROLS ARE} \end{array} \right\}$	$\left\{ \begin{array}{l} \text{data-name-1 [, data-name-2]} \ldots \\ \text{FINAL [, data-name-1 [, data-name-2]} \ldots \end{array} \right\}$

Data-name-1 and data-name-2 must not be defined in the Report Section. FINAL, if specified, is the highest control; data-name-1 is the major control; data-name-2 is an intermediate control, and so forth. The last data-name specified is the minor control.

A second option is:

GROUP INDICATE

The GROUP INDICATE clause specifies that the associated printable item is presented only on the first occurrence of the associated report group, after a control break or page advance.

A third format is as follows:

$$\text{LINE NUMBER IS} \left\{ \begin{array}{l} \text{integer-1 [ON \underline{NEXT} \underline{PAGE}]} \\ \underline{\text{PLUS}}\ \text{integer-2} \end{array} \right\}$$

This clause specifies vertical positioning information for the associated report group. The following rules apply:

1 Integer-1 and integer-2 must not be specified in such a way as to cause any line of a report group to be presented outside of the vertical subdivisions of the page designated for the report group type, as defined by the PAGE clause (see discussion of the PAGE clause).

2 Within a given report group, an entry that contains a LINE NUMBER clause must not contain a subordinate entry that also contains a LINE NUMBER clause.

3 Within a given report description entry, a NEXT PAGE phrase can appear only once and, if present, must be in the first LINE NUMBER clause in that report group.

4 A LINE NUMBER clause with the NEXT PAGE phrase can appear only in the description of the CONTROL HEADING, DETAIL, CONTROL FOOTING, and REPORT FOOTING groups.

5 The first LINE NUMBER clause specified within a PAGE FOOTING report group must be an absolute LINE NUMBER clause.

A fourth clause is:

$$\underline{\text{NEXT}}\ \text{GROUP IS} \left\{ \begin{array}{l} \text{integer-1} \\ \underline{\text{PLUS}}\ \text{integer-2} \\ \underline{\text{NEXT}}\ \underline{\text{PAGE}} \end{array} \right\}$$

The NEXT GROUP clause specifies information for vertical positioning following presentation of the last line of a report group. However, it is ignored when it is specified on a CONTROL FOOTING report group that is at a level other than the highest level at which a control break is detected. These two rules apply:

1   The NEXT PAGE phrase of the NEXT GROUP clause must not be specified in a PAGE FOOTING report group.

2   The NEXT GROUP clause must not be specified in a REPORT FOOTING or PAGE HEADING report group.

A fifth format is as follows:

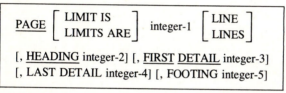

The PAGE clause defines the length of a page and the vertical subdivisions within which report groups are presented. The order of writing HEADING, FIRST DETAIL, LAST DETAIL, and FOOTING is immaterial. Use of the PAGE clause defines certain page regions that are described in this format. The integer-1, integer-2, and so on, refer to the operands of the PAGE clause. As an illustration of using the table, notice that CONTROL FOOTING report groups are allocated the region between integer-3 and integer-5. Thus, if the PAGE clause had contained FIRST DETAIL 6, FOOTING 20, the CONTROL FOOTING report group description should not contain, for example, an absolute LINE NUMBER clause referring to line 22.

A sixth option is:

```
SOURCE IS identifier-1
```

The SOURCE clause identifies the sending data item that is moved to an associated printable item defined within a report group description entry. Identifier-1 may be defined in any section of the DATA DIVISION. If identifier-1 is a REPORT SECTION item, it can only be PAGE-COUNTER, LINE-COUNTER, or a sum counter.

A seventh clause looks like this:

```
{SUM identifier-1 [, identifier-2] . . .

    [UPON data-name-1 [, data-name-2] . . . ]} . . .

⎡                   ⎧ data-name-3 ⎫  ⎤
⎢ RESET ON          ⎨             ⎬  ⎥
⎣                   ⎩ FINAL       ⎭  ⎦
```

The SUM clause establishes a sum counter and names the data items to be summed. When more than one identifier is used, the sum counter is incremented by the sum of the identifiers. Thus:

03 EX-TOTAL PIC Z(6).99 SUM DAT1, DAT2

indicates that EX-TOTAL will be incremented by both the value of DAT1 and DAT2 each time a summation is indicated. If DAT1 and DAT2 are items described in the same report group and on the same line, we refer to this sum as a *crossfooting,* as in this example:

DAT1	DAT2	EX-TOTAL
20	30	50

In contrast to crossfooting, we refer to *rolling forward* as the summation of sum counters at a lower hierarchical level. Thus:

02 DEPT-TOTAL PIC ZZ,ZZZ,ZZ9.99 COLUMN 69
    SUM MONTH-TOTAL

where MONTH-TOTAL was a sum counter specified earlier, represents an example of a *rolling forward* total.

The following rules apply:

1 A SUM clause can appear only in the description of a CONTROL FOOT-ING report group.
2 The UPON phrase provides the capability to accomplish selective subtotaling for the detail report groups named in the phrase.
3 The RESET option inhibits automatic resetting to zero upon the occurrence of a control break. Thus the sum counter can be zeroed only when a control break occurs for data-name-3, or on the occurrence of FINAL. The latter case represents an accumulation for the entire report.

An eighth format is:

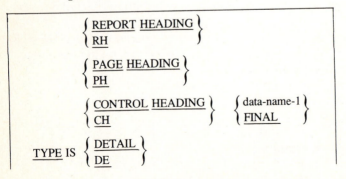

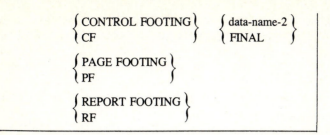

The TYPE clause specifies the particular type of report group that is described by this entry. Each option can be abbreviated in a two-letter reserved COBOL word, as shown. In a complete report format, the following general outline occurs:

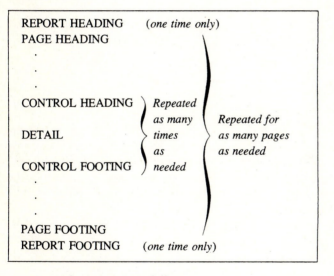

A ninth option is as follows:

The INITIATE statement causes the system to begin processing a report. As part of the initialization procedure, all sum counters are set to zero, and so is PAGE-COUNTER and LINE-COUNTER.

A tenth format is:

$$
\underline{GENERATE} \left\{ \begin{array}{l} \text{data-name} \\ \text{report-name} \end{array} \right\}
$$

The GENERATE statement directs the production of a report in accordance with the report description in the REPORT SECTION of the DATA DIVISION. Data-name is a TYPE DETAIL report group. If report-name is used, no detail report groups are printed; instead, we produce what is called a summary report. The GENERATE statement causes report generation, including handling of control breaks, the start of page procedures, and so forth. A report may contain more than one type of detail report group. In such a case there will be more than one GENERATE statement in the PROCEDURE DIVISION, each referencing the proper detail group.

An eleventh statement is:

> TERMINATE report-name

The TERMINATE statement causes the completion of the report processing. All CONTROL FOOTING and REPORT FOOTING groups are produced.

A twelfth format is as follows:

> USE BEFORE REPORTING identifier

The USE statement specifies PROCEDURE DIVISION statements that are executed just before a report group named in the REPORT SECTION of the DATA DIVISION is produced. The USE statement, when present, must follow immediately a section header in the declaratives section, and must be followed by a period and a space. The identifier is a report group.

EXERCISES

16.1 A card file contains data pertaining to student grades. Each card record consists of:

COLUMNS	CONTENT
1–15	Student name
16–27	Course name
28	Credits
29	Grade (A, B, C, D, or F)

Create a program whereby we can print a report as outlined on the following print chart.

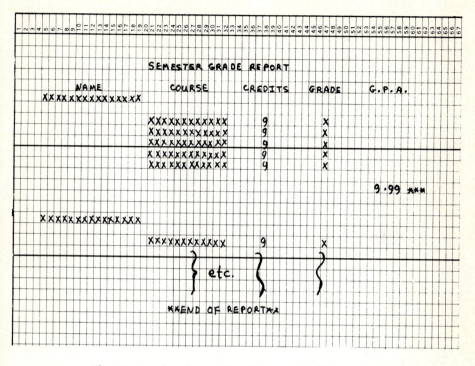

The report heading "SEMESTER GRADE REPORT" will be printed on the first page only.

For page size limits use:

PAGE LIMIT IS 40 LINES
HEADING 3
FIRST DETAIL 5
LAST DETAIL 37.

Each student is enrolled in five courses.

A report footing is printed at the end of the report, as shown.

The grade point average (GPA) is computed by considering A = 4, B = 3, C = 2, D = 1, F = 0 points.

Hint: You may find it useful to use two DECLARATIVES procedures; one to compute the GPA before printing the line containing the GPA, and one to clear the total credits accumulator which you will need to sum up the credits for each student.

16.2 Incorporate the report writer feature into a program that you have already written.

A

ANS COBOL reserved words

ACCEPT	CF	DATE
ACCESS	CH	DATE-COMPILED
ADD	CHARACTER	DATE-WRITTEN
ADVANCING	CHARACTERS	DAY
AFTER	CLOCK-UNITS	DE
ALL	CLOSE	DEBUG-CONTENTS
ALPHABETIC	COBOL	DEBUG-ITEM
ALSO	CODE	DEBUG-LINE
ALTER	CODE-SET	DEBUG-NAME
ALTERNATE	COLLATING	DEBUG-SUB-1
AND	COLUMN	DEBUG-SUB-2
ARE	COMMA	DEBUG-SUB-3
AREA	COMMUNICATION	DEBUGGING
AREAS	COMP	DECIMAL-POINT
ASCENDING	COMPUTATIONAL	DECLARATIVES
ASSIGN	COMPUTE	DELETE
AT	CONFIGURATION	DELIMITED
AUTHOR	CONTAINS	DELIMITER
BEFORE	CONTROL	DEPENDING
BLANK	CONTROLS	DESCENDING
BLOCK	COPY	DESTINATION
BOTTOM	CORR	DETAIL
BY	CORRESPONDING	DISABLE
CALL	COUNT	DISPLAY
CANCEL	CURRENCY	DIVIDE
CD	DATA	DIVISION

DOWN
DUPLICATES
DYNAMIC
EGI
ELSE
EMI
ENABLE
END
END-OF-PAGE
ENTER
ENVIRONMENT
EOP
EQUAL
ERROR ESI
EVERY
EXCEPTION
EXIT
EXTEND
FD
FILE
FILE-CONTROL
FILLER
FINAL
FIRST
FOOTING
FOR
FROM
GENERATE
GIVING
GO
GREATER
GROUP
HEADING
HIGH-VALUE
HIGH-VALUES
I-O
I-O-CONTROL
IDENTIFICATION
IF
IN
INDEX
INDEXED

INDICATE
INITIAL
INITIATE
INPUT
INPUT-OUTPUT
INSPECT
INSTALLATION
INTO
INVALID
IS
JUST
JUSTIFIED
KEY
LABEL
LAST
LEADING
LEFT
LENGTH
LESS
LIMIT
LIMITS
LINAGE
LINAGE-COUNTER
LINE
LINE-COUNTER
LINES
LINKAGE
LOCK
LOW-VALUE
LOW-VALUES
MEMORY
MERGE
MESSAGE
MODE
MODULES
MOVE
MULTIPLE
MULTIPLY
NATIVE
NEGATIVE
NEXT
NO

NOT
NUMBER
NUMERIC
OBJECT-COMPUTER
OCCURS
OF
OFF
OMITTED
ON
OPEN
OPTIONAL
OR
ORGANIZATION
OUTPUT
OVERFLOW
PAGE
PAGE-COUNTER
PERFORM
PF
PH
PIC
PICTURE
PLUS
POINTER
POSITION
POSITIVE
PRINTING
PROCEDURE
PROCEDURES
PROCEED
PROGRAM
PROGRAM-ID
QUEUE
QUOTE
QUOTES
RANDOM
RD
READ
RECEIVE
RECORD
RECORDS
REDEFINES

REEL	SEQUENCE	THROUGH
REFERENCES	SEQUENTIAL	THRU
RELATIVE	SET	TIME
RELEASE	SIGN	TIMES
REMAINDER	SIZE	TO
REMOVAL	SORT	TOP
RENAMES	SORT-MERGE	TRAILING
REPLACING	SOURCE	TYPE
REPORT	SOURCE-COMPUTER	UNIT
REPORTING	SPACE	UNSTRING
REPORTS	SPACES	UNTIL
RERUN	SPECIAL-NAMES	UP
RESERVE	STANDARD	UPON
RESET	STANDARD-1	USAGE
RETURN	START	USE
REVERSED	STATUS	USING
REWIND	STOP	VALUE
REWRITE	STRING	VALUES
RF	SUB-QUEUE-1	VARYING
RH	SUB-QUEUE-2	WHEN
RIGHT	SUB-QUEUE-3	WITH
ROUNDED	SUBTRACT	WORDS
RUN	SUM	WORKING-STORAGE
SAME	SUPPRESS	WRITE
SD	SYMBOLIC	ZERO
SEARCH	SYNC	ZEROES
SECTION	SYNCHRONIZED	ZEROS
SECURITY	TABLE	+
SEGMENT	TALLYING	−
SEGMENT-LIMIT	TAPE	*
SELECT	TERMINAL	/
SEND	TERMINATE	**
SENTENCE	TEXT	>
SEPARATE	THAN	<
		=

B

Complete ANS COBOL language formats

The following set of conventions is followed in the format statements:

1 Words presented in uppercase are always reserved COBOL words.

2 Uppercase words that are underlined are words that are required in the type of program statement being described. Uppercase words that are not underlined are optional and are used only to improve the readability of the program.

3 Lowercase words are used to indicate the points at which data-names or constants are to be supplied by the programmer. In addition to the words "data-name" and "literal," the term "identifier" is used to indicate a data-name, but it has a slightly broader meaning. It refers to either of the following cases: data-names that are unique in themselves, or data-names that are not unique in themselves but are made unique through qualification. Qualification is discussed in Chapter 8. Other lowercase words used to indicate items to be inserted by the programmer are:

file-name
record-name
integer
formula
condition
statement
any imperative statement
any sentence

4   Items enclosed in braces { } indicate that one of the enclosed items must be used.

5   Items enclosed in brackets[ ] indicate that the items are optional, and one of them may be used, at the discretion of the programmer.

6   An ellipsis (. . .) indicates that further information may be included in the program instruction, usually in the form of repeating the immediately preceding element any desired number of times.

GENERAL FORMAT FOR IDENTIFICATION DIVISION

IDENTIFICATION DIVISION.
PROGRAM-ID.   program-name.

[AUTHOR. [comment-entry] . . .]

[INSTALLATION. [comment-entry] . . .]

[DATE-WRITTEN. [comment-entry] . . .]

[DATE-COMPILED. [comment-entry] . . .]

[SECURITY. [comment-entry] . . .]

GENERAL FORMAT FOR ENVIRONMENT DIVISION

ENVIRONMENT DIVISION.

CONFIGURATION SECTION.

SOURCE-COMPUTER.   computer-name   [WITH DEBUGGING MODE].

OBJECT-COMPUTER.   computer-name

$$\left[, \text{MEMORY SIZE integer} \left\{ \begin{array}{l} \text{WORDS} \\ \text{CHARACTERS} \\ \text{MODULES} \end{array} \right\} \right]$$

[, PROGRAM COLLATING SEQUENCE IS alphabet-name]

[, SEGMENT-LIMIT IS segment-number].

[SPECIAL-NAMES.   [, implementor-name

$$\left\{ \begin{array}{l} \text{IS mnemonic name [, } \underline{\text{ON}} \text{ STATUS } \underline{\text{IS}} \text{ condition-name-1} \\ \quad \text{[, } \underline{\text{OFF}} \text{ STATUS } \underline{\text{IS}} \text{ condition-name-2]]} \\ \text{IS mnemonic-name [, } \underline{\text{OFF}} \text{ STATUS } \underline{\text{IS}} \text{ condition-name-2} \\ \quad \text{[, } \underline{\text{ON}} \text{ STATUS } \underline{\text{IS}} \text{ condition-name-1]]} \\ \underline{\text{ON}} \text{ STATUS } \underline{\text{IS}} \text{ condition-name-1 [, } \underline{\text{OFF}} \text{ STATUS } \underline{\text{IS}} \text{ condition-name-2]} \\ \underline{\text{OFF}} \text{ STATUS } \underline{\text{IS}} \text{ condition-name-2 [, } \underline{\text{ON}} \text{ STATUS } \underline{\text{IS}} \text{ condition-name-1]} \end{array} \right\} \right] \quad \ldots$$

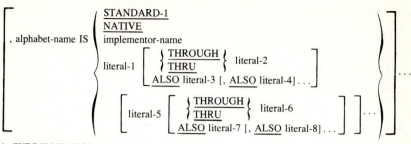

[, CURRENCY SIGN IS literal-9]

[, DECIMAL-POINT IS COMMA].

[INPUT-OUTPUT SECTION.

FILE-CONTROL.

    {file-control-entry} . . .

[I-O-CONTROL.

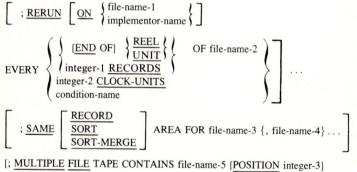

[; MULTIPLE FILE TAPE CONTAINS file-name-5 [POSITION integer-3]

   [, file-name-6 [POSITION integer-4]] . . .] . . .   .]]

GENERAL FORMAT FOR FILE CONTROL ENTRY

FORMAT 1

SELECT [OPTIONAL] file-name

   ASSIGN TO implementor-name-1 [, implementor-name-2] . . .

   $\begin{bmatrix} ; \underline{RESERVE} \text{ integer-1} \begin{bmatrix} AREA \\ AREAS \end{bmatrix} \end{bmatrix}$

  [; ORGANIZATION IS SEQUENTIAL]

[; <u>ACCESS</u> MODE IS <u>SEQUENTIAL</u>]

[; FILE <u>STATUS</u> IS data-name-1]

FORMAT 2

<u>SELECT</u> file-name

   <u>ASSIGN</u> TO implementor-name-1 [, implementor-name-2] . . .

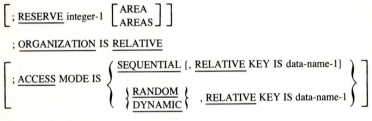

   ; <u>ORGANIZATION</u> IS <u>RELATIVE</u>

   [; FILE <u>STATUS</u> IS data-name-2]

FORMAT 3

<u>SELECT</u> file-name

   <u>ASSIGN</u> TO implementor-name-1 [, implementor-name-2] . . .

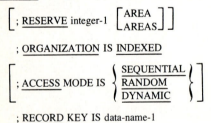

   ; <u>ORGANIZATION</u> IS <u>INDEXED</u>

   ; <u>RECORD</u> KEY IS data-name-1

   [; ALTERNATE <u>RECORD</u> KEY IS data-name-2 [WITH <u>DUPLICATES</u>]] . . .

   [; FILE <u>STATUS</u> IS data-name-3].

FORMAT 4

<u>SELECT</u> file-name <u>ASSIGN</u> TO implementor-name-1 [, implementor-name-2] . . .

GENERAL FORMAT FOR DATA DIVISION

DATA DIVISION.

[FILE SECTION.

[FD   file-name

$$\left[\; ; \text{BLOCK CONTAINS} \quad [\text{integer-1 TO}] \quad \text{integer-2} \left\{ \begin{array}{l} \text{RECORDS} \\ \text{CHARACTERS} \end{array} \right\} \right]$$

[; RECORD CONTAINS   [integer-3 TO]   integer-4 CHARACTERS]

$$\; ; \text{LABEL} \left\{ \begin{array}{l} \text{RECORD IS} \\ \text{RECORDS ARE} \end{array} \right\} \left\{ \begin{array}{l} \text{STANDARD} \\ \text{OMITTED} \end{array} \right\}$$

$$\left[\; ; \text{VALUE OF implementor-name-1 IS} \left\{ \begin{array}{l} \text{data-name-1} \\ \text{literal-1} \end{array} \right\} \right.$$

$$\left. \left[, \text{implementor-name-2 IS} \left\{ \begin{array}{l} \text{data-name-2} \\ \text{literal-2} \end{array} \right\} \right] \quad \dots \right]$$

$$\left[\; ; \underline{\text{DATA}} \left\{ \begin{array}{l} \text{RECORD IS} \\ \text{RECORDS ARE} \end{array} \right\} \text{data-name-3} \quad [, \text{data-name-4}] \dots \right]$$

$$\left[\; ; \underline{\text{LINAGE}} \text{ IS} \left\{ \begin{array}{l} \text{data-name-5} \\ \text{integer-5} \end{array} \right\} \text{LINES} \left[, \text{WITH} \underline{\text{FOOTING}} \text{ AT} \left\{ \begin{array}{l} \text{data-name-6} \\ \text{integer-6} \end{array} \right\} \right] \right.$$

$$\left. \left[, \text{LINES AT} \underline{\text{TOP}} \left\{ \begin{array}{l} \text{data-name-7} \\ \text{integer-7} \end{array} \right\} \right] \left[, \text{LINES AT} \underline{\text{BOTTOM}} \left\{ \begin{array}{l} \text{data-name-8} \\ \text{integer-8} \end{array} \right\} \right] \right]$$

[; CODE-SET IS alphabet-name]

$$\left[; \left\{ \begin{array}{l} \text{REPORT IS} \\ \text{REPORTS ARE} \end{array} \right\} \text{report-name-1} \quad [, \text{report-name-2}] \dots \right] .$$

[record-description-entry] . . .] . . .

[SD   file-name

[; RECORD CONTAINS [integer-1 TO] integer-2 CHARACTERS]

$$\left[\; ; \underline{\text{DATA}} \left\{ \begin{array}{l} \text{RECORD IS} \\ \text{RECORDS ARE} \end{array} \right\} \text{data-name-1} \quad [, \text{data-name-2}] \dots \right]$$

{record-description-entry} . . .] . . .

[WORKING-STORAGE SECTION.

$$\left[\begin{array}{l} \text{77-level-description-entry} \\ \text{record-description-entry} \end{array} \right] \quad \dots \right]$$

[LINKAGE SECTION.

$$\left[\begin{array}{l} \text{77-level-description-entry} \\ \text{record-description-entry} \end{array} \right] \quad \dots \right]$$

[COMMUNICATION SECTION.

[communication-description-entry

[record-description-entry] . . .] . . .]

[REPORT SECTION.

[RD report-name

[; CODE literal-1]

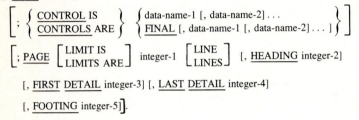

$$\left[\; ; \begin{Bmatrix} \underline{CONTROL} \; IS \\ \underline{CONTROLS} \; ARE \end{Bmatrix} \begin{Bmatrix} data\text{-}name\text{-}1 \; [, data\text{-}name\text{-}2] \ldots \\ \underline{FINAL} \; [, data\text{-}name\text{-}1 \; [, data\text{-}name\text{-}2] \ldots] \end{Bmatrix} \right]$$

$$\left[\; ; \underline{PAGE} \begin{bmatrix} \underline{LIMIT} \; IS \\ \underline{LIMITS} \; ARE \end{bmatrix} integer\text{-}1 \begin{bmatrix} \underline{LINE} \\ \underline{LINES} \end{bmatrix} [, \underline{HEADING} \; integer\text{-}2] \right.$$

[, FIRST DETAIL integer-3] [, LAST DETAIL integer-4]

[, FOOTING integer-5]].

{report-group-description-entry} . . .] . . .]

GENERAL FORMAT FOR DATA DESCRIPTION ENTRY

FORMAT 1

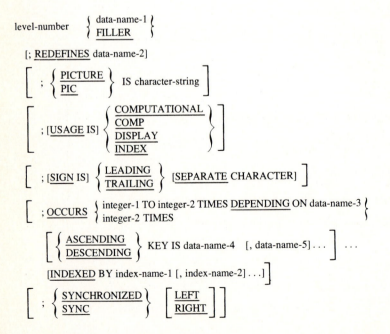

level-number $\begin{Bmatrix} data\text{-}name\text{-}1 \\ \underline{FILLER} \end{Bmatrix}$

[; REDEFINES data-name-2]

$$\left[\; ; \begin{Bmatrix} \underline{PICTURE} \\ \underline{PIC} \end{Bmatrix} IS \; character\text{-}string \right]$$

$$\left[\; ; [\underline{USAGE} \; IS] \begin{Bmatrix} \underline{COMPUTATIONAL} \\ \underline{COMP} \\ \underline{DISPLAY} \\ \underline{INDEX} \end{Bmatrix} \right]$$

$$\left[\; ; [\underline{SIGN} \; IS] \begin{Bmatrix} \underline{LEADING} \\ \underline{TRAILING} \end{Bmatrix} [\underline{SEPARATE} \; CHARACTER] \right]$$

$$\left[\; ; \underline{OCCURS} \begin{Bmatrix} integer\text{-}1 \; TO \; integer\text{-}2 \; TIMES \; \underline{DEPENDING} \; ON \; data\text{-}name\text{-}3 \\ integer\text{-}2 \; TIMES \end{Bmatrix} \right.$$

$$\left[\begin{Bmatrix} \underline{ASCENDING} \\ \underline{DESCENDING} \end{Bmatrix} KEY \; IS \; data\text{-}name\text{-}4 \; [, data\text{-}name\text{-}5] \ldots \right] \ldots$$

[INDEXED BY index-name-1 [, index-name-2] . . .]]

$$\left[\; ; \begin{Bmatrix} \underline{SYNCHRONIZED} \\ \underline{SYNC} \end{Bmatrix} \begin{bmatrix} \underline{LEFT} \\ \underline{RIGHT} \end{bmatrix} \right]$$

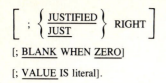

$$\left[\quad ; \left\{ \begin{array}{c} \underline{JUSTIFIED} \\ \underline{JUST} \end{array} \right\} RIGHT \right]$$

[; <u>BLANK</u> WHEN <u>ZERO</u>]

[; <u>VALUE</u> IS literal].

FORMAT 2

66   data-name-1; <u>RENAMES</u> data-name-2 $\left[\left\{ \begin{array}{c} \underline{THROUGH} \\ \underline{THRU} \end{array} \right\} \text{data-name-3} \right]$.

FORMAT 3

88   condition-name; $\left\{ \begin{array}{c} \underline{VALUE} \text{ IS} \\ \underline{VALUES} \text{ ARE} \end{array} \right\}$ literal-1 $\left[\left\{ \begin{array}{c} \underline{THROUGH} \\ \underline{THRU} \end{array} \right\} \text{literal-2} \right]$

$\left[\text{, literal-3} \left[\left\{ \begin{array}{c} \underline{THROUGH} \\ \underline{THRU} \end{array} \right\} \text{literal-4} \right] \right]$ ... .

GENERAL FORMAT FOR COMMUNICATION DESCRIPTION ENTRY

FORMAT 1

<u>CD</u>   cd-name;

FOR [INITIAL] INPUT

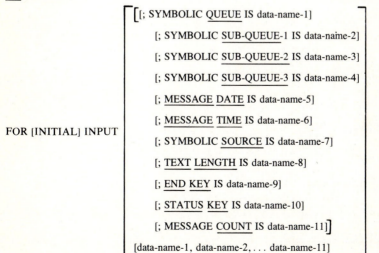

[; SYMBOLIC <u>QUEUE</u> IS data-name-1]

[; SYMBOLIC <u>SUB-QUEUE</u>-1 IS data-name-2]

[; SYMBOLIC <u>SUB-QUEUE</u>-2 IS data-name-3]

[; SYMBOLIC <u>SUB-QUEUE</u>-3 IS data-name-4]

[; <u>MESSAGE</u> DATE IS data-name-5]

[; <u>MESSAGE</u> TIME IS data-name-6]

[; SYMBOLIC <u>SOURCE</u> IS data-name-7]

[; <u>TEXT</u> <u>LENGTH</u> IS data-name-8]

[; <u>END</u> KEY IS data-name-9]

[; <u>STATUS</u> <u>KEY</u> IS data-name-10]

[; MESSAGE <u>COUNT</u> IS data-name-11]

[data-name-1, data-name-2, ... data-name-11]

FORMAT 2

<u>CD</u>   cd-name; FOR <u>OUTPUT</u>

[; <u>DESTINATION COUNT</u> IS data-name-1]

[; <u>TEXT LENGTH</u> IS data-name-2]

[; <u>STATUS KEY</u> IS data-name-3]

[; <u>DESTINATION TABLE OCCURS</u> integer-2 TIMES

$\left[\text{: } \underline{\text{INDEXED}} \text{ BY index-name-1 [, index-name-2]} \dots \right]\Big]$

[; <u>ERROR KEY</u> IS data-name-4]

[; SYMBOLIC <u>DESTINATION</u> IS data-name-5].

GENERAL FORMAT FOR REPORT GROUP DESCRIPTION ENTRY

FORMAT 1

01   [data-name-1]

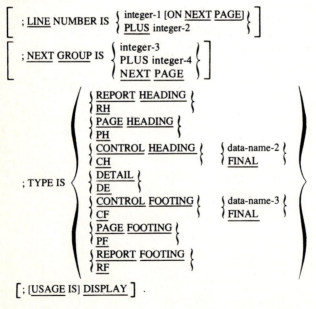

FORMAT 2

level-number [data-name-1]

$$\left[\; ;\; \underline{\text{LINE}} \text{ NUMBER IS } \left\{ \begin{array}{l} \text{integer-1 [ON } \underline{\text{NEXT PAGE}}\text{]} \\ \underline{\text{PLUS}} \text{ integer-2} \end{array} \right\} \right]$$

$$\left[\; ;\; [\underline{\text{USAGE}} \text{ IS}] \; \underline{\text{DISPLAY}} \; \right] \; .$$

FORMAT 3

level-number   [data-name-1]

[; <u>BLANK</u> WHEN <u>ZERO</u>]

[; <u>GROUP</u> INDICATE]

$$\left[\; ;\; \left\{ \begin{array}{l} \underline{\text{JUSTIFIED}} \\ \underline{\text{JUST}} \end{array} \right\} \; \text{RIGHT} \right]$$

$$\left[\; ;\; \underline{\text{LINE}} \text{ NUMBER IS } \left\{ \begin{array}{l} \text{integer-1 [ON } \underline{\text{NEXT PAGE}}\text{]} \\ \underline{\text{PLUS}} \text{ integer-2} \end{array} \right\} \right]$$

[; <u>COLUMN</u> NUMBER IS integer-3]

$$;\; \left\{ \begin{array}{l} \underline{\text{PICTURE}} \\ \underline{\text{PIC}} \end{array} \right\} \; \text{IS character-string}$$

$$\left\{ \begin{array}{l} ;\; \underline{\text{SOURCE}} \text{ IS identifier-1} \\ ;\; \underline{\text{VALUE}} \text{ IS literal} \\ \{\; ;\; \underline{\text{SUM}} \text{ identifier-2 [, identifier-3]} \dots \\ \quad [\underline{\text{UPON}} \text{ data-name-2 [, data-name-3]} \dots]\} \dots \\ \quad \left[\underline{\text{RESET}} \text{ ON } \left\{ \begin{array}{l} \text{data-name-4} \\ \underline{\text{FINAL}} \end{array} \right\} \right] \end{array} \right\}$$

[; [<u>USAGE</u> IS] <u>DISPLAY</u>].

GENERAL FORMAT FOR PROCEDURE DIVISION

FORMAT 1

<u>PROCEDURE</u> <u>DIVISION</u> [<u>USING</u> data-name-1 [, **data-name-2**] ...].

[<u>DECLARATIVES</u>.

{section-name <u>SECTION</u> [segment-number].   declarative-sentence

[paragraph-name.   [sentence] . . .] . . . } . . .

<u>END</u> <u>DECLARATIVES</u>.]

{section-name <u>SECTION</u> [segment-number].

[paragraph-name.   [sentence] . . .] . . . } . . .

FORMAT 2

<u>PROCEDURE</u> <u>DIVISION</u> [<u>USING</u> data-name-1 [, data-name-2] . . .].

{paragraph-name.   [sentence] . . . } . . .

GENERAL FORMAT FOR VERBS

<u>ACCEPT</u> identifier [<u>FROM</u> mnemonic-name]

$$\underline{\text{ACCEPT}} \text{ identifier } \underline{\text{FROM}} \left\{ \begin{array}{l} \underline{\text{DATE}} \\ \underline{\text{DAY}} \\ \underline{\text{TIME}} \end{array} \right\}$$

<u>ACCEPT</u> cd-name MESSAGE <u>COUNT</u>

$$\underline{\text{ADD}} \left\{ \begin{array}{l} \text{identifier-1} \\ \text{literal-1} \end{array} \right\} \quad \left[\begin{array}{l} , \text{ identifier-2} \\ , \text{ literal-2} \end{array} \right] \quad \ldots \underline{\text{TO}} \text{ identifier-m } [\underline{\text{ROUNDED}}]$$

[, identifier-n [<u>ROUNDED</u>]]   . . . [; ON <u>SIZE</u> <u>ERROR</u> imperative-statement]

$$\underline{\text{ADD}} \left\{ \begin{array}{l} \text{identifier-1} \\ \text{literal-1} \end{array} \right\} , \left\{ \begin{array}{l} \text{identifier-2} \\ \text{literal-2} \end{array} \right\} \left[\begin{array}{l} , \text{ identifier-3} \\ , \text{ literal-3} \end{array} \right] \ldots$$

<u>GIVING</u> identifier-m [<u>ROUNDED</u>] [, identifier-n [<u>ROUNDED</u>]] . . .

[; ON <u>SIZE</u> <u>ERROR</u> imperative-statement]

$$\underline{\text{ADD}} \left\{ \begin{array}{l} \underline{\text{CORRESPONDING}} \\ \underline{\text{CORR}} \end{array} \right\} \text{ identifier-1 } \underline{\text{TO}} \text{ identifier-2 } [\underline{\text{ROUNDED}}]$$

[; ON <u>SIZE</u> <u>ERROR</u> imperative-statement]

<u>ALTER</u> procedure-name-1 <u>TO</u> [<u>PROCEED</u> <u>TO</u>] procedure-name-2

[, procedure-name-3 <u>TO</u> [<u>PROCEED</u> <u>TO</u>] procedure-name-4] . . .

$$\underline{\text{CALL}} \left\{ \begin{array}{l} \text{identifier-1} \\ \text{literal-1} \end{array} \right\} [\underline{\text{USING}} \text{ data-name-1 } [, \text{ data-name-2}] \ldots]$$

[; ON <u>OVERFLOW</u> imperative-statement]

<u>CANCEL</u> $\begin{Bmatrix} \text{identifier-1} \\ \text{literal-1} \end{Bmatrix}$ $\begin{bmatrix} \text{, identifier-2} \\ \text{, literal-2} \end{bmatrix}$ . . .

<u>CLOSE</u> file-name-1 $\begin{bmatrix} \begin{bmatrix} \begin{Bmatrix} \underline{\text{REEL}} \\ \underline{\text{UNIT}} \end{Bmatrix} & \begin{bmatrix} \text{WITH } \underline{\text{NO}} \text{ REWIND} \\ \text{FOR } \underline{\text{REMOVAL}} \end{bmatrix} \end{bmatrix} \\ \text{WITH } \begin{Bmatrix} \underline{\text{NO}} \text{ REWIND} \\ \underline{\text{LOCK}} \end{Bmatrix} \end{bmatrix}$

$\begin{bmatrix} \text{, file-name-2} \begin{bmatrix} \begin{bmatrix} \begin{Bmatrix} \underline{\text{REEL}} \\ \underline{\text{UNIT}} \end{Bmatrix} & \begin{bmatrix} \text{WITH } \underline{\text{NO}} \text{ REWIND} \\ \text{FOR } \underline{\text{REMOVAL}} \end{bmatrix} \end{bmatrix} \\ \text{WITH } \begin{Bmatrix} \underline{\text{NO}} \text{ REWIND} \\ \underline{\text{LOCK}} \end{Bmatrix} \end{bmatrix} \end{bmatrix}$ . . .

<u>CLOSE</u> file-name-1 [WITH <u>LOCK</u>] $\big[$, file-name-2 [WITH <u>LOCK</u>]$\big]$ . . .

<u>COMPUTE</u> identifier-1 [<u>ROUNDED</u>] [, identifier-2 [<u>ROUNDED</u>]] . . .

= arithmetic-expression [; ON <u>SIZE</u> <u>ERROR</u> imperative-statement]

<u>DELETE</u> file-name RECORD [; <u>INVALID</u> KEY imperative-statement]

<u>DISABLE</u> $\begin{Bmatrix} \underline{\text{INPUT}} \text{ [TERMINAL]} \\ \underline{\text{OUTPUT}} \end{Bmatrix}$ cd-name WITH <u>KEY</u> $\begin{Bmatrix} \text{identifier-1} \\ \text{literal-1} \end{Bmatrix}$

<u>DISPLAY</u> $\begin{Bmatrix} \text{identifier-1} \\ \text{literal-1} \end{Bmatrix}$ $\begin{Bmatrix} \text{, identifier-2} \\ \text{, literal-2} \end{Bmatrix}$ . . . [<u>UPON</u> mnemonic-name]

<u>DIVIDE</u> $\begin{Bmatrix} \text{identifier-1} \\ \text{literal-1} \end{Bmatrix}$ <u>INTO</u> identifier-2 [<u>ROUNDED</u>]

[, identifier-3 [<u>ROUNDED</u>]] . . . [; ON <u>SIZE</u> <u>ERROR</u> imperative-statement]

<u>DIVIDE</u> $\begin{Bmatrix} \text{identifier-1} \\ \text{literal-1} \end{Bmatrix}$ <u>INTO</u> $\begin{Bmatrix} \text{identifier-2} \\ \text{literal-2} \end{Bmatrix}$ <u>GIVING</u> identifier-3 [<u>ROUNDED</u>]

[, identifier-4 [<u>ROUNDED</u>]] . . . [; ON <u>SIZE</u> <u>ERROR</u> imperative-statement]

<u>DIVIDE</u> $\begin{Bmatrix} \text{identifier-1} \\ \text{literal-1} \end{Bmatrix}$ <u>BY</u> $\begin{Bmatrix} \text{identifier-2} \\ \text{literal-2} \end{Bmatrix}$ <u>GIVING</u> identifier-3 [<u>ROUNDED</u>]

[, identifier-4 [<u>ROUNDED</u>]] . . . [; ON <u>SIZE</u> <u>ERROR</u> imperative-statement]

<u>DIVIDE</u> $\begin{Bmatrix} \text{identifier-1} \\ \text{literal-1} \end{Bmatrix}$ <u>INTO</u> $\begin{Bmatrix} \text{identifier-2} \\ \text{literal-2} \end{Bmatrix}$ <u>GIVING</u> identifier-3 [<u>ROUNDED</u>]

<u>REMAINDER</u> identifier-4 [; ON <u>SIZE</u> <u>ERROR</u> imperative-statement]

$\underline{\text{DIVIDE}} \left\{ \begin{array}{l} \text{identifier-1} \\ \text{literal-1} \end{array} \right\} \underline{\text{BY}} \left\{ \begin{array}{l} \text{identifier-2} \\ \text{literal-2} \end{array} \right\} \underline{\text{GIVING}} \text{ identifier-3 } [\underline{\text{ROUNDED}}]$

$\underline{\text{REMAINDER}} \text{ identifier-4 [; ON } \underline{\text{SIZE}} \underline{\text{ERROR}} \text{ imperative-statement]}$

$\underline{\text{ENABLE}} \left\{ \begin{array}{l} \underline{\text{INPUT}} [\underline{\text{TERMINAL}}] \\ \underline{\text{OUTPUT}} \end{array} \right\} \text{ cd-name WITH } \underline{\text{KEY}} \left\{ \begin{array}{l} \text{identifier-1} \\ \text{literal-1} \end{array} \right\}$

$\underline{\text{ENTER}} \text{ language-name [routine-name].}$

$\underline{\text{EXIT}} [\underline{\text{PROGRAM}}].$

$\underline{\text{GENERATE}} \left\{ \begin{array}{l} \text{data-name} \\ \text{report-name} \end{array} \right\}$

$\underline{\text{GO}} \text{ TO [procedure-name-1]}$

$\underline{\text{GO}} \text{ TO procedure-name-1 [, procedure-name-2] } \ldots \text{ , procedure name-n}$

$\quad \underline{\text{DEPENDING}} \text{ ON identifier}$

$\underline{\text{IF}} \text{ condition; } \left\{ \begin{array}{l} \text{statement-1} \\ \underline{\text{NEXT}} \underline{\text{SENTENCE}} \end{array} \right\} \left\{ \begin{array}{l} \text{; } \underline{\text{ELSE}} \text{ statement-2} \\ \text{; } \underline{\text{ELSE}} \underline{\text{NEXT}} \underline{\text{SENTENCE}} \end{array} \right\}$

$\underline{\text{INITIATE}} \text{ report-name-1 [, report-name-2] } \ldots$

$\underline{\text{INSPECT}} \text{ identifier-1 } \underline{\text{TALLYING}}$

$\left\{ \text{, identifier-2 } \underline{\text{FOR}} \right\} , \left\{ \begin{array}{l} \underline{\text{ALL}} \\ \underline{\text{LEADING}} \\ \underline{\text{CHARACTERS}} \end{array} \right\} \left\{ \begin{array}{l} \text{identifier-3} \\ \text{literal-1} \end{array} \right\}$

$\left[\left\{ \begin{array}{l} \underline{\text{BEFORE}} \\ \underline{\text{AFTER}} \end{array} \right\} \text{ INITIAL } \left\{ \begin{array}{l} \text{identifier-4} \\ \text{literal-2} \end{array} \right\} \right] \ldots \right\} \ldots \right\}$

$\underline{\text{INSPECT}} \text{ identifier-1 } \underline{\text{REPLACING}}$

$\left\{ \underline{\text{CHARACTERS}} \underline{\text{BY}} \left\{ \begin{array}{l} \text{identifier-6} \\ \text{literal-4} \end{array} \right\} \left[\left\{ \begin{array}{l} \underline{\text{BEFORE}} \\ \underline{\text{AFTER}} \end{array} \right\} \text{ INITIAL } \left\{ \begin{array}{l} \text{identifier-7} \\ \text{literal-5} \end{array} \right\} \right] \right.$

$\left\{ , \left\{ \begin{array}{l} \underline{\text{ALL}} \\ \underline{\text{LEADING}} \\ \underline{\text{FIRST}} \end{array} \right\} \right\} , \left\{ \begin{array}{l} \text{identifier-5} \\ \text{literal-3} \end{array} \right\} \underline{\text{BY}} \left\{ \begin{array}{l} \text{identifier-6} \\ \text{literal-4} \end{array} \right\}$

$\left[\left\{ \begin{array}{l} \underline{\text{BEFORE}} \\ \underline{\text{AFTER}} \end{array} \right\} \text{ INITIAL } \left\{ \begin{array}{l} \text{identifier-7} \\ \text{literal-5} \end{array} \right\} \right] \right\} \ldots \right\} \ldots \right\}$

$\underline{\text{INSPECT}} \text{ identifier-1 } \underline{\text{TALLYING}}$

$\left\{ \text{, identifier-2 } \underline{\text{FOR}} \right\} , \left\{ \begin{array}{l} \underline{\text{ALL}} \\ \underline{\text{LEADING}} \\ \underline{\text{CHARACTERS}} \end{array} \right\} \left\{ \begin{array}{l} \text{identifier-3} \\ \text{literal-1} \end{array} \right\}$

$$\left[\left\{ \begin{array}{c} \underline{BEFORE} \\ \underline{AFTER} \end{array} \right\} \text{INITIAL} \left\{ \begin{array}{c} \text{identifier-4} \\ \text{literal-2} \end{array} \right\} \right] \cdots \left\{ \cdots \right.$$

<u>REPLACING</u>

$$\left\{ \underline{CHARACTERS} \; \underline{BY} \left\{ \begin{array}{c} \text{identifier-6} \\ \text{literal-4} \end{array} \right\} \quad \left\{ \begin{array}{c} \underline{BEFORE} \\ \underline{AFTER} \end{array} \right\} \text{INITIAL} \left\{ \begin{array}{c} \text{identifier-7} \\ \text{literal-5} \end{array} \right\} \right]$$

$$\left\{ \; , \left\{ \begin{array}{c} \underline{ALL} \\ \underline{LEADING} \\ \underline{FIRST} \end{array} \right\} \; \right\} \; , \left\{ \begin{array}{c} \text{identifier-5} \\ \text{literal-3} \end{array} \right\} \; \underline{BY} \left\{ \begin{array}{c} \text{identifier-6} \\ \text{literal-4} \end{array} \right\}$$

$$\left[\left\{ \begin{array}{c} \underline{BEFORE} \\ \underline{AFTER} \end{array} \right\} \text{INITIAL} \left\{ \begin{array}{c} \text{identifier-7} \\ \text{literal-5} \end{array} \right\} \right] \right\} \cdots \left\{ \cdots \right.$$

<u>MERGE</u> file-name-1   ON $\left\{ \begin{array}{c} \underline{ASCENDING} \\ \underline{DESCENDING} \end{array} \right\}$ KEY data-name-1 [, data-name-2] . . .

$$\left[\text{ON} \left\{ \begin{array}{c} \underline{ASCENDING} \\ \underline{DESCENDING} \end{array} \right\} \text{KEY data-name-3 [, data-name-4] } \ldots \right] \ldots$$

[COLLATING <u>SEQUENCE</u> IS alphabet-name]

<u>USING</u> file-name-2, file-name-3 [, file-name-4] . . .

$$\left\{ \begin{array}{l} \underline{OUTPUT} \; \underline{PROCEDURE} \; \text{IS section-name-1} \left[\left\{ \begin{array}{c} \underline{THROUGH} \\ \underline{THRU} \end{array} \right\} \text{section-name-2} \right] \\ \underline{GIVING} \text{ file-name-5} \end{array} \right\}$$

<u>MOVE</u> $\left\{ \begin{array}{c} \text{identifier-1} \\ \text{literal} \end{array} \right\}$ <u>TO</u> identifier-2 [, identifier-3] . . .

<u>MOVE</u> $\left\{ \begin{array}{c} \underline{CORRESPONDING} \\ \underline{CORR} \end{array} \right\}$ identifier-1 <u>TO</u> identifier-2

<u>MULTIPLY</u> $\left\{ \begin{array}{c} \text{identifier-1} \\ \text{literal-1} \end{array} \right\}$ <u>BY</u> identifier-2 [<u>ROUNDED</u>]

$$\left[, \text{identifier-3 } [\underline{ROUNDED}] \right] \ldots [; \text{ON} \; \underline{SIZE} \; \underline{ERROR} \; \text{imperative-statement}]$$

<u>MULTIPLY</u> $\left\{ \begin{array}{c} \text{identifier-1} \\ \text{literal-1} \end{array} \right\}$ <u>BY</u> $\left\{ \begin{array}{c} \text{identifier-2} \\ \text{literal-2} \end{array} \right\}$ <u>GIVING</u> identifier-3 [<u>ROUNDED</u>]

$$\left[, \text{identifier-4 } [\underline{ROUNDED}] \right] \ldots [; \text{ON} \; \underline{SIZE} \; \underline{ERROR} \; \text{imperative-statement}]$$

<u>OPEN</u> $\left\{ \; \underline{INPUT} \text{ file-name-1} \left[\begin{array}{c} \underline{REVERSED} \\ \underline{WITH} \; \underline{NO} \; \underline{REWIND} \end{array} \right] \right.$

$$\left. \left[\; , \text{file-name-2} \left[\begin{array}{c} \underline{REVERSED} \\ \underline{WITH} \; \underline{NO} \; \underline{REWIND} \end{array} \right] \right] \; \ldots \right.$$

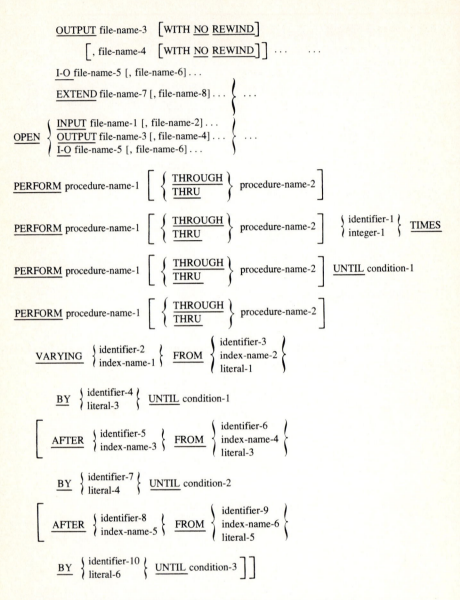

$$\text{OPEN} \left\{ \begin{array}{l} \underline{\text{OUTPUT}} \text{ file-name-3 } \left[\text{WITH } \underline{\text{NO}} \text{ REWIND} \right] \\ \qquad \left[\text{, file-name-4 } \left[\text{WITH } \underline{\text{NO}} \text{ REWIND} \right] \right] \ldots \qquad \ldots \\ \underline{\text{I-O}} \text{ file-name-5 } [\text{, file-name-6}] \ldots \\ \underline{\text{EXTEND}} \text{ file-name-7 } [\text{, file-name-8}] \ldots \end{array} \right\} \ldots$$

$$\underline{\text{OPEN}} \left\{ \begin{array}{l} \underline{\text{INPUT}} \text{ file-name-1 } [\text{, file-name-2}] \ldots \\ \underline{\text{OUTPUT}} \text{ file-name-3 } [\text{, file-name-4}] \ldots \\ \underline{\text{I-O}} \text{ file-name-5 } [\text{, file-name-6}] \ldots \end{array} \right\} \ldots$$

$$\underline{\text{PERFORM}} \text{ procedure-name-1 } \left[\left\{ \begin{array}{l} \underline{\text{THROUGH}} \\ \underline{\text{THRU}} \end{array} \right\} \text{ procedure-name-2} \right]$$

$$\underline{\text{PERFORM}} \text{ procedure-name-1 } \left[\left\{ \begin{array}{l} \underline{\text{THROUGH}} \\ \underline{\text{THRU}} \end{array} \right\} \text{ procedure-name-2} \right] \left\{ \begin{array}{l} \text{identifier-1} \\ \text{integer-1} \end{array} \right\} \underline{\text{TIMES}}$$

$$\underline{\text{PERFORM}} \text{ procedure-name-1 } \left[\left\{ \begin{array}{l} \underline{\text{THROUGH}} \\ \underline{\text{THRU}} \end{array} \right\} \text{ procedure-name-2} \right] \underline{\text{UNTIL}} \text{ condition-1}$$

$$\underline{\text{PERFORM}} \text{ procedure-name-1 } \left[\left\{ \begin{array}{l} \underline{\text{THROUGH}} \\ \underline{\text{THRU}} \end{array} \right\} \text{ procedure-name-2} \right]$$

$$\underline{\text{VARYING}} \left\{ \begin{array}{l} \text{identifier-2} \\ \text{index-name-1} \end{array} \right\} \underline{\text{FROM}} \left\{ \begin{array}{l} \text{identifier-3} \\ \text{index-name-2} \\ \text{literal-1} \end{array} \right\}$$

$$\underline{\text{BY}} \left\{ \begin{array}{l} \text{identifier-4} \\ \text{literal-3} \end{array} \right\} \underline{\text{UNTIL}} \text{ condition-1}$$

$$\left[\underline{\text{AFTER}} \left\{ \begin{array}{l} \text{identifier-5} \\ \text{index-name-3} \end{array} \right\} \underline{\text{FROM}} \left\{ \begin{array}{l} \text{identifier-6} \\ \text{index-name-4} \\ \text{literal-3} \end{array} \right\} \right.$$

$$\underline{\text{BY}} \left\{ \begin{array}{l} \text{identifier-7} \\ \text{literal-4} \end{array} \right\} \underline{\text{UNTIL}} \text{ condition-2}$$

$$\left[\underline{\text{AFTER}} \left\{ \begin{array}{l} \text{identifier-8} \\ \text{index-name-5} \end{array} \right\} \underline{\text{FROM}} \left\{ \begin{array}{l} \text{identifier-9} \\ \text{index-name-6} \\ \text{literal-5} \end{array} \right\} \right.$$

$$\left. \left. \underline{\text{BY}} \left\{ \begin{array}{l} \text{identifier-10} \\ \text{literal-6} \end{array} \right\} \underline{\text{UNTIL}} \text{ condition-3} \right] \right]$$

$\underline{\text{READ}}$ file-name RECORD [$\underline{\text{INTO}}$ identifier] [; AT $\underline{\text{END}}$ imperative-statement]

$\underline{\text{READ}}$ file-name [$\underline{\text{NEXT}}$] RECORD [$\underline{\text{INTO}}$ identifier]

[; AT $\underline{\text{END}}$ imperative-statement]

$\underline{\text{READ}}$ file-name RECORD [$\underline{\text{INTO}}$ identifier] [; $\underline{\text{INVALID}}$ KEY imperative-statement]

<u>READ</u> file-name RECORD [<u>INTO</u> identifier]

    [; <u>KEY</u> IS data-name]

    [; <u>INVALID</u> KEY imperative statement]

<u>RECEIVE</u> cd-name $\left\{ \begin{array}{c} \underline{\text{MESSAGE}} \\ \underline{\text{SEGMENT}} \end{array} \right\}$ <u>INTO</u> identifier-1 [; <u>NO DATA</u> imperative-statement]

<u>RELEASE</u> record-name [<u>FROM</u> identifier]

<u>RETURN</u> file-name RECORD [<u>INTO</u> identifier] ; AT <u>END</u> imperative-statement

<u>REWRITE</u> record-name [<u>FROM</u> identifier]

<u>REWRITE</u> record-name [<u>FROM</u> identifier] [; <u>INVALID</u> KEY imperative-statement]

<u>SEARCH</u> identifier-1 $\left[\underline{\text{VARYING}} \left\{ \begin{array}{c} \text{identifier-2} \\ \text{index-name-1} \end{array} \right\} \right]$ [; AT <u>END</u> imperative-statement-1]

    ; <u>WHEN</u> condition-1 $\left\{ \begin{array}{c} \text{imperative-statement-2} \\ \underline{\text{NEXT}}\ \underline{\text{SENTENCE}} \end{array} \right\}$

    $\left[;\ \underline{\text{WHEN}}\ \text{condition-2} \left\{ \begin{array}{c} \text{imperative-statement-3} \\ \underline{\text{NEXT}}\ \underline{\text{SENTENCE}} \end{array} \right\} \right]$ ...

<u>SEARCH</u> ALL identifier-1 [; AT <u>END</u> imperative-statement-1]

    ; <u>WHEN</u> $\left\{ \begin{array}{c} \text{data-name-1} \left\{ \begin{array}{c} \text{IS } \underline{\text{EQUAL}} \text{ TO} \\ \text{IS } \underline{=} \end{array} \right\} \left\{ \begin{array}{c} \text{identifier-3} \\ \text{literal-1} \\ \text{arithmetic-expression-1} \end{array} \right\} \\ \text{condition-name-1} \end{array} \right\}$

    $\left[\underline{\text{AND}} \left\{ \begin{array}{c} \text{data-name-2} \left\{ \begin{array}{c} \text{IS } \underline{\text{EQUAL}} \text{ TO} \\ \text{IS } = \end{array} \right\} \left\{ \begin{array}{c} \text{identifier-4} \\ \text{literal-2} \\ \text{arithmetic-expression-2} \end{array} \right\} \\ \text{condition-name-2} \end{array} \right\} \right]$ ...

    $\left\{ \begin{array}{c} \text{imperative-statement-2} \\ \underline{\text{NEXT}}\ \underline{\text{SENTENCE}} \end{array} \right\}$

<u>SEND</u> cd-name <u>FROM</u> identifier-1

<u>SEND</u> cd-name [<u>FROM</u> identifier-1] $\left\{ \begin{array}{c} \text{WITH identifier-2} \\ \text{WITH ESI} \\ \text{WITH } \underline{\text{EMI}} \\ \text{WITH } \underline{\text{EGI}} \end{array} \right\}$

    $\left[\left\{ \begin{array}{c} \underline{\text{BEFORE}} \\ \underline{\text{AFTER}} \end{array} \right\} \text{ADVANCING} \left\{ \begin{array}{c} \left\{ \begin{array}{c} \text{identifier-3} \\ \text{integer} \end{array} \right\} \left[\begin{array}{c} \text{LINE} \\ \text{LINES} \end{array} \right] \\ \left\{ \begin{array}{c} \text{mnemonic-name} \\ \underline{\text{PAGE}} \end{array} \right\} \end{array} \right\} \right]$

$$\underline{\text{SET}} \left\{ \begin{array}{l} \text{identifier-1 [, identifier-2]} \ldots \\ \text{index-name-1 [, index-name-2]} \ldots \end{array} \right\} \quad \underline{\text{TO}} \quad \left\{ \begin{array}{l} \text{identifier-3} \\ \text{index-name-3} \\ \text{integer-1} \end{array} \right\}$$

$$\underline{\text{SET}} \text{ index-name-4 [, index-name-5]} \ldots \left\{ \begin{array}{l} \underline{\text{UP BY}} \\ \underline{\text{DOWN}} \text{ BY} \end{array} \right\} \quad \left\{ \begin{array}{l} \text{identifier-4} \\ \text{integer-2} \end{array} \right\}$$

$$\underline{\text{SORT}} \text{ file-name-1} \quad \text{ON} \left\{ \begin{array}{l} \underline{\text{ASCENDING}} \\ \underline{\text{DESCENDING}} \end{array} \right\} \text{ KEY data-name-1 [, data-name-2]} \ldots$$

$$\left[\text{ON} \left\{ \begin{array}{l} \underline{\text{ASCENDING}} \\ \underline{\text{DESCENDING}} \end{array} \right\} \text{ KEY data-name-3 [, data-name-4]} \ldots \right] \ldots$$

[COLLATING <u>SEQUENCE</u> IS alphabet-name]

$$\left\{ \begin{array}{l} \underline{\text{INPUT PROCEDURE}} \text{ IS section-name-1} \quad \left[\left\{ \begin{array}{l} \underline{\text{THROUGH}} \\ \underline{\text{THRU}} \end{array} \right\} \text{ section-name-2} \right] \\ \text{USING file-name-2 [, file-name-3]} \ldots \end{array} \right\}$$

$$\left\{ \begin{array}{l} \underline{\text{OUTPUT PROCEDURE}} \text{ IS section-name-3} \quad \left[\left\{ \begin{array}{l} \underline{\text{THROUGH}} \\ \underline{\text{THRU}} \end{array} \right\} \text{ section-name-4} \right] \\ \underline{\text{GIVING}} \text{ file-name-4} \end{array} \right\}$$

$$\underline{\text{START}} \text{ file-name} \left[\underline{\text{KEY}} \left\{ \begin{array}{l} \text{IS } \underline{\text{EQUAL TO}} \\ \text{IS } \underline{=} \\ \text{IS } \underline{\text{GREATER}} \text{ THAN} \\ \text{IS } \underline{>} \\ \text{IS } \underline{\text{NOT LESS}} \text{ THAN} \\ \text{IS } \underline{\text{NOT}} < \end{array} \right\} \text{ data-name} \right]$$

[; INVALID KEY imperative-statement]

$$\underline{\text{STOP}} \left\{ \begin{array}{l} \underline{\text{RUN}} \\ \text{literal} \end{array} \right\}$$

$$\underline{\text{STRING}} \left\{ \begin{array}{l} \text{identifier-1} \\ \text{literal-1} \end{array} \right\} \quad \left[\begin{array}{l} \text{, identifier-2} \\ \text{, literal-2} \end{array} \right] \ldots \underline{\text{DELIMITED}} \text{ BY} \left\{ \begin{array}{l} \text{identifier-3} \\ \text{literal-3} \\ \underline{\text{SIZE}} \end{array} \right\}$$

$$\left[, \left\{ \begin{array}{l} \text{identifier-4} \\ \text{literal-4} \end{array} \right\} \quad \left[\begin{array}{l} \text{, identifier-5} \\ \text{, literal-5} \end{array} \right] \ldots \underline{\text{DELIMITED}} \text{ BY} \left\{ \begin{array}{l} \text{identifier-6} \\ \text{literal-6} \\ \underline{\text{SIZE}} \end{array} \right\} \right] \ldots$$

<u>INTO</u> identifier-7 [WITH <u>POINTER</u> identifier-8]

[; ON <u>OVERFLOW</u> imperative-statement]

$$\underline{\text{SUBTRACT}} \left\{ \begin{array}{l} \text{identifier-1} \\ \text{literal-1} \end{array} \right\} \quad \left[\begin{array}{l} \text{, identifier-2} \\ \text{, literal-2} \end{array} \right] \ldots \underline{\text{FROM}} \text{ identifier-m [\underline{ROUNDED}]}$$

$$\left[, \text{ identifier-n [\underline{ROUNDED}]} \right] \ldots [; \text{ ON } \underline{\text{SIZE ERROR}} \text{ imperative-statement}]$$

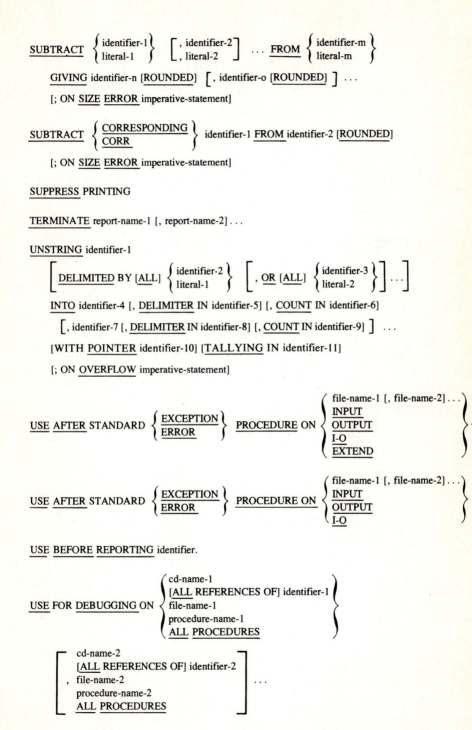

SUBTRACT $\begin{Bmatrix} \text{identifier-1} \\ \text{literal-1} \end{Bmatrix}$ $\begin{bmatrix} \text{, identifier-2} \\ \text{, literal-2} \end{bmatrix}$ ... <u>FROM</u> $\begin{Bmatrix} \text{identifier-m} \\ \text{literal-m} \end{Bmatrix}$

  <u>GIVING</u> identifier-n [<u>ROUNDED</u>] [, identifier-o [<u>ROUNDED</u>]] ...

  [; ON <u>SIZE</u> <u>ERROR</u> imperative-statement]

<u>SUBTRACT</u> $\begin{Bmatrix} \underline{\text{CORRESPONDING}} \\ \underline{\text{CORR}} \end{Bmatrix}$ identifier-1 <u>FROM</u> identifier-2 [<u>ROUNDED</u>]

  [; ON <u>SIZE</u> <u>ERROR</u> imperative-statement]

<u>SUPPRESS</u> PRINTING

<u>TERMINATE</u> report-name-1 [, report-name-2] ...

<u>UNSTRING</u> identifier-1

$\left[\underline{\text{DELIMITED}} \text{ BY [ALL]} \begin{Bmatrix} \text{identifier-2} \\ \text{literal-1} \end{Bmatrix} \left[, \underline{\text{OR}} \text{ [ALL]} \begin{Bmatrix} \text{identifier-3} \\ \text{literal-2} \end{Bmatrix} \right] ... \right]$

  <u>INTO</u> identifier-4 [, <u>DELIMITER</u> IN identifier-5] [, <u>COUNT</u> IN identifier-6]

   $\left[, \text{identifier-7} [, \underline{\text{DELIMITER}} \text{ IN identifier-8}] [, \underline{\text{COUNT}} \text{ IN identifier-9}] \right]$ ...

  [WITH <u>POINTER</u> identifier-10] [<u>TALLYING</u> IN identifier-11]

  [; ON <u>OVERFLOW</u> imperative-statement]

<u>USE</u> <u>AFTER</u> STANDARD $\begin{Bmatrix} \underline{\text{EXCEPTION}} \\ \underline{\text{ERROR}} \end{Bmatrix}$ <u>PROCEDURE</u> ON $\begin{Bmatrix} \text{file-name-1 [, file-name-2]} ... \\ \text{INPUT} \\ \underline{\text{OUTPUT}} \\ \underline{\text{I-O}} \\ \underline{\text{EXTEND}} \end{Bmatrix}$.

<u>USE</u> <u>AFTER</u> STANDARD $\begin{Bmatrix} \underline{\text{EXCEPTION}} \\ \underline{\text{ERROR}} \end{Bmatrix}$ <u>PROCEDURE</u> ON $\begin{Bmatrix} \text{file-name-1 [, file-name-2]} ... \\ \text{INPUT} \\ \underline{\text{OUTPUT}} \\ \underline{\text{I-O}} \end{Bmatrix}$.

<u>USE</u> BEFORE <u>REPORTING</u> identifier.

<u>USE</u> FOR <u>DEBUGGING</u> ON $\begin{Bmatrix} \text{cd-name-1} \\ \text{[ALL REFERENCES OF] identifier-1} \\ \text{file-name-1} \\ \text{procedure-name-1} \\ \underline{\text{ALL}} \underline{\text{PROCEDURES}} \end{Bmatrix}$

  $\left[, \begin{matrix} \text{cd-name-2} \\ \text{[\underline{ALL} REFERENCES OF] identifier-2} \\ \text{file-name-2} \\ \text{procedure-name-2} \\ \underline{\text{ALL}} \underline{\text{PROCEDURES}} \end{matrix} \right]$ ...

WRITE record-name [FROM identifier-1]

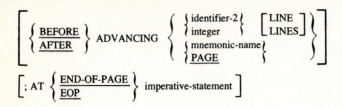

WRITE record-name [FROM identifier] [; INVALID KEY imperative-statement]

GENERAL FORMAT FOR CONDITIONS

RELATION CONDITION

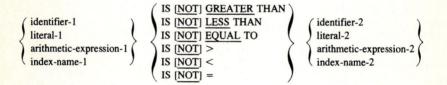

CLASS CONDITION

$$\text{identifier is [NOT]} \left\{ \begin{array}{l} \text{NUMERIC} \\ \text{ALPHABETIC} \end{array} \right\}$$

SIGN CONDITION

$$\text{arithmetic-expression is [NOT]} \left\{ \begin{array}{l} \text{POSITIVE} \\ \text{NEGATIVE} \\ \text{ZERO} \end{array} \right\}$$

CONDITION-NAME CONDITION

condition-name

SWITCH-STATUS CONDITION

condition-name

NEGATED SIMPLE CONDITION

<u>NOT</u> simple-condition

COMBINED CONDITION

condition $\left\{ \left\{ \dfrac{\text{AND}}{\text{OR}} \right\} \text{ condition} \right\}$ ...

ABBREVIATED COMBINED RELATION CONDITION

relation-condition $\left\{ \left\{ \dfrac{\text{AND}}{\text{OR}} \right\} \text{ [NOT] [relational-operator] object} \right\}$ ...

MISCELLANEOUS FORMATS

QUALIFICATION

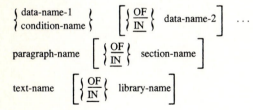

$\left\{ \begin{array}{l} \text{data-name-1} \\ \text{condition-name} \end{array} \right\}$ $\left[\left\{ \dfrac{\text{OF}}{\text{IN}} \right\} \text{ data-name-2} \right]$ ...

paragraph-name $\left[\left\{ \dfrac{\text{OF}}{\text{IN}} \right\} \text{ section-name} \right]$

text-name $\left[\left\{ \dfrac{\text{OF}}{\text{IN}} \right\} \text{ library-name} \right]$

SUBSCRIPTING

$\left\{ \begin{array}{l} \text{data-name} \\ \text{condition-name} \end{array} \right\}$ (subscript-1 [, subscript-2 [, subscript-3]])

INDEXING

$\left\{ \begin{array}{l} \text{data-name} \\ \text{condition-name} \end{array} \right\}$ $\left(\left\{ \begin{array}{l} \text{index-name-1 } [\{\pm\} \text{ literal-2}] \\ \text{literal-1} \end{array} \right\} \right.$

$\left[\text{, } \left\{ \begin{array}{l} \text{index-name-2 } [\{\pm\} \text{ literal-4}] \\ \text{literal-3} \end{array} \right\} \right.$ $\left. \left[\text{, } \left\{ \begin{array}{l} \text{index-name-3 } [\{\pm\} \text{ literal-6}] \\ \text{literal-5} \end{array} \right\} \right] \right] \Big)$

IDENTIFIER: FORMAT 1

data-name-1 $\left[\left\{\dfrac{OF}{IN}\right\}\ \text{data-name-2}\right]$ ... $\Big[$ (subscript-1 [, subscript-2

[, subscript-3]]) $\Big]$

IDENTIFIER: FORMAT 2

data-name-1 $\left[\left\{\dfrac{OF}{IN}\right\}\ \text{data-name-2}\right]$ ... $\left[\left(\left\{\begin{array}{l}\text{index-name-1 }[\{\pm\}\text{ literal-2}]\\ \text{literal-1}\end{array}\right\}\right.\right.$

$\left[\ ,\ \left\{\begin{array}{l}\text{index-name-2 }[\{\pm\}\text{ literal-4}]\\ \text{literal-3}\end{array}\right\}\right.$ $\left.\left[\ ,\ \left\{\begin{array}{l}\text{index-name-3 }[\{\pm\}\text{ literal-6}]\\ \text{literal-5}\end{array}\right\}\right]\right]\Big)\Big]$

GENERAL FORMAT FOR COPY STATEMENT

$\underline{\text{COPY}}$ text-name $\left[\left\{\dfrac{OF}{IN}\right\}\ \text{library-name}\right]$

$\left[\ \underline{\text{REPLACING}}\ \left\{,\ \left\{\begin{array}{l}==\text{pseudo-text-1}==\\ \text{identifier-1}\\ \text{literal-1}\\ \text{word-1}\end{array}\right\}\ \underline{\text{BY}}\ \left\{\begin{array}{l}==\text{pseudo-text-2}==\\ \text{identifier-2}\\ \text{literal-2}\\ \text{word-2}\end{array}\right\}\right\}\ ...\ \right]$

INDEX